Praise for Jacuzzi...

"Kenneth Jacuzzi and his family are a very much respected American story. His book about his life and family is of great interest to all who keep abreast and enjoy reading the struggles and successes that immigrants and their families encounter. In Mr. Jacuzzi's case, of even more interest is the manner in which Ken and members of his family overcame not only problems that immigrants face, like discrimination and disorientation due to language and culture differences, but also physical difficulties by disabilities as they relate to physical health. Mr. Jacuzzi lays out in clear terms many of the problems that he and members of his family encountered.

I have known Ken Jacuzzi for more than 25 years and have admired and worked with him in the political and social service area in Arizona. He represents the good things that have come from immigrant families that make America so strong today."

—Sen. Dennis DeConcini, retired U.S. Senator for Arizona.

"If you want to understand the words 'courage, perseverance, and determination,' you must read Ken Jacuzzi's autobiography. His amazing life is an inspiration."

—Jana Bommersbach, author and journalist.

"This is a book that, first, looks back on the life of a family crammed with such activity and achievement as to make it globally famous as a household name and symbolic of American quality living. It also provides a vivid self-portrait by the author, and a description of the challenges he has faced through severe disablement. The result is both refreshing and fascinating. It is simply the story of a struggle for survival—courageous, deeply sensitive, sharply observant—but one that is triumphant in the end, and captures the imagination.

The author describes his extraordinary background and antecedents, his remarkable parents, his early experience, and the strength that can come from close family life. He ties together family and personal strands in a compelling narrative which illuminates and unravels the complexities of a degree of disablement that would crush many another person. Vigorously written, candid, and self-revealing, it is as concerned with the substance of policy as with personal reminiscence, and we are presented, happily, with a thoughtful and well-written reflection on a most fulfilling life despite the severest physical constraints. Throughout the reader is made aware in an account both honest and generous of the realities of such a life, and how it culminated in a happy marriage. The result, in an eminently lucid and entirely undoctrinaire way, is an important social document.

Whilst Britain's Minister for the Navy in the 'seventies and President of NATO's Parliamentary Assembly in the 'eighties, I was a constant visitor to the Pentagon, the State Department and Capitol Hill, where I often sat in on meetings of the Armed Services committees of the House and Senate. I worked closely during those dark days of the Cold War with senior military as well as major figures in public life in America and elsewhere in the Western Alliance. I rarely encountered anyone as impressive as the author, or anyone who could match his incisive intellect, insatiable curiosity and relentless questioning. The intellectual and moral command, the insights, the common sense, the kindness and the sense of humor that appear in this unflinching book—and of which his friends have always been aware—are the true characteristics of its author."

—Sir Patrick Duffy, Ph.D.

"Ken Jacuzzi's engaging writing style draws the reader into an open and honest picture of the complexities of the day-to-day struggles of living with a disability and the resulting challenges and tensions that plague family, friends, and care-givers. Along the way, he tells a fascinating story of an entrepreneurial Italian immigrant family. The successes, the failures, the missed opportunities, the family in-fighting are all present. There is much to be learned from this book about disabilities, about family businesses, but most importantly, about being human."

—Regina Wentzel Wolfe, Ph.D., Christopher Chair in Business Ethics, Dominican University.

"Ken Jacuzzi has added an extraordinary book to an extraordinary life. His graphic yet matter-of-fact descriptions of leading a meaningful life despite daunting disabilities are an example for anyone who has ever felt sorry for himself."

—Dino J. DeConcini, attorney, businessman, civic activist.

"This is a landmark story of how an invention for arthritis made the Jacuzzi name famous worldwide, starting with the immigration of the Jacuzzi family from Italy to Ken's struggle to help others with disabilities. This Horatio Alger story of invention derived from a father's determination to reduce his young son's pain from juvenile rheumatoid arthritis. Here you can glimpse the Jacuzzi family from their early invention of the first enclosed cabin

monoplane to the world's most recognized brand of whirlpool baths and spas."

—Barbara Barrett, attorney and Chairman, U.S. Advisory Commission on Public Diplomacy.

"Readers with and without disabilities will appreciate the different journey Ken has taken through life. Ken Jacuzzi elegantly carries us through the challenging and rewarding times of his life. He fosters disability culture by his direct, thoughtful discussion of living with a disability with dignity and honesty. What a hero to us all!"

—John D. Kemp, Esq., lawyer and author of *Reflections From A Different Journey: What People With Disabilities Wish All Parents Knew.*

"Before I met Ken Jacuzzi personally, his life had impacted mine. In the hippie days when I had moved to California, hot tubs with "Jacuzzis" were the rage. None of us knew of the irony that these "pleasure machines" had been invented as a therapeutic device for a debilitating condition. Thanks, Ken. I am grateful for your human story now being available in your book."

—Kenneth Ray Stubbs, Ph.D., author and sexologist.

"Ken Jacuzzi has meant a great deal to me in the six years that I've known him. He taught me a lot about being a human being in a wheelchair. When I was first told that I was going to meet Ken, I did not know that we had so much in common, such as that he used an electric wheelchair or that he and I knew a lot about history and other school subjects. Ken has inspired me to become more serious about getting a good job and good life and sticking to

those goals. Ken makes me feel calm and relaxed and it's always interesting to talk with him about various subjects."

—Aaron Wake, student and Goodwill worker, age 24.

Jacuzzi

Jacuzzi

◆

A Father's Invention to Ease a Son's Pain

Ken Jacuzzi
With Dr. Diane Holloway

iUniverse, Inc.
New York Lincoln Shanghai

Jacuzzi
A Father's Invention to Ease a Son's Pain

Copyright © 2005 by Kenneth A. Jacuzzi

All rights reserved. No part of this book may be used or reproduced by any means, graphic, electronic, or mechanical, including photocopying, recording, taping or by any information storage retrieval system without the written permission of the publisher except in the case of brief quotations embodied in critical articles and reviews.

iUniverse books may be ordered through booksellers or by contacting:

iUniverse
2021 Pine Lake Road, Suite 100
Lincoln, NE 68512
www.iuniverse.com
1-800-Authors (1-800-288-4677)

ISBN-13: 978-0-595-37097-9 (pbk)
ISBN-13: 978-0-595-81498-5 (ebk)
ISBN-10: 0-595-37097-7 (pbk)
ISBN-10: 0-595-81498-0 (ebk)

Printed in the United States of America

This book is dedicated to four very special people: Father Pat Robinson; my aunt (zia) Gilia Peruzzo, the last surviving first generation of Jacuzzis in America; my brother-in-law, Peter Kosta; and my spouse, Daniela.

Fr. Pat, Zia Gilia, Pete, and Daniela share common traits: they are all exceptional, yet very down-to-earth persons. Like you and me, they are not without their foibles or idiosyncrasies, but they each are dedicated to what they do with their entire hearts and souls—my Aunt Gilia to helping her family and friends; Fr. Pat to serving the people of his parish, The Community of the Blessed Sacrament; Pete the Greek who taught me how to tie a tie, develop a business budget and so much more; and Daniela to giving of herself to me and others unselfishly. Each day, their lives reflect the love, giving, and humanity taught us by Jesus.

Contents

Cast Your Fate to the Wind (song by Vince Guaraldi) xvii
Preface xix
Introduction xxiii

Part I IMMIGRATION OF THE JACUZZIS

Chapter 1 The Jacuzzis Come to America 3
Chapter 2 The End of the Airplane 33
Chapter 3 How My Parents Met 41

Part II FREE-FOR-ALL WITH A DISABILITY

Chapter 4 Candido Jacuzzi's Family 61
Chapter 5 America's Dirty Little Secret: Italian Internment Camps 80
Chapter 6 My Limitations 86
Chapter 7 Premature Sexuality 104
Chapter 8 Rehabilitation Was My "Work" 125
Chapter 9 Adolescence 139
Chapter 10 Dependent Forever! 153
Chapter 11 The Disability "Cause" 172
Chapter 12 Leaving Home 198

Chapter 13	I'm a Man!	220
Chapter 14	The Bathing Suit	241
Chapter 15	My First Real Job	244
Chapter 16	Italian Businessman	259

Part III LEARNING, MARRIAGE, AND STUFF

Chapter 17	Meeting My Future Wife	317
Chapter 18	Marriage	329
Chapter 19	My Father's Disability	335
Chapter 20	Return to America: Fast vs. Slow	347
Chapter 21	Another Slant on Things	352
Chapter 22	Identity Crisis	366
Chapter 23	Being Different	378
Chapter 24	Being Small	387
Chapter 25	This Is Your Life, Ken Jacuzzi!	394
Chapter 26	"Call No Man Happy Until He is Dead!"	412

Appendix A	Resources	425
Appendix B	Jacuzzi Family Tree	445
Sources		493
Index		495

Acknowledgments

Toys are good. Toys mean play and fun. All are good things. Dying with a nice number of toys isn't bad either. However, a man's lifetime wealth is not in the number of his toys, but his stories…and the best stories involve other people. K.J.

How and where does one begin writing acknowledgments? This was a tough nut to crack for me. I mean—Jesus, Mary and Joseph—I cannot begin to truly express the kindnesses, generosity, thoughtfulness, sacrifices and lessons of the myriad of individuals who have nourished me throughout my life and contributed to this book.

From my very earliest years, I remember Dad always saying that a person's best, most important lessons in life, the finest source of the richest knowledge, was, quite simply, people. The next most important source for enriching that gray matter between one's ears, according to Dad, was travel, whether in your own town, country, or the world. He was quick to add, of course, that what made travel so worthwhile was all the folks you met along the way.

There is no other way to say it: Dad was right. All the richness of my life, all that I have learned and experienced—from the nurse who comforted this frightened, lonely two-year-old child in hospital to those who gave so much and made this life, this book, possible—can only be attributed to an incredible spouse, family, friends, and countless people I met along my way.

Over the last several decades, many wonderful people assisted me in the research, drafting and eventual completion of this memoir. I cannot adequately express my appreciation for the many contributions made by Al Baccari, Joan Penl, Phil Rulon, Karen Hitchcock and Teresa Moore. To each and every one of them I am deeply grateful. I'm especially thankful for Daniel Brawner's extensive work, especially with respect to his research on my family. Additionally, I doubt a completed memoir would have been realizable without the vision and wise counsel of my dear, late friend, Peggy Spaw, and the insight and savvy of Francine Hardaway.

Additionally, I want to thank some people who have helped produce this book: photographer John Beckett, and his assistant, Julie Koeth, for the cover photos, and Randy Harper for the interior photos. I very much appreciate Phil

Whitmarsh and Cecilia Cuevas of iUniverse Publishing who have been so helpful in the final preparation of this book.

I want to especially thank Ralph Jansen, the kind of friend who never expects or asks for anything in return, who spent countless hours editing the book and helping me improve it in many ways.

I will be forever grateful, too, for the untold kindnesses given me by wonderful friends and members of my extensive Jacuzzi family. The inspiration, information, and personal stories so generously shared with me have proven to be enriching, touching, and invaluable. This book couldn't have been done without the exceptional contributions of Joe Scafetta, Anne, Richard, Tom, Julie, Susan, Pete, Ruth, Bruce, Egidio, Bill, Abel and Pat. And special thanks are owed my aunts Cirilla, Armanda, Stella, Rosie, and Gilia, my uncles Rachele, Frank, and Joseph, and my cousins Lola, Nilda, Teresa, Lydia, Silviano, Bob, Don, Aldo, Virgil, Giocondo, Victor, and my brother, John, to name just a few.

There are several other individuals who deserve special recognition for their share in the completion of this book. The first is my sister, Alba, who continued, year after year, to push me relentlessly to get the damn thing done. Next is Irene, my other beautiful sister, who, even years after her too early death, kept me going during my worst down times. I am especially indebted to my cousin Lydia Negherbon who drove me and my mother to innumerable doctor's appointments throughout the Bay Area, including San Francisco and beyond. And finally, there would be no memoir without the tireless support and encouragement of my wife, Daniela.

However, the single most determining person in my memoir's completion can be none other than my collaborator extraordinaire and co-author, Dr. Diane Holloway. Diane's patience—particularly with yours truly—savvy and genius made possible the otherwise improbable: the relatively rational putting together of several decades of research, recollections and my myriad of written meanderings. Besides, it was relatively easy (for me) completing the writing assignments she gave me because saying no to her sexy Texas lilt was impossible.

Cast Your Fate to the Wind

A month of nights, a year of days
Octobers drifting into Mays
You set your sail when the tide comes in
And you cast your fate to the wind.

You shift your course along the breeze
Won't sail upwind on memories
The empty sky is your best friend
And you just cast your fate to the wind.

That time has such a way of changing a man throughout the years
And now you're rearranging your life through all your tears
Alone, alone.

There never was, there couldn't be
A place in time for men to be
Who'd drink the dark and laugh at day
And let their wildest dreams blow away.

So now you're old, you're wise, you're smart
You're just a man with half a heart
You wonder how it might have been
Had you not cast your fate to the wind.

This 1962 song by fellow Italian-American Vince Guaraldi is one of my favorite jazz pieces and a sort of theme song for my life.

Preface

I think I first heard of the "Jacuzzi" when I often found my mother watching a TV show in the mid-50s called *Queen for a Day*. Several women would appear with sob stories and the audience would vote on the neediest woman to become "Queen for a Day" and receive gifts. If she had a medical problem, she might receive a Jacuzzi Whirlpool Bath along with other gifts. It was kind of like Jerry Springer or similar shows today where people describe sad plights and receive advice or gifts for all their suffering.

I had no idea that the Jacuzzi Whirlpool Bath was designed by Candido Jacuzzi for his son Kenneth, who had arthritis and severe pain from the age of two. I learned that from Ken when I met him some time ago in Arizona.

I had heard from a friend that Jacuzzi wanted to write the story of his family and how they came to America and began to invent things such as airplanes and water pumps. He also wanted to explain what life was like for those with disabilities. He wanted to describe the inner life of disabled persons in hopes of removing common stereotypes.

I had worked first as a nurse and then as a psychologist and crime consultant. I had written several books, including the memoir of the judge who tried Jack Ruby for killing Lee Harvey Oswald. I had also helped some other writers prepare their autobiographies but I was unprepared for the extraordinary Ken Jacuzzi.

At the request of my friend, I called Ken Jacuzzi to see if I could help. Having found his picture on the internet, a short man in a wheel chair with non-functional limbs, I was surprised by his candor, wit, and enthusiasm when we first met. He had already been at work on his memoir for some time and had assembled taped and written interviews of family members to aid his memory. He furnished me with abundant notes of his busy life, and requested me to use a pruning knife. He disparaged his writing, but I was not only intrigued with his work, I was fascinated by his creativity and the willingness to expose reactions to disability.

Ken described his first recollections of a time when children were isolated in hospital wards because of their severe disabilities. Ken was no different than other children and wanted to be as normal as possible, but that was denied him because of his dependency upon others to do the simplest of things; even to use the toilet.

Now people with similar problems are beginning to be valued in the community. However, that was not the case when the multiply-disabled Kenneth Jacuzzi grew up. He poignantly described being the cause of arguments which began to divide his parents from each other. In addition, they stayed away from family and acquaintances as they dealt with a child they wanted to help but also wanted to hide.

Jacuzzi owed much to the influence of his father, who was not only an inventor but a tremendous salesman for Jacuzzi products. His memories of his father are passionate and fierce as he weaves together the stories of himself and his family.

Ken, however, was the source of frustration for his family, as well as for many in the medical profession. His description of his struggles to try to walk, to undergo experimental treatments, to oblige his doctors by submitting to hormonal treatment creating a sensual man in a child's body, shows his resilience and humor as he tried to associate with boys and girls and conquers the heart.

His rocky relationships with women are disclosed with humor and longing, until he finally landed the love of his life, an Italian beauty. Nevertheless, life was not always a bowl of cherries, either in Italy where he managed the family company, or in this country where he managed other businesses. He describes achingly how he had to come to terms with his disability and his wife's care-taking role that gradually changed his relationship with her.

Along the way, Ken speaks four languages and corresponds with people at all levels of life across the world. He obtained, with great difficulty, bachelor's and master's degrees in business, and coaches people and companies about disability-related issues.

The Italian concept of togetherness brought his family much success in early years, but failed in the individually competitive American economy. The Jacuzzi family company finally broke apart and was taken over by non-family entrepreneurs who now use the name. The disintegration of lives and family camaraderie is heartbreaking.

Ken writes like an artist, and creates a cast of unusual characters among family, friends, and aides that defy imagination. Part history, part romance, part globe-trekking adventure, this book answers numerous questions about the Jacuzzis, their dreams and inventions, and the ongoing quests of this outspoken man, who happens to be disabled.

I hope that in editing this book, I have not omitted anything that is likely to be interesting or instructive. I must add that everything was submitted for his correction and received his final approval.

I believe that family, friends, medical workers, and people in public service or policy positions will better understand their roles in the lives of the disabled when they read this book. Those with disabilities, as well as their parents and family members, will benefit from this book and will be inspired by Ken.

This story allows the reader to appreciate the life-changing nature of severe illness as Ken Jacuzzi reveals the details of his predicament. Those with disabilities want to hear about others who have made it, and we all respond well to good role models, good news, and encouragement.

Ken shares anti-establishment views openly in this book. He feels that the medical profession is geared to "cure" people rather than to help those with permanent medical problems. As a lifetime consumer of medical care, he has much to say about the shortcomings of American medicine. He thinks we spend too much for too little, that too many are uninsured or underinsured. He believes that we should consider the quality and quantity of health care in other advanced nations. In addition, he believes the health system in America is built on the unquestionable authority of the physician. Those authorities discourage patients from asking, participating, and becoming a role player in their own healthcare.

This memoir helps us redefine the word "hero," but Ken doesn't like that title for himself, nor do most of the 50 million disabled people. They argue that there is nothing heroic about wanting to live life to the fullest. They get irritated, however, when people imply that they should stay home or in an institution or forget about trying to use restaurants, libraries, universities, buildings, and other places.

In fact, they usually say, like Ken, "I've got a spouse, a house, and bills to pay just like you, so I'm not so special! What's more, we'll all be disabled sooner or later, now that we live longer and start losing abilities we had earlier, so I'm sure not alone."

This is a book for those interested in human rights, social justice, and learning the strength to face formidable obstacles.

Diane Holloway, Ph.D.

Introduction

I write faster than I speak, which is still more rapid than my walk. Of course, that's easy to figure out 'cause I don't walk and I haven't walked for decades. And when I did walk, it was mostly during my teens and twenties, using platform crutches and primarily for exercise, not mobility. After a couple of dozen surgeries and for a short stretch of a couple of years during my mid-teens, I could even walk short distances without crutches. Visualize one of the floundering juveniles from the movie *March of the Penguins*.

I didn't start out that way. I came into this world a healthy, 10-pound baby boy on April 22, 1941. Seven months and days later (December 7th), the Japanese bombed Pearl Harbor. It was a hell of a year for our country and the world—and my family and me.

About nine months after my birth, I graduated quickly from crawling to walking and then running. I was impatient then, more so now. Then, some time in the winter of 1942–43, before my second birthday, I contracted a streptococcal infection in my throat. My body took an irreversible giant hit. The strep throat put my body on a daily roller coaster of spiking and falling fever, vacillating between 105°F and 99°F. Soon I was diagnosed as having developed rheumatic fever.

The terrible fever slowly evened out and returned to normal. Evidence of the rheumatic fever started to recede. But by then I was toast and my body emerged crippled from neck to ankles, with swollen painful joints, even at the touch of my loving parents. A specialist diagnosed me as having contracted Still's Disease, a shortened way to say severe systemic Juvenile Rheumatoid Arthritis (JRA).

"Systemic" is a real efficient way of saying that the whole body, not just the joints, is affected—muscles, heart, lungs, you name it. It's the no-cost, extra-equipment package that often comes with top-of-the-line rheumatoid arthritis.

When I was about seven years old—this was in the late 1940s—my doctor prescribed hydrotherapy treatments, followed by physical therapy, at a local hospital in Berkeley, California, twice a week. My parents and therapists noted that after the treatments, the warm water and massage gave me a greater ability to move my limbs with less pain. Being good Italian parents, they thought that more must be better. You know how pushy Italians are: "Mangia, mangia!"—"Eat, eat!" However, each time I traveled to a hospital for hydrotherapy, I was vulnerable to cold and flu germs.

That is why my mother, Inez, urged my father, Candido Jacuzzi, to invent a whirlpool pump for my everyday use at home—which he did. Subsequently, he and his brothers, who ran a commercial water irrigation pump manufacturing business, started building and marketing whirlpool baths in the early 1950s.

I've already lived longer at 63 than what an average male's life expectancy was in the United States at the time of my birth. Either I'm a miracle of medical science, one hardheaded son of a bitch, or God's putting off taking me. I suspect it's a combination of all three. But I'm digressing from the introduction. *Perdonami*, pardon me, I do meander at times.

So how did I make it this far? I haven't the foggiest idea. But planet Earth is stuck with me, at least for a while. For me, getting to the here and now wasn't easy or painless, something I think I share with most folks. During my life's problem-filled journey, I didn't refrain from doing my share of bitchin' and hollerin.' Dammit! When it hurts bad, it hurts bad.

It wasn't just the pain from the arthritis that upset me; my anger arose from the endless limits the pain and crippling placed on my life. Many times throughout these last 60 plus years, I recall being told that I wanted or expected too much of myself, I was a complainer, or that I had a chip on my shoulder. I love the "chip on my shoulder" comment. It's one of the many things that I, as well as others with disabilities like me, share with minorities of color.

After all, what right do I have, a person physically dependent upon the help of others to meet my daily personal care needs, to expect the *same* opportunities for an education, work and housing as someone who's *able-bodied?* It's just not practical. It would cost society far too much money. Besides, it just couldn't be done. Maybe in 100 or 200 years when medical science has *cured* illness and *stops* people from being born with or later developing disabilities will a more "equal" world be possible. Yes, I've heard all the arguments for denying things to the disabled. You'll meet them, just as I did, as I tell my story.

"So what's your problem?" you ask. How about a few examples? Heck, you knew I couldn't resist. Let's start with "number one." That was the euphemism for taking a pee when I was a little boy. I think it still is. It was easy then. Mom was around to help me, as is the case with most little children the first couple of years of their lives. So my taking a pee wasn't so much different from other little boys and girls. After age two, however, when the rheumatoid arthritis affected my ability to walk, stand and even use my hands, the pee bottle (urinal) became my elimination device of choice. "Number two," the "other" bodily elimination system, I describe adequately elsewhere in this book, so I'll skip it for now. I bet that's a *relief* for ya. Love them double meanings!

What about a few of my other daily ins and outs, ups and downs…like sex?

"Hey, Mabel, this guy's talking about takin' a whiz when he was a little fart, then in the next breath he's already doin' the nasty. *I wonder how easy this arthritis is to catch?*"

Well, I'll get to more…much more of sex later, too. For now, what you need to know is that sex has always been a driving force in my life, and also the source of a lot of frustration. The frustration stems from the fact that, for one thing, there's a host of mechanical issues for a crip to resolve to just have sex. Whatever is involved, sex is worth it. You know the pain and crippling you get from the arthritis? You betcha! Sex not only feels good but it alleviates some of those nasty symptoms, too. By the way, that's not just me talking. There's a host of accumulated scientific data showing that, indeed, sex is good for arthritis.

The trouble is, however, I possessed for many years a nagging doubt that I could ever interest a woman in having sex with me. The exception, of course, was sex in exchange for money, which I didn't like the idea of at all. I wanted to be with a woman who wanted to be with me, and I think I share that wish with most men.

In retrospect, I must also admit—without having the least idea why—that I have had the privilege over my lifetime of knowing (some in the biblical sense, others platonically, all closely) a number of strikingly creative, caring, gorgeous women. They all gave to me in different ways, but much more than I gave them. Some were friends, a few were personal caregivers, some family members and several colleagues.

Some other lovely ladies have been very special to me throughout my life: my second mom and "older" sister Alba (she hates it when I call her that, but it's a standing brother-sister tease between us) and my sister, Irene. Irene had the look and beauty of Sofia Loren and was the only sibling who could stand up to our Dad. She could also handle me like an expert. Suddenly, stealthily, cancer took Irene in her prime, at 51. They were all loves of my life. But the greatest love, of course, has been my wife, Daniela. You will hear much about her as we proceed.

From my early childhood years, I have had the good fortune, too, of developing friendships with a host of different, but incredible guys who taught me much and were there for me, time and again. Unfortunately, although I was encouraged to have friends from an early age, thanks to the encouragement of my parents, the peer male friendships of most of my elementary school and adolescent years were limited to home and outside the common interaction environment of young boys and teens.

In my preteen years, not only couldn't I participate in the physical stuff that kids do—running, jumping, playing ball, discovering—my schooling was either in home or hospital. And although I did finally go to public school when I was in my teens—thanks to the insistence of my sister and brother-in-law, Alba and Pete—attendance the first several years was minimal because I was, yep, in hospital so much of the time for surgeries.

It really wasn't until I was in my late teens to mid-twenties that I slowly came to fully appreciate the preciousness of my friends. That time of my life was particularly fraught with emotional turmoil and lapses into depression. I had contemplated suicide and even took first steps at one attempt, but I backed myself down before it was too late. But somewhere from the muddy bottom of this despair, I experienced a time of personal growth and maturing. The gifts of my friends, the love they gave me and the unending things I could still learn from them and their friendship came into focus. "From the mud grows the lotus." (Alan Watts)

Shifting gears, I think I'll put aside for now going up and down one or more stairs. Forget it in a wheelchair. Turning light switches on or off. Most are too high. Entering or exiting public buildings or bathrooms unaided. Impossible for me, unless the doors are motorized. Maneuvering through store aisles, especially during the holidays. Not a good idea in a wheelchair, unless you like the attention you get when you topple merchandise and/or get stuck and can't move. Attempting to eat and carry on a conversation with friends in a restaurant that only has elevated tables or booths. In such a scenario, it is not uncommon for the waitress to ask my wife or one of my friends, despite having heard me speak, "Would the man in the wheelchair like a tray or something for his lap?" My personal favorite: "What would *he* like to order?"

Since I'm a crip and a small person—politically correct term for dwarf—a result of being immobilized in an entire body cast for nearly a year when I was about three, I've learned to deal with other things, too.

About the only articles of clothing that I can ever buy off the rack—but very carefully—are socks, underwear, T-shirts, swimming trunks, and the occasional necktie, which I detest, but have to wear at times. Trousers, shirts, jackets, suits, and shoes I have to have custom-made. Finding a tailor or seamstress that can decently dress a pretzel-like, shrimp body like mine isn't easy or easy on the pocketbook. To this day, I still get a little knot in my gut when walking (wheelchair users say "walking" like everyone else, not "riding") through the men's section of a department store, and realize I can't buy a damn thing on the racks. Except—wouldn't you know it—neckties.

This book is also about how I changed over time. My evolution as a person with a Hummer-sized disability came from the lessons of my mistakes and screw-ups, some of which I regret to say, were repeats or three-peats. My teen years were lived during the 1950s. Then, I was a crippled, disabled or handicapped person, the latter being the "genteel" term. Isn't "genteel" a great word? Other people, by the way, were "normal." Then, I began to have real problems with the qualitative significance that some people seemed prone to attach to certain physical disabilities. It was like, "My physical disease/disability is worse than yours and, therefore, needs more attention." To me, the blockbuster crippling or blindness or deafness that resulted from an accident, arthritis, polio, or birth defect, were all the shits.

I began to think of television's new addition, the telethons, as being a money-raising distortion, a shell game, of what might really help people badly diseased and/or handicapped. Weren't all cripples just cripples?

In the first several decades of my life, I bought into the "medical model" of my illness and resulting disability, hook, line and sinker. My parents bought into it, too. How could one help not doing otherwise? The "medical model" was drilled into the cabezas of all doctors and health practitioners. The "medical model" goes something like this: if we doctors cannot cure or fix you, we can't help you. Ergo, you're hopeless, or at least a reasonable facsimile of hopeless.

The alternative plan? Gee, Mabel, beats the hell out of me! So if hopelessness doesn't do it for us, it's back to the old total "cure" or nothing. Doctors were the nearest thing to God that could be found, and they wanted to return you to the state of perfection into which you were born—or supposed to be born. They were puzzled and unprepared if they could not do that.

It took me one hell of a long time, and some really hard knocks, but I finally realized the bill of goods I had been sold by the "Medical Model Corporation" wasn't just defective—which I felt instinctively all along—but never really worked to begin with. Just ask someone with multiple sclerosis, cerebral palsy, muscular dystrophy, Parkinson's, bipolar syndrome, blindness, post-polio syndrome, acute attention deficit disorder, schizophrenia, deafness, autism...Well, I think you get it.

The trouble is that the "Medical Model Corporation" is still thriving because of its monopolistic grip on what's taught in medical schools. Christopher Reeve, God rest his soul, was a very brave man and a strong advocate for people with disabilities. He was also a champion of spinal cord injury research. But the overemphasis on a "cure" perpetuated by the "medical model" made even Christopher ignore the importance of the daily business of living one's life with a major disability. Did his focus on a "cure" contribute to his death?

It takes decades of learning and exposure to the world of disability to get to the level of understanding that I have today. While I was growing up, many "normal" people who encountered me for the first time involuntarily cringed and/or turned away if they could. But I didn't exactly welcome with open arms either people who had intellectual learning differences or mental disabilities. Gradually and later in life, I came to realize that whether the disability was mental and/or physical, all of us with disabilities were in the same damn boat. We shared significant challenges in living our lives, in being respected members of society, despite being marginalized or worse, and even sometimes feared.

It is my fervent desire, too, that those who are influential in corporate America, and happen to read this book, will finally begin to GET IT! What do I mean? Well, for one thing, corporate executives should begin taking more to heart the old cliché, "Necessity is the mother of invention," and finally learn what this tells them about designing products and services to meet their customers' needs, not their own. I'm certain they'll discover, much more frequently than not, customers want products that not only do more and do it better, but that also don't waste their time and are simpler and easier to use.

Well, the persons who are quintessentially equipped to create and design products and services that do more and are easier to use are people with disabilities, especially those with significant mobility, sensory, and even cognitive disabilities. I think that industry—as well as government—should immediately snatch up people with disabilities to help them create truly better products and services for the 21st century. That's what an old, worn-out cripple like me thinks!

As I said earlier, this book contains a good deal of sex. If you will excuse the irresistible metaphor, it's rather like getting a whole lot of banana in your oatmeal. Sex, for me, is vital because it is such an important part of what made me who I am. For a man and, I believe, for a woman, too, sex is a powerful life force. This life force does not go away when one becomes even severely disabled.

To attempt to diminish, deny, or relegate to the "irrelevant" column, any person's sexuality because of disability, disfigurement or some other similar "reason" is hogwash. How can one who becomes severely disabled, whether from accident, illness, or war, be expected to fully rehabilitate while simultaneously being life-force starved? It is sad to say, but the relegation of the sexual life force to immaterial status for tens of millions of people is exactly what is still being done every day by otherwise well-meaning doctors, parents and families.

It is difficult to understand fully what I just said when we still live in a society that drapes a nude statue of, say, *Venus* or *David* in a public building. That is as sick as hiding the sexual force in people with disabilities and deformities in closets. A similar craziness wants to keep youth from viewing human nudity while letting them view all manner of human violence and depravity. We do these things because we don't take time to listen. Doctors don't listen to patients, husbands don't listen to wives, parents don't listen to children, and, of course, vice versa. So, my friends, there is a goodly amount of sex in this book. I want you to get it—no pun intended.

My hope and prayer is that those reading this book who are blessed with a well-functioning, fit body and mind may come away with an appreciation of how tenuous and temporal that blessing is. Next year, next month, tomorrow, anyone—you included—can find yourself thrust to the bottom of an unimaginably steep canyon by an auto accident, the big "C," or the feeling of sudden loss of control, desperate, alone. The climb back is never easy. The prejudices and fears of our brothers and sisters make the return more difficult, sometimes unbearably so. Instead, with true understanding and compassion, the journey becomes more endurable. We feel, we know, we're in the same boat—ALL of us.

Now I've gotta be honest. I've been a nasty kid, a spoiled brat, and I share that because I want to paint a truthful picture of myself. I suppose we all start off being pretty self-centered. We try to grow out of that. I hope I have. But I recognize that I've always had a propensity to justify my actions. It's not to insist that I was right but simply to explain that there was no perverse intention and no secret dislike for others at the bottom of my impulses. So you will hear how and what I think as we travel along together.

Actually there are several themes in this book. The first is how the Jacuzzis came to America and began inventing airplanes, pumps and whirlpool baths, which my father initially invented for me. The second is how people with disabilities live and deal with their baggage. The third is the tragedy of how an immigrant family came to America from Italy with values that worked there but not always here. The fourth is how some of us must change our thinking to accommodate our need to live completely when we finally realize we can't all be cured. In that respect, in the appendix I have included a number of organizations and the type of help they offer to those with disabilities. The fifth is the correction of some misinformation about our family portrayed in the media after the family sold the Jacuzzi business and rights to the name. The sixth is the presentation of the most current family tree of the Jacuzzis available at this time.

As my friend, attorney Tom S. noted, the first generation of Jacuzzis came to America with little more than each other. They worked together to build a remarkably successful multinational business, but their success destroyed them, or at least their original dream. They ended with little more than money and a power struggle. Today, there is not one Jacuzzi in a position of importance in the corporation that was so central to the lives of its founders. The name Jacuzzi is associated in the public mind with a luxury product, although it was developed almost accidentally by a father to help a son, crippled from arthritis: moi. The experiences of my family, good and bad, shed much light on what has happened in America and the world in the last one hundred years.

I also must apologize to the rest of the Jacuzzi relatives if I have presented anything that does not match their recollections of the family. I've tried to do my best to recall things factually and to get friends and family to give input to this account. But just as two people will never describe the same sunset or an accident in the same way, so may people differ with my depiction of some things in this book.

I think, nevertheless, it is a bit more accurate than some of the information stated in the print media over the past several decades about the family and the business that bears its name. The basic thing I fault the press for, however, is their propensity to gobble up at face value what's handed to them by public relations companies hired to stroke the ego of people who may feel incomplete, despite their power and money.

The result of melding public relations and press, the blending of fact and fiction, the fogging over of what's true in 21st-century American business and politics means that a lot of important information and facts are left floating out there in the twilight zone, unavailable, unknown. But elaborating that story is for another time and place.

To me, it seems like my life has a kinship to a series of environmental and atmospheric phenomena, an earthquake here, and a hurricane there, that sort of thing. So, not only do I love the song cited above about casting one's fate to the winds, but I think it is an accurate reflection of the kind of life I have lived. Therefore, I've divided the chapters of this book according to the type of storm, or nature's little surprises that appeared and engulfed me at various stages of my life.

You will also note that here and there in various parts of the book, you will find poems and dreams, rather than straight narrative. I did this for several reasons. I wanted to somehow give the reader a different perspective or insight that might clarify the conflicts and feelings I was experiencing at the time.

These venues gave me a greater creative range while allowing me to forgo the needless dredging up of old skeletons that best be left buried, disintegrating into earthly nutrients. Suffice it to say, for better or worse, everything in this book comes from one place, one intention: the truth of the life and essence of Ken Jacuzzi. I hope I did that.

Part I
Immigration of the Jacuzzis

1

The Jacuzzis Come to America

El Nino: Immense shift in ocean currents over a long period of time.

It was the beginning of summer in 1914 in Sarajevo in the Austro-Hungarian Empire. Riding leisurely through the streets in an open car were Franz Ferdinand, his spouse, Sophie Chotek, and Governor Potiorek. An onlooker, a poor 27-year-old Muslim carpenter, decided at the last minute not to use the bomb he was carrying. Not far away stood a fidgety school dropout, his finger on the trigger of a concealed revolver. He, too, did nothing as the car passed in front of him, fearing a stray bullet might hit Sophie. Without warning, a bomb was thrown by one of the other passersby, but it hit and exploded in the car following the intended target. The young man who launched the bomb swallowed poison and jumped into a nearby waterway. The open car with its intended victim continued on, unscathed. Away from the chaos of the moment, another rebel, a 19-year-old school dropout by the name of Princip heard the explosion of the bomb, but couldn't see it and could only surmise what had happened.

Not long afterwards Princip learned of the bungled attempt and started to walk back home, disillusioned and angry. The open car's returning trek missed a turn and had to stop to go back. Princip happened to be walking on the same road at the same time. He retrieved his revolver and fired two shots, killing the heir to the Austrian-Hungarian Empire, Ferdinand, and his wife, Sophie. The objective of the seven young ragtag plotters had been achieved. Theirs was an act of symbolic protest against regimes and leadership they considered threatening to their own way of life and existence. Little did they know or realize at the time that this act would light the fuse of a devastating five-year conflict, eventually involving nation states throughout the world. Thus began World War I, which ended up involving over 20 countries, leaving nearly 2 million missing, wounding 21 million more, and killing 8 million people.

Yes, royalty from one of the then nation states of Europe had been assassinated. It was a despicable act of murder. But what happened that caused the "Great War" to evolve from that one act? Was it the belief that such an act of murder deserved something significantly greater in response? Was it fear that one nation would gain an upper hand over another? Was the participation of many nation states motivated primarily by the desire for economic conquest and dominance? Were the consequences of the escalating acts of individual nation states often badly calculated? Did ethnic issues and prejudices fuel the fire that kept the war going? Were many countries, although opposed to an escalating conflict, reluctantly swept into the war because of alliances, actual or perceived? There is one answer to all of those questions: yes.

At the time of Archduke Ferdinand's assassination, my father, Candido, was little more than 11 years old. He would very soon find himself, his sisters and parents in the midst of much more than just the widespread, near-poverty environment of the northeastern region of Italy in which he and his family lived. Far sooner than they would all like to remember, my dad, aunts, uncles, and grandparents had to contend with much more than tending their family's small farm, eating beans and cornmeal mush, and eking out a modest existence. They had to survive while the currents of war swept over, around and through their household and endangered their lives.

◆　　◆　　◆

I don't know where I'm going, but I know where I've been.

That's one of the few ways I'm like you. Not that I haven't spent my life trying to be like you, to fit in, to be one of the guys. But it hasn't worked very well.

So where have I been? When people write about me or introduce me, they say things like, "Kenneth Jacuzzi grew up with wealth, intelligence, and a loving family. He became fluent in four languages, painted portraits, jet-setted across Europe, managed a family business in Italy, crusaded for causes, developed a software business, married a wonderful Italian lady, and enjoys gourmet food."

They usually don't mention that I'm one of the "hidden population" of the United States, one of the 50 million men, women, and children who have a physical disability, and a major one! They do say that my father, Candido Jacuzzi, invented the "Jacuzzi" whirlpool bath for me when I was severely ill as a child.

The *American Heritage Dictionary* defined "Jacuzzi" as: "A trademark for a device that swirls water in a bath." The Jacuzzi name has become synonymous with whirlpool baths and hot tubs, and is found in accommodation descriptions across the world. However, few know about our Italian family, our agonies and our ecstasies. I know about them because their story is part of my story. So I can tell you not only where *I've* been, but where *we've* been.

Before I get started, let me tell you what recently happened to the company. In 1979, the Jacuzzi family sold the family business, Jacuzzi Bros. Inc., "JBI," to Kidde, a company known for its emergency fire extinguishers. At the time, the stock markets had been dealt a disastrous blow from the Arab oil embargo, soaring energy prices, resulting double-digit inflation, and the Watergate break-in that triggered President Nixon's resignation. About six years later, Kidde sold its portfolio holdings, including Jacuzzi, to Hanson, a British conglomerate. Around 1993, Hanson spun off a separate U.S. company including, yep, Jacuzzi. When the stock market bubble burst, Hanson Industries tumbled from a $6 billion plus company to something valued a little over one billion. The chairman and CEO, David Clark, decided that the company needed a high-recognition name to expand into the 21st century. Hence, in 2003, "Jacuzzi Brands, Inc." was born and "JBI" was quoted on the New York Stock Exchange.

As of mid-June 2005, JBI was valued at approximately $10 per share, but the Jacuzzi family has no more connection with the company. You'll hear the whole sordid story, but I'm rather intrigued that what goes around comes around and JBI is now back to JBI in 2005.

As I begin this book and its revelations, I am reminded that reading books is like peeking into the bedroom to see what really goes on between people in there. "Hey, Mabel, I'm just starting and I'm already peekin' in their bedroom."

We read about people because we are curious about them—and about ourselves. Only by reading do we discover whether our thoughts are similar to others or really weird. I will open that private door for those who wish to view the dramatic rise and tragic fall of a successful and inventive family, and the secret life of a person with a severe disability.

So where did my father and his people come from? My grandparents were Giovanni (1855–1929) and Teresa (1865–1943) Jacuzzi. Grandpa was born in Casarsa, Italy. My Grandma was born the last year of the American Civil War, when the world learned the news that beleaguered President Lincoln was assassinated in the United States. My grandparents met life from a threshold of domesticity. Against invasions, war, the calamities of nature or the pains of separation, the family within the home provided a fixed point from which fortune, good or bad, could be acceptable.

My grandfather, Giovanni Jacuzzi, was the son of Francesco and Angela Jacuzzi. His father died when he was a child and Giovanni early took over some of his father's role as a breadwinner and helpmate. He became a woodworker, a laborer and helped his mother grow and sell produce. He and his mother moved to the seaport of Trieste for some years before coming back to Casarsa.

James Joyce lived in Trieste while he wrote his first great work, *A Portrait of the Artist as a Young Man*. Fierce winds are a common condition of climate in Trieste, and poles, with steel chains attached are placed throughout the city, so that walkers can grab and hold when the gusts are at their most violent.

In Trieste, Giovanni was just one of thousands like himself; young and sturdy, they supplied the brawn and energy required of the rankless teams of unskilled who worked as loaders and laborers around the seaport docks. Home, after a 12 or 16-hour workday, he would wash up before he ate. The pay he'd pull out of his pocket might be one lire, if he'd been lucky, just enough to buy the day's food on the plate before him, with a little left over.

The little left over eventually amounted to enough to buy a train ticket toward a new and permanent way of life. He and his mother moved back to Casarsa and to the little hamlet of San Lorenzo.

The little village of Casarsa della Delizia and the hamlet of San Lorenzo are in northeastern Italy in the Friuli region. Friuli is a province that is bordered by Switzerland, Austria and Yugoslavia, basically a province of peasants. At that time it was in the province of Udine, but is now in the province of Pordenone. Wars keep changing borders in Europe. The countryside is dotted with hamlets, hand-laid stone houses, chapels and round and square castles built during the crusades and medieval times. These landmarks have never astounded natives as much as tourists, because the residents simply take them for granted.

Friuli is between Venice and Trieste, not far from the Austrian border on the north, so it was vulnerable to invasion. Therefore, castles were built in Austrian and German style as well as Italian and Roman. When Venice conquered Friuli, the decline of the castles began. They were not destroyed by artillery and are well preserved, but they deteriorated through negligence. As time passed, although Friuli was beautiful in its faded glory, it became severely economically depressed by the time my family arrived.

When my grandfather and his mother came back from Trieste, they opened a store selling fruit and other things next to the church in Casarsa. Grandpa was of medium height, about 5 feet, 9 inches tall, and had blond curly hair and blue eyes. He carried himself well and was a careful dresser, I've heard. Sadly, I didn't get to know him.

Among those passing their shop, Grandpa took notice of a pretty girl on her way to church. It didn't take him long to realize that he wanted to take her hand in marriage. Her stepmother took a liking to Grandpa and considered him a great catch for her stepdaughter. Grandma's family was considered well to do, and Grandpa didn't seem to have much, but both Giovanni and Teresa could read and write well.

Grandma was petite, a little over five feet, with brown hair, brown eyes, slight build and was very pretty. Despite Giovanni's lack of worldly goods, the marriage was approved by her father and they were married.

In Italian patriarchal tradition, Grandpa was ten years older than Grandma, which made it easier to impress her and to tell her what to do! He was his own man and also quite dapper, unlike the usual farmers that Teresa knew. But Grandma maintained her independence in some ways, such as signing her maiden name (Arman Teresa Jacuzzi) and being sure that her name was on all contracts of ownership along with Grandpa's signature, as co-owners.

She was the daughter of farmers Giuseppe and Felicita Arman. Grandpa Giovanni and Grandma Teresa were married January 30, 1886. For their honeymoon, Giovanni and Teresa chose Venice, which would seem like an unusual choice. However, my grandfather was an unusual man and this was an unusual time for Venice. They married the year that Venice became part of Italy after a long history of being part of Austria. Perhaps the unique town with its waterways and gondolas captured their hearts as it has captured the hearts of so many, including mine.

Those who visit Venice see it the same way my grandparents saw it, by boat and gondola, and on foot; the same way it will always be visited. Venice never changes, except that it sinks a little deeper into the water with each passing year.

Thomas Mann found Venice irresistible and placed his dying professor in the dying city of Venice to experience passionate love for the first time in *Death in Venice*.

Even Kathryn Hepburn couldn't resist falling in love with Rosanno Brazzi in the movie *Summertime*, filmed beautifully in Venice. I'm sure my grandparents found it just as irresistible on their honeymoon. They had other things to occupy them besides beautiful Venice since their first child, my uncle Rachele, was born nine months later.

My grandparents began their marriage in the village of San Lorenzo near Casarsa where my grandmother had inherited some property. Little did they know that they would gradually shift their entire household to the United States between 1907 and 1921. This major family shift seemed to me like the large current shift of *El Nino*. The batterings the family took along this journey to America were not dissimilar to the ravages often inflicted by *La Bora,* the violent winter winds of Trieste.

My grandparents' first abode in tiny San Lorenzo was a little house that belonged to Nonna (Grandmother) Raffin. There they lived until 1890 and had their first two sons, Racaele (Rachele) and Valeriano (Valerio). With a third child on the way, the house seemed cramped. Grandma got another inheritance that required a little money. It was three hectares of land in a place called Comunale or San Vito al Tagliamento, about a mile from Casarsa.

Grandpa took out a loan for 9,000 lire from the Bank of San Vito al Tagliamento. They sold the property in San Lorenzo and the store in Casarsa. Grandpa made some good deals and they thought there were enough lire to pay for the land and build a house.

Much time elapsed before the house was completed and my grandparents ran out of money before the roof was built. Grandma knew where some money was—her papa. Unfortunately, Giovanni didn't get along well with his father-in-law. Most importantly, this rebel flaunted tradition and had not named the children after their grandfathers. He was, as we say in Italian, *testa dura* or hard-headed.

Despite this, Grandma went to her father. My Aunt Gilia told us about this meeting. It was market day in San Vito and Teresa knew that her father would be going to town. She took off and caught up to him. Both walked to San Vito where the banks were. She simply told him another baby was coming and they needed money to finish the roof before winter.

Her father sternly said, "I am not surprised. Giovanni should provide for you and your children. He doesn't work in the fields. He wears shoes made of leather and he dresses himself like he was going to church every day. He goes to the barber for a shave! Not only that. How come you named the boys strange names, not honoring their grandfathers—not honoring me?"

"Well," Grandma said to him, "remember that you consented that I marry him. You knew that he would not work in the fields. He earns his money in a different way. He does work and earn money, but not in the field. But Papa, we need the roof on the house. And now, I promise that for the next baby and for all that might come after; we will follow traditions in naming the children."

Shrewd negotiator that she was, Grandma got the money. Beginning with the third child, Francesco, they were named after their grandfathers (Francesco and Giuseppe). The first two girls (Felicita and Angelina) were also named for their paternal and maternal grandmothers. Candido (my dad) and Cirilla were named for saints because a priest complained that none of the children had saints' names.

With the help of Nonno (Grandfather) Arman, they were able to build a three-story, six-room house.

Meanwhile, the fourth child, Giuseppe was born. The harsh Friuli wind, rain and snow managed to enter through the windows not yet quite finished due to the lack of money. But still the family kept growing despite their poverty. My Grandma's parents adored Giovanni and Teresa, and gave them a sack of cornmeal to make polenta, or wheat to make bread or pasta whenever they could afford it.

Giovanni and Teresa were both great storytellers and their children loved to listen to them talk. Grandpa had read a lot and kept himself well informed, as did Grandma. Their storytelling tradition was seen at family reunions when the Jacuzzis gave anecdotes from their past.

What kind of woman must my Grandma Teresa have been? She was obviously very busy with so many children. Just to wash their diapers, she had to go out in the winter cold and break blocks of ice apart for water when the nearby creek was frozen over. She gathered wood to make fires for warmth and cooking in the fireplace. She taught her own and neighborhood children subjects such as church liturgy, the *Ten Commandments,* and prayers. She also raised chickens, rabbits, and a goat for milk. At first a cow was just too expensive but eventually they purchased one. Sometimes a pig would be slaughtered for food and fat or sold for money to purchase important needs.

One time, my grandfather really upset my grandmother. According to Aunt Gilia, one day he brought home seven little pigs that were not yet weaned. She was already taking care of five children, who needed all the milk their cow produced. She was dismayed at the prospect of feeding milk to the little newborn pigs with a teaspoon. Grandma solved the problem easily. Young pork is very tender and makes a meal that's *lecca baffi*—mustache lickin' good!

My grandfather had a strange way of thinking about his government. First, I should explain that the nation of Italy had only become unified in the 1860s after the work of Giuseppe Mazzini, Giuseppe Garibaldi and supporters such as operatic composer Giuseppe Verdi. The unification *(Risorgimento)* tied together areas like Sardinia, Lombardy, Parma, Venezia, Modena, Tuscany, Umbria, Romagna, the Papal States, and the kingdom of the two Sicilies. The first king of Italy was Victor Emmanuel II.

In the early 1900s, many juices were fermenting in Italy besides vino. They began to colonize, expand, and annex countries like many of their European neighbors. If everybody else was colonizing, why shouldn't Italy?

Wages and working conditions were tough at home and many Italians believed the Socialist party might help workers. It gained popularity when it claimed that the reigning royal family, the House of Savoy, was corrupt and cared little for the working class. Benito Mussolini began to publish a newspaper about these issues and went so far as to advocate *armed* neutrality against Austria-Hungary. In this atmosphere of inequality and countries moving in on each other, war was eminent.

My grandfather did not trust the new and unpredictable Italian government. He feared that leaders would drag the country into war, taking along all the young men. So he tried to outsmart the government. He was like so many Italians who viewed the government as an enemy or at least an institution to be leery of. His view led to some decisions that still affect our family today.

Meanwhile, the Jacuzzis were becoming very entrepreneurial, according to Aunt Gilia. As the boys grew up, their farming yielded a bumper crop of grapes and produced more than enough wine for the family. The family decided to open an osteria (tavern). Grandma was a pretty good cook and Grandpa helped run the place.

But alas, some customers became drunk and brawled. The little Jacuzzi girls had to be in the tavern near their parents. Giovanni and Teresa did not think it was a good environment for the girls so that was the end of their adventure in the hospitality business. *Peccato*—what a shame. Eating and drinking establishments are my kind of places and I'm sure theirs would've become Casarsa's joint of choice.

Grandpa was quite a carpenter and would teach my father that trade. He made the furniture that was needed in their house, such as tables, benches, cabinets, bedsteads, chests, sideboards, and many more things. Grandma did fine sewing, made over clothes, made slippers and knitted stockings. She was thrifty, kept a well-run house, and helped tend the animals.

Racaele, usually called Rachele, the firstborn son, loved to read and study. Giovanni wanted to encourage his son's fertile mind. By the time my Grandpa was 36 years old, he had six children, five boys, a girl, and a wife to look after. Hardly a week went by that Teresa didn't report some sign of extraordinary brightness she had observed in Rachele. They decided he should be sent to grammar school.

After Rachele completed elementary school, which in those days was three years of schooling, he continued to read and study during the night by candlelight, because there was no electricity. But income was needed, so by day he sold newspapers for his papa at the train station where Grandpa worked part-time.

In those days, the train was the queen of transportation. Townspeople came to watch the train come in and let their imaginations enhance the lives of passengers whom they watched but would never know. Grandpa Giovanni worked hard to become a personable mediator between the familiar and the rest of the world. Company policy required that he wear a starched white collar and tie on the job. He was the messenger between important persons on board and the telegrapher, who delivered the written route instructions up to the engineer, who rode in the little engine cabin.

Giovanni loved to tell his children about the passengers of exceptional note: a Cardinal, who'd made the sign of the cross over him that day; four musicians from Pordenone who'd been hired to play at a rich man's party; a Chaucerian lady traveling with three servants who'd been sent to Paris by her lover in Germany; and local boys who soothed their mothers and sweethearts as they boarded for Udine to enlist in the King's Army.

When Rachele was 14, he got around on a bicycle which he had converted into something of an archetype. A fin was attached to the back of the bike, and a swinging movement, operated by the conventional pedals, propelled the bike forward. At the time, Rachele's simple management of air flow to create propulsion won him the outspoken praise of his father.

It was the summer of his 14th year that Grandpa urged Rachele to go out of the country for better pay. So Rachele went to a brick factory in Munich, Germany, with brother Valeriano who was just 13. The entire family saw them off and they were financed by Rachele, who had apprenticed to the telegrapher, and now had a full time job. They worked during the summer making bricks. This became an annual summer job for other Jacuzzi brothers as well.

Besides needing financial help from the boys, my grandfather sent them to Germany so they wouldn't be in Italy when war was brewing. It wasn't that my grandparents minded them serving in the military, it was that nobody wants their children to be injured or killed in a war. So they encouraged the boys to leave Italy as they approached draft age. This began a family tradition of trying to outthink the government. It also developed an interest in going to other countries, and eventually led to emigration.

My uncle Rachele, always the quintessential intellectual, became a telegraph operator when he was 19, at the same railway station where my grandfather worked. At that time, the telegraph was a system of dots and dashes recorded on a tape at the receiving end. It was later (after 1913) that telegraphs were automated so that they could be sent by key and received by ear. Rachele's quickness to learn and interest in new inventions grew with this experience.

After Giuseppe, Gelindo, Giocondo, Felicita, Angelina, and Ancilla were born, Cirilla, Candido, Stella, and Gilia were to come later. I know, I know, this is like a Russian novel with so many names. And as if that's not enough, when they came to the United States, many of them changed their names to American ones.

Meanwhile, Grandma inherited various "vaults" (land parcels) from her side of the family. Grandpa, ever the entrepreneur, had the good fortune of being the broker for the sale of a property called Casa Matta that belonged to Count Zoppola. Now this begins to sound like a movie from Transylvania with Count Dracula, but I promise it's not.

Grandpa received a tidy sum of money that he used to buy a rather large piece of land called La Marcia. Today, the remains of the Castle of Zoppola can be visited in the Valvasone area of Friuli. The Casa Matta is currently occupied by a discothèque lounge. Thank God Grandma and Grandpa can't see it now. But since Grandma and Grandpa loved music and dancing so much, maybe they'd think *stupendo*, right on!

They purchased still other pieces of land called Latina Seconda, Ciampignon, Scodelaris, and Ciamput over different time periods with the help of Grandma's inheritance. The land of Friuli was fertile and provided much work for everybody, from the little ones to the adults.

My father, Candido, was born in 1903. That year, bicycle maker Orville Wright was the first man to fly a powered heavier-than-air machine in which he stayed aloft for all of 12 seconds. Rachele, 17 by that time, would have paid attention to the news about such an invention, because he was so interested in scientific things. At that time, our family had no idea that they would soon be making airplane history.

The following year, as news of the Wright brothers and dirigible flights spread, Ren Shields and George Evans wrote the song *Come Take a Trip in My Air-Ship,* which was actually more about love than airships. One must guess that an airship (a blimp kind of thing) can be flown by a mere finger, leaving a pilot plenty of room to kiss a girl.

> I love a sailor, the sailor loves me,
> And sails ev'ry night to my home.

He's not a sailor that sails o'er the sea,
Or the wild briny foam,
For he owns an airship and sails up on high;
He's just like a bird on the wing,
And when the shadows of evening draw nigh,
He'll sail to my window and sing:
Come take a trip in my airship,
Come take a sail 'mong the stars,
Come have a ride around Venus,
Come have a spin around Mars.
No one to watch while we're kissing
No one to see while we spoon,
Come take a trip in my airship,
And we'll visit the man in the moon.

An even larger family house in Casarsa was started in 1905, but during several years of scarcity, it was hard to complete. The small house my grandfather bought was a two-story flagstone place with a red tile roof. It is still standing, remodeled into a family library by my father, but no longer a Jacuzzi possession. I sold it, under financial pressures, when I was managing the Jacuzzi-Italy operation many years ago. At the front of the house, there was a feature of some dimension, an elaborate iron gate. Viewed for its separate merit, it was quite a structure, but taken at the whole, its proportions overwhelmed the little house. The few acres that went with the house were planted with corn, beans, grains for the cow and chickens, and strawberries.

My Aunt Cirilla was born in 1905, the year that the Industrial Workers of the World (IWW) was founded as a universal working class movement to improve conditions for workers. The oppression of workers by profiteers was making news in the U.S., Soviet Union, and much of Europe. Unions were springing up everywhere to protect poor overworked underprivileged laborers. In Italy, children were regarded as rewards, not punishments. The Italians, particularly those who worked the land for a living, might not understand today's antiseptic processes for spacing and reducing the size of a family.

My grandmother knew about labor. She had a child almost every year, and probably nursed them all until they grew teeth. Altogether, my grandparents had 21 children but only seven boys and six girls managed to survive to adulthood.

She and Grandpa must have suffered much heartbreak with the loss of eight children. Those who survived were Rachele (1886–1937), Valeriano (1887–1973), Francesco (1889–1973), Giuseppe (1891–1965), Gelindo (1894–1950), Giocondo (1895–1921), Felicita (1897–1978), Angelina (1899–1990), Ancilla (1901–1949), Candido (1903–1986), Cirilla (1905–2000), Stella (1907–2003) and Gilia (1908–?).

My Aunt Gilia, the only one of my father's siblings still alive, is still razor-sharp and she will not hesitate to share her views on everything from whether Catholic priests should marry (yes, if they want to) to U.S. politics and presidential campaigns (don't ask).

In 1906 at age 20, Rachele joined or was drafted by the Italian Army and was assigned to the Communication Corps enabling him to use his telegraphy trade. During this time he attended a Florence training school for a year and then served out his three years of enlistment at a post in Asmara, the capital of Eritrea, in what is now Ethiopia in eastern Africa. Asmara was a well-equipped post, and off duty, he spent hours reading available military manuals about a phenomenal new dynamic called air power.

A look at the history of Italy showed me that Italy had tried to colonize this area but in July 1906, reluctantly granted independence to Ethiopia in a pact with Great Britain and France. Troops (including Rachele) were sent in to aid a smooth transfer of leadership when the Ethiopian leader died. Ethiopian issues caused much unrest within Italy and anarchists bombed St. Peter's Cathedral in Rome four months after the pact was signed. Terrorists are neither an exclusive nor recent invention of the 21st century.

I've heard that around this time, many Friulani were so disgusted with the Italian government, limited economic opportunities and war posturing that they emigrated to Canada and South America. During Rachele's military service, at Grandpa Giovanni's urging, Valeriano and Francesco got out of Italy and came to America in 1907 at ages 20 and 18.

The year before they came, San Francisco had suffered the largest earthquake in American history. Valeriano and Francesco sailed from Le Havre to Ellis Island on October 4, 1907. They chose to travel from New York on to the West Coast because many Italian farmers and fishermen were finding it prosperous. They first went to Spokane, Washington where they worked with a railroad construction crew.

They were soon attracted to California, and went to work in a copper mine in the Shasta area. Then Francesco broke his hip, crushed between two coal cars. During a year of recuperation, he worked for a family in Watsonville who needed help with their apple orchard. During that time, Valeriano left the mine to work in an oil refinery near San Luis Obispo.

Upon Francesco's recovery, the brothers decided to shake the coal dust off their feet forever and head for Southern California to pick oranges for a living, arriving there around 1910.

A year earlier, Orville Wright had made big news in 1909 when he tested the first U.S. Army airplane and flew it one hour and twelve minutes. It impressed the Army and they accepted the first delivery of a military airplane. Later that year, the Army Air Corps was formed with the first delivery of planes from the Wright brothers.

My aunt told us that after Rachele's hitch in the Army, he went to Milan to study engineering and aeronautics, and became excited about airplanes. She also remembered that when Rachele brought home fireworks and launched them, the loud, explosive sounds startled and frightened her so much that she didn't want to look up at them. She mentioned that this was about the same time a brilliant comet was visible in the western sky. That would have been Halley's Comet, which was visible May 8, 1910.

Meanwhile, in 1910 Congress attempted to purify the flood of immigrants arriving in the country. They amended the Immigration Act of 1907 to exclude paupers, criminals, anarchists and diseased persons.

Thrift was not a virtue that Rachele ever learned to practice. His Army discharge money was in his pocket, and the amount he got for his work in the Milan engine shop raised the count. There were two new sisters whom he had yet to see in Casarsa, Stella and Gilia. He loaded up with gifts for everyone and the train brought the poor but happy young man into the depot at Casarsa in 1910.

When Rachele read the letters from his two brothers in American, he became fired up with enthusiasm from his aeronautics training, and wanted to go to America and join his brothers. He heard that in Los Angeles, individuals were experimenting with new ideas in aviation. He wanted to see for himself what they were doing. He hocked his gold watch to raise money for the passage and left for the west coast of the United States.

The first U.S. Air Meet was held at Los Angeles in 1910. Audiences averaged 35,000 per day and watched air speed records be broken by a Frenchman and Glenn Curtiss of the U.S. Perhaps the Air Meet inspired Alfred Bryan and Fred Fisher, because in 1910 they wrote the most famous airplane song ever written.

> Come Josephine in my flying machine,
> Going up she goes; up she goes!

> Balance yourself like a bird on a beam,
> In the air she goes, there she goes!
> Up, up, a little bit higher.
> Oh, my, the moon is on fire.
> Come Josephine in my flying machine,
> Going up, all on, 'goodbye.'

Rachele settled in Los Angeles at the age of 24 where aviation action was, but first worked picking oranges like the other brothers. However, he shortly found work in a machine shop. The immigration of the Jacuzzis to America ran like a trans-ocean pulley: as soon as the price of passage was earned in America and the chances for work looked decent, another brother was sent the money and drawn into the country.

In 1911, the war in Tripoli, Libya, had just begun. Since Italy was an ally, Giuseppe was at risk of being drafted by the Italian Army to defend Tripoli against the Turks. Planes were used for the first time in a military capacity on August 3, 1911, when Italians reconnoitered Turkish lines near Tripoli. Grandpa managed to scrape together enough to send Giuseppe to America.

My aunt Cirilla told us that Grandpa Jacuzzi was criticized by neighbors for sending his sons to America to avoid the draft. He was told that he was not patriotic. Never one to please others, he was satisfied that he was doing the right thing for his family. At that point, Rachele, Valeriano, Francesco, and Giuseppe were in America while the rest of the children were in Italy working the land with their parents.

With the older boys gone and because of poverty, my father attended only five years of school and then quit to help out on the farm. At that time in Italy, schooling was mandatory only through the third grade. It wasn't unusual for pre-teen children to begin working, especially if their parents owned farms.

Felicita and Angelina were still young. Grandma taught them to sew for their family members. None of the family bought ready-made clothes except for shoes, which they took good care of. When the land was dry, they wore shoes inside the house, but never upstairs. When it was muddy, raining or snowing, they wore zoccoli, a clog made from wood in the shape of the foot, or ciabate, a slipper popular in Friuli. Aunt Cirilla told us that the shoes we wear today were only worn then by the very rich. They were too costly for farmers. But no one really cared because their neighbors were all alike. They all made do with the little they had.

From the youngest to the oldest, each child in Casarsa had his or her job to do. The Jacuzzis worked the land, gathered the harvest, tended the beasts, raised the silkworms and made silk, and did countless other things to provide for all of their needs. My father and my aunts and uncles remembered the voracious appetite of the silkworms that Grandma kept up in the attic.

Silkworms were fed with mulberry leaves. Their greedy munching jaws could be heard all over the house. When they were ready to spin, they were given branches to attach their cocoons to, and covered with cloths so they would be in the dark. They are sensitive and any small temperature change made them swell up and sweat a milky substance that might kill them. They had to be kept warm so the family set out iron pots *(bacinelle di braci)* filled with embers made from dried corn cobs.

Sudden loud noises made them turn their heads sharply and snap their threads. If a thunderstorm came during the spinning season, someone always went to the attic and set up a constant percussion on tin so the thunderclaps would pass unnoticed. This care is one reason that Italian silk is so precious and famous throughout the world.

My father told me that life was not all work. People sang, whistled, played musical instruments and danced for entertainment. Sometimes Grandpa would sing and whistle for hours. He had a beautiful voice, I've been told. Grandma was not equally blessed. But still some evenings they would sing duets of popular songs like "O Ce Biel Cis'cel a Udin" or "Tanto Tempo Che tu mi Conosci," and the beautiful "Assunta Inglese." Dad continued this tradition and everyone enjoyed having him for dinner when he would burst into song at the table.

Perhaps they kept themselves happy to endure their meager means. My Grandma loved to read, and she would often explain to the family about the stories in the Bible, or history, romances, and poetry. Books alone have not been needed to tell the children about the history of their region. For them, the parents have always been around to repeat their legends to ready little ears. During May and October, there were devotions and prayers, and after dinner everyone would get on their knees and say the Rosary.

During the icy cold winter evenings, not even the fireplace was enough to warm them. They would all go into the stables with the farm animals to benefit from their warmth. It certainly was not a perfumery. As the Italians say, "When necessary, one learns to live with it." To endure the stable aroma, someone was always telling a story or singing. When Grandpa told stories, he liked to scare the children with mysteries and killings, sprinkled between fairy tales.

On traditional and special occasions such as New Year's Day, the children would run early in the morning to wish each other happy new year in Grandma and Grandpa's bedroom. Each child was given a piece of torrone (nougat) or other traditional sweets such as biscotti or torts.

The Carnevale, which starts on Fat Thursday and culminates on Fat Tuesday (Martedi Grasso), was celebrated just before Lent. Everyone would dress up in masks and gather with the neighbors to eat thin, sweet fritters called Crostoli, drinking wine, singing and dancing together.

There were special times for prayers and fasting on Fridays during Lent with the celebration of Easter. It began with Easter Mass when they dressed up in newly made clothes. After Mass the family would end their Easter dinner with panettone (a high cake) from Milan, which Grandpa would buy.

As Easter slipped away, so would the icy cold of winter. The blossoms of springtime and the slowly warming sun would usher in, day by day, the beautiful season of summer. The youngest of the kids would run and play hopscotch and other games with neighbors. The parents would sit around, gossip and discuss all manner of things from weather to politics to the latest farming tools and machinery.

About harvest time was "la Sagra," the celebration (la festa) of Casarsa for the harvest. There were carnival rides for kids and expositions of some of the latest farm machines. The celebration of the picking of the grapes (vendemmia) was the highlight of la Sagra. There was beautiful singing from the local choral group, accordion music, dancing and plenty of wine to drink.

As the leaves turned colors, from green to red, yellow and brown, the chill of rapidly approaching winter rains and winds soon filled the air. During the time of *Tutti i Santi*—All Saints Day—they would attend Mass and walk in procession to visit and pray at the gravesites of deceased family members and friends. Later they cheered their spirits by eating freshly roasted chestnuts and drinking vin brulè by a warm fire.

Just as a certain exuberance filled the air during Easter celebrations following Lent, la Sagra in the early fall led to excesses occasionally…frequently. Okay, let's face it. Italians invented phrases about Lent such as, "He leapt upon his wife like a friar leaps upon a ham at the end of Lent." Self-sacrifice is not exactly an Italian trait and while some truly fast there are always some Italians who fast only by skipping dessert.

Twenty-one Jacuzzi kids didn't just happen along, at least not without some attendant pleasantries first taking place. Yes, Grandma and Grandpa had a deep religious faith, respect for family and each other, the old country, and conservative values. But with what I've heard of their joy for life and love for each other, I can easily picture them f...g each others' brains out. Now that's Italian! That's amore!

The end of the year brought Christmas and all of the pious functions and adorations that went with this religious season, especially those centered on the manger (Presepio) and the birth of Jesus. Everyone hung their socks on Christmas Eve alongside the staircase in hopes that they be filled them with goodies. Sometimes they found things like a whistle or harmonica for the boys, a doll made from rags or ribbons for the girls and maybe an orange, an apple and a piece of torrone (almond nougat).

My Aunt Gilia recalled that at Christmas, the children would go to neighbors to wish them Merry Christmas and might be given a few coins. Once Gilia was given a doll made of confections and goodies, the only doll she ever had or so she said. She loved to tragically tell how the pig ate her doll up!

Shoes had to be worn to attend church. During cold weather, hats and coats were usually not worn because shawls kept out the cold air. Long sleeves, long stockings, long pants or dresses, petticoats, and undershirts kept children warm. They also carried a handkerchief (veleta or velo) to cover their head for church.

Following Christmas and New Year's was the celebration of the Epiphany on January 6. The townspeople of Casarsa would gather and build a giant, bell-shaped fire at the town's crossroads. They called this Festa "Paccancavin." At the fire's center, a large cross was erected with a bale of pine twigs hung at each end of the cross. Around the periphery of the fire, many bales of corn stalks were arranged so that the fire would burn at least two hours. Before being lit, the priest would circle the fire, blessing it with holy water and then lighting it at four places, like the cardinal points of a compass. Meanwhile the town's choir sang religious and popular songs.

After the fire was lit, everyone would drink new wine made from the recently harvested grapes and enjoy the music provided by the accordion and the voices. As the fire rose from the bottom of the woodpile up through to the cross, everyone watched anxiously to see in which direction the smoke would go. That would foretell the abundance of the coming harvest as well as the marriages of the young men and women. When the smoke direction was fortuitous, you could hear shrieks of joy and laughter from the young people, but when the smoke went the other way; many could be heard saying their prayers.

That was daily life at that time in Friuli. My aunt wasn't sure if all of these traditions continue today in Friuli, but she hoped so.

The brothers in America were sending money to Italy to help my Grandpa pay off the mortgage on the house. My grandfather's idea was always to have the family united for he believed the united family was a strong family. He made his house big for this purpose. His dream was always that the boys who were in America would return to Italy.

That dream was dashed by their oldest brightest child. Rachele wrote his father that in Chino, California, near Los Angeles, there was an orange ranch for sale. He thought it would be a good idea to sell everything in Italy so the rest of the family could come to America to be together and live on this orange ranch.

Grandpa thought the whole idea was rather strange and ridiculous. It was a very big step to take. Grandma was dead set against it, having worked so hard to acquire property from her ancestors. But Grandpa was the patriarch, the older man, and he would make the decision.

He, therefore, decided to leave for America himself to see what this idea was all about before considering such a big move. Grandpa Jacuzzi traveled to Ellis Island arriving February 10, 1911, at age 55. Without knowing a word of English, he traveled to Los Angeles to visit his sons and listen to their idea for moving the entire family to America. Rachele was making a good income repairing airplanes and building propellers. Giovanni liked what he saw, and yearned to have his family together once again.

After returning to Italy, Grandpa decided that everything in Italy should be sold to buy this orange ranch in Chino. Grandma Teresa was not convinced, however, because they were well established in Italy and she was afraid to move. She was happy when it became difficult to sell the property immediately and had to put the move on hold for some time. It was extremely hard for her to leave and she made Grandpa agree that they could come back one day. He not only acquiesced but left a little furniture in the house for future visits.

It was hard on all the family to consider moving to America. My aunt Cirilla said:

> Rachele wrote to us that all of the brothers were now living in Berkeley, California, and that they were all married, some with children, and that they would not be returning any more to Italy.
>
> Rachele said that if Papa still had the idea to reunite the family that it would be up to us to come to America. I cannot tell you how much anguish we suffered and our parents suffered knowing that their boys were going to stay in America and would not return anymore to Italy. All this followed suffering and working so hard to build up something in Italy, to build a house and to have acquired the land to work.

The idea of moving to America was welcomed by some of the family. My uncle Giocondo really did not like being a farm hand so he had found a job at the train station in Casarsa just as his father and brothers had done. Therefore, he was elated at the prospect of going to America, land of opportunity, and leaving the world of farming behind him.

Grandpa Giovanni, who always had the final say, eventually convinced Teresa to put most of the property up for sale. At this time, the rumor of eminent war on Italian soil was quite strong. Because of this, Grandpa sent Gelindo and Giocondo on to America, and received new criticisms from everyone in town. Gelindo had worked on the farm in Udine, Italy, where he experimented with commercial fertilizers. In his spare time, he raced bicycles and also worked as a brick mason in Germany, as had his brothers. But he was perhaps the most interested in farming among the boys and would finally, in America, have his own farm.

Gelindo and Giocondo arrived at Ellis Island on December 21, 1912, when Gelindo was 18 and Giocondo was 17 years old. There may have been some greater fear about sailing because the "unsinkable" *Titanic* had gone down six months earlier on April 14th but they were undaunted.

They went on to Southern California where first Gelindo picked oranges and sharpened knives and scissors on Los Angeles streets. He used a sharpening stone mounted on wheels, which he constructed himself. He also washed dishes for a restaurant. Instead of being paid, the restaurant owners gave him a lot in Beverly Hills, which he later sold for a nice profit. It seemed like everything was coming up roses (or oranges)!

Francesco had gone to work for Standard Oil and soon leased a ranch where Giuseppe, Gelindo and Giocondo worked. However, after two hard years of farming, Frank gave up the ranch and went to work as a cabinetmaker (which he had learned from Grandpa) in Los Angeles. Giuseppe also headed back to the city to search for work. Francesco then switched to building automobile bodies for two years.

Meanwhile in Italy, the sale of the family property was suspended because buyers feared impending major war in the face of two small Balkan wars of 1912–1913. Since the house couldn't be sold, the rest of the family remained in Italy somewhat longer.

Those left in Casarsa had to work the farmland without the stronger older boys to help. It was hard to find farmhands as Europe entered World War I. Then the assassination of Archduke Ferdinand and his wife by a Serb in 1914 touched off the tensions between countries. As each country entered the fray, they pulled with them other countries who were involved in alliances to protect each other.

My Aunt Stella's first recollection of the war was in 1914 when she was seven. They saw many soldiers all going in the same direction and Grandma told them the men were going to war.

My aunts and uncles remembered long columns of marching and singing soldiers passing in front of the house. They saw some Bersaglieri (sharpshooters) who wore uniforms and black feathers in their hats that glistened in the sun and their marches were more the speed of jogging. Some rode bicycles. The soldiers camped along the way overnight and ate boiled meat, soup, coffee, wine, canned milk, and other items. They bound their legs with a long band, a part of their uniform.

Schools were shut down right away and for four years there was no school except their mother's teachings.

Grandpa Giovanni was almost killed in that year, according to Aunt Stella. Two Austrian soldiers passed by. One wanted to take the watch Grandpa had earned for his work at the railroad station. The soldier pointed a gun at Giovanni's chest, ready to shoot. The other soldier pulled him away and saved my Grandpa. As Stella said, "If that soldier had killed Papa, none of us would be here today!"

According to the law at the time, because the oldest son Rachele had already served in the Armed Forces, the next sons were permitted to avoid the draft. Assuming he would not be drafted, in 1915, Valeriano returned to Italy. He went to help out on the farm and prepare the remaining family members for their trip to America, teaching them some English.

When he returned to Italy, he brought the first canned food the family had ever seen; peaches and pears. They could not understand how canned food could possibly be of interest when people could raise their own fresh fruit and produce, or easily buy it at the market.

Grandpa bought some new modern farm equipment to work the land and horses to pull plows, so the work was easier. But as the war heated up, the government sequestered their horses and some of their cows. With the cows that remained, they pulled the implements to work the land.

The cloud of war and darkness settled upon them, full of cold, dark, sickness, ignorance and want. The Italian people underwent a terrible grinding; a grinding that left young men old. Children were given ancient faces and grave voices. Hunger stared down and filled up empty streets. The corrupt Italian government had gotten them into this mess and could not get them out.

As the war went on, the law about calling up other brothers was waived. Therefore, Valeriano was called into the service. Thus, the sisters and my father, Candido, were left to work the land. They all did the best they could. The mail to and from America was halted because of the war. And then the very thing that my Grandpa always feared happened!

Valeriano suffered a bad head injury and was sent home from the Army. The Red Cross marked certain trains that brought back injured men. Gilia remembered the day that her papa got the telegram about Valeriano being injured. Giovanni went to visit his son in the hospital. Valeriano finally came home on one of the marked trains with a bandage around his head and dark eyeglasses. He could not work for many years during his convalescence.

The war was right at my father's doorstep. Candido grew up feeling the same as Grandpa about trying to protect his sons from the draft. Dad told me about what happened to his dog during the war.

He had a sweet dog that he loved very much, named Milecca, which means, "she licks me." During World War I, the Germans often used my grandparents' house as a first aid or way station and they were usually pretty decent, Dad said. But one day, Milecca growled at a German soldier. The officer shot the beloved dog. My father told me he hated war after that. And the suffering of his older brother Valeriano from his wound compounded that.

Back in the safety of America, Rachele worked in the machine shop, and sat up half the night reading technical books to supplement his third-grade education. Like Jules Verne and Leonardo da Vinci, Rachele Jacuzzi had a mind that seethed with fantastic visions of future technology. He had created a special propeller for adventurous young R. L. Remington of Los Angeles. The job ended when Remington's father died in 1914. Rachele then took a job as a mechanic with the Christoferson Aviation Company in San Francisco. But it was not until the 1915 Panama-Pacific International Exposition in San Francisco that his creative energies found a focus.

The Exposition had begun the previous year to celebrate the opening of the Panama Canal. It displayed some of the world's latest scientific achievements, but Rachele was fascinated most by the "aero plane." It was a machine so extraordinary that it seemed to epitomize imagination itself. And yet, the "aero plane" was clearly still in its infancy, a feeble child that would require much nurturing before it could begin to live out its purpose.

Rachele made another unique propeller for a flyer he met at the Fair. It was so successful that he soon received orders for more from others in the Bay Area such as the Union Gas Engine Company, Corham Aviation School, and the Hall-

Scott Motor Car Company. An Italian import merchant, G. Tarola, advanced Rachele money to provide the equipment to fill propeller orders.

Gelindo joined Rachele in 1915. They worked on the design and building of airplane propellers. The two brothers spent hours conferring with Mills College professors at the Lick Observatory in Oakland, in quest of scientific information.

Meanwhile, even though America did not enter World War I until 1917, the Jacuzzi brothers were awarded a contract in 1915 to make propellers for the fledgling U.S. Air Force. The propeller shop was in full production during World War I, keeping all the brothers busy. They moved from a small rented building in Oakland, California, to two stores in Berkeley in 1917.

I cannot believe the many talents of my extraordinary uncles. In the early mornings before going to work, Gelindo picked chickens for a San Francisco poultry house. At night he took up boxing, and sometimes sparred with the famous boxer, Jack Dempsey, during the champ's gym workouts. In addition, he became an avid devotee of the opera. He was a very well-rounded man.

Uncle Giocondo was interested in art. He attended an art school for a while, but soon joined his brothers building propellers. He continued painting as a hobby and remained an artist at heart. Before he left Italy, Giocondo had brought home a mandolin, which he used to strum, and then he acquired a zither. According to my Aunt Gilia, he was the musician of the family, the only one "who could get a tune out of it."

Uncle Rachele married Olympia Calugi in 1916, when he was 30 and she was 35. He did not follow the tradition of marrying a younger girl, and probably lived to regret it. Meanwhile, his four brothers moved into Rachele's home in typical close-knit Italian fashion.

Rachele and his wife found that they could not have children. In desperation, after 12 years of marriage they adopted a baby boy named Gordon. Olympia was 47 when she finally had a child upon whom to shower affections. Everybody said she doted on Gordon, and criticized how she treated Rachele, making his henpecked life lamentable on many levels. Rachele's joy was his creativity. At least in the family, the younger brothers listened to what he had to say, whether his wife did or not.

How many married guys out there resemble that remark? Hey, guys, our ladies probably feel we leave a lot to be desired, too. I wonder what my Uncle Rachele would tell me about the fair sex if we could sit down and chat over a bottle of wine?

In 1917, Lee Scott of the Hall-Scott Motor Company visited the Jacuzzi shop to see the work on propellers he had ordered. He was so impressed that he invited the Jacuzzi brothers to move closer to his plant in Berkeley to supply them with propellers to fulfill a contract for airplanes with the Russian government for use in WWI. In September, 1917, the brothers rented two stores on San Pablo Avenue and Addison Street in Berkeley for the propeller shop.

Rachele created a way of laminating layers of tough wood to make a thin propeller, which was nicknamed "the toothpick." The "toothpick" propeller became so significant to the aviation industry that it now stands in the Smithsonian Institution alongside Lindbergh's "Spirit of St. Louis" and other aviation landmarks. The propeller on display there was built during WWI for a seaplane, which was flown for five years.

As Rachele worked with the parts for airplanes, it was a pleasant experience, like undressing a willing woman. As the fragile machines gradually revealed themselves, their smell of lacquer on wood, leather, isinglass and castor oil was its own pleasant reward.

Rachele was driven to play a role in the new world of aviation, so dramatically portrayed in Hollywood movies. The movies, many of which were made only 200 miles away, featured World War I pilots who thrilled audiences as much as cowboys and Valentino.

The first movie to use an airplane in the plot was a 12-minute Mack Sennett 1912 comedy called *A Dash through the Clouds* with Mabel Normand. A Wright brother's plane, the Wright Model B, was flown in the movie by one of the Wright team of pilots, Philip O. Parmalee, who died in a crash later that year.

Next, comedian Roscoe "Fatty" Arbuckle directed and starred in a one-reel comedy called *The Sky Pirate*.

In 1915, a major film called *The Girl of Yesterday* came out with Donald Crisp and Mary Pickford. Aerial flying and stunts were done by pilot Lincoln Beachey who was killed later that year in a plane crash. Another 1915 movie, *Out of the Air*, featured an airplane to train transfer done by a stunt pilot.

Secret of the Submarine was a 15-part serial made in 1916 with some aerial scenes. *The Flying Torpedo* was made in 1916 with Erich Von Stroheim playing, what else, an evil German officer. *A Romance in the Air* made in 1918 was about a WWI flying ace, Lt. Bert Hall, who played himself. His real girlfriend was his love. This theme picked up on the many popular songs about lovers flying through the clouds together.

In 1919, Harry Houdini was in *The Grim Game*. The magician was unjustly jailed and escaped, using an airplane, to seek the real villains. His stunt pilot double, WWI pilot and wing-walker Robert Kennedy was nearly killed when a midair collision occurred. Houdini always claimed that he was actually in the plane when it crashed but he was not.

The following year, WWI pilots and stunt flyers Ormer Locklear and Milton Elliott were not so lucky. While filming the final night scene in *The Skywayman*, they flew a plane into the ground and died when movie searchlights blinded them. The crash was kept in the movie, as was the crash in *The Grim Game*, drawing audiences to see the horrific events.

Rachele's laminated propeller was selected for the first U.S. transcontinental mail flight. Using his own shop in Berkeley, he enlisted his brothers to help in the manufacture of the "Jacuzzi Toothpick." In 1919, Jacuzzi Brothers, Inc. was formed as a company name, and the boys were able to help buy passage to the United States for their parents and the rest of the siblings in Italy.

Rachele's English was passable but most of the family floundered in the language, which marked them as foreigners, requiring that they huddle together like a separate species in fear of extinction. Their only associations outside the family were usually with other Italian immigrants like themselves, socially stereotyped as ignorant, overzealous foreigners who stole jobs from the "natives" and maybe stole a lot more besides.

My father and aunts were still in Italy enduring terrible moments during WWI such as the retreat (ritirata) from Caporetto, made famous additionally by Ernest Hemingway's, *A Farewell to Arms*. They said that even though it was raining day and night, people abandoned their homes for fear of the enemy. Everywhere were implements of war, people lost and abandoned, wandering aimlessly around the countryside, with dead bodies lying everywhere.

The Jacuzzi family tried to escape over the bridge spanning the Tagliamento River. Just as they reached it, the bridge was bombed. Everything and everyone on it crashed into the river below and many people were swept away in the torrent of the river. When they could not cross, the family returned home with their two cows and horse pulling a cart with their belongings. Their home had been ransacked and someone was trying to walk off with the remaining cows just as they returned, but family members ran them off.

My Aunt Cirilla described the war years movingly:

> I see that horror today as clearly and as terribly as it occurred those many, many years ago. I was still a girl at the time and I remember those explosions and bombs to the left and to the right that lit up the night sky like artificial fireworks. The Germans advanced into Italy and we were under their control and occupation for over a year. Many lives were lost as were many animals and much of the harvest. The Germans did not have much to eat so they confis-

cated everything we had. Many, many people came down from the mountains because they, too, had very little to eat.

On one of these occasions, Giuseppina (who later married Valeriano) came to our house together with her cousin, Pasquetta. We gave the young girls what they needed to live and eat. In exchange they helped us with the work of the house and the farm.

We passed many days together like sisters. Everyone was afraid but the little ones like us did not recognize some of the dangers that were around us. We would play with the explosives and the shells as if they were toys. I look back now and I think that there must have been some good God that protected us in those terrible moments.

At times, the land, animals, and vineyards produced great quantities. Mother sold everything: butter, milk, cheese, eggs, chickens, rabbits, pigs, veal, vegetables of every type and quality. Everything was very much sought after. We had enough to bring everything to the central market where Father was the salesman. With the money that Papa made, he was able to finish the payments on the house and the end of the war finally came.

The Italian government paid us some money for damages we suffered during the war. Then came the first letter from America after such a long time of interrupted mail.

After his long convalescence, Valeriano was able to once more work and in the meantime had fallen in love with Giuseppina (Pina). They were married and their first son, Virgil, was born and became the grand joy of the family. In America, our brothers continued to write us to reunite the family in America. Sisters Felicita and Angelina were already engaged in Italy. Father did not want them to marry in Italy because he was concerned about how to make this trip and re-unite the family.

My Aunt Gilia remembered that her father sometimes brought home eggs, sugar, salt and cheese that had been dumped out of trains. More and more patrols came by the house. Once Grandma offered them milk to drink. Because they feared being poisoned, they made her drink it first.

The family dug holes in the garden to hide potatoes, grain, copper, wine and other things. Grandma paid a teacher with eggs and a chicken to give the children lessons beyond what she could teach. Gilia said that they were so hungry; she tried to take some olive branches that had been blessed on Palm Sunday. When Grandpa Giovanni slapped her face, she didn't try to do that any more.

Gilia's memories include with shudders that everybody seemed to have lice and Grandma combed the children's hair hunting for them. The children saw terrible atrocities like an Italian prisoner forced by an Austrian officer to be washed with a stiff brush and soap, cutting his skin. The Italian swore that he would kill him if he got a chance.

They also saw Russian prisoners of war who were forced to fix roads but spent more time making trinkets to sell for food than working.

Aunt Gilia's first memory of the American flag was in 1917, when she was nine years old. The Americans had joined the Allies and some American soldiers were camped on a field across from the family home. She had not seen American soldiers before and ran out to see them and ask for chocolate candies. The soldiers were putting up a flag and one said, "This is the American flag."

As an aside, Gilia learned later from an American woman how the flag should be displayed. Gilia's husband led a parade for the National Recovery Act (NRA) in 1933 and carried the flag in the manner she had learned about. Many years later, in her community in Mill Creek Point, she noticed that a flag was incorrectly attached to a light pole. She proudly brought people together to get it mounted on the correct kind of pole.

At the end of World War I in 1918, Italy was insulted when they were given no part of the Hapsburg Empire after it was carved up and divided between several triumphant countries. Unemployment, ineffective government, a cost of living that rose more than 500% since 1914, and endless strikes plagued the nation during and after the war. These abominable conditions would lead to Mussolini taking over the government in 1922. Talk of more war continued and many more Italians left for America.

◆ ◆ ◆

After a flurry of activity in their California shop, the war ended in 1918 and the Jacuzzi propeller business declined sharply. The brothers kept one store and converted it into an auto and airplane repair shop. Rachele guided his brethren to conduct experiments on building airplanes. In 1920, the shop sign at 1450 San Pablo Avenue in Berkeley, California, read "Airplane Work."

Uncle Gelindo had become an expert mechanic and built his own hot-rod car from scratch, combining a Ford chassis, Reo radiator, and an engine put together from parts. He designed and built the body from aluminum sheets, and fitted it with red upholstery. He was the daredevil of the family, a mechanical craftsman, and brought his ingenuity to play in the development of an airplane.

As the Jacuzzi brothers tried to fit into the American dream, they began to use simpler names for themselves. Francesco was called Frank and Giuseppe was called Joseph. Five of my uncles (Frank, Joseph, Gelindo, Giocondo and Rachele) drew up articles of incorporation on May 3, 1920, "to manufacture, buy, sell, repair and deal in Airoplanes and Airoplane propellers."

It was during this time that the brothers together built a small monoplane called the "Mosquito." I would love to have been there to hear the conversation as they chose that name. They used a Model T engine that they rebuilt for greater power. After Gelindo successfully flew this plane, the brothers decided to build a bigger one. Then all the Jacuzzis got into the act.

It costs a lot to build an airplane. The Jacuzzi family fortune became heavily invested in the creation of this new larger airplane. The investment paid off in a way. United States aviation history recorded it as the first cabin monoplane ever built in America. The Jacuzzi Cabin Monoplane was built in 1920, had 200 horsepower, held seven passengers, and could fly at 100 miles per hour. It was notable in that it was designed for multi-passenger use. It's hard to imagine the excitement this generated as the Jacuzzis rode the crest of the most advanced technology in the world.

Grandpa Giovanni was enthusiastic to move the family to America where everyone could be in on the history-making events. He thought he would first send Felicita, Angelina, and Candido to America and the sisters Ancilla, Stella, Gilia, and Cirilla would temporarily stay behind. Gilia remembered that whenever family members went to America, they took food to eat on the trip and new shoes.

Life was grim for those left behind. The children who remained had to clean bed chamber pots, which must be inspected by older family members and be free of odors. When children had to stay home to help their parents, they lagged behind in school and were chastised through no fault of their own. When children went to school, teachers scared them with threats of the wooden ruler when they couldn't keep up.

There was not even the thrill of being around the opposite sex because girls had classes on one side of the school and boys had classes on the other side. Gilia took lessons in knitting and made socks of white string for her papa. She was very embarrassed because most of the class already knew how to knit. She had to stand in front of the class until she knitted properly. After learning trade skills like knitting, children were taught to read, write and do arithmetic. School buildings served as hospitals for war casualties, so schools that had been closed during WWI reopened in 1919.

During those bad years, water had to be carried to the vegetable garden by buckets. Apple growth was dwarfed by worms and disease. The children went snail hunting after rainstorms. They washed the snails before parboiling them, pulled the snail out of the shell and took the entrails out. Then they made an omelet with the cleaned snails.

The day finally came for my father to leave for America in March, 1920. He was 17 and departed with his older sisters. They arrived at Ellis Island on the *S.S. France*, built for the French Line. My father told me how he remembered seeing the Statue of Liberty while being processed at nearby Ellis Island.

He was asked by an American immigration officer if he could read. He feared that he might not get to the mainland if he said he couldn't read. By the time the guard discovered that he could read but only Italian, Dad was already past him. Nevertheless, the family was sent through quickly after it was learned that they were from Friuli, not Sicily where immigrants were being scrutinized for criminal and health risks. Their arrival was marred only by terrible seasickness.

They proceeded to California to join the rest of the family. My father first went to work for a cabinetmaker in Berkeley, California, having learned that skill from Grandpa Giovanni.

Then finally the rest of the family came to America in December, 1920. At a family reunion in 1958, Aunt Stella told the family about how hard it was to leave her home.

"We said goodbye to all our friends and were ready to get on the train to leave our birthplace," Stella said. "Papa had bought second-class tickets for the trip, which allowed the family to enter the United States without passing through Ellis Island, where someone could be sent back to the Old Country."

She described how she saw mountains on the trip for the first time, since there were none by the seashore where they lived in Casarsa, Italy. They spent a night in a hotel in Milan, where Grandpa took them to see the Duomo inside and out, as well as the great vistas. They bought Coca Colas to drink while looking around. Then they journeyed to Paris where she remembered seeing dresses in display windows as they passed by. After a night in Paris, they went to Le Havre and boarded a ship.

Stella told about their first glimpse of the Statue of Liberty. She said, "We were so happy to see her. It gave us a feeling of freedom to be in this land." Then they traveled on to Los Angeles, arriving on New Year's Eve. Some of the workers started shouting what sounded like "Happy Noia" and they answered the same way. From Los Angeles, they went to San Francisco, and then to Berkeley where the brothers were waiting. The boys had rented a house big enough for everyone to have a place to sleep.

Stella remembered that little Rina (Joseph's wife) had a bag full of rice and it burst right in the front door as they were all about to enter. She said, "We laughed and thought it was a good omen and that we should be happy in the house. And so we were for many years. My brothers had made a great big dining room table with benches on each side plus a chair on each end. We were very pleased with everything our brothers had done for us. My father eventually bought the house for $2,500 and fixed it up a little and all of us six girls and our youngest brother Candido were happily married in that house."

My Aunt Cirilla described her feelings about the move to America:

> Valeriano and his wife Pina and their small son Virgil and mother and father went on the boat. I was not very content to make this big change and thought that the value that was most worthwhile was to reunite the entire family. Father decided not to sell the property in case some of the children would eventually want to return.
>
> So we began to sell everything in the house, all the things that we had gathered over these many years, our remembrances, our knickknacks, our animals, our tools that we used to work the countryside, our furniture, everything. The only thing we left in the house was a room with the kitchen utensils and table in case someone would decide to return. I remember very well seeing all of these items leave the house, sold out from under us and how much I suffered even though I was already a big girl. I also had near me people who were dear to me, such as neighbors and friends that I hated to leave.
>
> I hated the idea of going into a new land that I knew nothing about and leaving the country. Our friends told us we were crazy to go. We were considered at the time one of the best off families in Casarsa. No one could understand why we were all leaving.
>
> It was incredible when the time came to finally leave Italy, our town, our friends and our loved ones. How many tears I shed at that last goodbye. At the same time, however, we were anxious and full of joy at the thought of reuniting all of our family and to know our new family members, the wives that they married in America and the children they had. It gave us the hope of a new beginning and a better future.
>
> I remember our trip to the "promised land." We had just given our last goodbye to the multitude of friends and loved ones. In my heart I felt a strange emptiness. I could not stop crying. Mother put her arms around me to give me comfort and she told me it was for a better beginning. We made this long trip by boat full of fear and very anxious about the unknown people that spoke a different language than us.

That last family group arrived at Ellis Island on December 29, 1920, on the *S.S. Rochambeau*. They reached Berkeley, California, on January 4, 1921. The entire family was so happy to be together again.

When my grandparents left Italy, they leased their property to farmers so the family had a little income, as farmers paid according to the sale of their crops. Grandpa was very shrewd when he decided to protect his income against inflation by tying the rental of the property to the cost of a specific number of bales of wheat, rather than a specific currency amount. My father had an oil painting of the family home made for each of his children and I still have the one he gave me in my home in Arizona.

The Jacuzzis got out of Italy just in time. The following year, Mussolini became Prime Minister under King Victor Emmanuel III (son of Victor Emmanuel II) and set up rules that all boys aged 6 to 21 must join Fascist groups and train to use firearms. Grandpa's fear that sons would be forced to fight was now a reality.

As the new Jacuzzi emigrants settled in Berkeley, California, the seven brothers operated the machine shop started by Rachele. My father left his work as a cabinetmaker and began work as an apprentice machinist at JBI, Jacuzzi Brothers, Inc.

The war was far behind them now. Tragedies and suffering lay in the past for the time being. As with all of us, unpleasant memories are often shoved to the back of our minds as we fill our lives with more pleasant activities. More suffering would lie ahead but, for now, life for the Jacuzzi family in their adopted country of America was getting rosier with each day.

2

The End of the Airplane

Thunderclap: A clap or loud crash of thunder.

The Jacuzzis stuck together in America, now even more tenaciously than they had in Italy. What did it matter that jobs were scarce? Rachele taught the brothers how to carve and laminate propellers. Then his voracious imagination, and the many willing hands of the Jacuzzi family, worked on the new and more demanding project: the cabin monoplane.

Probably Rachele had heard that the Russian aviator, Igor Sikorsky, had created a twin-engine plane that carried 17 passengers. Sikorsky would later create the first helicopter. Rachele realized the potential of a large airplane for carrying mail, equipment, and more passengers. He developed his monoplane with the goal of gaining a contract to carry mail, and did so.

United States Air Mail service had begun on May 15, 1918, under the direction of Gen. Otto Praeger, who wanted to prove that airplanes could deliver mail faster than trains. The pilots usually flew a little deHavilland DH-4, with a top speed of 120 mph and an open cockpit giving little protection from weather. The compass gave inaccurate readings, so pilots navigated by looking for roads, rivers, and railroad tracks. Since pilots couldn't see landmarks to fly at night, the mail was transferred to trains at dusk. Gradually pilots from WWI and barnstormers were added to the mail service and showed that they could fly over mountains, through fog, and even after dark.

Ingenious pilots risked life and limb. One pilot drove his plane on the ground across 35 miles of foggy prairie, rising into the air to hop the barbed-wire fences that stood in his way. Another used a half-empty whiskey bottle to tell whether his wings were level.

Between October 1919 and July 1921, 26 Air Mail employees died in plane crashes, more than one fatality per month. Starting in 1920, pilots were issued parachutes. At first, many complained about having to carry them. There were, of course, no towers or radio controls, no runways, no brakes, but lots of guts.

One of the earliest U.S. Air Mail pilots, Dean Smith, crashed in Iowa and sent this telegram to Air Mail headquarters. "On Trip 4 westbound. Flying low. Engine quit. Only place to land on cow. Killed cow. Wrecked plane. Scared me. Smith."

People asked Smith why he continued to fly with such dangers. He said, "It was so alive and rich a life that any other conceivable choice seemed dull, prosaic, and humdrum." Perhaps the Jacuzzis felt some of those thrills as they worked.

On April 16, 1921, a pilot of the U.S. Air Mail Service tested the new Jacuzzi monoplane since it was the first large, fully enclosed cabin and was perfect for carrying large mail loads. He took off from the Marina airfield in San Francisco headed for Reno, Nevada, 187 air miles away, across the towering Sierra Nevada Mountains. The pilot took the plane up easily to 14,000 feet to cross the treacherous mountains, averaging 90 miles per hour, never even pushing the plane to full speed. The aircraft and motor performed perfectly throughout the journey. The U.S. Air Mail Service was ready to sign a contract for mail service with the Jacuzzis.

Performance, safety features and the clean ultra-modern design of the craft had already been hailed earlier in the year by aircraft magazines in the United States, England and Germany. This was THE plane of the day, the prototype of commercial aircraft to come.

John Kauke of the *Aerial Age Weekly* wrote favorably in the February 7, 1921, issue about the fuselage and plywood roof. Another story appeared in *Aerial Age Weekly* in the issue of May 1921 stating:

> ...A particularly striking feature of the flight from a passenger-carrying standpoint was the relative comfort enjoyed by pilot and passengers in the Jacuzzi plane as compared to the ordinary cockpit job. The sedan-like cabin of the Jacuzzi plane made it possible for the pilot to wear nothing more than the clothes which one would wear were he to drive to Reno in a closed car.

The plane was 29 feet long with a wingspan of 52 feet, and weighed (without fuel) 1800 lbs. It held 80 gallons and used about 8–9 gallons of fuel per hour. The seats were arranged in three tandem rows, the first seating two (pilot and passenger or two pilots), the second held three and the third two. Large windows gave unobstructed views.

The plane was recorded in aviation history as the first successful, fully enclosed high-wing monoplane to be built and flown in the United States. The future of the Jacuzzi commercial cabin monoplane appeared bright. But fate stepped in and put an end to the aircraft manufacturing activities of my family.

Riding on that plane was every cent the Jacuzzis had and every cent they could borrow. Rachele's twelve brothers and sisters had devoted themselves to its construction. They would do anything he asked or believe anything he told them, no matter how wild or incomprehensible, because Rachele was the oldest. They knew he was a genius.

It had not been easy for the Jacuzzis in America. The stereotypes of Italians were built by a few bad incidents. In 1890, Sicilians battling over illegal waterfront operations killed David Hennessy, a New Orleans police chief. In that city of rough souls, officials claimed it was the work of the Mafia and, although a jury acquitted the nineteen defendants, a mob of leading citizens stormed the jail and lynched or shot eleven of the prisoners.

Italy was so outraged it broke off diplomatic relations with the U.S. until reparations were made. However, this did not keep stories of Mafia invasions from spreading across the country, intensifying in the early 1900s when Italian immigrants began pouring into America by the hundreds of thousands.

But the Jacuzzis were overcoming these stereotypes by their new invention. In test flights, it had lifted itself grandly into the air like a great California condor. Its stability was something out of an engineer's dream. If they'd been drinking champagne in the cockpit, they would not have spilled a drop.

Little thought was given to the danger involved. There was no official recording of air mishaps until 1920 and when reported, they downplayed fatal crashes, and had no accounting for the cause of the crash.

A few people of significance had newspaper coverage when they died in plane crashes over the years. There was Calbraith Rodgers, 33, a U.S. aviator who made the first transcontinental flight. He crashed into the Pacific during an air show on April 3, 1912, after hitting a seagull which fouled his controls.

Harriet Quimby, 37, a pioneer female aviator, died on July 1, 1912, when she was hurled out of a plane as it suddenly pitched forward during an air show demonstration. A friend, William Willard, was also killed with her.

Lincoln Beachey, a stunt and movie pilot, died on March 14, 1915. His plane plunged into San Francisco Bay at the Panama-Pacific International Exhibition that Rachele had attended. Rachele never mentioned seeing the crash, however.

During World War I, The Red Baron (Manfred von Richthofen) was shot down over enemy lines. Quentin Roosevelt, the son of President Theodore Roosevelt, died July 14, 1918, when he was shot down behind German lines. These fatalities did not deter the Jacuzzis, however.

When the plane was ready to fly before an august crowd, Rachele didn't want to be the pilot. He had been in a plane earlier when a pilot passed out and the terrified Rachele had to land the plane. He secured a pilot and the cabin monoplane was ready to take off.

"Contact!" commanded the pilot, Harold (Bud) Coffee. Rachele heaved his considerable bulk against the propeller and the engine quickly responded. With a powerful two-handed thrust of the wooden propeller, the specially built engine snapped into life, eliciting a chorus of gasps from the crowd of spectators gathered at the flying field, closely followed by a rhapsody of sighs from star-struck females as the exciting spectacle unfolded.

With a 52-foot wingspan and a top speed of 115 miles per hour, this sleek craft was a radical departure from the rickety, primitive descendants of the Wright brothers' "aero plane."

Although it was a big plane by 1921 standards, it nimbly pirouetted to face the runway. His heart undoubtedly pounded with a combination of pride and apprehension as Rachele gave the pilot the "thumbs up" sign and watched his brainchild sprint down the field for takeoff.

A fine spray of motor oil glazed the ring cowling around the engine and thick, gray exhaust cloaked the fuselage as the monoplane accelerated down the runway. For six years Rachele had been waiting for this moment, and now he could barely bring himself to watch. My grandfather, Giovanni, although skeptical of Rachele's obsession with flight, smiled with pride as the plane gained momentum.

Suddenly, the front fat-tired dual wheels lifted off the earth and the engine screamed in defiance of its adversary, gravity, as the rear skid wheel hopped lightly two times and left solid ground for good. The crowd cheered and the pilot waved.

Surely Rachele would have liked to be on board for the test flight, but while the plane was still in the experimental stage, they decided to limit seating to four, including the pilot, the man who was going to help finance the production of the new plane and his advisor. After the flight, the men intended to discuss the possibility of air transportation of visitors into the National Park at Yosemite.

The one seat remaining, Rachele gave to his brother, Giocondo, whose enthusiasm for aviation and especially the Jacuzzi plane was as great as Rachele's. As the majestic, alabaster craft vanished like a spirit in the haze blown in from the Bay, I'm sure my Uncle Rachele envied his brother Giocondo's adventure aboard the plane.

In Rachele's plane, the sound of the sputtering engine carried efficiently across the Bay to the throng who watched the plane rise. Rachele was enthralled with the performance but noticed how the wings flexed under the strain of the pilot's acrobatics, performed to dazzle the crowd. The stress did not seem to be evenly distributed.

But it was not until the next day that they heard how the pilot had disregarded orders from Jacuzzi engineer consultant Kauke and tried to land in Modesto to see his girlfriend and how the plane had burst into flames, killing everybody aboard on July 14, 1921.

The engine exploded as it crashed, it was said, and my Uncle Giocondo, only 26, was killed along with Kauke who wrote the article mentioned above for *Aerial Age Weekly*, the pilot and another man, a visiting aviator from England. The newspaper headline said, "Last Photograph of Four Aviators Killed at Modesto and Ill-fated Machine." The caption under the photograph read:

"The above photograph, found in the wreckage of the monoplane which fell in Modesto Thursday morning July 14, was taken at Yosemite Valley following the arrival of the machine there Tuesday evening, July 12. Left to right Giocondo Jacuzzi, John H. Kauke, A. Duncan McLeish and Harold L. (Bud) Coffee. The latter was the pilot and the others were passengers on the fatal trip from Yosemite Valley to Durant Field."

This sudden violent *thunderclap* of fate was both sad and ironic. Of all the Jacuzzi brothers, how strange it was that Giocondo was killed on that flight. Giocondo was very much unlike his other brothers in that he was cut from a different cloth; a dreamer intrigued by the arts, especially oil painting. His life cut prematurely short by this tragic accident, the little that remained of Giocondo's legacy was a small collection of his dark, but beautifully executed oil paintings. His brother, Francesco, named his first son Giocondo when the boy was born shortly afterwards on September 12, 1921.

My mother, recalling the tragic event, told about Rachele's difficulty in turning away from aviation toward the mundane pump business. She said,

> I went up in the first cabin plane. I said, 'My God, this is comfortable.' But it went down and burnt. We had to bury brother (Giocondo) right there. Not enough left to take away. In his spare time, Rachele would go and look at planes.
>
> When eggbeaters (helicopters) came, he wanted to do those, but couldn't. He sent a sister and me up to find out what it was like. I told him it was fun, but made a lot of racket. He never got planes, flying, out of his head.

After pumps came whirlpool. Years later, Ken's dentist was asked if we could make little motor or thing to clean teeth. Somebody else did it later—water pick. Jacuzzi on a stick.

My father recalled the day back in 1919 when Giocondo left their home in Casarsa, hoping to make his fortune in America.

"He was so happy! He was singing, going out of the house, saying, 'I hope I won't have to eat so many beans anymore!' Those were the last words he said to our mother before he left Italy."

Dad explained, "In our home, humble, poor, we ate a lot of beans. Mostly beans and polenta. Our mother was a good cook but, you know, Giocondo got tired of beans."

In the United States, Giocondo not only painted but entertained the rest of the family on the violin and other instruments. But like Rachele, he was infatuated with flying. To Giocondo, aviation seemed to exemplify the life he sought in America. It was a dramatic and profitable break from the past. After Rachele's invention of the seven-passenger cabin monoplane, Giocondo was more convinced than ever that the Jacuzzi brothers would be at the forefront of a thriving aviation industry. He insisted on taking part in what he believed would be an historic event, the test flight of Rachele's prototype.

Giocondo's little girl and his widow, Mary, were left with very little money and practically nothing to show for his hard work in the business except his nearly worthless shares in the company.

The Jacuzzi airplane had been a total family project; in fact, many of the wives of the brothers helped out in the actual construction of the airplane by hand sewing the canvas exterior of its wing. The loss was hard to bear by all.

◆ ◆ ◆

To my grandparents, Giovanni and Teresa, California was a very complex and confusing place. Why everyone wanted to go there, Giovanni wasn't sure. It was a nation of strangers, even to those who grew up there. In Casarsa Della Delizia, they never had much money but they were happy and their neighbors were old friends. They had worked so hard to get the family all back together and now this!

This American sojourn was not the dream that Giovanni had envisioned for his sons. Ever since his family began breaking up to look for work, he tried to reunite them. But now, Giocondo was dead. Giovanni was old and he did not know much about airplanes but he was still the papa, still the boss. Here is how he gave Rachele his marching orders, according to my relatives.

> Rachele, my son, you have a genius that few other men in this world can ever possess. I know you wish to fly, but our family has been given an omen with the death of your brother, Giocondo. We come from the land; we are farmers. Use your genius to help the farmer in our adopted California. Much of the soil here is rich and fertile, like that of our beloved Friuli. But they need water. You can do it, Rachele. You can find a way to give the farmer the water he needs. And that's how we will make our family prosper. Now, leave me my time for grief and let us hear nothing more of flying.

My Uncle Rachele felt responsible for the loss of his brother Giocondo through his invention of the passenger airplane. He helped raise Giocondo's two-year-old daughter, Anna. My aunt, Cirilla Jacuzzi Benassini, told me later that relatively soon after the airplane crash, they were able to sell the patents they had to the Wright brothers company, although Wilbur Wright had died in 1912.

The family did give up the aircraft business, some taking odd jobs for a few dollars a week, and some working in the shop making radio cabinets, grape crushers or whatever people wanted. Only Rachele did not work. The others would not let him. They knew that if they were ever to get out of debt and back in business, it was Rachele who would think of a way. They gave him room to mourn and to create.

Finding jobs was additionally difficult not only because of immigrants from the Old World but because the Chinese and Japanese were also pouring into California. To discourage immigration from Asia, California legislators prevented Orientals from marrying and prohibited their children from attending public schools. The situation with Italians was not much different. Even though the immigrants from Friuli were often light-skinned and blue-eyed, it made no difference. An Italian was an Italian!

Rachele thought of lots of inventions and ways to create a product, although many of them wouldn't work. He considered the citrus groves of Chino and invented what he called the Frostifugo, a contraption with propellers that would blow steam and hot air over the trees to prevent frost, replacing the smudge pots that blackened the fruit and the trees. Without the time and money to perfect the machine, he abandoned it for less imaginative inventions and for those more prosperous than himself to capitalize upon. Even though the venture wasn't much of a success at the time, Arizona and California use such fans in fruit orchards today for just the same purpose.

He invented a gas-turbine engine decades ahead of its time. It worked on paper, but there were no known metals that could withstand the heat and stress of the high revolutions per minute required of the gas turbine. Then there was the solar-powered generator that he invented and drew on paper but it would have cost a fortune to build. Investors were not interested then. Now it's a money-maker.

3

How My Parents Met

Microburst: A sudden updraft from winds sucking objects into a convexity, usually in a small area and lasting only seconds or minutes.

In 1925, my father, Candido Jacuzzi, married my mother, Inez Ranieri. They would have four children and I would be their last.

Mom lived in San Francisco, and told a friend that she had met a charming young man who wanted to marry her. She added, "He lives in Berkeley and that's so far from San Francisco." I think my father must have been a pretty good salesman because she married him anyway.

My mother came to the United States when she was three so she had no memory of Italy but they spoke Italian as she was growing up. Her mother was from Genoa but had my mother in Rapallo on the Mediterranean, near the town where Columbus was born. Mom's mother mingled with royalty because she ironed for the English in a resort town. English noblemen and kings arrived in yachts and needed their personal articles ironed.

My mother's father came from Turin, close to France toward the west and Switzerland was to the north. Turin was under France for 200 years so their Italian dialect has a lot of French in it. Mother's parents met shortly after Grandpa Ranieri finished serving in the Italian Army and went to Genoa. There he became a kind of policeman, a carabiniere, for which he was selected. This was a big honor and at the age of 21, he proudly marched in a parade. This strong, good-looking young man fell for my classy grandmother and they married. My grandmother had a girlfriend who moved to San Francisco and wrote her to come. My grandparents did just that when Mom was three.

Mom told me what happened to her sister when they came to America, in a recording which I possess and relish to this day.

I was already born, and mother had had another little girl but she didn't have enough milk to nurse, so it was the style to give baby to a wet nurse. There were people in the mountains that wet nursed 'cause they were so healthy, so when they decided to come they didn't want to take the baby away from the wet nurse 'til she was at least one year old. So she said, well, when she's ready to come.

Mother gave baby to her sister who had two little boys. She was a dressmaker, and she was going to take care of her until baby was able to travel with somebody. Later my grandmother decided she would come over and bring her. Grandmother had a good education, but she was an orphan early so they were living with the money my mother had saved from ironing for the wealthy. She was able to make the trip and bring my sister, who was then several years old. At that time, war had broken out so it was dangerous to make the trip. But my grandmother took a chance and made it.

When they got as far as Ellis Island they found out my sister had a little—in the eyes—redness. The inspectors thought it was catching and they sent her back. She returned to Italy with another couple that couldn't get in.

I learned more of the details of this sad event. My mother's grandparents sailed into New York Bay with my Mom's little sister. A gangplank was lowered to the terminus of the ferryboat, which took them to Ellis Island. Ellis Island was gray, overgrown with mold, and windows were barred with twisted iron. The doctors who examined immigrants were cruel as they used their power to separate families. With bundles in hand, family members were questioned in turn by clerks sitting on very high stools. The clerks wore black coats with shiny buttons and starched collars.

Suddenly, when my mother's little sister was being examined something stopped. The clerk stuttered in his anger, because the usual situation was violated when the child was found to have a physical problem. He tried to be helpful but he didn't know how to do that. Mother's grandmother (Suntina) began to cry, and tried to explain how important it was to keep the little girl with the family. The clerk did not care to listen any longer to this story of the child with the affliction, which affected him in some kind of painful manner. The grandmother's plea did no good.

The little girl ran after her grandmother like a newly hatched chick, crying as she was passed over to some other rejected passengers to return to Italy. We kids asked what happened to her little sister and my mother told us this.

> She went back to my mother's sister who raised her until the time that she could make it on her own. But by that time, ships were being bombarded during the war, so she kept waiting until she almost reached age eighteen.

Then mother became a citizen and she could send for her. There was a quota at this time. They set quotas of each nationality. (Immigration laws of 1921 accepted only 3% annually of each nationality, based on the population of that nationality already living in the U.S. according to the 1910 census). So she wrote daughter if you don't come now, you'll have to wait 'till age 25. But she didn't want to come.

She was raised like a queen over there. Mother used to send money to my sister, who became a tailor. She did all the latest fashions. My aunt was glad to have a girl to dress up 'cause she only had two boys. They all benefited by money my parents sent.

My mother didn't work here 'til I was about six years old and she had my other sister. She was in family way when she came over. They used to call the third daughter, "the one who got a free trip—the sardine"—so she became a citizen right away. She was born in San Francisco. My father found a job at Del Monte factory. Del Monte, he was also an immigrant.

In San Francisco where mother's family settled in 1911, there was an area called "little Italy." One street was all Genovese, one all Piemontese, and the ones from Sicily were all down by the wharf where they fished. It was five years after the 1906 San Francisco fire and they still had a few wooden sidewalks and horse-drawn buggies. Horses pulled the ice wagons.

My sister, Alba, recalled Suntina, Mom's grandmother, who must have been a very interesting old lady and lived her last years in San Francisco and Berkeley at our house on Ada Street. I only have a vague recollection of her because she died when I was around four years old. I do remember Mom always telling me that Great Grandma Suntina said I would go far in life because I had "la lingua lunga," or something to say about everything—in other words, a big mouth.

Alba recalled that she used snuff. In fact, when Alba coughed, Suntina gave her snuff. Alba said, "She was full of fun and jokes. She used to sit on the stoop after cleaning all the marble steps and she'd tell jokes. Her husband was a seaman who died at sea and was buried in Greece."

Who knows whether hearing this story had anything to do with the fact that Alba married Peter Kosta, whom almost everyone in our family ended up calling "Pete the Greek"?

Alba described our grandmother, who became polished through contact with her wealthy patrons. She left my grandfather when my Mom was about 12 or 13:

> She was a love. Very caring, couldn't do enough for people. Very sweet lady! Very nice housekeeper! Did everything herself, all her own cooking, worked, and raised the girls by herself. They were separated. My grandmother never spoke of my grandfather. She always prayed to the Blessed Mother. I used to

> love to go with grandmother and light candles. She took care of my great-grandmother, Suntina. She was a career lady, always dressed like a career lady with a hat, very San Francisco, dressy, a real lady. Important people knew her. She even bought many clothes for me, which I think upset my father. I adored her.

Alba remembered what Grandmother said when she married Pete. "Now that you're married, get up that fifteen minutes earlier in the morning. Always make sure your house is in order, beds made, dishes done and covered with tea cloth if you can't put them away. Always have a doily on table."

Alba heeded her advice. "To this day I have a doily on the table," she said.

Her grandmother always had fresh flowers in the bathroom and instructed Alba, "Always have house ready for company. Have fresh towels in bathroom."

My mother's parents must have been very hard workers. Mother told me more about their life in San Francisco.

> Father worked in a sort of coconut factory, where they squeezed the oil and made margarine. Mother got into the cannery because Dad was working there. She was peeling, putting things in jars, then they had to put in syrup. She was doing well because they had piecework. But then she developed cracks in her fingers and the doctor said she was allergic to the acid. They hated for her to go 'cause she was a good worker, so they made her inspector.
>
> After I graduated from elementary school, my Mom and Dad broke up. Mother was still working. We were old enough now to take care of ourselves, 12, 13 or so. My Grandmother Suntina would come and get us after school so we wouldn't walk by ourselves. She taught us how to cook.
>
> Our parents got separated. My father started to drink. Maybe he missed his family, who knows. They were always fighting because on weekends he used to get drunk and my mother got fed up. He died about two or three years after I got married.

Apparently, it was only by accident that my siblings and I came to be. I say this because I learned that my mother was not very responsive to my father at first. I think I have my grandmother to thank for my existence. Here is what my mother remembered about how she met my father.

> We were invited to go to the Veritas Club, a place for the Italians. Girls of Italian extraction could go without paying. They went either with their mother or older sister. My mother was sitting on a bench and we were sitting with her and then he came up. He (Candido Jacuzzi) asked me to dance but I said no. I didn't want to dance with anybody I didn't know. So he sat next to

my mother and asked her, "Why don't your daughter want to dance with me?"

My mother gave me hell. "You didn't come with no boyfriend. You should dance with people that ask you."

So I danced with him. So he says, "I live in Berkeley. To get here I have to take the ferry boat and cable car."

So he called me up and he wanted to come over and I said, "Look, we're moving next door and we haven't got time for that."

So he said, "Well, I'll help you move." So I told my mother. He came with a bouquet of flowers and a box of See's candy. My sister ate all of 'em. Could have slapped her.

He was working for cabinet makers, was superintendent. His dad used to be cabinet maker also, so he learned a lot. That's how we were able to marry. He said he wouldn't be able to afford a home. We'd have to live with his mother and dad in their house. Everybody had married. My husband was the last one. There were seven brothers and six sisters, and all brothers were married.

Candido started to cry and said, "I'm going to be all alone in that big house." Said to mother, "I don't know why she doesn't want to marry me."

I wanted to do what my grandma told me, and have fun. There were a lot of boys I wanted to know. Me and my sisters weren't allowed to go out separately. We weren't allowed to talk to any Irish or any other ethnic groups except Italians. We were too young to go without chaperone, and my mother couldn't go with us where we wanted to go, so my sister was my chaperone.

So we'd go as far as we could go, the show, and we dragged her to the park, or to church, then maybe eat over at the house. We had company, other people. Candido was a good singer. He had all these songs from Italy and all the American songs. All the songs from Ethiopia. (The Italians had occupied Ethiopia from 1889 to 1896).

We met in February. We were going together less than a year when he gave me the engagement ring. You didn't get married until you had an engagement ring. Was white gold. We had to finish paying for it. Put down a little money. He gave all his money to his father and mother 'cause he was living there. He thought maybe they'd leave it to us. But it didn't go to us. We had to do it the hard way.

We got married in 1925. We were supposed to get married Christmas Day but the priest refused. He said that too much was going on so we did it the next day. We got married in the new St. Peter and Paul Cathedral. Inside was finished but outside wasn't. My mother talked me into it. Said he was going to make a nice home so why don't you go get married. My grandma was against it but I listened to my mother. So we got married in church with a veil. His parents couldn't even make it. They sent the oldest brother and a couple of sisters. Candido's brother had one of those Tin Lizzies and was a lot of fun. I had my aunt there, representing my father's side.

After church, we went on a ferry, veil and all. Candido had gotten all my things the week before with a hope chest he made. My mother had everything. Seven sheets. Everything you'd need for a year. That was the style. Your dowry. His family believed in furnishing the bride. They bought all my outfit, shoes and all. His father came with him when we went to get the license. From there we went to the Emporium to get all my things. Candido's father paid for everything. My wedding dress was made of chiffon.

The day we got married, right after Christmas, was a Saturday. But we were already married without knowing about it. Two weeks before, when we went for license, his father and my mother went because I was underage. The judge thought we had to get married. My mother didn't know English. Candido paid the three dollars. Then they told us to go into the next room and we thought it was part of the licensing, but they married us.

Here's what happened in this sudden *microburst* of matrimony. When my parents married, they took my father's father and my mother's mother along as witnesses. They all went by boat from Berkeley to San Francisco since there was no San Francisco to Oakland Bay Bridge yet. At the courthouse, they filled out the forms as well as they could. Although they did not understand one word of the document, the elderly witnesses solemnly signed it. Candido gave the clerk some money and looked around for the exit.

The clerk directed them out the door with some words they did not understand. They looked at each other and dad asked mother in Italian what the man had said. Grandpa Giovanni just shrugged. He had never learned a word of English. And my Mom's mother knew only a little English.

Mom pointed down a hallway, saying, "We're supposed to go through this door here."

They dutifully trooped through the door, but instead of finding themselves outside, they were standing before a little man in a crumpled suit who asked to see their marriage license. He glanced at it quickly and, turning to my parents, he said, "Raise your right hands." He started talking, rapidly, and my parents stood patiently waiting for him to finish, never suspecting that at that very moment, they were being bound in holy matrimony. When he was through, the little man peered over the top of his wire-rimmed glasses and said, "Five dollars, please."

Candido said, "Gee, I just paid it." But he gave him the money and left.

Two weeks later, the couple went out to St. Peter and Paul's Church in San Francisco to make arrangements for their wedding. The priest met them at the door, looked at the marriage documents, and said, "What are you doing here? You're already married!"

They told the priest they wanted to be married in the church. Neither of them had realized all that talk in the courthouse was the wedding ceremony.

"Married for two weeks and I didn't even know it!" Dad, brought up to honor a woman's virginity before marriage, thought, "All that wasted time!" (The desire to "get down to business" was one of the things, I guess, that I did successfully inherit hook, line and sinker from my Dad).

Candido and Inez did get their church wedding in San Francisco. With all the relatives, there must have been over fifty people climbing off the boat from Berkeley, all laughing and chattering in Italian. Mother described the reception:

> My mother-in-law had the reception in the Jacuzzi family home. Got all the sisters and brothers from ranches at her house.
>
> Why did I marry him? I thought he was good looking. When you're young, you don't think about what love is. You think it's infatuation.
>
> We didn't leave for honeymoon that same day. The party lasted 'til too late, so we slept over that night. We had our room upstairs. Father-in-law had made all the furniture. Nice furnishings, 'cause he was a cabinet maker. He had made the set of mahogany and walnut and curly maple, including a bureau and mirror.
>
> We went for three days on a honeymoon. Know what kind of a honeymoon it was? Visiting relatives. They entertained as best they could. They were broke, too, but had ranches, wine and all kinds of food.
>
> Soon as we got married, wasn't even a month, the cabinet factory folded. Candido was out of work, but the brothers in meantime had just invented this pump and started making them. The family was beginning to recover from the loss of the aviation venture and followed Grandpa Jacuzzi's advice to develop irrigation pumps. So they asked him if he wanted to work for them. They would pay him a little bit, not much, but, living with his folks, we didn't have to pay rent. But we paid electric bill and water bill. But God, the house was so much to keep up. My husband helped on weekends—mopping up and such.
>
> I wanted my father to meet my husband. Father looked at him and said, "I don't see why you can't do better than that." At that time my husband was only working for his brothers. Father thought I should marry someone really wealthy.

By the time Dad was married at the age of twenty-two, his hair was as gray as his mother's. Five years later, it would be completely white, resembling a lion's mane, and he was nicknamed "the Lion." Some joked that since he was working so hard, he was aging more quickly. He looked very much like the famous Italian movie director, Vittorio DeSica, who directed *The Bicycle Thief* in 1948 and other movies.

In the same year that they married, 1925, while conducting experiments in fluid dynamics, Rachele hit upon the idea of moving water with water. One day, while working on heat exchange in airplane engines, Rachele realized how to improve his brother Gelindo's well, which was not producing much water. The principle was simple: water would be forced down a pipe, creating a vacuum and bringing water up. At that time, it was a novel idea to pump water from below 30 feet. Because there were no moving parts inside the well, it was virtually foolproof. When the brothers saw it in action, they immediately recognized this as the invention they had been waiting for. Rachele's pump would make their fortune.

Not only that, he also put much effort into exploring how to get heat from the sun to make steam. It soon became apparent to him that the principle of the steam injector could be applied to make a water injector. This principle led to the Jacuzzi Jet Ejector Pump and revolutionized the pump business almost overnight. It made Jacuzzi pumps more durable and efficient than other pumps.

Rachele may have been the genius of the family, but my father, the youngest male, was the salesman. His drive and faith in the company would later provide the foundation for a multi-million dollar company.

However, Dad did have one problem—he could hardly speak English. This did not stop him. He set out in his rickety Model-T Ford, scouring the countryside for mailboxes bearing Italian or Latin-sounding names. In those days, families with Latin-based names—French, Spanish, Portuguese and Italian, were often immigrants like he was. Candido knew instinctively that their English was not a whole lot better than his and they probably would be more forgiving, and a lot more willing to listen to his sales pitch. He was right.

Dad had remarkably good luck with this method, except for the time he was thrown out of a man's house, pump, and all, and told not to come back until he could speak "better American."

Although he would always retain a heavy Italian accent, which he feared hampered his effectiveness as a businessman and prejudiced certain people against him, Dad faithfully attended night classes in English, determined to master the language at least well enough to pass the naturalization exam. He did go back to the man who told him to speak "American" and got a sale. But an accent was always there, to the end of his life, and he seemed to think of it like a limp, a slight defect.

Although there was no American equivalent for certain names such as his own, Candido encouraged the others to adopt American names whenever possible. For the good of their families and the company, they all agreed to speak only English at home until their children were grown.

My father sold the pumps to farmers one at a time, just like the Fuller Brush Man who sold brushes to one household at a time. Initial Jacuzzi operations were carried out in the San Pablo shop in Berkeley, California, but the sign on the front now read, "Jacuzzi Pumps." It was later changed to "Jacuzzi Bros. Deep Well Pumps." Eventually Dad set up a Jacuzzi West Coast dealer network from Klamath Falls, Oregon, to San Diego, California.

The years from 1927 to 1930 were crucial for the company. They established policies, set prices, and developed performance tables. Much opposition came from other pump companies who criticized Jacuzzi pumps as being of unproven operating principles. My father eventually hired other salesmen. He trained them to answer questions and to extend the guarantee of the pump for an extra year, to help overcome the resistance to this new type of pump.

The phenomenal growth of California's San Joaquin Valley during this period of time paralleled the rapid growth of Jacuzzi Brothers. San Joaquin Valley soon became one of the premier agricultural growing areas for the United States. The Valley's thirst for water was phenomenal and Jacuzzi Pumps played an ever more important role in satisfying that thirst.

My Uncle Rachele continued to invent and patent new products. In 1927 he patented his pumping system, and in 1929 he patented his centrifugal force pump. But he could not give up the dream of aircraft so in 1930 he patented a "design for an aeroplane." It was hard for him to lay aside thoughts of that dynamically developing new industry. Those plans and designs look very much like today's helicopters with propellers above the cabin rather than in front like airplanes. However, he could not afford to go further to produce a model.

It must have been hard for Rachele to ignore the aviation industry. After all, it was constantly in the news. Charles Lindbergh had made headlines in 1927 when he became the first man to fly alone from New York to Paris. Over 30 songs were written about Lindbergh portraying him as Lucky Lindy, and even dances such as the Lindy Hop carried on the exciting theme. There were so many songs about Lindbergh that one song had a line in the lyrics that said, "This song is not about Lindbergh."

These were lean years and not the best of times to develop a business. The crash of 1929 was a major setback for growth. The brothers were determined not to borrow any more money until they were again solvent. So they would build one pump and sell it. With the proceeds, they would make two more and sell them, and so on.

Despite being the youngest of the seven brothers, Dad saw to it that Jacuzzi Brothers, Inc. continued to make sales and promote the pumps. This was rather untraditional since the oldest son usually took up the most important position in a family business. But in Italian fashion, Dad took his father's cue and set up the company to provide employment for the Jacuzzis. Candido could see that if the company intended to maintain this objective, it would have to keep expanding to supply jobs for the children of the thirteen founders, and their children, and so on.

It thrilled my uncles and my father when their jet pump was awarded a gold medal for "Meritorious Invention" by their home state of California at the 1930 State Fair in Sacramento. The award was for "inventions releasing availability and lowering the cost of water." Such a product was valuable in California, one of the greatest farm producers of the nation. In several pictures of Rachele, he was wearing that medal of which he was so proud.

Business began to slow down in 1931 as the Depression was being felt. Then in 1932, Rachele developed a large windmill for driving pumps, which was built and installed at a farm near Brentwood, California, and another was made for use on the ranch of Gelindo Jacuzzi.

These windmills towered 30 feet high and had a three-blade propeller, a product of the experience gained from the aircraft business. This wind motor drove, through a V-belt pulley arrangement, Jacuzzi deep well turbine pumps at speeds ranging from 1200 to 1800 rpm, depending upon wind velocity. These were similar to the many windmill generators seen in Southern California today along Interstate 10. Uncle Rachele was truly ahead of his time.

My mother recalled those years. Her recollections make it clear that my Grandma Teresa had gotten a little hard to take. She preferred to live under the roof of a son rather than a daughter. What might this tell generations of Italian females about the Italian psyche? Isn't it true that Sigmund Freud said mothers prefer sons and fathers prefer daughters?

Or it may have been because my Dad was such a loyal and generous son. Who knows? Mom, who by then had my older brother John and my older sister Alba, said,

> Then the Depression got bad. We were paying $30 a month rent. By then Johnny had been born. My mother-in-law (Teresa) used to like to go to the ranch to *visit* (her daughter and son-in-law) and come back the same day. But she didn't believe it was very stylish…That's why she came to live with us. But my mother-in-law liked to do a lot of preaching. She was bossy, very bossy.

> Alba was born ten months and thirteen days after we got married, 'cause we didn't know nothing about birth control, and my mother-in-law, she'd hardly seen me 'til then. After three days we were in that house. But I got to love Candido because he was a very good father and provider and he was a good man. And when he had learned the language, he kept wanting to do more and more and we kept getting nicer homes all the time. We lived in his parents' home for three years. Then his father died. One of the sisters said she'd move in with the mother and we had a chance to move out. We rented a house. By that time we had saved $500.

My sister, Alba, recently put in her two cents worth. She told me,

> Grandmother Teresa used to scold her adult sons when they didn't come to visit when she wanted them to come. Children best not forget her when Mother's Day or her birthday came. She was a lot more interested in seeing her own children than she was their spouses or other relatives.

Alba recalled that Grandma Teresa interceded for her sometimes. For example, Alba said, "I wanted to go to a dance but Daddy thought I was too young. Grandma Teresa said, 'If you're not going to take her, I'm going to take her' and she walked me to the school dance and walked me back. She also interceded for me to get a driver's license when I was 13 so I could drive her around. She ran the family."

Alba said "Grandpa Giovanni was very passive, sweet, and loving. Dad took a little from both—sweet and passive at home, but with other people very bossy. But he was always really nice to me, never mean, never home much. We would never disobey him."

Things gradually began to improve economically for my parents. My father told me in later years about how he first made trips for one week, then two weeks, then a month. He said, "And every time I came home, it was a honeymoon for Inez and me. I think we had a lot of fun. I used to call home if I was gone more than one week."

In 1933 California wine makers were impressed by the performance of the jet pump and asked for filters. They approached my creative family and soon the business expanded into making filters as well as pumps. They little realized what the filter business would hold for them in the future with the development of the Jacuzzi Whirlpool Bath, hot tubs and equipment for the swimming pool industry.

Even through the squeeze of the Depression, other experiments were started. The propeller turbine pump, a high-pressure car wash pump, solar power, high-pressure pumps with arm impellers, and multi-stage horizontal pumps for deep and shallow wells were undertaken in 1934.

During summer vacations, most of the Jacuzzi boys and a few of the girls over 12 would come into the company headquarters in Berkeley and help out. They usually worked in shipping or kept the premises clean. The older, more experienced boys were trained to work in the machine shop, usually with the drill press. The few girls were given clerical or janitorial jobs. It was also a way of getting the younger generation involved early on with the company that someday would be passed from the first brothers to their control.

During the '30s, the brothers who were most involved with the company's day-to-day operations were Rachele, Frank, Joseph, Gelindo and C.J., my Dad. Valeriano served on the Board of Directors, but his first love was his farm in Oakley, California. Likewise, Gelindo ran a successful nearby farm in Antioch that occupied much of his time, but he still managed to participate in the company where his main involvement was with water pressure systems.

Here the Italian patriarchal system began to break down because in America, people were paid according to their value to the company. In Italy, they were paid according to their seniority in the family.

Frank was concerned with both the engineering and manufacturing departments and focused a lot of his time on the lathes and milling machines as well as assembly. Joseph, who was almost always calm and very professional in his demeanor, gravitated towards the administrative end of the business.

Rachele, whose lofty dreams of designing aircraft were grounded forever by his father's decree, "no more flying," bought a ranch next to Gelindo's where he toyed with ideas for grand inventions. Most of these went unrealized for lack of money, little supportive technology, and no public interest. He was a bit too far ahead of his time and many of his concepts seemed fantasy-based and impossible.

Dad said, "Having our father tell him 'Lay off aviation' and having lost a brother in the plane he designed just kind of destroyed him in a way. He was not in love with pumps. He hated them! He wanted to stay with airplanes. He didn't want to sell; he didn't want to collect. He didn't want nothing to do with pumps. It was our fault for holding him back."

Rachele was the leader and de facto chief executive of the company. As the eldest, Rachele automatically assumed the role of president of the company. However, he had little tact and could irritate people. My father, youngest son, had been promoted from master machinist to sales manager in 1933 because of his English capabilities.

Dad's English was never very good, but with the exception of Rachele, he spoke better English than anybody else in the family and was also the best salesman. The combination of these two factors eventually made him, by unanimous consent, Jacuzzi Brothers de facto president, in a very un-Italian pecking order.

Rachele did not mind. He was drifting farther and farther from the company. The rest of the family worried about him. They told him that he smoked too much and that all the rich food his wife cooked was not good for him. But he was the oldest and the smartest and was devoted to the family. How could they criticize him?

He continued to explore unique ideas and often wrote treatises. In 1936, he wrote a piece called "Wind, Solar and Geologic Power," using the name J. V. Raquelote. You see, the controversial nature of some of his ideas made him decide to publish the booklets under a pen name.

He had this benign view that many Americans had about world leaders in that year. Italics are mine. I, of course, noticed his view that those who don't work—invalids—should have "no voice in public matters."

> Considering the commercial wealth of the world as the product of labor, and that labor must use it as his own tool for increasing the world's entropy, any theory of contrary-minded capitalists is doomed to absolute failure: *Hitler, Stalin, Mussolini, Roosevelt and Veltro* (another of Rachele's pen names) *protect labor. And he who does not work shall be called an invalid with no voice in public matters.*

What many Americans forget is that before the realities of the Holocaust became known worldwide, political leaders like Mussolini, Stalin, and Hitler appeared to represent protection for the working man and his labor. In the depths of a devastating, worldwide economic depression that was largely fueled by an ever widening gap between rich and poor, the working man and woman were literally starving for politicians who at least sounded like they honored work and respected workers.

The world soon learned the reality of men like Mussolini, Hitler, and Stalin. We've all learned a lot from them and from that time in our history. We've learned that it is up to us to keep our elected political leaders accountable. We must make sure that they not only do what they say they are going to do—keep their word—but that they do what we elected them to do.

The airplane industry had continued to grow and leaders such as Mussolini and Hitler had seen its potential for war. As Mussolini geared Italy up for war by beefing up their air force, he arranged for 24 Italian seaplanes to be displayed at the Chicago World's Fair in 1933. Rachele was always aware of world developments and airplanes, and would have known about this display.

My uncle had moved on beyond his helicopter-like design, and may have been thinking of his brother's plane crash and the deaths of other pilots when he wrote the following:

> Technical teachers and professors overlooked hydraulics, pneumatics, and aviation so much that turbine water pumps are not efficient, air turbo-compressors are very inefficient and flying machines are veritable death traps already killing people by the dozen.
>
> The flying machines of tomorrow will have no wings and no propellers. They will leave the ground vertically, stopping in the air at any height in order to give the pilot plenty of time to ascertain his whereabouts. He will be able to fly around at a rate of four or five miles an hour and rapidly accelerate his speed to 800 miles per hour. Through the assistance of a friend of mine, I can furnish the necessary technical data to make such a flying machine possible, economic and practical.

He looked for support in vain and none ever came. But he continued to sprout ideas. He described solar power in a pamphlet where he made a diagram of a "country house collecting solar power" with solar panels on a roof exactly like many such homes today. Such solar panels are also currently used to power lights and communication devices along major highways in most states. He wrote:

> Fifty horse power or more of the sun's heat can be collected from the roof of a house 18 feet wide and 15 feet long, as shown on the opposite page. It will be convenient for the house to have a 30-degree roof facing east and west so as to collect the same amount of solar radiation for 12 hours per day. Solar heat can be used to drive low pressure steam engines…and for heating large volumes of water…

The year before he died, he may have been more than a little eccentric. He wrote of peculiar ideas such as that more deaths occurred at night than day. In a pamphlet called "Creation," under the name of R. J. Veltro, he seemed to foresee the United Nations, which was formed after WWII. (Of course, the R. J. in his pen name stood for Rachele Jacuzzi). He wrote:

> Let us appoint a great giver of employment and relief like our President, F. D. Roosevelt, with his assistants and advisors, to draft an international constitution, representing numerically all people of any color or creed, to open and

legislate international emigration, industry, commerce, etc., with a spirit of justice and equality for all.

All nations may contribute ten per cent of their present war strength and appropriations to police the seas, liberate all the vacant lands not actually in use for immigration, and liberate all money and wealth not in use for immediate expansion of public works.

One of the more interesting "rules" in his suggestions was this one:

Matrimonial contracts shall be valid for only five years at a time until nature approves them with the birth of a child, thus eliminating the unable, unfit or malicious companions.

I cannot but wonder whether my Uncle Rachele secretly wanted to apply that rule to himself or would have applied it to me. He had no children of his own, nor did I. He eventually adopted a boy, Gordon, and took over the rearing of Anna, his brother Giocondo's daughter. But his wife, Olympia, hen-pecked him badly.

Anyway, my amazing uncle even foresaw the power of an atomic bomb and black holes in space when he wrote, "...any attempt to remove atomic energy will probably give us the annihilation of matter...everything would collapse into a cold, small body of tremendous density."

He also predicted satellites when he wrote, "Someday we will probably be able to build an asteroid that will fly around the earth from west to east."

Between supporting a family and endless experiments, it was difficult for Rachele to save money. In fact, he was always asking for donations for his inventions. For example, in his publication "Wind, Solar and Geologic Power," he invited donations for his pen name of "Veltro." He created a martyr-like character for a poor but talented "Veltro" and pled, "For more information, consult Veltro and lend your support to help him out of his present occupation in the Nevada mines, so that he can devote all of his time to science."

Rachele was not only a mechanical genius; he was a caring and loving man. After my grandfather Giovanni died, Rachele did everything he could to make his mother, Teresa, happy. No matter how hard she tried, she could never adjust to living in the United States. She said, "I have all my children here. Sometimes I think I have everything, but I don't have my home."

She always talked about her girlfriends in Italy, the beautiful summers and the wild strawberries. Neither she nor Grandpa Jacuzzi ever learned English and they kept their bedroom set and their house in Casarsa in hopes that someday they would return to Italy. As she spoke of such things with the light of excitement and expectancy, Rachele sometimes noticed tears leaving their trails down her cheeks.

Rachele's mother was grateful when he tried to spoil her with the little gifts he showered on her, but he knew there was only one thing she really wanted. Sacrificing some of his precious experiments, Rachele saved enough money to take his mama home to Italy for one last visit. But one morning, a few days before they were to leave, Rachele reached down to put on his shoes and dropped dead. Unfortunately, my uncle's unhealthy habits caught up with him and he died of a sudden massive heart attack just before his 51st birthday on August 24, 1937.

When Rachele died, Giuseppe became president of the company. But it wasn't long before my father, Candido, became the real force of the Jacuzzi family because of his salesmanship and sheer drive.

A couple of years later, in 1939, my sister Alba went to work for the Jacuzzi family business. She was 13 and worked in the office where Dad worked and she described him at that time.

> I saw my Dad in action. He was always at the office before anyone arrived in the morning. They better be on time and be dressed properly. I saw him send people home if shirts were not ironed properly. Dad's desk was always perfect. I remember him wanting all offices to look perfect. One night I'll never forget. He opened drawers in accounting and billing. They had thrown things in top drawers and not finished work. He was livid.
>
> A lot of people didn't like him but they respected him. He molded and groomed family members to work in certain places where there were openings so he could integrate them into the business. It took years to formulate these things. This is where he had the art and foresight to place them appropriately, whether they liked it or not.
>
> He liked being a powerful person, liked being able to make all the decisions. What drove him was family unity, keeping the family together. He did a marvelous job for so many years. Keeping the family together.
>
> He was always writing to the cousins and bringing them up to date with what was going on in the factory. When cousin Giocondo went on his first date, he loaned a company car to him. He was always very good to the boys. That was not the case with the girls. Girls were supposed to be at home—be homemakers.

I think my father was one of those old-world patriarchs like his own father—stubborn, independent, wanting to do things his own way. He wanted to run the family and the business without interference by young family upstarts or outsiders. He didn't want the government to interfere by taking the able-bodied boys to fight and maybe die in a war, or by taking his profits away in taxation. He wanted the American dream of success, while keeping his old-world mentality. Just as his own father set his cap to defy the Italian government, so did my father defy the American government. Perhaps he thought if any problems occurred, he could bribe a government official, but this was not Italy or Mexico, as he would learn.

PART II
FREE-FOR-ALL WITH A DISABILITY

4

Candido Jacuzzi's Family

Flood: An overflowing of water on land usually dry; inundation; or deluge overwhelming an area.

My Dad tried to make his mother happy. He built her a little apartment in his home and brought her breakfast in bed every morning. But it was hard for her to get over the shock of losing, with one stroke, the two things she loved most, her oldest boy and her final trip to Italy.

Dad threw himself vigorously into the business after the death of his oldest brother. Mom described the birth of my siblings and then how she dealt with my birth and medical problems.

> Alba was born at home with midwife. Alba was the 13th grandchild, born October 13, and there were 13 steps up to the room where she was born. John was born at Berkeley General Hospital, Irene at Albany Hospital. But when ready to have Kenny we needed a larger house and by then we could afford a bigger and better one and moved to Ada Street.
>
> At that time Candido found a house for sale for $3,800, brand new, but we still didn't have the down payment. His mother loaned us the $500 and we built her a little apartment onto it so she could be part of household but still on her own. Another daughter who lived close by came and did chores and she always came to eat with us. We lived in that house for nine years.

My father recalled those same years. He said, "It was an obsession with me, wanting always to do more. But more was not enough. It had to be more than more. The trips, the promotion…I generated the pressure myself. And I was away from my family so much."

After my father applied for his first two U.S. patents for agricultural well pumps, which formed the core of the family business, he was promoted from sales manager to general manager in 1940.

The business continued to grow and in 1941 the Jacuzzi Bros., Inc., purchased property in Richmond, California, for enlarged facilities. That was the year I was born and I'll get to that in a minute. It was around this time that my father acquired a station wagon for his sales travel. It sported the words "Jacuzzi Pumps" across the side of the car and was filled with pumps and equipment to demonstrate their wares from California to New York. It was also in that year that the brothers paid off their last loans, and they resolved never again to go into debt.

The Depression was over and California's economy was booming. More and more, Jacuzzi Brothers, Inc., came to rely on Candido's guidance. He now commanded the highest salary in the company. That was almost unheard of for the youngest in an Italian family business. Thanks to his drive and his brothers' support, they were all moving up in the world, although he was moving up the fastest.

By the time my mother had her second child, they had moved from Stannage Avenue to a new house on Ada Street in Berkeley. Compared to where they had been living, it was pure luxury. But why not? They felt they could afford it and that they were entitled to it!

Dad watched his son, my brother Johnny, in the back yard, lifting weights. He kidded that Johnny could eat more pancakes than any two grown men and still he was a puny kid. How my brother wanted to be big like his Dad and grow up to play football! Valerio already had three fine boys to carry on his name and his work with the company.

When I was born, they named me Kenneth Anthony Jacuzzi. Kenneth was the closest English equivalent to Candido they could find, and it was the name of my mother's doctor. Anthony was chosen because my father liked it and believed children should have middle names.

Since the company had recently opened a new factory at Richmond, and planned to open a third near St. Louis, Dad spent much time away from home. They also had a ranch in Saint Helena but he could not be everywhere at once. He had his duty to the company and to the future of his family. If that meant he sometimes had to be away from home on one of his children's birthdays or had to miss hearing them say their first words, Mom would tell him about it. She would complain, but she understood his reasons.

It was my father's dream to build a Jacuzzi dynasty like the Fords, the Mellons, and the Kaisers. The Jacuzzis would never again have to pick oranges to make a living. They would be executives and nobody would look down on them as Italian immigrants. They would speak perfect English. His children would never have to be embarrassed the way he was. He, Candido Jacuzzi, would see to it.

Dad cherished the moments he was able to spend with our family. He loved to romp in the big backyard with Johnny and our savage Doberman that was almost friendly as long as Johnny was present. Although I was not yet two years old, they tell me that I was able to toddle after them as they ran imaginary football plays.

Shortly before my second birthday, I came down with a cold. At least that was what one doctor thought it was. My mother, however, thought differently. Although she had faith in the miracles of modern medicine, she still thought her baby's fever was too high to be brought on by any ordinary cold, and it seemed to her that I had begun to limp. Here is how she described my illness to a friend.

> Dr. Thompson had delivered Kenny at Providence Hospital in Oakland. He left for war a couple of years later. I thought that if he had been around at the first sign of what they thought was a cold, he might have known what it was. He was a good doctor.
>
> He (Kenny) was nearly two years old. I called the pediatrician. I said my boy has an awfully high fever. Doctor came over. Examined. Said "coming down with a cold." Gave some pills and a shot. No penicillin.

Mother described what happened next when she called the doctor. "All right," the doctor acquiesced. "He may have the flu. I'll be over tomorrow and give him a shot."

The "shot" was the miracle drug, sulfa. Antibiotics were still in the experimental stage and not available to civilians; used almost exclusively in the war effort. The Japanese had bombed Pearl Harbor the year I was born and World War II was in full swing. Penicillin would be in short supply for another year until a new form of mold was discovered that produced ten times as much penicillin.

The shot did not help. My mother was right. What I had was not a cold, but strep throat. An insidious microbe called hemolytic streptococcus gathered its forces and invaded my bloodstream. Then rheumatic fever set in. My limp grew worse and my fever would not come down. I don't remember all this but my parents could never forget it.

My father told me, "When you refused to stand and always wanted to be carried, we didn't know what was wrong. One doctor said there was nothing wrong; another said you had polio. We noticed your feet were swelling and your hands could not pick up things."

Mother described the next stage of my illness:

> We watched him, gave him aspirin. Little better one day. Next day wouldn't eat much. He was losing weight, had burning fever. Temp went up at midnight, went down in day. So doctor never saw high temp. Couldn't believe it was going up to 105. So he came one night to see and found it was true. He was baffled. Kenny kept getting thinner. Went down to 21 pounds.
>
> Got him a specialist known in San Francisco for diagnosis. They put Kenny in hospital in Oakland. Doctor came from San Francisco to examine him.
>
> This doctor said he must have had strep throat. Must have dislodged from tonsils and gone into blood stream. Streptococcus can go to heart and enlarge heart. That could have killed him. Went to every joint and that's how he got the rheumatoid arthritis.

It was not until later that the doctors discovered that what they were finally up against was Still's disease or Juvenile Rheumatoid Arthritis. The doctor who treated me at the Children's Hospital in Oakland tried to comfort my mother, suggesting I might outgrow it someday. What he meant was perhaps I would someday stop getting worse. The damage being done was unavoidable and irreversible. Already I could turn my head only a few degrees and had to be fed through a straw or intravenously because I was unable to open my mouth. Soon, my fingers would stiffen and wither, rendering them useless.

My mother went on to describe my condition:

> Took him to another place for treatment. Looked at my husband and said if he's going to die, let's take him home. He's pining away. I have to cross the bay to see him. They couldn't do any more in hospital than they could at home. We took him home and took care of him as best as we could.
>
> Sleeping all the time, not eating. Took him back to children's hospital. Not eating, getting fed by transfusions. He had excruciating pain. They wanted to go in with needle to get water out from around heart. Dangerous. He stayed one year there in Children's Hospital under transfusions. He used to hate when they took blood. He was all drawn up. Got some better there. They gave him treatments that were used for Roosevelt. When some better, they put him in room with other children. When I came to read for him, they'd all listen. When I didn't come, they'd all call for "Nurse Jacuzzi."
>
> We used to go to library after school. Wasn't too far. Learned all about Oz. Came in 11 volumes. Bought those for Kenny when he was a little boy. Read a lot to Kenny 'cause he was ill for so long. You know, *The Little Train That Could*. Then there were the records—*Peter and the Wolf*.

The doctors put me in a complete body cast to try to maintain the straightness of my limbs before they contracted. It was terrible and it lasted for a whole year, in which I had virtually no physical contact because of this cocoon. Everybody needs to be touched!

One day, the doctors really upset my mother. "I don't think you should visit Kenny every day, Mrs. Jacuzzi," the doctor said, taking her aside one morning. "It might be better if you see the boy less. After you leave, he cries the rest of the day."

It went against her instincts but something in the doctor's tone led her to comply. Of course, I probably cried because of the pain. I just don't remember any more. Doctors so often give the impression that they know what is wrong with us, but nobody can wring it from them. They usually have the appearance of a man conscious of money in the savings bank. As time passes, it is finally impossible to associate a serious-looking doctor with an ordinary human being. So I'm sure my mother received a doctor's pronouncements like the word of God being handed down.

My father didn't like illness, didn't understand it, and it was my mother who always gave me medicine. But Dad got the good doctors for me. At first before the diagnosis was made, my mother blamed my father for it, saying that he had too many windows in the new house and I probably got sick from a draft. But, of course, that had nothing to do with my illness. Later, my mother still blamed my father for things connected with my illness, saying that he was always on a business trip and the bulk of care fell on her and fatigued her. I'm afraid that my illness created many arguments between them.

My mother saw me as her little boy who didn't understand what was happening to him while his whole body was being slowly twisted and contorted. Somewhere in the back of her mind, Mom suspected she was being weaned away from me in preparation for my death. She could see it in the doctors' faces and it made her suspicious. But she wanted to do things right, to cooperate. Even when my condition became less critical and I could eat solid food, mother let her sister-in-law take her place and visit me whenever she could, bringing me some of Mom's cooking. I missed that and my mother thought it was a shame to let me eat hospital food when she knew what I liked.

My sister Alba remembered what it was like for my parents when I was sick. She said, "I really did not understand why you got sick. The family at that time was filled with worry. Doctors in and out—and I saw Mom and Dad with tears so very often—it was very scary. Your stay at Children's Hospital was long. Lydia (Aunt Cirilla's oldest daughter) and I took turns staying with you at night."

"That boy is pining away for you," Inez's sister-in-law, Cirilla, told her. "It's not for the pain he cries. It is for you!"

Mom rushed to the hospital, the spell of deference to the doctors' superior knowledge broken. The doctor was not available, but some interns who knew her stopped to offer their advice. "You might just as well take him home, Mrs. Jacuzzi," said one from the tell-it-like-it-is school of amateur psychology. "Your son won't live to be three."

When she heard that, my mother said, "He's going home with me right now!" She couldn't actually pick me up as one might normally do a child. Any movement at the joints caused severe pain. She had to carry me out on a pillow. Of course, she had to take me back for treatments. Mother described that time.

> Finally decided to take him home. Would put him in the sun a little bit when we could. Rub with olive oil for calluses all over him. For exercise got a therapist from Finland three times a week. He played with a lot of toys on wheels. He could roll back and forth. We wanted to put him on tricycle but damn pedals in the way, so took it to bike shop and Bernie cut the pedals off. Father put paths all around house that he could use, protected by fences.
>
> By the time he was six or seven, we were taking Kenny to Berkeley General 'cause hospital in Oakland didn't have a Hubbard Tank. That was a small pool you could put one limb in for massage. But every time we took him over there for treatment, he'd catch a cold. Then we had to worry about leaving the youngest, Irene, home alone. Had to put her in convent and she wasn't happy.
>
> Three or four years later, I told my husband, "Jeez, can't you rig something up for a tub at home?" So he and engineers in the factory talked it over and decided to try reversing pumps they used in wells. This would throw rather than suck up the water. They rigged up a portable pump, just for him.
>
> We didn't think of putting it on market though it helped him a lot. One of our neighbors had a son who had polio. She wanted one, too. Candido said we can't do that. They had to go through the American Medical Association. He said we were not in business to make medical equipment. But one of doctors encouraged him to try. So they experimented and came up with a thing made of steel aluminum water pump shaped like torpedo. It plugged into wall, with grips on top for grounding it. So he started selling them here and there to help patients. He couldn't say it was a cure, could only say it would help like a hot pad would help.
>
> The first invention for Ken was a portable Jacuzzi. He used it for seven years before they were marketed. Would put in bath, attach to plumbing. Whole family used and enjoyed it. Kept his blood circulating good. Doctors were amazed at his good circulation. Limbs good, not deteriorating. Started to walk on crutches when he was 12. Then when got a little older, he had another attack.
>
> Had a teacher coming to house for schooling. He wanted to go to public school but he couldn't make it. Told him they'd get same teacher for him and when he was ready, he'd go to class with the others. Got a bigger house on just

one level and put in a swimming pool. We designed everything so Kenny could reach things, switches, etc. I taught him to float. Kids used to come all the time to swim, and played in rumpus room. He became so much older for his age because he talked so much to adults from every walk of life.

But going back to my earliest year, while the nation was focused on the war, families had their own concerns and my parents were concerned about me. The family was flooded, inundated, and overwhelmed by the constant bad news from physicians about my condition. They had felt so happy and fortunate in America until my illness. They hardly knew which direction to turn and every family member had advice for them.

My parents tried to care for me at home but I developed pneumonia and grew thinner every day. I wouldn't eat and it seemed horrible to force-feed a child, but they were obliged to do so. Finally, they had to admit they could not help me and took me once more to the hospital. There, doctors managed to drive out the pneumonia but soon a new assault was discovered on my already weakened body. This time, the pericardium was under attack.

Only weeks before, the doctors were saying how lucky I was not to have had the rheumatism settle in my heart. That would have been serious. But for somebody in my condition, pericarditis was usually fatal. The pericardium is a membranous sac that encloses the heart and its main vessels. It is anchored, at the base, to the diaphragm and from behind, to the bronchi and the esophagus. In pericarditis, this sac fills up with fluid and if the process is not reversed, the fluid overflows into the lungs and the victim drowns in his own internal fluids.

My mother was called into my hospital room. With a blue pen, they marked on my chest the battle plan. "Mrs. Jacuzzi," the doctor said, "tomorrow we have to stick the needle where the blue marks are in order to reduce the fluid level. I have to tell you, it is a very delicate operation because if we should hit the wrong spot..." the doctor's voice dropped "...the boy will die."

My mother didn't know what to do.

"But if we leave him this way, he'll die anyway," the doctor added.

She just stood there waiting for them to continue.

"There is another thing we could try." He didn't sound confident but she listened intently. "We could give him hot poultices tonight every so often, which might also relieve him. But we can't put off the operation beyond tomorrow morning."

Mother chose the latter and stayed up with me all night long, changing the poultices and praying. They say that I slept fitfully, sometimes waking suddenly and staring blankly at mother with wild, glassy eyes. Months before, the fever had turned my baby teeth black and some had fallen out. Toothless, twisted with arthritis, wracked with pain, I hardly looked like a child, my mother thought, much less her child. She had to fight the desire to gather me up in her arms because pain from the arthritis made the slightest touch cause me to scream in agony. She gently laid a fresh poultice on my chest and waited.

Just before dawn, I grew quieter. My breathing became deeper and more even. Were they winning or losing? Mother could not tell. She had reached that stage of exhaustion when her movements were automatic and mechanical. Slowly and precisely, she changed my poultice and sat back down on the edge of the narrow hospital bed and waited.

A few hours later, the doctor strode in, examined me and announced, "The crisis is over! Something happened. I don't know what, but the water around the heart is gone." He shrugged and left Mom to celebrate her victory alone.

My father could not concentrate. He tried to think of some solution to my illness. Whenever there was a problem at work, didn't they always come to Candido to solve it? Didn't he reduce their high transportation costs by opening new branches across the country, making them competitive with eastern pump companies? Didn't he always seem to patch up other people's mistakes? He sold our ranch in Saint Helena. So what if it was nicer than Valeriano's or Rachele's ranch and would be worth a fortune some day. He would sell it so he could spend more time with his little boy.

I was not the only one in the family experiencing difficulties. A few days after I became ill, my father's sister, Stella, was arrested, apparently deemed a Mussolini sympathizer. She and her family were sent to Grass Valley, California, to live in a four-room house in a detention camp. There was no telling what would happen next. The whole family might be rounded up and imprisoned for being Italian. My father was no different than many Italian immigrants who gradually felt paranoid toward the American government. Were these authorities in the medical profession really on his side and would they help?

I turned three in the hospital. The war was still on and the hospital was forced to ration the meat it served to patients. Since arthritics require extra protein in the diet, my mother gave the family's meat rations to me. I needed endless transfusions and, of course, blood was also hard to get. Sometimes when supplies ran low, mother would give me blood herself. Fortunately, we were not only the same blood type but also cross-matched. She knew everyone was doing all that could be done for me. I was not getting any worse, but I wasn't getting any better either.

The family doctor, Dr. Sweet, knew something about arthritis because his wife had it. He had some success treating her with gold salt shots so he recommended them for me. Nobody really knew why that worked, only that it could be a dangerous procedure. It was also an expensive one. But my folks figured the odds were already against them and it was worth a try. They brought me home again. Every two weeks I would get an injection of gold, but the results were not dramatic.

Then Mom heard about a Dr. Saunders, who, it was said, left his practice in Hawaii rather hurriedly and was now established in San Francisco. There were rumors that perhaps some lady had allowed him to bake a loaf in her oven, leaving her with an unnatural swelling that the Hawaiians called "nine months' dropsy."

Nevertheless, Saunders took to me right away. Like a good general, he quickly sized up the situation. "What your boy needs," he told Mom "is a special serum." There was a specialist, Dr. Jeffrey in Los Angeles, who could make up a serum out of a patient's own antibodies. Saunders did not make any claims about it, only that there was only a small percent chance it would increase the range of motion in my joints.

Dr. Sweet was a stubborn old Scotsman. "I do not think it will work," he growled. "It did not help me wife, and it may not help yer laddie." He refused to give it his blessing. "Do not waste yer time. It's nothin' but false hope. I would not bet me kilt on it, ya know! But..."

Sweet was competent; there was no doubt of that. And he was the type who let you know about it, in case you had any doubt. He had no tolerance for lay people theorizing about medicine without a license, especially mothers. They knew less than anyone. Mom always listened, but finally lost patience with his condescending attitude.

"Listen!" she blurted out. "You said you didn't know what causes arthritis. I don't either. So my guess as good as yours. They say he won't live to have another birthday and that nothing anybody does will help. But I'm his mother and I'm going to try!"

This may have been the first time anybody, much less a woman, had stood up to him and he respected her for it. He had to admit she was right. He did not know what would help and what would not. Nobody really did.

The procedure required a culture from my throat and a culture of my bowel movement. Dr. Jeffrey instructed her that the bowel movement had to be kept warm—all the way from Berkeley. A weaker woman might have been dismayed at the prospect, but my mother cheerfully placed me in the car and my bowel movement on a hot water bottle and headed off for Los Angeles. After two weeks, Dr. Jeffrey produced a small bottle of clear serum made from the specimens. And after only three treatments, I was able to turn my head halfway around. It was a miracle. A mother's faith and persistence paid off.

My fourth birthday rolled around. Mom had an idea. Berkeley could be cold and damp even in the summer. Why didn't they get a summer place in the Lake Country where I could be warm and get lots of sunshine and fresh vegetables? My Dad went for it but Dr. Sweet did not.

"You can not do that!" he ranted at Mom, but with a fair degree of respect. "Yer boy has to have his gold shots. You can not do it yerself. You need a therapist for him."

So Mom found a therapist, a Finnish woman who had learned the art of massage in Finland and also worked part-time at the local hospital. She located a doctor, Dr. Barr, a Seventh Day Adventist, who would be termed "holistic" if he were practicing today. He did not believe in giving patients a lot of medication, especially not children. And he had experience with arthritic kids. He and Mom saw eye to eye about the value of giving me fresh fruits and vegetables. Let God and nature work their magic. My mother even drove me 20 miles every other week to get my gold shots hoping they might begin to help. At the end of the summer, she took me to Dr. Sweet for a checkup.

When I was through, the doctor smiled and said, "Whatever you did for this laddie, you did wonderfully!" He leaned thoughtfully back in his chair and gave his pronouncement: "It is my recommendation that you take Kenny to the Lake Country every summer." With a perfectly straight face, too!

However, I could never be "normal." Although I was four years old, I looked barely half that age. I remained bent over and could not walk. If I continued to beat the odds and live to maturity, what kind of future could I look forward to? How could I compete with able-bodied children? Could I ever work? Could I ever get married and have a family? Would I ever be happy? One thing was certain: if I were even to survive, I would have to struggle for the rest of my life.

One week after they returned from the Lake Country, Dad, recently home from a business trip, rushed into the living room, carrying a newspaper and shouting, "The war is over! Japan surrendered! They all surrendered! It's finally over."

Mom always complained about Dad not giving more time to the family. She would say he didn't see the children grow up like she did. He gradually agreed more and more. He used to tell my brother and sisters to spend more time with their families. He warned that soon they would grow away from their parents and wouldn't know each other any more.

Dad and Mom wanted to hide me because my condition was so hard to explain. It was like they felt responsible for my illness and my defects, and wouldn't have to explain if nobody saw me. They stayed away from other people and even family members. They had their reasons or rationalizations, and may not have realized exactly why they stayed away from others.

Dad never played golf. "Silly game! Who wants to run after a ball?" So he didn't have to socialize much with family or business contacts. He never took trips except to promote business. His main concern outside of business was his family and inner circle.

"On long trips, I used to call home every week," he recalled. "Once, when Alba was dating Peter Kosta, they said they wanted to get married. But Inez and me, we thought they should wait until Pete was out of the Navy to have a nice wedding."

From Kansas City, Dad called home. Mom told him that Alba and Pete went out to Reno, Nevada, and got married. Dad sounded happy but the more he thought about it, the madder he got. His firstborn child ran off behind his back to get married. He didn't even get to see the wedding. Did his daughter and new husband have no respect for him? Pete was a nice boy but what he did was not a thing for a man to do!

When Dad arrived in Berkeley to meet his son-in-law on the Southern Pacific Railroad, Pete was waiting for him on the platform. All the way to California, Dad thought of what he would say to this boy who stole his daughter in this cowardly way. But when he stepped off the train, Pete threw his arms around him and said, "Hello, Pop!" And it made my father laugh.

Alba said that Pete was about to go into the military. Once married, he would get an allotment. She was in college and they had found a Navy apartment on the base that they both thought would be perfect.

Dad came around and offered them the suite his mother had used before she died, saying that they could still be in the house close to Mom and me. They did stay at the house for nearly two years. As Alba said, "It was hard to reason with Dad when he said something and I couldn't speak up for myself. We were there till after I was pregnant when we moved into an older house."

Dad didn't stop to think that almost nobody could stand up to him. He intimidated everyone and didn't hesitate to do so if it helped him win an argument. Later he and Mom found out that Alba and Pete did not elope to escape their disapproval but, since Peter was scheduled to be shipped to Japan, they were married so he would not have to go.

Alba described those years and I heard how much my illness was at the seat of conflicts between my parents. I learned later that most couples have trouble when a child has a major disability, and it's a miracle when they can hold their marriage together.

> Pete didn't know what he would do when the war was over. Dad asked him to come to work in the shop, install pumps, and then go into sales.
> Then he asked Pete to go to Mexico and help set up the factory there. Pete and I went down there for about six months but after that, it was stay or no job. That was the end of his career with the Jacuzzis. He went into electronics for some time in Stockton, California. After a while, Dad wanted him back. Dad wasn't sure he'd listen to his father-in-law so asked his brother, Joseph, to speak to Pete about coming back to take over marketing and selling of Jacuzzi. Pete did but I was unhappy because he was back in the family business.
> It used to hurt me to hear mother complain about how bad things were or about Kenny or someone who's ill. She always blamed others. She'd start off on one subject and quickly jump to another like this child, that child, your business, why do you travel, why am I at home? Kenny always came up, the fact that my father traveled and she was home alone and the sacrifices she made for Kenny. But mother had a tremendous amount of help and had aides for Kenny.

Our home, nestled in a quiet Berkeley neighborhood, was far from opulent, but was cozy and dignified. It was a two-story house, built in that red-tile-roof-white-stucco style so popular in California. It had a spiral staircase built of stone and a split-level living room. There was one bedroom on the ground floor and upstairs, three others, including the master bedroom and my bedroom.

I couldn't make it up the stairs and had to be carried to and from my room. I wasn't given the room on the lower floor because my parents wanted me to be nearer to them upstairs. For me, being dependent upon other people was a fundamental fact of life. Certainly, it caused frustrations from time to time but my family loved me and tried to help me whenever I needed it.

My parents' quest to improve my health sometimes led us to strange places, including a visit to an Indian medicine man in Chino, California. Friends had told my parents of miraculous cures by the old man. The face-to-face meeting of my father and the Indian might have evoked smiles if there had been onlookers. For the broken English of both made communication almost impossible. But Dad told his story and then waited impatiently for the deeply creased and impassive jaw of the tribal spokesman to move. After a long pause, the Indian said, "Give the boy goat's milk. That will cure him."

So Candido, the lion, went out and bought a goat and somebody in the family milked it every day. I couldn't stand the taste. Even when Mom told me that some people were allergic to cow's milk and that they were brought up on goat milk, it didn't ease the situation. I detested goat's milk. I had to endure many other doctors, physical therapists, and all kinds of supposed healers, but I drew the line at goat's milk!

I was a happy child but I wasn't getting any better and my mother was worried. My joints were twisting, and my muscles were atrophying. At the Children's Hospital in Berkeley, they were treating me with hot compresses known as "Kenny Packs," named after the Australian nurse "Sister" Kenny. Like most of the treatments that were suggested, they were less than miraculous and were done "just in case."

By now, the family pump business was doing very well and Dad, as general manager, was left with little time to spend with our family. Nevertheless, he personally took me to San Francisco every week, using the trips as an opportunity to get to know me better. My burly father would pack me around on his shoulders, giving me a lofty view from his secure perch. One of the few early memories I have of my father was of these trips and our lunches near Fisherman's Wharf. They served a dish called Cioppino, similar to bouillabaisse. To a boy used to Italian food, it was an exotic delight, although the shells that remained in the stew were hard for me to handle.

As time passed and I accompanied my father, these unusual meals became more common. Germans would say, they became as common as cherries in the Black Forest. Italians would say, they became as common as macaroni in Naples.

I loved my father dearly and looked forward to these shared adventures. Dad's crude version of the whirlpool that would someday make the name Jacuzzi famous around the world helped me. He took the basic sump pump design they had been using to remove water from basements, and used it to produce a water jet in a bathtub.

However, my Dad also added an air inlet to the water that mixed air with the water jet. Both the air and water jet outputs were adjustable. This air-water jet mix formed the basis for the patent for the Jacuzzi whirlpool bath. The motor was suspended above the water on a board that lay across the width of the bathtub. A shaft extended from the base of the motor to the bottom of the tub, terminating in the pump's impeller. It was a crude and homely contraption to have sitting on the bathtub.

Once it was built, Dad asked my doctor, Cecil Saunders, to see if it measured up to the one I used in the hospital. Dr. Saunders started fawning over its potential and encouraged my family to build and market Dad's whirlpool bath. He said it would be great for people with disabilities and the elderly who could benefit from daily hydrotherapy in their homes.

Dr. Saunders always took a personal interest in me. Many years after we met, he confided to my parents that he always thought of me as his own son. One time he held a luau at his golf course, complete with a door prize of a television set, an invention only recently made available to the public. Saunders did not attempt to hide his delight when the Jacuzzis won. He did, however, conceal the fact that he had fixed the contest. He knew I wouldn't be able to attend public school, and thought a TV would be an educational tool for me.

One physician who heard about the whirlpool from Saunders approached my Dad about making one for him.

"Sure," said Candido. "I'll give you one."

"No, I want to pay for it," the doctor said.

"But, one machine…"

"No," the doctor interrupted, "I'll need eight more."

This got my father to thinking that maybe there really was something of value in all this. A friend of the family had a wife with arthritis and was also making trips to San Francisco to use the Hubbard Tank. So Candido built him a whirlpool bath. Once more, the reaction was so positive that he thought of presenting the idea of putting it into production before the other Jacuzzi Brothers. They were accustomed to looking to Candido for direction but diversification was costly and the brothers had learned their lesson about borrowing money. Although mostly they were in favor of Dad's idea, a final decision had to be unanimous. He accepted this and kept refining the design and waiting.

At first, Dad wasn't sure if such a product had any kind of market potential. Mom, however, insisted that there were lots of people—not just those with disabilities—who could be helped by a whirlpool bath at home. What convinced Dad to support this product was nothing less than fear, the fear that can often spring from a father's love and concern for a chronically ill child.

When I went in for a checkup, Dr. Saunders was amazed at how good my muscle tone was for having so little movement in my joints. Dad explained and offered to demonstrate his invention. Being not only a fine physician but also a man with a sharp eye for business, Dr. Saunders became fascinated with the idea of a home whirlpool.

"Listen, Jacuzzi, you've got something here! You should try to market this thing."

Dr. Saunders' reputation, both professionally and otherwise, preceded him all the way from Hawaii where it was rumored he had been politely but firmly asked to leave for running an establishment of masculine pleasures on the side. He had other investments too, like a sumptuous golf course in Sonoma where he lived, commuting to his lively practice in San Francisco. His business dealings never made him rich, although they did make his wives happy. Nobody is sure just how many he had during his life. When he met our family, he was working on his fifth; after that, only his accountants kept up. Perhaps he imagined a partnership and a way to capitalize on my father's invention.

Dad was modest about his knowledge and reluctant to make money on something that was invented to help me. In fact, it was 1947 before my father and John Armstrong, one of Jacuzzi's engineers, developed the pump that created a swirling whirlpool in a bathtub to temporarily relieve my pain. But he didn't apply for or obtain U.S. patent No. 2,621,597 for the pump until December 16, 1952.

In that year, the Jacuzzi Company began a project with the Mount Diablo Therapy Center where I had been treated. They had a sheltered workshop in their rehabilitation center providing jobs with pay and benefits for patients. My father and his brothers arranged for patients to assemble a new invention, the famous Jet Charger pump used to pressurize water systems for home and farm, at the center.

Several employees went to the center to teach patients how to assemble it. Arrangements were made for delivery of parts to the Center, and pick up later. Although production problems arose, they were overcome. By the end of the three-month trial period, over 1,000 Jet Chargers had been assembled. I can't describe how proud I am of my Dad for this early effort to give work to disabled people.

This led to other companies giving business contracts to people with disabilities and rehabilitation workshops. In the San Francisco Bay Area, hospitals sent their hypodermic needles to be sharpened by workshop patients. This was interesting to me because the following year (1953), I would be introduced to my first job—sharpening hypodermic needles. Sister Mary Ellen gave me that assignment when I was a hospital patient. Unbeknownst to me at the time, it was our family company in the California area that opened the door to permitting those with disabilities to do such jobs.

Five years after the Mount Diablo Therapy Center began producing the Jet Charger, 35 occupational therapy patients were turning out approximately 3,200 units per week with no rejects because the quality of workmanship was so high. A decision was made to let the Therapy Center assemble the new tiny Mijet. In addition, patients at the Center had turned out 60,000 flappers for valves, with only one reject.

I always thought my family dropped the ball because the Jacuzzi Bros., Inc., (JBI) never did honor people with disabilities in any meaningful way. I just didn't appreciate my father's early efforts. I thought the company could have created a nonprofit foundation to research new technologies and products to enhance independent living for people with disabilities. But I'm glad they did do some innovative things for people with handicaps.

The original hydrotherapy apparatus that Dad created for me was made of shiny chrome-plated steel and was suspended about halfway in the water from a ladder-type frame. The frame rested on the left and right edges of the bathtub, straddling the feet of whoever was in the tub. (This original Jacuzzi Whirlpool Bath currently resides somewhere in the bowels of the Smithsonian Museum in Washington, D.C.)

Dad was a determined, hardheaded negotiator and, when required, a fearless son-of-a-bitch. I didn't understand how hard it was for Dad to interest the family in turning his invention into a source of income for me in the long run. With more than five years of healthcare expenses for me, Dad was afraid that when I reached adulthood, there would be no money to pay for my medical care. As his child, I was covered under the group insurance paid for by Jacuzzi Bros., Inc. But the day would eventually arrive when that coverage would no longer exist.

In the 1940s, few thought a severely "disabled" child could become a productive, working adult. Dad was no exception. Furthermore, Medicare and other forms of government-subsidized healthcare coverage for people with disabilities didn't exist.

Increasingly, Dad began to visualize the Jacuzzi Whirlpool Bath as a viable product that could eventually provide me with lifetime healthcare insurance coverage. That "kill-two-birds-with-one-stone" benefit was all the motivation Dad required. He pulled no punches with his family and insisted that the company produce this product. Dad won the battle and Jacuzzi Research, Inc., the division created to manufacture and market the Jacuzzi Whirlpool Bath, was born.

Meanwhile, I was getting the benefit of the prototype. Without knowing it, I had also entered into my first position as a consultant for the family business. Each time an alteration was made, Dad would have me try it out, taking careful note of my comments and making adjustments accordingly. This process continued for the next seven years.

Little did Dad know that his invention for me, the Jacuzzi Whirlpool Bath, would make the family name famous worldwide. In the early 1950s, a few production prototypes were tested on me in our home bathtub. Several unique patents were applied for and granted—among them, an original water Venturi-jet. This design allowed the user to vary the size, mix and intensity of air bubbles and water pressure. The Jacuzzi Whirlpool Bath was officially launched in the U.S. marketplace. A year prior, the Jacuzzi Whirlpool Bath was test marketed in California and a few dealerships were established.

One of the first to open a Jacuzzi dealership was former Dodgers' baseball player and Mets' coach, "Cookie" Lavagetto. I don't know how he did it but he got a baseball autographed by New York Yankees team members, including Mickey Mantle. He gave it to my Dad to give to me. I still have that ball although the signatures are badly faded.

Meanwhile, Dad wanted a good person to run the Whirlpool Bath division of Jacuzzi Research, Inc. My cousin, Lydia Benassini, had married Frank Negherbon. Dad asked him to manage Jacuzzi research. He saw Frank as a strong salesperson. Frank turned him down, probably because they were too much alike. Frank wanted to make his own mark in the world and did later when he purchased an auto dealership. He went on to purchase more and became one of Oakland's leading entrepreneurs.

When Frank turned the job down, Dad wanted to ask Peter. But he felt it would be more diplomatic if his brother, Joseph, asked Pete, rather than his father-in-law. When Joseph approached Pete, I'm happy to say that he accepted.

The company had hired a freelance sports writer by the name of Ray Schwartz. Ray was an in-law of my cousin, Giocondo, who ran the JBI operation out of New Jersey. Giocondo knew that Ray didn't know a damn thing about pumps or hydrotherapy devices. But he was an excellent writer, based out of southern California, who knew scores of people in the sporting world and entertainment industry, mostly on a first-name basis. Ray's contacts included major league players, Hollywood stars, and many originators of the new television industry. Giocondo also knew that Ray had a very bad heart and, being a freelance writer, had neither healthcare nor life insurance coverage.

Giocondo was right. Ray Schwartz came on board because he knew just how bad his heart was and that it probably wouldn't be long before he "bought the farm." Ray, as is often true of talented writers, didn't have much and wanted to leave his wife, Francine, with at least something, which the company's life insurance permitted him to do.

Soon after joining the company, Ray got the Jacuzzi Whirlpool Bath photographed with the most renowned celebrities of the day, including Joe Di Maggio, Rita Hayworth, Jayne Mansfield, Marilyn Monroe, Admiral Chester Nimitz, Charlton Heston, and many others. But, by far, the very best thing Ray Schwartz did for Jacuzzi was to get it on the daytime television show, *Queen for a Day*, emceed by Jack Bailey.

On this TV show, broadcast from Hollywood before a live audience, three women, usually homemakers, would tell their individual "hard-luck" stories. The one who had the greatest tearjerker and received the most applause from the studio audience would be named *Queen for a Day*. The lucky lady would receive a complete beauty makeover, wardrobe, and night on the town with limousine, and a host of more practical prizes, usually appliances like stoves, washers, dryers, etc.

Since *Queen for a Day* was broadcast Monday through Friday, the chances were excellent that on two or three of those five days, a *Queen* would be selected who had a health-related problem in her family. Whenever that would occur, one of the *Queen's* prizes would be a Jacuzzi Whirlpool Bath.

Prior to exposure on this nationwide television show, hardly anyone I knew could come even close to pronouncing the name Jacuzzi. It was called everything from *Choosy* to *Jersey* to *Juicy* to a lot of other things, but rarely, if ever, Jacuzzi. Within less than a year of exposure on *Queen for a Day* with 20 million viewers, everyone not only pronounced Jacuzzi correctly, but it also became a household word synonymous with whirlpool bath. Ah, the power of television!

It wasn't many months later that Ray Schwartz, one hell of a writer and creative, media-savvy guy, died. It was only as I grew older that I came to fully appreciate the magnitude of what Ray achieved in such a short time. Dad invented a much-needed product and brought it to market. Ray made its name famous. Their creativity and successes were born from the same value—caring.

The Jacuzzis kept adapting the whirlpool bath to meet the needs for mass production and safety, and the finished product was marketed beginning in 1953. Later the whirlpool pump was developed for bathtubs and incorporated into large baths called hot tubs or spas. My family took risks that other business owners didn't, and my mother described some of those risks.

> We put a factory in Little Rock in the 1960s because government was encouraging industry. It gave the Jacuzzi Brothers a lot for nothing. Then we could

distribute to eastern markets the deep well pumps and the whirlpool. We had big party when we opened the plant. The Governor came. A priest blessed it. We brought men in from California to teach workers. We had a couple of black men. Ticklish situation. We were famous in a way for introducing black men into the work force.

Local people didn't like that we were paying workers more than normal wage. We were paying them California wages. They wouldn't join unions. Unions didn't like it and tried to sabotage the plant. They put salt in car tanks in the parking lot, and shot through a window at Candido.

I think my mother enjoyed all this notoriety and excitement. She loved Dad's success and the lifestyle it gave her. She wasn't a bad wife, but she had a temper. Years of temper in a "palace" were probably easier for Dad to take than years of temper in a shack because he could get some distance from Mom.

My dear friend Tom S., who spent many afternoons a week tutoring and studying with me in high school, described my mother. He said:

> Inez was a tiger when it came to protecting her young. She was a "stay at home" mom of the old school, who took good care of her home and family. Her pride was her cooking. Nobody at her table ever went hungry. I remember her with much affection.
>
> She was a middle-aged woman whose physical appeal was fading. For this reason, her husband essentially had put her in a pleasant bird cage and possibly sought comfort elsewhere. As far as I know, she endured this situation in silence.
>
> I believe in later years she was not living with or even near Ken's father. Once her youngest child, Ken, was on his own, it was unnecessary for her to continue the pretense of happy married life.

Of course, Tom was making guesses and nobody knows whether those guesses were correct or not. I have no evidence, nor does anyone in our family, that my parents were unfaithful to each other. But I'm sure we've all wondered, because they had the Italian habit of being so open about their likes and dislikes. Have you ever seen an Italian who was subtle?

5

America's Dirty Little Secret: Italian Internment Camps

Drought: Destructive prolonged absence of rain and moisture

About the time I got sick, my Aunt Stella's family was ordered by the government to pack up and leave their residence during WWII. She apparently was taken to be a Mussolini sympathizer. They were sent from the West Coast of California inland to Grass Valley. Her family of four was set up in a sort of internment camp in a four-room house. It scared my family and especially my father, and affected all the Jacuzzis for years to come, so I wanted to understand how that could happen.

By the 1930's, Italians comprised the largest immigrant group in California. Hardships of the Depression caused many, especially immigrants reading Italian newspapers, to favor Mussolini's totalitarian policies to help workers and unions. Mussolini was seen by many as a hero because he was turning Italy into a modern nation.

Beginning on December 7, 1941, Japanese, German and Italians who had not yet become American citizens, and some who had, were arrested by the F.B.I. After Pearl Harbor, "dangerous" aliens were evacuated from the West Coast and either prohibited free movement or restricted by curfews. The Alien and Sedition Acts gave the government power to detain aliens in times of emergency. U.S. military authorities worried that sabotage, espionage or subversion might be carried out by persons of Italian, German or Japanese ancestry.

Roosevelt's possible prejudices, revealed in accidental remarks, may have had something to do with repression of these ethnic groups. He destroyed much Italian support when he called Italy a "back-stabbing nation" for their alliance with Germany. Then he showed disrespect when he said, "We don't have to worry about the Italians. They're not a dangerous people; they're just a nation of opera singers."

First came the arrests. Hundreds of Italians were arrested in the months immediately after Pearl Harbor. About 250 individuals were interned for up to two years in military camps in Montana, Oklahoma, Tennessee and Texas.

Most of the men arrested in the San Francisco area had served in World War I for Italy, when Italy and America were allies. But after that war, the Federation of Italian War Veterans collected funds for war widows and orphans in Italy. Those who contributed, as years went by, came under surveillance whether they were fascist or not.

The early months of 1942 were filled with fear and confusion for Italian and German Americans, as well as Japanese. Fears of a Japanese invasion of the West Coast flourished. After a Japanese submarine fired some torpedoes in Santa Barbara, the pressure to move the Japanese population away from the coast escalated.

In January 1942, "enemy aliens" were required to register at local post offices around the country. Although all resident aliens had been required to register in 1940 under the Smith Act, they were now fingerprinted, photographed, and required to carry an "enemy alien registration card" with their photo. Those on the West Coast were limited to traveling no more than five miles from home, and had to turn in firearms, radios, cameras, flashlights and all "signaling devices." A curfew went into effect confining them to their homes from 8:00 pm to 6:00 am.

Mothers could not visit their children in hospitals if they were more than five miles away. Families could not attend a relative's funeral past the five mile limit. Aliens could not visit distant friends including their own sons serving at military bases, if they were beyond that distance.

German and Italian Americans became jittery and soon their worst fears materialized. President Roosevelt signed an executive order on February 19, 1942, authorizing the Army to bar "enemy aliens" from 86 restricted areas on the West Coast. Many were removed from their homes to internment camps for simply living too close to an important military base. On February 24, 1942, General John DeWitt, the head of the Western Defense Command, used Executive Order 9066 to evacuate, intern and confine "enemy alien" German and Italian immigrants and even American-born Japanese.

Arrests in San Francisco were probably similar to what occurred in other areas. F.B.I. agents arrived at night, searched homes, and took individuals to an Immigration Service detention facility. The family was not informed about why the arrest was made or what would happen. Many arrestees were moved to facilities such as Sharp Park in San Francisco, where Quonset huts were quickly assembled on a golf course. Later, Italian prisoners of war were brought back from Europe and also held at Sharp Park. Most of the arrestees were then shipped by train to Fort Missoula, Montana, where over 1,000 Italian nationals had been interned since 1941.

In Montana, the interned aliens were given hearings before boards of military officers and lay citizens. They were not informed of the charges against them, nor were they represented by legal counsel. The boards used F.B.I. reports containing errors, lack of rumor verification, and misinterpretations of innocent acts.

Internment camps were set up nationwide for the nearly 30,000 persons processed by the Immigration Service. Most that were relocated were sent to camps in Crossville, Tennessee; McAlester, Oklahoma; Livingston, Louisiana; Trinidad, Colorado; Opelika, Alabama; Florence, Arizona; Concordia, Kansas; Houlton, Maine; Scottsbluff, Nebraska; Mexia, Texas; and Ellis Island, New York. There were additional places such as Grass Valley, California, where Aunt Stella was sent.

Many were simply told to move, assigned to specific towns, and required to report in to the F.B.I. authorities within ten days. There were restrictions and curfews, but they were not treated very harshly.

Some could not bear the separation from home and family. Among several suicides was a 65 year old man who threw himself in front of a train on February 21, 1942.

These evacuations virtually destroyed California's fishing fleet. Italians in Monterey, Santa Cruz, Pittsburg, and San Francisco made up most of the fishermen, restaurant workers, and janitors, creating serious employment and food supply problems. Those who fished only within San Francisco Bay were able to continue. But most who fished ocean waters, including Joe DiMaggio's father, were restricted.

Ironically, posters could be seen urging people to eat more fish, since meat was being rationed for military use. One such poster said, "Fish is a fighting food. We need more!" But the fishing industry was suffering by the loss of Italian fishermen on the Pacific Coast.

At the elegant St. Francis Hotel in San Francisco, the State Legislature's Un-American Activities Committee, or Tenney Committee (named after chairman state Senator Jack Tenney) met in May of 1942. They concluded that community leaders of the *L'Italia* newspaper and the Italian language school Dopo Scuola (which means *after regular school hours*) were "leaders of the Fascist movement in California."

On the very appropriate holiday of Columbus Day, October 12, 1942, Italians were removed from the enemy alien classification. That did not stop local officials, however. Some naturalized citizens were still ordered to move away from California. They had to move out of the designated zones within ten days. Italian mothers who had sent their sons off to fight in the war had to leave their homes. Even some who lost sons in Pearl Harbor were forced to leave their residences.

Overall some 600,000 Italian Americans were considered "enemy aliens" because they lacked citizenship, and often simply because they did not know the English language, such as my grandparents. American women who married Italian immigrants lost their citizenship and were branded "enemy aliens" as well.

Unfortunately, America had a prejudice about Italians that came to a white hot heat during World War II. It had been mostly dormant and surfaced mainly in jokes, insulting nicknames, songs mocking Italians, and vaudeville. The force of this prejudice once exposed caused many Italians to change their names and abandon their native language.

U.S. Government posters associated the use of a foreign language with disloyalty. One poster said, "Don't speak the Enemy's Language! Speak American!" This wish to fit in caused many Italians to avoid emphasis on their Italian identity thereafter. This created a *drought* or drying up of pride in Italian Americans, who let their heritage evaporate out of fear of the government. Earlier, my family enjoyed being Italian and that was always a fixed point of reference on their personal compass.

Those who had been removed (called "excludes") were allowed to return to their homes at the end of 1943, after Italy surrendered in September. Most spent a little over a year in exile, having had to report regularly to F.B.I. offices even if they weren't confined in a camp. Often because of poor English skills and lack of proper notification, Italian Americans did not know they could return home. Often the notices of their release were simply posted in local post offices.

My Aunt Stella was married to Rino Marin and they had two sons, aged 8 and 16 at the time they had to move. In addition to Stella having been identified as a Mussolini sympathizer, they were living in an area of sensitive U.S. security, in Richmond, California, on the East Bay of Berkeley. She was not yet a citizen but was working on it. They had to immediately move inland to Grass Valley, not far from the Nevada border and the town of Truckee. She described the 1942 experience and what happened when she was notified she had to move.

> Quickly we stored the non-essential furniture and with only the bare necessities loaded on one of my brother's trucks, we were moved in fast; for we were

not given time to make different plans. Bearcreek Road passed in front of our house with good and frequent bus service to Colfax Grass Valley School or shopping to satisfy us very well. The children went to school and so did I for my final American citizen paper, which I was happy to receive from the Superior Court Judge of Nevada City, the capital of that county.

We lived in Grass Valley almost a year. Now I was an American citizen. Restriction of movements was lifted so we decided to go back to the city where my husband's job was. Everyone was working because the American industrial giant stood up and no one could stop its mass.

At this time, we suffered a great loss. Our dear mother left us because of a heart attack on August 8, 1943. The whole family was devastated because she was the center of all our getting together, our adviser and our giver of peace.

Now because of the war effort, my brothers' factory also had many orders to do anything they could with the equipment they had. Another change also took place in the family. All our brothers' and sisters' sons of draft age were in the service, all nine of them, also another nine that were husbands to the daughters of our brothers and sisters were also drafted for service in the American forces.

All 18 of them were giving their best. We prayed for all of them. Some had very close calls in the thick of battles. Some came home with scars. Many good young men never came back and our hearts felt very deeply for their families even after so many years, because a loss is forever.

The terrible war of many million dead was over but in the fall of 1945, it took America's atomic bomb to convince Japan to put down its arms. Hitler and Mussolini were already dead. Now it was time for peace amongst all the former enemies. So, as usual, America, very generous all the time, came up with the Marshall Plan. General George Marshall's plan of operation was to reconstruct the devastation left behind. First was law and order provided by the American service men, then hospitals and utilities.

Most Italians seemed to be reluctant to talk about their experience during this time. I never understood this reaction until I read an article about the internment of Ezio Pinza written by his granddaughter, Sarah Goodyear. He was a famous basso of the Metropolitan Opera, and star of the musical, *South Pacific*, with Mary Martin.

In March of 1942, F.B.I. agents entered his house without knocking and arrested him, without stating charges. He was confined at Ellis Island. His alleged "crime" was making admiring comments about Mussolini and receiving letters and magazines from Italy. His wife thought his accusers were envious opera singers.

He was lucky in that he was released after only 11 weeks due to letters on his behalf by writer Thomas Mann and anti-Fascist leader Carlo Tresca. Pinza was paroled on condition that he report weekly to a reliable American citizen. His physician was chosen to be that person since his physical and mental health had deteriorated during his confinement.

He and his wife did not discuss this internment with their own children until they were grown, because they were so ashamed. Ezio told family members that it was so disturbing, he wanted to forget it.

Joseph Scelsa, Dean of the Italian-American Institute at Queens College, said, "It's the nature of the Italian American psyche. We never bring shame to ourselves, even though we were the victims. It's a cultural legacy of taking it on the chin, of being quiet about it."

I think that Scelsa was very accurate in describing this trait, which I've seen at work in my own family, and especially in my own father.

After 1942, in the West, arrests, internments, curfews, and confiscations caused fear, suspicion, and more. People wondered if family, friends, neighbors or workers had informed on them. Animosities grew and became permanent. This whole episode in American history probably did little for security, but sowed the seeds for distrust of the government.

In the 1990s, the American Italian Historical Association of Bolinas, California, produced an exhibit called *Una Storia Segreta, A Secret Story*. After six years of travel and public attention, President Bill Clinton signed the Wartime Violation of Italian American Civil Liberties into Public Law #106–451 on November 7, 2000.

A year later, the U. S. Department of Justice issued a report entitled *Report to the Congress of the United States: A Review of the Restrictions on Persons of Italian Ancestry During World War II*. It acknowledged events that were long denied, especially the mass evacuation of California. Alas, this came too late to help my Aunt Stella who died in 2003 unaware of the report.

6

My Limitations

Blizzard: A severe snowstorm with high wind diminishing visibility.

My life was very self-centered. My family did not want to bother me with much news of the outside world. Our discussions were usually focused on my condition and my therapy. Whirlpool treatments became part of my daily ritual. The treatments made me feel better and discussing design improvements made me feel useful and more adult.

Although I was somewhat spoiled by all the attention lavished on me, I tried to be sensitive to other people's problems. Mine was a problem-oriented world. There was the problem of getting across the room, the problem of getting up even a single step, of getting dressed, or going to the bathroom. Naturally, I often had to have help in getting these things done and this, too, was a problem. It is a problem to show your anger at an older brother or sister when in five minutes you need one of them to carry you upstairs. A person in this position must learn to be extra diplomatic and not insist too strongly on his point of view. And it is of great importance to become considerate of other people.

My mother did most of the work around the house, but with me to take care of, there was more than she could do. She eventually hired a maid who also acted as a kind of attendant for me. She was one of those fanatically dutiful Swedish housekeepers. Everything had to be spotless and in its proper place. She absolutely loved little children, although she didn't quite understand me. She imagined me to be much more fragile than I was, with one foot in the grave and the other on my tricycle. She felt pity for me, an emotion I dimly recognized even then, and one I would later learn to spot a mile away.

When I called for something, she would drop whatever she was doing and run to me to see what I needed. Her dedication was exemplary but she was not a young woman. Her intentions were good but she might have ended up spoiling me if she had stayed on, because she didn't know how to set limits on me.

Of course, I took advantage of her. It amused me to see the way she bounded, graying blonde and big-boned, across the room, wide-eyed and so very serious, just because I called her name. Sometimes I would fabricate excuses for calling her, having her fetch me this or that, or pick up something I had dropped and couldn't reach. I was never malicious. The fact is I liked her. It would have been hard not to. She had that Ingrid Bergman kind of militant vulnerability that all men, even very, very young men, find irresistible.

One day I called to her, as usual, on some thin pretense, and she appeared, careening frantically across the well-furnished living room as if to dispute the theory that the shortest distance between two points is following a straight line. It was almost inevitable that she would trip, but my fascination turned to horror when I saw her fall face first, twisting unnaturally as she extended her full and considerable length across the carpet. She let out only a small, almost apologetic yelp.

Her ankle was broken in three places. When I discovered that a broken ankle means you cannot walk, I was overwhelmed with guilt. If I had not been so demanding, she would still be able to walk. I imagined how she would now have to have people bring her things and carry her into the bathroom, all because of me. All my life, I would never forget it.

And yet, life went on. An impression was made, though I could still be a brat. What does a bright little five-year-old do when his brothers and sisters get to go to school and he has to stay home? My parents always encouraged me to use my hands. By now, I was sketching quite a lot and even showing some talent. Still, sometimes this was not enough. I always did and always would want to make things. Although I would later deny it, other family members said that Rachele and I had a great deal in common.

I loved trains. Surrounded by my trains, I was in my element. I had an intricate maze of tracks plotted across the massive hobby table. With my blue-striped, duck-billed conductor's cap and an elaborate arrangement of switches, I took myself very seriously. This was my private domain. I was in complete control.

Occasionally, like any child, I would become bored and frustrated and expressed myself with a tantrum. I was not physically able to fly into a violent rage. But I discovered I could inspire a similar response in others by throwing things for them to pick up. Mother was incredibly patient and it took a good deal of ingenuity to get her mad. However, I found that I could eventually provoke a conflict by throwing various railroad cars about the room. Heck, I even threw miniature telephone poles, warning signs, and plastic cows.

Mom had already gone through this with her three older children. She knew when she was being baited. She was older and calmer now. And then, too, I was different. One had to be gentler, more understanding with me, she thought. She would pick up the cars and plastic cows with the patient perseverance only mothers seem to have. This, of course, only fanned the flames, and presented me with a challenge. My entire youthful life was devoted to problem solving and I set to work at once on this one.

I would let Mother pick up all my toys and give me a modulated lecture, and then I'd wait about half an hour before I did it all over again. With perverse satisfaction, I imagined what would happen to my sister Irene if she were so bold as to pull a stunt like this. Something awful, probably! I couldn't remember any of the kids ever being spanked; Dad did not believe in it. He remembered his own gentle father in Italy who lovingly raised thirteen respectful children and never once lifted his hand against them.

Even saints and guards at Buckingham Palace have their limits. I finally picked the wrong day to test my mother's patience. After strewing my toys from one end of the room to the other in a chaotic Jackson Pollock pattern, I waited with grim relish for Mother to start her routine. She took one look at the mess, set her jaw, and told me she was not going to pick up my toys any more. She turned and started out of the room when another of my defiant clatters stopped her in her tracks. Surprising herself as well as me, she wheeled around and almost before she knew it, delivered a light but unmistakably punitive thump to my arm. I was stunned for a moment. Then with a triumphant smile, I said, "I'm a regular boy, now!"

Testing the limits had paid off. I found I couldn't fool her. She knew how to control me. I wasn't going to be able get my way because of my disabilities. I needed to know that.

◆   ◆   ◆

Over the years, Jacuzzi Bros., Inc., was progressively increasing in international status. The sons of my six uncles and six aunts, along with my brother, John, were growing up with the assurance that a career in the family company was waiting for them when they were ready. It was my lot to observe their vigor and development from my own corner, which consisted of my crutches, my wheelchair, my seemingly endless frustrations, and, still, my dreams.

At home, I was the object of love without stint. But I was summarily excused from becoming a useful commodity in the tight, multi-national corporation that was the rapidly evolving Jacuzzi family enterprise. The unwritten policy of Jacuzzi Bros., Inc., was my deterrent: A "crip" didn't qualify as "manpower".

I spent the first 30 years of my life as primarily a spectator with a huge inner rage to perform. Friendships, travel, my broken body, attempts at an advanced education, and my share of sometimes magnificent, but mostly passing love affairs only mollified and chopped in half the many hopes I had as a growing child.

Mine were the commonplace wants of millions of men. But, when I aspired to them, they became uncommon because, physically, I was and am a person with profound disabilities.

But I'm a survivor of a disorder that can kill children. And, what does such a survivor look like? My face seems about right for a man born in 1941, except I have J.R.A.'s telltale signs of a short, stiff neck and receding chin. My clothing and shoes are, by necessity, custom-made to my size, which is approximately 4 feet two inches in height (I'm getting shorter all the time). I have very limited flexion and extension in my fingers, wrists, elbows, hips, knees, and ankles. The ligaments in my hips and knees have been surgically rearranged and their joints repositioned.

As of today, I've had surgical fusions performed on my cervical and thoracic spine. My neck rotation is limited to about 5–10 degrees, right and left. Both of my ankles are fused. I have light brown, but graying hair, "big and beautiful" hazel-brown eyes (at least that's what a few fems have told me), and I show some good and mean looking teeth when I smile.

My Still's Disease "burned out" about the time I entered full-blown puberty, but not before it left me with another lasting condition. My heart and lungs, although of fairly good quality, are subnormal in size due to the constricted expansion of my rib cage, which also was a fringe benefit of J.R.A. This particular condition has added hazard and intrigue to the probability of my survival from any really serious illness or major surgery. To date, I have had 14 major operations. There will probably be more, and there were some during the writing of this book.

From childhood to early manhood, my affliction stayed around like a cruel jailer. (It wasn't until I was well into my 40s before I realized that, thanks to the disability community in the United States, and our own Civil Rights Movement to gain equality, I had a disability, not an "affliction," which was largely a state-of-mind possessed and promulgated by fearful able-bodied people. At intervals, which might last a month or a year, I would be thrown back into misery. The doctors called these episodes "relapses," and they sometimes climaxed (not the feel good kind) with a session of repair surgery.

These operations gave me a few years in which I was able to move about on platform crutches in a marginal way. I could get in and out of a building (sometimes), in and out of bed, use a bathroom (also, sometimes), or enter a very low-to-the-ground car with the pull-and-lift gate of a stiff-kneed user of crutches.

Growing up at our home on Ada Street in Berkeley, California, was, for me, a mixed bag. There was laughter, good Italian food, and always lots of relatives coming and going. Alba, my oldest sister, was now married to Pete "the Greek" Kosta, an ex-Navy guy with a big heart. They have always been among my favorite persons.

Pete, when I was three and four, would often take me to the train tracks that ran along the west side of Spenger's fish market and restaurant on the Bay Shore in Berkeley. There, Pete and I would look and wave at the "choo-choo" trains as they came into the yard, or were passing through, heading north to Oregon and Washington. One day, Pete got one of the conductors to give me his gray and white striped cap. I wanted to ride and work on the railroads for a long time after that.

There were also frightening times when my parents were angry and yelling at each other. Actually, my mother did most of the yelling. Dad would remain intransigent and unyielding throughout their marital fight. Inside, I always felt fearful and insecure, wondering if they would separate and leave my sister, Irene, and me or force us to choose between them. Oftentimes, I and my disability seemed to be the reason they were fighting. More and more, every time these explosions happened, I wanted to be on my own and no longer the cause of their bitterness or troubles. I sure didn't like having to depend on everyone for everything. And I definitely wasn't enamored with being the crip who caused so much grief among the people I loved most. I still don't.

Sometimes on Saturdays, my sister Irene and I would get fed up with the bickering and retreat to her room to listen to radio programs like "Let's Pretend." Once in a while, cousins or girlfriends of Irene would drop over on these Saturday mornings, and we'd all end up in bed, one happy, silly group of kids, with me getting more than my share of attention.

As I transitioned from early to later childhood, these group encounters, in my sister's bed with a bundle of carefree soft and pretty females, started feeling good for reasons other than the imaginative stories on the radio. I must admit that I grew to like the way girls looked, felt, and smelled from a very early age. Alas, from about the age of 9 or 10, I was invited less and less frequently to climb into

Irene's bed when her girlfriends and cousins came over for their weekend morning gabfests. I guess they could see in my eyes, and elsewhere, that I was growing up.

When I wasn't being carried around the house in someone's arms, I physically motored about on a tricycle. However, the pain and stiffness in my knee joints made it difficult to use the tricycle's pedals. My Dad easily solved that problem by cutting off the pedals. I was now able to scoot around on the tricycle by "pulling" myself with my feet on the floor. The only thing I couldn't do with that damn tricycle was ascend the four or five stairs that went up to the bedroom level of our house. This newly added independence gave me an insatiable appetite for even more. Tricycle mobility also gave me my first sweet taste of something else.

During the day, my Mom wasn't unlike most middle-class housewives during the mid-1940s who cleaned, cooked, and otherwise managed the business of the family "estate." This continuing occupation was not without its moments of rest 'n relaxation (R&R), however. Frequently, one or two ladies from the neighborhood would stop by for a cup of coffee and, of course, a healthy exchange of gossip. Sometimes, one of the next-door neighbors would also bring in tow a son or daughter who wasn't yet attending public school.

On an especially warm and sparkling-clear day in Berkeley, our neighbor down the street came over to chat with Mom, escorted by her four-year-old daughter, Penny. Well, almost as soon as they arrived, the two moms retreated into the kitchen for their coffee, cookies, and animated gab. Meanwhile, Penny and I were left to our own devices in the living-room area to entertain ourselves. On this particular day, I took the lead.

"Penny, what do you want to play?" I asked this very pretty little girl with silky blond hair and hypnotically blue eyes, which I remember so well even after all this time.

"Let's play house," she said.

"Okay. How do you play house?"

"You go off to work, and then come back home to me and give me a hug and a kiss. Then I'll cook you dinner."

Penny's instructions to me were quite detailed and precise. (Lucky me). Penny must have also intuitively tuned in to the fact that I was Italian, when she told me that awaiting me at home was a kiss and food.

We mutually decided that "work" would be in the living room and our "home" would be under the large dining room table. Hurriedly, I scooted myself off to work on my tricycle. Heavy drapes hung on either side of the window overlooking Ada Street and overstuffed furniture and bric-a-brac filled up most of the living room.

Outside, down on the lawn in view from this window, were two cats scratching, clawing, and tussling fervently with one another. I became mesmerized when their continuing dance evolved into one of the cats dominating the other by berthing himself on top of the other's body and rhythmically, ceaselessly moving his rump back and forth like a piston on a steam engine leaving the train station. I may have figured out the secret of life at that moment. Something strange but amazing that I never felt before began tingling within my four-year-old body. Naw, it wasn't hormones yet, but it was exciting.

My "work" environment, although familiar and warm, suddenly wasn't as captivating as this feeling within me. But the fragrant, delicately arranged cut flowers on the living room coffee table and my inner tingle fused to kindle an imagined kiss from Penny's tempting, petal-shaped mouth awaiting my return home. I abruptly made an about-face on my tricycle and returned to our hideaway under the dining room table, and Penny. I carefully maneuvered my tricycle so that I could get as close as possible to where Penny was sitting on her child's chair. My little heart became a schizoid honeybee before a lush springtime garden, and my eyes could only see the most beautiful pair of lips ever beheld. But, unlike the honeybee, I didn't exactly know what to do.

Penny, perhaps sensing that I needed to be shown the way, deftly and quickly took on the role of my teacher. Although neither of us knew anything about sex, the business of children is to practice what their parents do, and we did. Actually, I learned a whole lot from her that special day in Berkeley, California. Penny's priceless lesson became an indelible and incredible part of my permanent memory bank. My teacher, despite her tender years, instinctively knew how to make learning easy. Penny didn't tell me what to do, but, instead, revealed her sensual secrets by physical demonstration. I felt as though she was lifting and guiding me up through the hidden side of a buoyant, endless field of cumulus clouds. She gently cuddled my face between her soft hands and very slowly brought our two faces together until our lips almost were touching.

As Penny guided our bodies en masse, I couldn't help but again notice that she was an extremely beautiful girl, a curly-haired blond with hair like silk and the most gorgeous, pale blue eyes one could imagine. I suppose my imagination, always powered by isolation from my peers and wishes to be with them, have elaborated on these innocent events. I also have to admit that in my world where my body was such a problem, only a few people came close enough to have physical contact with me, so this was a very special occasion.

All I knew was that I really, really, liked her taking charge and moving herself closer to me. It was like a doctor who authoritatively puts his hands where no one else does and somehow, it's welcome.

I could feel her warm, gentle breath on my face and see those eyes of hers looking at me in a strange, new way; almost as if she was very happy but wanted to be even closer to me at the same time. Penny moved again, suddenly but effortlessly, so that her mouth was now a fraction of an inch from mine. Mary, Joseph, and Jesus! (Catholics learn very early the names of the Holy family).

For what seemed like a very long time, but in reality, lasted less than minutes, Penny and I remained frozen in that nirvana of closeness. Time stopped. My mind flashed to the cats copulating outside the living room window. And I hadn't even been sure what they were doing, much less what we were doing.

Then, pure magic! Penny kissed me. No mother, aunt, sister, relative, or friend ever kissed me like that before. Her warm, slightly damp lips felt like tiny alive silk pillows being pressed in undulating waves against my mouth.

As we slowly kissed and breathed, I could smell the scent of floral soap and little girl entering my nostrils, making its way into my brain and the rest of my body. The sky above the clouds wasn't possible to imagine. Kissing and smelling Penny's being was overpowering. I didn't want to stop. Something else was going on at the same time as we were kissing. Our arms had fallen around each other, bringing our bodies together in a delicate embrace. Although we were children, and it would be years before we would know adulthood's special pleasures, the feelings generated by our two breathing and moving bodies were new and terribly exciting. There no longer existed the distancing frame of the tricycle, just my body and hers. Obviously, the sensory isolation in a body cast for a year at age three had left me wanting to touch and be touched.

Somewhere deep in my soul arose a feeling that called me to fuse myself with Penny—to be part of her. I didn't understand. I didn't care. Someday this day would live again, and both of us would understand and complete the ecstatic coital merging, which we could not do as children.

Penny, you see, taught me that it's the kiss and everything else that brings man and woman together, which makes loving and sex so miraculous. Beautiful Penny imparted so much of what I needed to know about kissing lips and mouths. Well, almost everything. We were still too young to intuitively graduate to the drama of that most secret kiss. But, "A Kiss Is Still a Kiss" and a torrent of joyous tears accompany my memory of those first luscious kisses. I shall always wonder what it would be like to suddenly meet Penny today.

My first grade school teacher also imparted the pleasure of the senses, especially touch and sight, to me. She was a middle-aged woman who was dispatched by the local public school system to teach, in their respective homes, boys and girls with disabilities. Unfortunately, I can't recall her name, but I do remember what she looked like. She had fairly curly, rather long blond hair that was streaked with gray, and her face had the many wrinkles and lines of a much older woman. But her eyes twinkled merrily and her dress and demeanor were that of a colorful, playful, nonconforming gypsy, not a schoolteacher.

I was about five years old at the time and was already pretty good at reading children's books because Mom had always read stories and books to me from as far back as I can remember. Consequently, I wasn't bad at picking up all the readin,' writin,' and 'rithmetic lessons she threw at me.

However, what I really enjoyed most from this fantastic lady was our finger painting sessions together. Here she would go on and on about "black" not being a real color and that when we saw something that looked dark to us we should reproduce it using purples, browns, and anything else but black. This even included the delineating lines around objects, animals, persons, and so forth. The bottom line: black was out, purples were in!

What these art lessons taught me was an appreciation of, and lifelong fondness for, the infinite rainbow of colors that surround us, and their innate ability to add texture, flavor, and dimension to a painting or drawing. But the medium my teacher chose to share with me—finger painting—couldn't have been a better choice for my little curved and twisted arthritic fingers. The feel of my fingers and hands working with the cool, thick finger paint on the painting surface was an almost inexplicable delight. I could actually manipulate and create something with these substandard tools called hands that nature and God had bestowed upon me. Between Penny's soft, willing lips, and the creations from my fingertips, life as a little crip unexpectedly was looking up. Thank you, dear God, thank you for two firsts: Penny and my first grade schoolteacher.

◆ ◆ ◆

After the harshness and deprivation of war, people sought relief and pleasure. This (especially in California) made swimming pool equipment an attractive market. The family company started manufacturing and marketing swimming pool pumps, filters, systems and accessories in the late forties. That was three or four years before the Jacuzzi Whirlpool Bath began to be marketed. Thus my father's invention of the Jacuzzi would fit nicely into this niche.

In 1947, the brothers built a $2,500,000 factory on ten acres at Richmond, California, on the East Bay of Berkeley. At the same time, the company expanded its St. Louis plant to serve states east of the Rockies. In the early 1950s, the old Berkeley plant on San Pablo was converted into the first manufacturing and marketing facility for the Jacuzzi Whirlpool Bath as sales skyrocketed for this device.

My Uncle Gelindo died prematurely and Valeriano spent more and more of his time building his farm. From the 1940s on, it was principally Frank and Joseph, with my father at the helm, who took the company from a Berkeley, California-based operation to a transnational, then multinational enterprise.

Dad and his brothers knew that they had no alternative but to grow if they were to provide work for all the members of an ever-expanding family. But more than anyone else, it was Dad who had the world vision of the enterprise and promoted the establishment of manufacturing and large distribution operations in Richmond, California; St. Louis, Missouri; Hackensack, New Jersey; Little Rock, Arkansas; Monterrey, Mexico; Toronto, Canada; Sao Paulo, Brazil; Buenos Aires, Argentina; and last but not least Valvasone, Italy, in the homeland they left behind during the early part of the 20th century.

As these operations were established, Dad would assign the older, more experienced nephews to head them up: Dante in St. Louis; Giocondo in Hackensack; Virgil in Toronto; my brother, John, in Monterrey; Harold in Sao Paulo and so on. Dad couldn't have done it without extremely wide shoulders for he was chided and berated more than once by very angry sisters and sisters-in-law for moving their men to faraway places and foreign countries. How dare he split up their family like that, they would ask. Why couldn't their son or husband be given a nice job in California? After all, they'd frequently add, wasn't the company making money?

However, Dad's vision, determination and charisma won out over the grumbling and fuming of worried mothers and wives who almost always relinquished their destiny in the end. All assignments outside of California brought with them some degree of sacrifice, but especially those outside of the United States. Nevertheless, those who were given overseas assignments were very nicely compensated for those sacrifices. In fact, it didn't take too long before those same protesting mothers and wives rather welcomed the periodic, company-paid sojourns to visit their sons and husbands abroad.

◆　　◆　　◆

Candido saw my inclination to create and was happy to help it develop. He built me a workbench, a desk-like thing with five drawers and a raised section used for storage. It stood against the wall with shelves and an overhead light. On the right hand side was a vise for securing pieces of wood or plastic to be cut out, sanded, or glued. There was also a small electric sander and grinder along with a set of razor-sharp wooden carving knives. I sorely wanted a proper set of power tools, complete with drill press and lathe, customized for my physical limitations. But my parents felt this would overextend the bounds of parental indulgence into the realm of flirting with disaster. All I needed was one less finger. They knew that my cousin, Roy, who played with my knife, cut his finger badly (I felt so guilty) and they thought it was just too dangerous for me.

Of course, my brother John could use any tool he wanted to. He could even run the lawn mower. And not just him, but lots of kids could work with electric tools. Why did I always have to be different? Why was there always a different set of rules for me? My parents did all they could to help me lead a normal life, but they really thought of me as "handicapped."

That label stereotyped me as one who deserves pity, handouts, is abnormal, and may even be feared. Words can be powerful and produce negative reactions or negative attitudes that damage the ego of a person with a disability. Later, much later, I would become part of movements to remove damaging labels from people.

These stereotypes were from the Southern European mentality in which my parents had grown up. Then they surrounded themselves with others like them once they got to the United States. They recognized there were exceptions like Franklin D. Roosevelt, who was paralyzed from polio, but he was "special." So it never occurred to them that if FDR could do it, perhaps their son could, too. Additionally, his disability was always disguised and minimized. In fact, I think the world knows almost nothing of people with disabilities, unless they go on to win something—like an election, or an Oscar, or a Nobel Prize.

Not only did the storm of my illness blind me to many parts of life, but it blinded my parents to the possibilities of my living a fairly normal life. They couldn't see through this *blizzard* so I didn't view myself as normal. I found little restricted areas, little niches where I could find some outlet, some self-expression, or some value.

Soon after we moved into our Lafayette home, around 1950, I was in our swimming pool in the shallow end one day. I enjoyed it because I was buoyant in the water. I was bouncing around on the steps and I fell down on my face with my head underwater. I tried to swim up to get my head above water but I couldn't do it. I was starting to panic. Dad saw me and pulled me out, and laid me down on a lounge chair. My whole body was tingling from shock like pins and needles. That's when it was decided to get me a swimming instructor.

Mother had always been the one to teach her own children to swim, but her instruction could only go so far. I needed more instruction than the average person. They hired a teacher who even taught me to dive by sitting on the edge of the pool to fall over. Unfortunately, I developed a terrible inner ear infection that required lancing—awful experience.

In that same year of 1950, Mom and Dad marked their 25th wedding anniversary. To celebrate the event, Dad threw a fantastic party, inviting all the relatives to share in his happiness and prosperity. Even my brother John was there, having flown up from Mexico City where he had been living for the past three years. I was only nine years old at the time.

After everybody had had a chance to see the house and have a couple of drinks, Dad gathered his brothers together in the study. Earlier I referred to how difficult it was to convince his brothers to manufacture whirlpools. It was at this event that he managed to talk them into producing and marketing the whirlpool.

His brothers knew all about his whirlpool prototypes and how effective the water massage had been in relieving the swelling from my arthritis. He had shown them the orders for whirlpool baths he received from hospitals and private physicians, but not all of the brothers had been convinced the product would be commercially successful. Now Dad opened a bottle of very fine wine and filled their glasses to the brim. I remember what he said on that day very well, as do some other family members. He was about to explain the greater possibilities of the whirlpool bath beyond the medical uses.

"Gentlemen," my father said, "in the past, we have had our differences concerning whether or not we're gonna manufacture the whirlpool bath. I think today we should decide once and for all to start the New Year with a new product line."

The lion stood before them, stocky and energetic, his thick mane of white hair swept back, emphasizing the resolution in his eyes.

One of the brothers spoke. "Candido, I don't know about this. Maybe the market for whirlpools is small. It may not be worth it to tool up for production."

Dad let the pause draw out for almost a half a minute. "I remember when you were afraid to build the factory in Richmond. Now look at that factory. Let me ask you something. Have you ever tried a whirlpool bath? Well, you should! I'll make one for you. It's fantastic. You don't have to be sick to use one. Everybody does not need a pump, but everybody needs a whirlpool bath."

A brother's son broke the silence. "We're doing pretty good with pumps. Why should we take a chance on something new?"

"Let's stop talking like farmers! Diversity is the name of the game. You stop growing and you die." A long pause. "We all got jobs. And our children, they all got jobs if they want them. But what about two, three generations from now? The business has to keep up with the family."

Perhaps Dad's brothers were beginning to feel their age and no longer had the spirit to oppose him. Or maybe he had proved himself right so many times to their mutual enrichment that they suspected if they merely kept quiet, they would be better off. It could also be that Dad, in spite of the domineering control he exerted over the company, was their brother and they loved him enough to let him have his way, believing he would never let them down. Whatever their reasons, they agreed to manufacture the whirlpool, although on a very limited budget.

This suited Dad. All he wanted was a chance to show what the whirlpool could do. He had dreamed of this moment for years. Now it was over so quickly and with so little trouble. Of course, I was glad to hear that Jacuzzi Brothers, Inc., would now manufacture the whirlpool, which, in a way, I had helped to redesign. Then and there in his moment of triumph, Dad decided to propose at the next board meeting that since the whirlpool had been inspired by me, I should receive a small percentage of the royalties.

Later, Dad was in an awkward position because as the youngest son of Giovanni and Teresa Jacuzzi, he drew the largest salary from Jacuzzi Brothers, Inc. Added to that was resentment that a "non-productive" person like me was going to get a one percent royalty on whirlpool products. Bitterness began to grow in the family from the time of that anniversary party. But there was one more problem that arose at the party that would rankle family members no end against my father.

Dad was congratulating his brothers on their decision to market whirlpools when my mother burst into the room, waving a letter in her hand. Johnny followed close behind.

"Read this!" Mom demanded, handing my father a neatly opened envelope bearing a U.S. Government stamp.

"What is this? Can't it wait?"
"No! Read it now."
"Inez, we have guests."
"For God's sake, Johnny's been drafted!"

Now the room was deadly silent except the sounds of distant revelry that drifted through the open door. The color drained from Dad's face. He looked down at the letter in his hand as if it were his own obituary, and then handed it back to Mom without reading it.

"He's not going!"

"But, Pa, I don't have a choice," John said coolly. "I have to go."

Dad laid his hand on his son's shoulder. "Johnny, you're right. You don't have no choice. You're not going to war!"

That pronouncement would come back to haunt my brother and my father in the future. I don't think Dad thought about the fact that most of his siblings had sons who went through military service in World War II. Even though their father, Giovanni, had tried to help the boys dodge the draft in Italy, none of the sons and husbands had dodged the draft in America.

Dad's point of view was this. There was not one of the Jacuzzi brothers who did not have some experience with war. Valeriano fought for Italy in World War I and was injured severely and spent several months in the hospital in Milan. Frank's son, Giocondo, served in World War II as did Joseph's son, Aldo. Their sisters' children had to fight in the last war. Every one of the thirteen brothers and sisters had been forced to live under the terror of war.

On my mother's side, she had two siblings, Zita and Armanda. Zita married Louis Ansani and they had two children, Sheila and Louis, Jr. Their son was eventually drafted into the Korean War, and came back a completely changed man, an emotional hurricane. The change eventually destroyed him and snuffed out his still young life.

Valeriano, who had suffered so after being wounded in WWI, stepped to Candido's other side. His lower lip trembled as he spoke. "You wanna serve your country, Johnny? Make pumps! Make good pumps!"

I felt very sorry for my father. I know that he had a very hard time trying to make everyone happy. This party and the important matters that were discussed were the beginning of the decline of the Jacuzzi Brothers' cooperation with each other. In his older years, Dad told me some of his feelings about the family.

Traditionally the oldest brother in an Italian family assumes the position of leadership along with all its rights and privileges. Therefore, with Rachele gone, Valeriano, the next oldest, should rightfully have been awarded the presidency and the company's highest salary. But this was America and they had started an American company. Employees should be paid according to what they were worth to the company.

Valeriano worked in the shop only part-time and was, by his own admission, a farmer, spending most of his time at his ranch. Valeriano, unlike Gelindo and Frank, was incapable of performing the complex duties of company president. But Valeriano recognized only that he was now the oldest brother and felt that the president's salary was his birthright. The brothers tried to reason with him but it did not do any good. He supported my Dad about John, but he didn't want to be given short shrift in the company.

Dad said that Giuseppe was known as the quiet brother, a hard worker, dedicated to the factory, first in Berkeley and later in Little Rock, Arkansas. While the other founding members of JBI thought of themselves as corporate executives, Joseph had no such pretensions or aspirations. He was a manual laborer and was not ashamed of it. Power did not interest him. After he was elected president at one of the board meetings, he walked calmly back to the shop and went on with his work. Joseph got along well with the other brothers and respected their authority, yet he was insistent when he believed he was right.

So, each week Joseph would hand Valeriano his relatively small check and each week, Valeriano would refuse it. Joseph stood his ground. Finally, after the checks had piled up for over a year, Valeriano must have realized there was no point in holding out any longer because one day he gathered up his back pay and never said another word about it.

This was the beginning of an understanding among the brothers that each of them would be paid what he was worth. It was after this incident that, Candido, although the youngest, began receiving the highest salary. The majority of the family decided this should happen because he was the best salesman and he did almost all of the traveling for the company.

"Francesco was a great guy," my father recalled. "Happy all the time. He was the only one of the brothers who said, 'I think I'm being overpaid.' Frank told the others, 'I work in the shop. You can get men to do the same work for less than what you're paying me.'"

Candido said, "You're a shareholder. You're entitled to it."

"No," he said, "I'm not worth it."

To justify his salary, Frank later picked up and moved to the new plant in Monterrey, Mexico, where he spent three years with my brother John, helping him set up the shop and the foundry.

My Dad, who was not very modest, said in his later years, "Frankie and I got along very, very well. He used to say, 'Candido is the one responsible for getting this family out of the gutter when we had nothing.' When he died, he called my name and mother's. He called my name first and then he said, 'Mother is coming to get me.' And he died. He was a very strong supporter."
Dad continued,

> Even Valeriano was a strong supporter, although he had a different point of view. His family was first, in every respect. He was very upset that Johnny had a responsible position, higher than his son, Virgil. He told me, "You know," he says, "Virgil is older than Johnny. He should have a bigger job."
>
> At this time we were thinking about Canada. I said, "Valerio, (I called Valeriano this) there is Canada. We'll give it to Virgil. I know he's a good, capable man. He'll go to Canada and make a fortune!" And Valerio lived long enough to know that Virgil did make a fortune, not only for himself but for the company. But Valerio, he had this idea that his children had to be tops. They had to be above the others. He even brought up the fact that his son, Dante, had more education than Johnny, therefore he should be making more. You see, I had to contend with all of that. And much more!
>
> Then I had the women! No woman would like to see her children go away from home to South America, Mexico, New York, Brazil, and Canada. I put the best guy in the position to best promote the company. Just imagine all the nephews in one area like Richmond, California, or later Little Rock, Arkansas! There wouldn't be anything for nobody! There wouldn't be a company. I always looked ahead and saw the next crop of nephews coming up. Some of them I knew were pretty damned good because I talked to them.
>
> My sister, Cirilla, had a son, Harold, who became manager at Portland. She complained he did not have enough responsibility in Oregon. He was making less money than Johnny or Virgil because the sales were less than Johnny had in Mexico or Virgil had in Canada.
>
> I said, "Harold, there's an opportunity in Brazil. You want it? Take it. It's coming up. I think you're qualified."
>
> Harold sweated it out in Brazil for seven years, trying to keep the company afloat while political turmoil rocked the country. After seven tough years, Harold was able to finally show a small profit.
>
> But the pressure from my sister, complaining that he was, at that time, her only boy and he had to be so far away from his mother and father. And Harold's wife was not happy in Brazil. She wanted to come back. And on and on and on with this pressure!

In the interest of peace, my Dad recalled Harold Benassini from Brazil replacing him with another of Valeriano's sons, Remo Jacuzzi. Harold was stunned. He thought he had been doing a fine job and now he was being denied the benefits of his seven years of hard work. That company had never made a profit until he became manager and now the "Old Man," my Dad, was going to take it away from him.

Remo was pleased but, again, his parents were not. Dad said, as he recalled the operation in the 1960s and 1970s,

> When we promoted Remo, I had a big argument with my sister-in-law, Pina (Valeriano's wife and Remo's mother). Actually, it was not an argument. She didn't talk to me for a long time, a year—maybe two. She said, "You're pushing my family away from me. You're breaking up my family!"
>
> True. But who was I serving? Her? Valeriano? The family? The company? In the 1970s, Remo was very happy in Brazil, making more than $60,000 a year plus fringe benefits, plus profit sharing. Very happy! They make trips down there once or twice a year. He makes trips to California once or twice a year. Very happy!
>
> Valeriano was not happy with me promoting his boys. He didn't see it as promotion. All he saw was that his boys were not living in Richmond any more. But there was no room in Richmond for all the boys coming up.

My father transferred only the bright, aggressive men. The others stayed with the mother company. Virgil's parents were not too upset when Candido sent him to Sacramento. He did so well in Sacramento that Candido told him they were thinking about opening a branch in Binghamton, New York, and would like him to manage it.

"Holy Mackerel," he said. "That far?"

"On an airplane, it's not very far," my Dad coaxed. "Maybe you'd like to improve yourself. Sacramento is doing $10,000 a month in sales; Binghamton could be $100,000 a month in sales. That means more money for you. I know you can do it."

Virgil considered this a moment and said, "How can I sell this to my wife?"

Dad said, "I don't know. That's your job."

Virgil did take the offer but he could not sell his wife on the idea of moving to New York. Dad did not like this arrangement because Virgil was forever flying back and forth to California to see his family and not devoting enough time to the new branch. His wife did not like it either. She was jealous, knowing that a handsome, successful man like Virgil living in motels has many opportunities to relieve his loneliness. And, of course, who should bear the blame for the situation but my father.

When they opened the factory in Canada, Dad asked Virgil to manage it, hoping, at the same time, to make the factory flourish and make the relatives happy.

Virgil said, "That's just as bad as Binghamton, isn't it?"

"Go there and find out," Candido said.

But Virgil was able to see the opportunities before him. He sold his home in Lafayette and moved his family to Ontario permanently, although they never did get used to the winters, which is why they bought a second home in Florida.

Dad remembered flying to the Canadian factory with Virgil one winter. As they were leaving California, Virgil complained, "Look down there," pointing at the lush patchwork below them. "That's the last green grass you'll see now for a long time."

My father laughed as he said, "Now Virgil's making over $100,000 a year! And I was the 'bad guy' who promoted him to Canada."

During his long tenure as company president, my father was determined to be democratic. "I tried to treat them all alike. When you have six brothers and six sisters, it's hard to be impartial. Some have more talent! Some are harder workers! I was very affectionate towards Rachele. I felt very bad when he died. And very affectionate towards Gelindo! Ah, but he was a good-looking man! His wife Rose was very jealous because many women liked Gelindo. In Italy, he had girls all over him."

Dad said, "I went to see him in San Francisco at the U. C. Hospital where he was dying to give him the latest news. We talked awhile and finally I said, 'Gelindo, we have opened a new branch in Portland.' And he smiled like he was saying, 'That's nice.' But he didn't say it. He couldn't say it. So before I left, I kissed him. He made an extreme effort to put his arms around me—but he had no strength—and kissed me. I'll never forget that. The next morning he died. Cancer of the liver."

The family dynasty was crumbling. And so was I, as I soon learned not long after.

7

Premature Sexuality

Heat Wave: Unusually hot weather resulting from a slow moving air mass of relatively high temperature over a region for a long time, baking it.

Although I thanked God for Penny, my first grade teacher, and art, there were many things that I could not thank God for, such as the endless hospitalizations and medical treatments. There were always side issues that plagued me, but sometimes I figured out a solution or two. I put this solution into a poem.

Remote Control

It's 1952, and I'm eleven going on twelve
Or maybe 30 something is more real.
On my back I lie,
In body cast, from heart to heel.
The docs have sliced
Hamstrings, hips, knees,
And given me holes to take craps and pees.
Their slices and many a cut,
Gave me nasty bugs.
They stole lots of my blood.
To kill the bad guys,
They shot antibiotics in my butt.
They pumped in the blood of drunks,
Replacing what they've sucked.
To watch my black-and-white two channel TV,

I Jimmy-rigged a piece of broomstick
And toilet plunger and wow, I've got my own remote!
But as days pass, infections go away,
Leaving itchies and no one to say,
"I'll scratch it for you!"
Then soon I discover what else my remote could do,
Including doing to those
Itchies what no one else could do.
And wouldn't you know, while scratching
An itch remote connected with pubic bone.
Little guy stirred, grew,
Making a teepee in the sheet,
Rolling eyes back, and me
Gasping for air,
'Cause I didn't care
As long as I didn't have to quit.
Oh, shit!
What if a nurse…a nun will see
What's now on my cast, my sheet, and me?
"Tepee"

I was 12 that particular summer, a relatively shy anomaly in a gathering of hormonally-charged youngsters who were around my age, but, in some cases, almost twice my height, including many of the girls. I had not yet attended any school, public or private, outside of my home. Up until then, a tutor from the public school system was delivering my education.

In 1952, Dad and Mom were able to take their first vacation together in 27 years of marriage. Irene was now a reasonably responsible 17-year-old and my arthritis appeared to have stabilized. Jacuzzi Brothers, Inc., was still far from self-propelled. But with the new whirlpool division making good progress in the competent hands of Alba's husband, Pete, Dad felt comfortable about taking the trip, leaving Alba and Pete in charge of the Jacuzzi mansion and me.

I was not able to care for myself, and Pete and Alba had their own house to look after. So, my current physical therapist, Elmer S., and his wife moved in for the interim. Elmer was a strict man, an Evangelical Christian, who believed right was right and wrong could be avoided.

Elmer also taught Pete how to stretch my arms and legs and that was very painful for me. But Pete would perform the therapist's duties when he was absent.

I would patiently attempt to explain to Elmer that there were many things I could not do. For many years, my mother had carried me from room to room. She had to hand me things I could not reach. I could not dress myself, tie my shoes, or walk. My therapists at the hospital understood these things and my parents understood these things. I was not normal! Why couldn't Elmer understand that?

Elmer understood two things very well: one, that he was responsible for my physical therapy and, two, that everybody can always achieve a little more.

"Can't does not exist in your vocabulary!" He would shout at me as I lay panting on the carpet. "Can't does not exist!" Visualize Arnold Schwarzenegger admonishing you in a booming voice, "Don't be a 'girly man.'"

To watch one of my therapy sessions, one might get the impression that Elmer was the worst kind of sadist. In every joint, my comfortable range of motion was limited to a few degrees. To increase the range of motion, Elmer had to stretch my limbs to the point of almost intolerable pain. When I would shriek, Elmer winced as if he was the one in pain but he would not allow either of us to give up.

The strengthening exercises were not as painful as the stretching, but just as important and requiring a greater involvement of my will. Elmer would go through a series of controlled wrestling exercises in which I would flex or extend a muscle while Elmer gave resistance. I had so little strength to begin with that sometimes it took everything I had to simply turn over in bed. After a few of these exercises with Elmer, I would collapse on the carpet.

"I can't do any more, Elmer," I gasped.

"What was that word you said? I don't think I heard you right."

"Can't," I whispered.

"But can't does...not...exist!"

Then why did everybody say, "Kenny can't go to school?" For years, I had listened to my brother and sisters talk about public school and I sensed I was missing out. I had always enjoyed my tutors, like the art teacher who did not believe in black and Mr. Hoten who first fired my interest in politics.

Hoten, a Democrat, described in detail the vast differences between the shimmering intellect of Adlai Stevenson and the affable plodding of Dwight Eisenhower. However, I did enjoy Eisenhower's comment when he was trying to wield peace between countries after WWII. He said, "Some people wanted champagne and caviar when they should have had beer and hot dogs."

Hoten was careful to prepare me for the occasional unfairness of politics. He explained that although Stevenson was brighter and might make a better president, Eisenhower had been a great general, which would be more reassuring to a nation then in the midst of the Korean War.

Hoten told his students about Adlai Stevenson's wonderful recipe for fish and I shall never forget it. Adlai said, "Take a 1–2 pound carp, and allow it to swim in clear water for 24 hours. Kill the carp, then scale and fillet it. Rub the fillets with butter and season them with salt and pepper. Place them on a board and bake in a moderate oven for 20 minutes. Then throw away the carp and eat the board."

Ike won the election and Hoten faded from the scene after a little incident during a camping trip. He dumped me and his son at his mountain cabin while he paid a visit to a local bar and an out-of-town girl. Hoten's wife was the suspicious type and had driven all the way up the mountain to say "hello," only to find him gone.

Mom thought it was funny, but Dad growled something about how you couldn't expect much more from a public school teacher. I had always insisted on my tutors being public school teachers. It was my way of fitting in with the other kids. In 1952, there was no such thing as wheelchair accessibility in the schools—or anywhere else for that matter. My parents never considered it an option to send me to public school. I could not get up and down the stairs, participate in sports, or ride the school bus. I would always be left out and might become bitter and withdrawn, they thought. The worst of it would be if I did put out the effort and do well; I might be told that there was no place for a person with a severe disability.

It seemed the only way I would ever make it to public school was if I somehow built myself up to the point where I could walk with crutches. I possessed the will to do it, but not the method. Pete Kosta had enough insight to recognize this. He suggested that I learn to walk in time to meet Dad at the door when he and Mom returned from Europe. The idea appealed to me. All my life, I wanted that hardnosed old man to be proud of me, the way he was proud of John, not just for being Candido's son, but for something I accomplished that took guts and brains. Now that I was on my way to becoming a man, I did not want to be thought of as "little Kenny" or "Baby." It was true I was still small. I always would be. But I was growing up and I wanted my father to know it.

When I accepted the challenge of walking for my father's return, Elmer could not have been more pleased. He considered he had received his orders, marching around the house, shouting, "There is no such word as can't!" It was like General Douglas MacArthur shouting, "There is no substitute for victory!" He worked me harder than ever. I would scream with pain and frustration but Elmer was determined to keep me on schedule.

Soon I was able to stand alone and maintain my balance with platform crutches. But the pain of resting my weight on my deteriorated joints was unbelievable. I felt I was on stilts, and the reckless joy of standing, more or less on my own two feet, almost gave me vertigo. I tried to take a step forward the way Elmer showed me, by shifting my weight to one side while throwing the opposite foot and crutch forward, but the additional pressure on the joint caused me such agony that tears came to my eyes and I was afraid I would lose my balance.

Elmer remained undeterred. "That just means you're not loose enough yet." And back we went to the floor exercises.

A week before my parents were scheduled to return, I had managed to take a couple of steps without falling, a thing to be feared for a person in my condition. An able-bodied person can brace himself when he falls but I lacked the strength in my arms to break my fall and prevent injury. Elmer and I worked up until the last day to get ready for my feat. Elmer was beginning to wonder if he had pushed me too hard. I had such a long way to go when we started. What kind of psychological damage would be done if I tried to walk for my father and failed? Elmer suggested that I rest the last day. I, however, sensed that Elmer had begun to doubt my ability and I insisted on an especially tough workout the day before my parents' return.

Pete was like a motion picture director, telling everybody where to stand, making sure they had their cues right and double-checking my timing. Dad and Mom were already an hour late and I was beginning to feel the adrenalin poisoning my system. But I waited, poised like an athlete, crutches ready, staring intently at the door.

Suddenly, without warning, a car door slammed and they were walking rapidly toward the front door. They seemed to be arguing loudly as they approached.

Just before Dad reached for the doorknob, Pete pulled the door open, stepping aside like a butler. I gritted my teeth against the pain and took a step forward swinging my weight to the other side. I steadied myself and took another step. My father was frozen in his tracks, his mouth open in amazement. Mom was trying rather unsuccessfully to see around him. Pete, Alba, and Irene all seemed to be holding their breath. Elmer grinned broadly.

Sweat started to course down my face. I was determined to walk the distance and not show that it hurt. I faltered slightly and my father reached out to me, not to catch me, but slowly, confident I would make it. This man who flung his cousins and nephews around the world like puppets, whose iron will no board member had the courage to oppose, stood silently with tears streaming down his cheeks as I made the final step into his arms.

◆   ◆   ◆

My dear sister Alba reminded me not long ago, "When I moved back to the Bay Area and lived in Lafayette, my dream was to get you into school. Your home teacher also thought it was a good idea. So when Mom and Dad took off for one of their long trips, Peter and I were in charge. So off I went to the school board and got you into school (Vallecito Junior High School). You loved it. And most of the time I took you, and always picked you up in the afternoons; also with some of your buddies."

Outside the sporadic company of my numerous cousins, and several newly discovered acquaintances I had made in the Boy Scouts once I turned 11, I had few really close friends. It was my sister Alba's idea to cart me off to Cathay Gardens this specific Saturday afternoon to "get to know some more kids your own age." Of course, Alba's venturesome task was facilitated by the fact that my folks were traveling in Europe and weren't around to offer any protestations or interfere with her socialization plans for me.

Alba and Pete drove me to this "debut" at Cathay Gardens in their well worn, but still trusty, Mercury. On the way, as was the norm for her, Alba kept assuring me that I was going to have a good time and make many new friends. Her heart was in the right place but I just knew that this wasn't going to happen. I was so petrified with apprehension about meeting the nonstop glances of "normal" kids in a place meant only for competent limbs, that I said nothing. I fantasized that the Mercury would be stopped in its tracks by a blowout, sparing me what was going to be an excruciating ordeal. It was kind of like Robert Benchley's essay about the horror of going to the dentist and the wish that he might fall into an open manhole on the way there.

A few yards from the entrance door, but between columns of decorative oleanders and hidden from the stare of curious onlookers, I asked Pete to stop the car and let me out with my walker. Alba turned around in the front seat and said to me, "Kenny, you're not going to back out of this, are you?"

"No," I said. "I just want to get out here and go in by myself."

Alba started to protest, but Pete stopped her cold. "For Christ's sake, Alba, let the kid be; let him go in alone." (I must say that my apprehension momentarily gave way to amusement. Pete rarely got visibly agitated, but when he got pissed off, you knew it!)

After I was certain that Pete's Mercury had driven off, I proceeded to the ticket booth, bought my ticket, and entered Cathay Gardens, as quickly and unobtrusively as I could. I sat down on a bench at the end of the dance floor, positioning my walker alongside of me. I spent the entire two hours I was there watching kids dance. I was especially drawn to the high, firm breasts and long, luscious legs of the teenage girls. The bent, distorted shape of my body and limbs, and my painfully dysfunctional, weight-bearing arthritic joints, couldn't conspire to diminish the stirring, insistent heat eating up my atmosphere.

Thankfully, Pete came to pick me up at 3:00 p.m. During those two hours before he picked me up, I had spoken to no one with anything more than a furtively returned, defensive glance. And, no one had spoken to me.

Resigned, I repeated this social penance a second Saturday afternoon. I kept my logistics the same. I sat in exactly the same spot, but at the beginning of hour two, someone smiled at me as she danced by. When the music stopped, she left her group and walked over to me. She introduced herself; her name was Pat P. She had seen me here last Saturday. I found out that Pat was my age and went to junior high school in Lafayette. She had honey blond hair, cut short in back like a duck's tail. Her mouth was full, like that of Marilyn Monroe. Pat's skin was a pale, porcelain white, and her eyes an equally pale, limpid blue. Her body was already shaped like a woman's. She brought over several of her friends for me to meet, but I didn't remember their names. I did remember her.

Pat told someone later about her impression of me at that time. She said,

> Kenny was like all of us trying to grow up in the seventh grade. He was trying to fit in, to be one of the guys, and felt terribly different. We became good friends and I visited his house and met his parents. His sister, Irene, and her husband Don took us out sometimes. Ken tried to walk more in those adolescent years. In fact, he pushed himself too much. I can't imagine what pain he went through to do that walking.
>
> His parents were very nice, friendly, and unpretentious. Even though they had maids and lived in an exclusive area, his mother was shucking peas one day and brought them in to do them in the living room while she talked with us. I thought that was very down to earth.
>
> They had a pool with a fence around it. Now that everybody does that, I see how they were ahead of their time to think of doing that. I'll never forget being shocked when I saw his mother's underwear hanging by the pool. I learned that she liked to go skinny-dipping at night in the pool.

◆   ◆   ◆

There was another reason that I remember being 11 years old. Although I was 11, my physical body was more the size of a 6 or 7 year-old boy. My build was average, neither thin nor chubby, but my hands, limbs, and body had been badly bent and crippled.

During weekdays, my routine started with breakfast, then bathing, stretching and exercise, and then an hour of free time before lunch. Following that, a public school teacher would come to the house for a couple of hours to teach me. After school, I'd rest for a half hour, even though I thought it was a waste of time, and then do the homework. I couldn't wait to get the homework over with so I could work on my model cars and airplanes, read, or just do one of my favorite things—daydream.

In my fantasy world, I did everything I couldn't do with the body I got stuck with. I'd go camping alone and with my buddies, take long hikes, climb mountains, swim and skin-dive with the fish in the ocean. My phantom body was as agile and swift as a panther, primed to leap, and free of pain.

My material body was different. Every day, to keep me going, I was given very warm baths in a Jacuzzi, one to two dozen aspirins, and several prescription medications to help relieve the constant stiffness and pain in my joints and torso.

One day, after the teacher had gone and my boring homework was done, I started rummaging in the study for something different to read. I discovered my folks' 1926 book called *Ideal Marriage* by Dr. Theodoor van de Velde. Each page of this book drew me further in, and mesmerized me with its detailed explanations of everything imaginable that a man and a woman could do together. Fully-arrived puberty, mixed with oodles of curiosity and some of the collateral effects of the prescribed steroids and hormones I was taking to hasten puberty and hopefully cause a burn-out of active J.R.A. made *Ideal Marriage*, and a couple of other books I found, a mandatory part of my daily reading.

Two prescription drugs I was taking at the time intensified my "pubescent situation." The still quasi-experimental drug called "cortisone" was one of the medications. Cortisone, I learned many years later, can really do a number on humans. Although I didn't realize it then, cortisone was turning my face into a balloon, my bones into oatmeal mush, and, if that weren't enough for a 12-year-old kid, making me hornier than a drunken sailor after a six-month tour of duty.

Besides the cortisone, my good ol' doc had also given me hormones to accelerate my puberty. The reasoning behind this treatment was based on observations by a few rheumatologists that there seemed to occur in some young people following puberty a "burning out" or subsiding of the more severe inflammatory aspects of the arthritis. Hence, bring on that puberty! So the *Heat Wave* began.

This one morning wasn't very much different than most others. It was a wet morning, the sort of weather in which snails cut their paths. The rising sun played peek-a-boo with airy, fast-moving northern California clouds as the moist, early morning air conveyed its chill into my too-soon antiquated bones. My pokey trek to the kitchen leaning on my walker was chaperoned by the Rice Krispies rattle coming from my hips and knees. Finally I arrived and plunked myself down on a chair at the kitchen table.

It was the job of Anita, our live-out nanny and housekeeper, to give me my bath every weekday morning before beginning her house cleaning duties. After each bath, Anita would massage my legs and arms and put me through a series of range-of-motion exercises and stretching. Then, she'd help me get dressed and send me outside on my three-wheel tricycle or walker to enjoy the warm sun.

Anita turned on the Zenith tabletop stereo and started playing a couple of my favorite LPs, movie soundtracks from *High Noon* and *The Thief*, while she fixed my breakfast of scrambled eggs, whole-wheat toast, and grapefruit juice. As the music lilted through the air and I munched joyously on the Jamaican-spiced eggs, the sliding glass doors before me unveiled a Mexican-tiled patio surging with red and white carnations, purple bougainvillea, and a brightening blue sky. This would always be my most relished time—when the intensifying heat and light of the sun dissipated morning fog and dampness and painted the day with new hope.

When I returned to my room, Anita helped me take off my PJs and get into a steaming bath. As customary, she left me alone to relax in the pulsating whirlpool for about 20 minutes. The scalding, spellbinding water warmed my sore limbs and torso and I drifted into a reverie of sea spraying my face as I steered an electric-blue sailboat through pounding surf.

"Twenty minutes are up. Time to get out," Anita announced upon her return. She then turned off the whirlpool, washed and rinsed me with the telephone-type shower spray, and helped me out of the tub and onto an adjacent bench used for drying me off and doing my exercises. As usual, Anita helped me lie down and began drying me with a big bath towel. Even though Anita's cheeks were pockmarked with acne scars, her ample mouth, shamrock-green eyes, gentle nose, and lush, coal-black hair, combed back in a long ponytail, gave her a young but elegant beauty that melted my preteen heart. The way Anita's pale orange jersey dress clung to her chocolate skin and firm, slender body made me notice her as I had never done before now.

As she began drying my thighs and area around my groin, I looked, for some reason, directly into her roomy eyes and from somewhere unknown, a low, sandpaper moan escaped from me. I felt my face become red as a beet. I couldn't move or speak. Anita continued drying me, not saying a word. The echo of my heart rumbled in my head. Substance wouldn't surrender.

From that same strange depth within me, words began escaping from my mouth without consciousness of what I was saying. "Anita, show me...how to make love. I...I don't think I'll ever find a girl...who'll, you know...Maybe ...someday. I don't know. I don't think so. But...I gotta know. Can someone like me...do it? Could I make a woman happy? I read that women want men to give them pleasure. I just don't know if a cripple like me could..."

No matter how much I try, I can't remember the exact words I used. I only know that's about what I said. After I stopped speaking, Anita looked into my eyes for what seemed like forever, but said nothing. She then started speaking in a whispered voice, never once removing her eyes from me.

"Kenny, I'll teach you how to love a woman. But only under certain conditions. Are you willing to do that? No ifs, ands, or buts?"

"Anything you want, Anita, I'll do it. I promise."

"All right, Kenny, I believe you. But listen to me, carefully. First, this must be our secret. You mustn't tell anyone, including your parents or friends, that this ever happened. You're only a kid and I'm probably twice your age. If anyone found out, I'd probably be fired in half a minute, and I need this job."

"I won't tell anyone, Anita."

"I hope you mean it. Now, if you want to learn, Kenny, you must pay attention to everything I say. And you must do everything—I mean everything—I tell you. Also, you must make me another promise. On the Cross of Jesus, you'll always be respectful of all women. Those who are poor, like me, or alone, or don't have a perfect body, like you. Do you promise on Jesus' Cross?"

"Yes, I promise."

Anita, without saying anything further, assisted me into my walker and pointed me in the direction of my bed. I felt like I was in a dense fog. I must have been some figure, my body curved like the letter "S," leaning naked on the walker, the heavy weight of my hardening thing dangling before me like some kind of hotdog. I don't really know how I got up and onto the bed. But there I was, lying on my back, my curled hands and bent arms folded against my chest with my mindless matter bouncing on my belly.

I could hear the seconds ticking loudly in my ear from the clock on the other side of the room. My mind was racing and standing still. I was stark naked, staring at the ceiling, scrambled like my breakfast eggs.

Minutes passed—many minutes—but Anita couldn't be seen or heard moving. I was anxious; my skin and insides feverish. Everything was centered on a weighty piece of meat waving in the air. The only sounds came from my beating heart and that damned clock.

I nearly fell off the bed with fright when Anita, like a sly cat, slipped onto the bed and lay down beside me! Another flush rose from my thighs to my chest as I realized it was Anita's warm nude flesh pressing against my side. She slowly turned and raised her torso and head above mine.

"Kenny, follow closely what I tell you with my words, with my eyes, with my movements. Do you understand?"

I said nothing. I couldn't. I could barely nod my head up and down in affirmation. I couldn't move anything else despite the fact I desperately wanted to grasp her head and bring her moist, scarlet lips down against mine. Penny's first kiss when we were both four flashed before me.

My heart jumped. I wanted Anita as badly as I wanted anything—to be normal, walking, or running like my buddies. But my hang-up was that I had never been with a woman. I didn't know what I should or shouldn't do or even if I could. The sun's golden rays were raining on me this day, since Anita seemed to anticipate my thoughts and fears in what she did, and moves she made.

"In making love, the kiss is the crown jewel. And before the kiss comes the touch. But there are two more things preceding the touch. Do you know what they are, Kenny?"

"I...No, I don't know. Maybe what you say?"

"Yes, that's perfect! What do you think comes before 'what you say?'"

"Gosh. What?"

"How you look at the woman and she looks at you."

"I don't understand. You mean I have to look at her a certain way?"

"No, no, Kenny. You should never have to look at or do anything 'a certain way' when loving someone else. But if you are attracted to someone, and want to know her better, you must look at her with your heart, tell her what you feel. For a woman, if you're timid, you're weak and not a man. Remember, Kenny, the strength a woman looks for is in the man's heart, not his body. Do you understand?"

"I think so. You mean I shouldn't be afraid a woman won't like me because I'm crippled?"

"Exactly. What a woman wants to see in a man's heart is courage and love. A woman sees those things in your eyes. You understand courage. Do you know what love is?"

I was perplexed over the answer to Anita's question. Then I noticed the sparkling lights in her eyes, the quiet curve of her mouth, and felt the warmth radiating from my recesses. "Is love like wanting to be close to that person?"

"That's not all of it, but you've got the idea. Let's try this a different way. What do you think love is not?"

"I don't know. Maybe if it's not love, it's anger or yelling or something like that. But that's stupid, eh?"

"No, it isn't, and you're right. If what's in your heart is selfish, or cruel, that's not love. You cannot love a woman with your body, Kenny, if it doesn't come from deep in your spirit."

"Okay, Anita, but then what? What do I say? I can hardly talk to you."

"Don't fret, Kenny. You'll be old with gray hair before you will begin to understand how to talk to a woman. But we have the same problem talking to men. You'll just have to learn gradually, making lots of goofy mistakes along the way. The best thing I can tell you is to be yourself. Never be an asshole."

"What's 'being an asshole?'"

"That's simple. You know, the guy who brags a lot or likes to impress people with his good looks or all the money he has? That's being an asshole—and women hate 'em."

"All women?" I asked, wondering.

"All women who are desirable—especially to someone with a pure heart, like you, Kenny. But I'm afraid you'll have to learn a lot of this from experience, as you get older."

Before realizing what was happening, Anita brushed her lips down my cheek and across my chin. Then, she positioned her mouth above mine, as if she were about to kiss me. But she didn't. She just probed my eyes with her comforting look that was also admonishing me to pay attention. It was a look that almost made me recoil in fear, yet also turned my manhood to stone. I was a confused boy-about-to-become-man who happened to also have a shitty disability. No matter the confusion, I was in heaven!

She kissed me then, like a feather landing on a ball of cotton. Her mouth was tentative, but didn't remove itself from mine. Instead, her warm, velvety soft lips seemed to tiptoe across my mouth, from one end to the other. Ever so slightly she increased the pressure of her lips against mine. As she caressed my mouth with hers, her firm, apricot-sweet tongue darted between my lips. But Anita wasn't in a hurry. She wanted me to "feel" everything. The pressure of her mouth against mine would increase and diminish like an evening tide that ebbs and flows over a seaside beach. Anita's kisses were so different, incredible, my chest, belly, limbs became one jumbo pressure-cooker.

"Anita," I begged her, "I can't stand it…I've got to…touch you, hold you. Please…!"

"Just breathe. Slowly. Deeply. That's right, Kenny…keep calm, very calm. Make it last. That's how love is made. It should be like a thousand mile roller coaster that always surprises and delights to the end. Kissing is only a part of the ride, and we've only begun that. Relax, Kenny. Enjoy."

My heart raced, my temples pounded and I felt feverish but held back. I obeyed. I felt light headed, but I didn't move. My member remained a stubborn piece of slow-roasting meat. At its base, my testicles were pulled up in tight, hard little balls. The tip-to-root skyscraper, down to the depths of my ass, ached and bewildered me.

Anita's kisses pressed harder against my lips as her tongue pulsed and caressed the inside of my mouth. While she continued to kiss me, her hands lightly stroked my arms, neck and body. She stopped kissing me long enough to ask me to caress her in the same way she was stroking me.

She again adjusted her body to position her torso above my chest, making her firm, silky breasts accessible to the touch of my hands. I began exploring her coffee-with-milk nectarines and brown erect buds with my fingers and hands, caressing and kneading them, first tentatively, then more aggressively. I couldn't believe how wonderful her beautiful, naked body felt in my hands, pressed against me. Something deep within me wanted to possess her, to screw her brains out, but I didn't know how. I stopped.

"I…I feel stupid, like I don't know how to touch you."

"You're doing fine, Kenny. Remember your grasping exercises; when you pick up pennies, nickels, and dimes from the table? That's a good pressure to use when pinching or caressing my nipples or breasts. You can vary from there, harder or softer, whatever I like."

"But how will I know?"

"Don't worry. Let your heart teach your eyes, guide your hands and lips. Now try. Hmm…That's nice. There's no 'right way'; you can use the back of your hands and fingers, too. Oooh, yes, Kenny, yes…"

It always seemed Anita knew what I was thinking and what she needed to do to enhance my learning or, should I say, her *sorcery*. She wouldn't need to say much, but just move her body, repositioning herself, imperceptibly at times, to tell me what she wanted and expected. When the heat and pressure began to reach the seething point within me, Anita would coyly, surreptitiously offer a new part of her glorious anatomy to my hungry mouth or hands. And she would move in a way that told me what she wanted and how she wanted it. As she offered her deliciously erect breasts and nipples to my hands and mouth, waves of unknown pleasure would sweep over and throughout my body.

Dragsters and drivers fiercely clasp onto each other, melding screeching, burning rubber tires, demanding engines to breathe only fire and commit to a deafening steel battle to victory or death.

A new, intense, throbbing bliss, far different than any orgasm I had experienced masturbating, was invading me. Without my knowing, Anita was not only teaching me a lesson in manhood, but how to prolong, intensify and feel a special kind of pleasure. Something secret that's within every woman, but few men are ever taught to experience.

"Kenny, no matter where you kiss me, remember to also taste and smell me, too. You can only know me, or any woman best when you use all God gave you. All your being. When you do, you increase the pleasure for both you and me." As Anita spoke these words, I noticed that her breathing was becoming heavier and her gentle, feminine voice deeper, more insistent. I had never before caressed a woman's breasts, let alone tasted or smelled them! The taste, fragrance and texture of those warm, firm, peach-sized breasts cannot be described. Did I sense the air at Clear Lake after a rain, sweet pineapple, or something else? I felt transported far away, suspended.

I felt 90 percent cock, hands and mouth, 10 percent everything else. Play, Kenny, play like you've never played before, I thought, as I feasted on Anita's burnt cream body. With her magical, cat-like movement, Anita teasingly pulled herself away from me. What did she have in mind for me now, I wondered? I didn't have to wait long. With the stealthy movements of a karate black-belt, Anita rose to a kneeling position above my face. I couldn't believe what I saw. The rose color of her sex was inches away from my face. Anita's vaginal lips were as beautiful and mesmerizing as her mouth, maybe more so. Her flesh here seemed even silkier and softer than her face or breasts. And Anita had little pubic hair. *Jesus*, I thought, *Jesus*. A hoarse, bottomless moan again escaped from inside me.

As beads of perspiration formed on my forehead, Anita began slowly undulating and lowering her vaginal beauty ever closer to my lips. I could see the crevice between her lips part ever so slightly. The center of that mysterious crevice was a rainbow of deep pinks and reds, and delicately dusted with drops of something pearlescent, like morning dew. Again, the scent of pineapple and wet grass filled my nostrils.

Ever so slowly she continued lowering her sex closer and closer to my mouth. Anita knew how to tease me to the point of torture. I could feel the heat of her thighs and vaginal lips radiating against my nose and mouth. She was now very wet. Beads of sweet dew appeared on the edges of her lips, like drops of water forming on the inside of a cave. Then, without warning, she lowered her vagina to within a fraction of an inch from my mouth. Instinctively, my lips parted and I received the liquids from her. The taste was both sweet and salty. At least, that was my first impression of these strange, intoxicating juices.

Ever so slowly I raised my mouth to meet and kiss her wet, filmy lips. As I raised up my mouth she lowered herself so that our 'kisses' would meet. Anita embodied so many new, spellbinding experiences. I couldn't avoid the growing dizziness in my head. From this moment, the only *drink* I would ever desire, for the rest of my life, would be the intoxication of sex with an intense, loving woman.

Anita, oh Anita, what you're doing to me! Please, I thought, *don't stop, ever.* Ohhhhh sounds escaped from my throat but were muzzled by the slow, persistent offering of Anita's treasure. Ohhhhh, Mary, Joseph and Jesus, don't let her stop. All these words, feelings were afire in my skull! I was in purgatory and paradise. I felt overwhelmed with the fear of being severed from this woman at any instant.

Jesus, what an emotionally complicated son-of-a-bitch I was. Was I thinking, then, as I still occasionally do today, that I was too reliant to receive pleasure, especially from such a gorgeous female? Or was it my slowly diminishing sense of self-worth? Whatever it was, I was convinced that I was headed straight to the devil!

Anita detached herself from my hungry mouth and began creeping backwards on her hands and knees as if she were an anticipatory cat, ready to pounce on her bird of prey. Ever so seductively, Anita berthed her delicious lips, oozing with her heat and moisture, at the tip of my hardness.

My hips contracted in an uncontrollable spasm, thrusting my hardwood upward. But Anita's practiced loins were swifter than my body's instinctive response, and she raised herself just in time to avoid penetration. She was so expert, however, that as my lunging spasms subsided, I could still feel the moisture and heat of her sex deposit droplets on my little guy's head.

"Slowly, Kenny. Let me guide you inside me, inch by inch. Feel how the walls of my flesh ripple and squeeze as you enter into me. Don't move. Let me do it. Oh…, yes, Kenny…"

My member felt like the piston of a steam locomotive pulling a long train up a steep mountain. My awareness of everything else, including the always-present pain from the arthritis, evaporated in the engine's steam. No other world existed. As my hips again spasmed upward, infusing her to the root, a furor surging from my heart, rained a thunderstorm of a billion sticky-milk cells. Repeated, violent spasms overtook me.

I awoke in a start as the contractions continued spraying my essence over my chest and shoulders and into the bubbling water like an uncontrolled fire hose. My milky, sticky melding of sweat and semen splattered on the bathroom tile and floated in gobs on the whirling water. A good part of the tub's water had splashed on the floor from my repeated spasms.

Abruptly, Anita stopped singing and ran into my bathroom, her mop in one hand.

"What's this splashing and moaning I heard over the noise of the whirlpool? You okay, Kenny?" Then, she noticed the water-covered floor and, looking directly at me in the tub, she saw my erection still sluggishly convulsing, bobbing up and down on the water, drops of ejaculate splattered everywhere. In what seemed like one fluid move, she stepped out of the water, grabbed her mop bucket, and mopped up the floor. She then shut off the whirlpool and came over to help me get onto the nearby bench. Gently, Anita began drying off my body.

"Last night, my boyfriend, Tony, was layin' on the bed with a big ol' hard thing, just like yours. Said it wouldn't go away. Just had to put it somewhere. Men. Big or little, you're all the same."

With my dream compelling my brain, my thing still stubborn, I groaned, "Would you show me how to…do it? To love, Anita?"

"Yeah, I'll show you, Kenny. Not now. Someday. As soon as you're bigger an' able to spread your legs an' get on top like a real man. You try to rest a little now, before I get you up." Anita went out to continue her housework.

The crushing, killing feeling of isolation and quarantine wasn't new. It wouldn't be the last, either.

Although her name was changed, Anita and the event were real. In looking back on my life, I only wish *the dream* would've actually been a reality. It would've taught me lessons and given me the self-confidence I could've used to make better choices much earlier in my life. Así es la vida! Such is life!

◆   ◆   ◆

In the late summer of 1952 or 1953, Mom and Dad left on a European vacation again leaving me in the care of Alba and Pete. It was the chance Alba had been waiting for. Alba and Pete wasted no time in enrolling me in the seventh grade at Lafayette's Stanley Junior High School. It was then that my life really began. I later remembered that first year as a kind of primal experience, being introduced for the first time to competition, both scholastic and sexual.

The first day of school was like a combination of being released after a long prison sentence and the first day of kindergarten. There were so many people rushing around, bells ringing and school buses docking and unloading hordes of children, all strangers to me. I had to find somebody to push my chair, help me find classes and get oriented.

"Hey, Buddy, what do you say?"

A big, athletic kid towered above my wheel chair blocking out the sun.

"Name's Richard," he said extending his monstrous paw in my direction. I realized that I had met him in Cub or Boy Scouts several years earlier.

I shifted in my chair, throwing my right shoulder forward. In reaching out, I was not able to straighten my arm or uncurl my fingers, but it was the best I could do and I was used to it.

"Hi! I'm Ken."

"Are you just here to look at the girls or are you going to school?"

"Do I have a choice?"

"Don't worry about the broads, kid. I'll fix you up." He saw my short arms would not reach the wheels of my chair. "Here, let me give you a lift." And we were off.

Richard was as good a guide as I could ask for. He knew everybody and every place at school. I was never late to class with Richard at the helm. This was the source of some discomfort for me because it reminded me of the way my father used my wheelchair as a battering ram in getting me through a crowd to the front row at parades and rodeos so I could see what was going on. I knew my father was only doing it to make me happy, but as much as I hated missing the action, I would rather wait on the periphery than force people to accommodate me. I felt my father's use of the wheelchair was separating me more from other people.

"You ever been camping?" Richard asked me one day.

"Sure. I used to go up to the mountains once in a while with my tutor and his son."

"Where'd you sleep?"
"In a bed."
"What! How the hell did you get a bed up the goddamn mountain?"
"It was already there...in the cabin."
"Oh, Christ!" He pretended to keel over. "A cabin! I thought you said you've been camping. Cabins are for pussies!"

To be considered a fool is tough to swallow, but "pussy" is a fighting word! I scowled.

"All right, no offense." Richard held up two big mitts in protest.

"Everything's fine. I just thought you might like to know, though, what real camping is like."

You could see he was gearing up for what must have been a well-worn routine, but it was grand, nonetheless.

He leaned his bulk on the armrest of my wheelchair and it complained meekly.

He stared like Rasputin into my face. "When you get deep into the wilderness, I mean deep, where nobody has set foot practically since time began; where no bastard has dropped a beer can or snuffed out a cigar, then you can hear Nature's heartbeat! It's so beautiful; it'll make your peter hard!"

So it was that I and Richard and Richard's dad went camping—really camping. We slept out in sleeping bags—not a cabin. My father never was much of a sportsman. Any activity that wasn't related to the business or to his family, he regarded as frivolous. For this reason, he never cared to camp alone with the boys. But he encouraged my interest in camping and even went along on camp-outs when I joined the Boy Scouts. Like the trips to the seafood restaurant in San Francisco, these were among the rare moments Dad and I would spend together.

I had always been a perceptive and hardworking student but was surprised to find public school more demanding than my tutorials had been. It was not simply that the teachers expected more of me, although that was certainly true. I had been allowed to work at a comfortable pace within the calm and security of my own home, and now my studies were more strictly regimented with very little individual attention. But what was absent in my home life and startlingly present at public school was a kind of social Darwinism, that keen edge of competition that compels human beings to demonstrate and perpetuate their abilities. Suddenly, this previously dormant instinct began to assert itself and take precedence over purely academic considerations.

At the eighth grade level, the most likely candidate for fullback of the high school team is narrowed down to just a few. Already, the most beautiful women and the most promising scholars are beginning to emerge. I began to wonder how I could ever fit into this kind of a world. What would I do for a living? How could I find a girl who would want me the way I was? Confined to a wheelchair, how could I ever get a university education?

These were abstract fears, that is, except for the girl part. My friends and I would spend tireless hours discussing the relative merits of the eighth and ninth grade nymphets and the remote possibility of getting one of them to help enact our adolescent fantasies.

As is fitting with any good initiation into manhood, the Boy Scouts did its part to help dispel spurious theories of female anatomy and physiology conceived in the undergarment section of the Sears Roebuck catalog, spawned in the locker room, and tested in the back seat of dad's Buick by only a fortunate few. When the Coleman lanterns went out and the older men would go off to sleep or sneak away to the scoutmaster's tent for a snort, out would come the flashlights and the "dirty" magazines. Of course, in the 1950's genuine pornography was contraband and the only accessible substitutes were the rather tame girlie magazines with healthy looking ladies wearing diaper-like bikinis. Once in a while you could find a really racy shot of a girl without a bra. Even though these had that funny airbrushed quality you find today on cheeseburger ads, it was a tremendous turn-on.

The first picture of a really naked lady I ever saw was in Perry A.'s cabin. Where he got his collection of obscene photographs he would not reveal, but since he shared my obsession with girls, he was generous enough to share his pornography. When Perry got out of high school, he went to live like Marlon Brando's Mr. Christian in Tahiti, leading the charge for the sexual revolution. Apparently Perry got what he wanted, living happily on Tahiti with a native until he died of cancer.

Being good old world Catholics, my parents never talked to their children about sex. It wouldn't have been proper. When I was ten years old, involved in physical and occupational therapy, the therapist could see I was preoccupied with sex and advised counseling for me, unaware that I was being given hormones to hasten puberty. He was from the self-improvement school of life. If something bugs you, chuck it out, talk about it. Let a therapist refurbish your mind.

But my father wouldn't have it. Giving me counseling would be like admitting I was crazy. I might have gotten an enlightened counselor who could have reassured me and strengthened my self-image, or I might have gotten somebody who would put out the flame, ending the frustration, but also the desire to reach out.

"There is nothing wrong with the boy's mind," Dad proclaimed. "He has arthritis, nothing more." And that was the end of that. I'm not sure Dad ever realized that the medicines were making me hornier than the average boy, but perhaps he didn't want to deal with that one.

I had several surgical operations before the seventh grade. But by this time, Dr. Saunders thought my arthritis had mostly burned itself out and now would be a good time to do some corrective surgery. With the new physical demands of attending public school, I needed more mobility. I could still move my neck only a few degrees and my tendons had shortened, causing me to hunch over. The problem was that no doctor in San Francisco was willing to operate on a rheumatoid arthritic for fear of reactivating the condition. Eventually, they discovered Dr. J. Donald Francis, later recognized as one of the finest surgeons in the United States. From the time I was 11 until I reached 23, Dr. Francis would perform 10 brilliant operations.

My schoolmate Richard was thrilled. "Well, all right! The Wizard of Oz is going to make a new man out of you. There won't be a girl safe within five miles."

I told him there would not be any guarantees, but his excitement fired my own and I could not help but fantasize about what new capabilities I might have. The doctors were forever telling my parents, "A cure is just around the corner." Of course, they believed it. Science could do anything. They were licking polio and killing infections with antibiotics. The future was bright.

Richard was winding up, "Hey, this is going to be great! Listen, when you get out, we are going to San Francisco and check out the whorehouse. I mean it. My treat."

The guys kept grinning all the way back to the schoolyard. I was certain that they had something up their sleeves. It was a sunny warm afternoon and students lounged on the grass beneath the trees or tossed baseballs back and forth. Boys and girls furtively checked each other out, pretending to be unaffected by the reckless exuberance in the air. Nobody wanted lunch break to end.

Richard wheeled me around a corner where a V-shaped angle in the building traditionally provided anonymity for after-school fights. Five or six boys, mostly eighth graders, leaned against the near wall, with barely suppressed leers of anticipation. Around the far wall came three girls. One of them, Rae Ann, was an early bloomer, whose name and crude image appeared like primitive cave drawings, idolized in the boiler room, given burnt offering and peculiar sacrifice in the boys' room. The more goal-oriented high school boys sought her favors like goats in rut.

The students began to drift like chromosomes during cell division toward the convergence of the two walls. The two girls accompanying Rae Ann broke away from her laughing, leaving her confused amidst a tightening circle of boys. They aimed me at the center of the action.

Because I couldn't turn my neck, I did not see the triumphant smile on Richard's face. "What's going on?" I asked.

I felt the cornered girl's fear as they pinned her bronze arms behind her, making her already prominent breasts stand out stiffly beneath her nearly transparent bra and blouse. Some of them leered and snickered.

"She sticks out her tits like a whore," one boy said.

I replied, "I noticed you guys always look."

"Sure we look," said another. "A man can't help it. I tell you, the bitch is asking for it!"

By now she was begging to be released but the boys held her tight. All eyes, including hers, were on me as they rammed the wheelchair between the girl's legs while they held her ankles.

"She's all yours!" another boy hooted.

Another shouted, "Go ahead. Feel her up!"

They bent the girl over so her breasts were within my limited reach. They cheered.

"Let her go!" I said, almost in tears. "Let her go, goddamn it!"

The bell rang for the end of lunch break and the group dissipated, casually, as if they had been playing basketball.

Recalling the incident almost 30 years later, I have to admit that I wanted to touch her very badly, but the situation seemed revolting to me. I wanted that girl, almost any girl, but I also wanted to be wanted, which unfortunately did not happen then and there.

8

Rehabilitation Was My "Work"

Maelstrom: A large or violent whirlpool in a small area; nearby can be calm.

My life and hospitalizations continued. The variety of patients and hospital staff were endless and often quite interesting.

When I wheeled up to Santa Rosa Hospital, Dr. Francis, kind of like St. Peter at the gate, met me. There were no promises, but if all went well, I hoped that I might leave on foot. I was immobile, dependent, but I also longed to be accepted and loved like any boy my age.

Hospitals had been my home away from home ever since I could remember. The sour effluvium of disinfectant, the colorless walls, and the drugged plodding of the patients had long since lost any negative association they might once have had, neutralized by familiarity. There was some unpleasantness that came with the territory, like submitting to numerous blood tests in which the nurse would invariably miss the vein because, since I could not straighten my arm, the vein would move, making it necessary to stab at it repeatedly. The anesthetic gas they used in those early operations had a foul smell. The rubber mask smelled like rotten fish and was enough to make anybody gag. But because I had always come away from the hospital in better condition than I went in, I thought of the hospital as a liberating place.

As the orderly steered me toward the lobby, a wiry old Irishwoman named Kay Flynn bustled around the corner from the opposite direction, muttering something deprecating about doctors and the "daft errands" they sent her on. After coming to America to look for work, Kay had found a good husband and a good position owning several dress shops and boutiques. The first, she lost to pneumonia and the second, she lost to her drinking. With the help of Alcoholics Anonymous, she rebuilt her life and got a job as a nurse's aide. When she looked at me, a small, helpless boy in a wheelchair, drawing stares from every corner of the room, her heart went out to me.

Recalling that moment, she said, "It was a fine, sunny afternoon that ye came to me in Santa Rosa. When a new patient comes into the hospital, there's naturally a little gawkin'. I think you were eleven, although you looked much younger. You were only about three or four feet tall. Yer wee little arms and legs had never grown. I went over there and to meself I said, 'I'll take care of ye.' And so I did."

Kay had her regular duties at the hospital, but always found time to see me. She appointed herself my personal aide and protector. She was jealous of anybody who took me outside for fresh air or even washed my clothes.

And God help anyone who mistreated me! When I came back from the fairgrounds one day with a bad case of fleas, not a soul dared to laugh when Kay was around. I've noted during my years as a patient that there has been a trend toward more aggressive female nurses and nurses' aides. I think it's a healthy trend and I appreciated it in Kay. I guess it's been depicted in nurses like "Hot Lips" Hoolihan in *MASH*. "Big Nurse" Ratchet dramatized it negatively in *One Flew Over the Cuckoo's Nest*. But I think that the fictional stereotypes of docile and devoted nurses like my parents sought gave way to the officious, spunky nurses during and after WWII.

I had my own temperament to deal with. It's so tough to be a rebellious preteen trying to become an adult when you are totally dependent on others. I was not without my antagonists, and for a good reason. I was at a stage in my development that my cousin Silviano Marin called "mean." I felt like I had three personalities kind of like Joanne Woodward in *The Three Faces of Eve*. There was my depressed withdrawn side, my hormonal flirty side, and a side that felt guilty for resisting parents, medical authorities, and cool kids who lived a "normal" life.

My surgeon, Dr. Francis, was a brilliant and tough little Welshman who refused to waste time pampering his patients. As a result, I dubbed him "Buck-a-Minute Francis." Once, when he entered my room and took a few minutes to look over my chart, I warned him, "Careful now, Dr. Francis, buck-a-minute for your services. Make it quick!"

Kay used to smile and warn the staff about me, "Ah, the little bastard is a joy to know!" Even she was sometimes the target of my vitriolic temper.

I had this damned radio in my room. I was too weak to work the dial and I wanted her to find my favorite station. Well, she'd try, but couldn't get it to my satisfaction. I'd say, "It's not right. It's not right!"

Finally, she said, "Goddamn it, Kenny! I'm goin' to go and burn three two-bit candles to the Virgin Mary, askin' for forgiveness because I'm *not* goin' to take care of ye any more."

I said, "Flynn, give me the six bits. I'll take care of it."

But she never turned her back on me. I guess she liked my spirit, even when I was rude. One day, she got a chance to put that spiritedness to work. My education had always been sporadic and often inadequate, so when Mrs. Peters, an instructor from one of the local high schools, began tutoring some of the children at Santa Rosa Memorial, Kay was quick to tell me about her.

She said to me, "Mrs. Peters is a Phi Beta Kappa. Yer a little sassy, so don't act so intelligent."

Later Kay said, "Without Mrs. Peters, I do na' think ye would have been ready for high school."

My father probably did not mind my being tutored in the hospital as much as he minded Kay Flynn presuming to raise his son. Kay later said, "Mr. Jacuzzi thought I was buttin' in. He did na' like the fact that I was givin' you advice and was only a nurse's aide. But that was all right. I'd pay no attention to 'im."

My father had plenty of other things to think about besides my attachment to members of the hospital staff. For one thing, my hospital bills were costing him a fortune. He said,

> The doctors tried to help you—and they all tried earnestly because they loved you. But the sickness was so severe that they just did the best they could. And I don't mind telling you that they charged me plenty. They knew I had a good job and was making good money. Every year I had deductions of $20,000, $40,000. I was questioned by the Internal Revenue right and left. They couldn't believe it. Not possible, to see all these bills, this list of all these doctors.
>
> Dr. Francis sent me a bill for $7,500 for one operation! I said, "Doctor, be reasonable."
>
> He said, "You know, I do a lot of operations and I don't charge a penny. People can't afford it."
>
> I said, "Doctor, do you realize that this has been going on for years and years and years and it's costing me a lot of money? True, perhaps I should help some of those you do for nothing. But this seems to me a little bit high."
>
> But I was happy to pay it in a way because Dr. Francis had succeeded in straightening you up.

J. Donald Francis at Santa Rosa Memorial did not have to justify his fees. They were out of sight, but then so were his results. What he performed on me was not just surgery, it was engineering. Both of my hip flexors had shrunk, causing me to hunch over. These were cut and released. My arthritic knees permitted my legs to straighten only to about a 45° angle. Dr. Francis modified the range of motion by cutting a wedge just below the joint. This did not increase my range of motion, but it allowed me to straighten my legs out completely.

These operations were part of a major overhaul that was to last until I was 23 and included the tendon releases of both ankles, the fusion of both wrists and both ankles. Later, following my earlier surgical fusion, when I was at San Francisco U.C. Medical Center, the flexors and extensors of my right hand were switched to facilitate extension of my fingers.

A Childhood Memory

Four white beds,
Two on either side of this
Our room, our home.

An old man, breathing furtively,
Lies in the corner near one window,
Smelling of something strange
While outside birds' chirping
Serenades the kitchen crew.

Across from him a veteran from the Korean War
Recounts an adventure of another sort.

In front of me a boy nearer my age
Sits on his bed, playing cards, whistling.

I've just arrived from Recovery,
Pain claws me from inside where they cut,
But a fever also pulses on my head.

A nurse comes in to take my blood.
I cannot straighten my arms
And the veins in my feet are weak.

She stands above me and to my side
With a foot-long needle

> And syringe poised vertically
> Above my groin, telling me not to move.
>
> Deftly, she stabs the needle
> Deeply into my flesh.
> I scream.
> She says, "That's okay,
> I'm sorry...really sorry."

You see, it wasn't all dreams and loneliness. Often at that age of twelve or so, people surrounded me who wanted to inflict pain. Well, maybe they didn't want to, but did it anyway. In my little world, my little *maelstrom*, I was going through a great deal that threatened to suck me down into the depths of depression. But the staff around me was relatively calm and that helped me bear up.

Sometimes, the only way to quickly draw a large amount of blood is with a femoral puncture. It's an ugly experience. You lie flat on your back with your thighs spread-eagle. The technician or nurse drawing the blood admonishes you to not move a muscle. You feel knowing fingers probing your groin for the precise location of the femoral artery. Then you see it: a huge syringe, bayoneted with an eight-inch needle, fiercely clenched and poised vertically above your groin. An extraterrestrial hand swabs the target with alcohol, icing skin and viscera.

She was petite, almost dwarf size and didn't look like someone who would, or even could, hurt you. Even though the nuns ran the place, she never wore her uniform longer than mid-thigh and no one said anything about it. Whenever she came around—and that was often for long-terms like yours truly, or the new transients who forever chugged in and out—she'd be called *bloodsucker* or *vampire*, but she would toss her golden hair like a rag doll and giggle, lifting you with her music and blue-magic eyes.

She'd then say something like, "Oh, Kenny, I wouldn't hurt you, ever." She was right, too, most of the time. Yeah, she'd hurt a little when drawing blood, but she was eternally gentle and knew how to take it from anywhere when she had to—your foot, behind knees, under forearms, the back of your hands—the place that hurt me the least. The doctors called on her to do things they couldn't do themselves and treated her with the respect they only gave one other woman: Mother Superior.

"This will *hurt a little*, Kenny, I can't help it; but you must not *move*! Do you understand?"

You say nothing—you can't. For an instant, time and the universe stops. In that hidden, tender spot where the skin of your testicle meets the valley of your thigh, steel lacerates your innocence with fearful agony. You look down and see this monstrous medical weapon wedged in your body, sucking blood and life from your soul. Time creeps, sweat droplets torture your eyes, and you wonder which will cease first: the flow of your maroon sustenance or your life itself?

It's over, finally; but fingers anchoring another cotton swab on your groin remind you of the horror journeyed. You lie still...still. Fingers, cotton swabs, and other foreign objects discard their intimate contact with you. You serve their objective no further. You're now free...free to cover your violated flesh, cocoon your body from the pain...the fear, even though, deep in your brain, you know it could happen again...at any time.

"I'm so sorry, Kenny, but I *had* to do it. They need a lot of blood to test so that the right antibiotic can be used to treat your infection and get you well again. I hope it didn't hurt too much. You get some rest now."

I lie on my side, curled, defensive of further onslaughts. Two of the other five beds are occupied. The third and fifth patiently wait like white, starched, sleeping automatons. Most transients come and go in days or weeks, but I stay months. The real nature of this place manifests in its empty rooms—eerie, especially around midnight, making you think this is what might greet you at the doors of hell. The only signs of life are the transients and townspeople found within its shell. Oh, there are also the visitors, but they usually are lowlifes or hopeless bores. I remain unmoving, fogged by medicines, but still seeing with my eyes and ears the transients and townspeople coming and going.

There was one bedmate I'll never forget. He was about 25 or 30 years beyond my 12. His leg was in a full cast, suspended in midair by an erector-set-like-contraption of pulleys, ropes, and weights. He didn't speak; he bellowed and boasted of his life-risking deeds and female conquests. He loved detailing how, during his stint in the still-in-progress Korean War, this trollop he was riding to victory worked a knotted rag into his rectum and, at just the right moment, yanked it out, giving him the orgasm to end all orgasms. I wasn't even sure what an orgasm was.

This old Korean vet, on the other hand, was a transient who hardly spoke at all. He knew no more than a fish knows about higher mathematics. Big, hairy all over like a bear. His voice, when he did speak, was soft and timid. He was old and crippled and could hardly get up and walk to the bathroom on his own. His arm was broken when he fell chasing one of his roosters. He raised chickens. What worried him the most, he said, was his bad heart and not being able to work and support his family. Some of the townspeople and transients didn't like him because he was poor and uneducated. I don't know why, but he was always nice to me, helping me or handing me the urinal when townspeople aren't around.

Eventually, they put us in a semi-private room together.

I had a Japanese therapy assistant at Santa Rosa Memorial who seemed to take special interest in me. I loved to hear the sound of her light, quick step approaching. She was very small, and she spoke in a careful, sing-song manner, sincere as well as musical. She kept me posted on all the news of the day, like how Eisenhower twice turned down the Julius and Ethel Rosenberg appeals, making their execution certain, and what Senator Joe McCarthy was doing. She admitted she was a little afraid of Eisenhower. With the wars with Japan and then Korea still fresh in people's minds, there were those who thought of all Orientals as the enemy.

I was amazed when she told how her parents were among those Japanese rounded up and put into detention camps in California for fear they might be Japanese sympathizers. I had heard horror stories about the Nazi concentration camps and although she assured me that nobody was tortured or killed, I felt a little ashamed that my country could have done something so unfair. It was not until years later that I was told how my Aunt Stella had been in a similar detention camp also in California with other Italians who were sympathetic to Mussolini.

One of the nuns, a mechanical Florence Nightingale, used to give me blood transfusions. This was a familiar procedure to me since I had been given transfusions for anemia ever since I came down with arthritis. I hardly noticed any more the sharp metallic intrusion of the thick needle or the sensation of the cold blood seeping into my arm. In those days, blood was stored in glass bottles with rubber tops that had to be punctured with the needle at the other end of the transfusion kit.

One day, I heard the solid military click of the transfusion nun's feet. Soon, in her quick, efficient manner, she had extended my circulatory system to include several feet of tubing and a pint bottle of blood on loan from some stranger. A good deal of it would probably end up on rubber gloves and surgical sponges at the next operation. The rest would be mine to keep. I wondered if after all those transfusions I still possessed any of my own vital fluid. I imagined that I must have had a good cross-section of blood brothers: blacks, Mexicans, rich and poor. By now, I was probably related to half the people in California.

After the first bottle of viscous, red fluid had drained into my arm, the nun took down the "empty" and snatched up another bottle. I'm not sure what happened after this. It was all over in a matter of two or three seconds. Very likely, she hit the air valve release on the bottle because suddenly there was blood everywhere, but most especially on the nun's immaculate starched white habit. The contrast was stunningly brilliant, the effect almost patriotic. The nun let out a little gasp, but managed to keep her composure remarkably well. She left the door open when she went out for another bottle, and an orderly stuck his head in.

"Jesus Christ! What happened? Did somebody have an aneurysm or something?"

I explained what happened and asked what an aneurysm was. The orderly explained that an aneurysm involves the weakening of a blood vessel due to heart disease. He said the vessel blows up like a balloon full of blood and will usually burst under the pressure. I shuddered.

The nun returned complete with a fresh habit and a full bottle. I stared at the ceiling, listening to the languid slopping sound of the orderly's mop on the floor and felt the cool flow of the new blood entering my body. Blood had splattered the walls and ceiling, too. After the excitement of the punctured bottle, the room seemed strangely peaceful. To pass the time, I took pieces of Kleenex, wet and wadded them up and blew them through my glass drinking straw so they stuck on the ceiling with the splattered red blood. That gave the walls a chicken pox look. Dinner trays would be arriving soon.

My roommate started gasping for breath and I began buzzing the nurses' station nonstop. The head nurse charged in, yelling at me for leaning on the buzzer. I told her that I thought he needed help. She looked at him for a few seconds then ran out to get the on-call doctor. When they got back she shoved closed the curtain between us. Minutes later he died. No one told me, but I knew what was happening. A little while later they wheeled me, bed and all, to the alcove in the hall used as the backup room when all the other rooms are full.

Then there was the orderly. He shuffled surprisingly fast, all the way down the hall from the nurses' station to my bedside. Wiry, aging and almost bald, his large hooked nose dominated his wrinkled, sea-mariner face. No one knows when he came to northern California from Appalachia, where he was raised and how alcohol got the best of him. He'd been off the booze a long time, but the only work he could get was the grunt jobs like the one he was doing in this place.

"Time to wash your ugly face and get your lazy ass up. Breakfast will be here any minute. They put you in the *closet*, eh? Chicken farmer must've croaked. Had t' happen. Everyone knew his heart wasn't worth *sheeet*. When'd he die? Poor white trash just like 'em damn fool black bastards; never see a doctor 'til it's too late. Here, take this goddamn washcloth and wipe 'em buggers off your *sheeet-face, eye-talian* nose."

I missed him when he wasn't on duty.

The delicate, but swift clickity clackity of his expensive, Italian shoes coming down the hall gave away the doctor's identity. He was of average stature and unassuming, dressed impeccably, and was always nice to everybody, me, even the nurses. He was thought of highly by all the crew, kind of a doctor's doctor. Several years later, one of this doctor's sons killed himself.

Time passed. Finally, when the day came to wriggle out of my plaster cocoon, I felt like a new man *only* in my ability to register new dimensions in pain. But I was not expecting to struggle quickly to my feet and gallop down the hospital halls, joyously scuffing the soles of my shoes for the first time in my life. I had spent half my life in hospitals and therapy centers and understood that doctors could perform only half the miracle. The other half was up to me.

I've always felt that you cannot delegate the responsibility to the doctor or therapist. They only have so much time and they don't know what's going on in your head.

I had to get into training for my new life. My goals: to be able to dress and undress myself and to walk with the aid of platform crutches. If I worked hard and was very lucky, this might be accomplished in a few months. My therapists were kind but merciless. They sympathized with the extraordinary pain I was in, but they continued to stretch my arms and legs even when I screamed with the pain. My arthritic joints sent pain shooting through my body when they were moved beyond their accustomed limit, not to mention the fact that I was still sore from the surgery.

Again, time passed. And even more time passed. But every day, I began the torturous process all over again. I never refused to go on because, as I have told people, "Rehabilitation was my work." In my home, work was recognized as the only way one person could distinguish himself from another and live according to his dreams.

Candido and his brothers had come to America, poor immigrants who could barely speak the language, and built a good business from the ground up. Certainly inventiveness helped, but it was plain hard work that made it happen. Dad, too, had been "handicapped" in a way. He had almost no capital, his English was very poor, and he had little formal education. When he came to America, he didn't know anybody outside his own family, who were all in the same predicament. He did not even have his brother Rachele's intellect. Equipped only with his willpower, Dad set out to become the company salesman, trying to convince people he did not know, in a language he did not adequately understand, to buy a pump. It was painful at times being misunderstood or laughed at by farmers suspicious of foreigners, but he persisted and overcame his "handicap".

I respected this concept of work, not only for what it had done for my father, but because it lent dignity and purpose to my own daily ordeal. It is difficult for any healthy, able-bodied person to comprehend the courage it takes to willfully submit to a process that feels like dismemberment day after day, each day knowing the pain will be just as terrible as the day before and that the treatments will probably go on for months. But it was my "work." I had no other! Each day wore itself out.

One day, on the edge of the shade cast by the giant oak tree under which I was sitting, a well-nourished, blue and gray bird was gathering tiny twigs and other wind-blown leftovers, carting them one-by-one up to the nest it was building above me.

Like a running, shallow brook hiccupping now and then by pebbled dams, my daydreaming drifted from the intensely warm March Santa Rosa day to my wicker cane wheelchair to the expansive courtyard, its own manicured planet with Kelly-green lawns, rainbow flowers, and shrewd, trusting trees to wondering if the surgeries would free me to….

From a distance a thump intruded my reverie and through swinging doors emerged a white dove striding deliberately in my direction.

Coming to pause at my side, a ghostly figure save for the school-girl freckled skin, orchid smile, and dazzling blue eyes peering out from the shrouded habit and through me like one skewered apple.

"Good afternoon, Ken. What are you doing this fine day?"

"Hi, Sister Mary Ellen. Just watchin' the birds."

"How would you like to help me in Central Supply three days a week while you're here?"

"Great, Sister, but what could I do? What about the doctors, nurses, Mother Superior?"

"Don't worry; I'll take care of everything. After physical therapy and lunch tomorrow, come down to Central and I'll show you. Okay?"

"Okay, Sister. I'll be there."

Sister Mary Ellen swooshed away as quickly as she had appeared. Moments after the dust settled, little blue-gray bird returned, continuing, as if uninterrupted, its calculated nest building. I had been in and out of hospital enough to know the rudiments of Central Supply, the warehouse lifeline furnishing everything needed from aspirins to x-ray film to everyone from nighttime janitor to brain surgeon.

But I asked myself over and over again, how could a kid stuck in a wheelchair, who's never worked before, help in a place like Central Supply? The thought made me a little edgy, tuning up my senses several notches. Soon bird finished its construction job and took off into the reddening sky. The p.m. shift had come on duty hours before. Grace, one of the nurses from my floor, came down to get me for dinner.

"You've been around here so long, Ken; no one missed you for dinner. I only noticed your empty bed when Jack, the new guy in your ward, asked where you were. Don't worry; I saved your tray. It even looks decent tonight, hamburger and French fries."

"Thanks, Grace."

That night nothing could take my mind off of Central Supply, not even hamburgers, French fries, being forgotten by the staff or one of my TV favorites, Milton Berle, known as *Uncle Miltie*.

Everything was kind of a daze until 1:00 p.m. the next day when a Candy Striper finally wheeled me into Central Supply. Without looking up from what she was doing, Sister Mary Ellen told the Candy Striper to wheel me over to the table by the window overlooking the courtyard, thanked her, said hello to me, but remained fixed at her job, loading the autoclave. After she set the high temperature sterilizer up to run, Sister Mary Ellen came over to my table setting piles of pieces of surgical gauze in front of me.

"Pay attention, Ken. I'm going to show you how to properly prepare and fold a surgical sponge. It has to be done precisely as I'm doing it each and every time. Same measurements, no mistakes. When you think you've got it, tell me and I'll let you make a few." Then she demonstrated.

"I think I can do it, Sister."

"Okay, do it."

My first couple of tries were pretty good, I thought, but my measurements varied slightly, causing Sister Mary Ellen to remind me emphatically how critical sponges were in every surgical procedure. After three or four more attempts, my folded sponges finally met with her approval. She then matter-of-factly placed enough pieces of gauze in front of me to make more than 300 surgical sponges. Two hours later, I had completed 300 sponges that passed Sister Mary Ellen's inspection. I was floating and more pain free than I remember ever being.

The next day was a Central Supply repeat, except I had to learn a new, even more demanding skill, and one which I relished doing. Sister Mary Ellen taught me how to sharpen and recycle syringe needles. Sterilized used needles were placed to one side of my work area. I would pick one, inspect it, making sure it wasn't too short—less than two and one half inches long—then I'd sharpen it, using a high-speed, extremely fine electric grinder. The angle of the sharpened needle would have to be kept at a precise forty-five degrees and contain absolutely no rough spots or metal burrs. When the needle was sharpened, I'd place it in a special receptacle while the unusable needles were to be discarded into another container.

By the end of that spring I was dumbfounded thinking how much medicine and human blood were delivered, withdrawn, absorbed by the thousands of surgical sponges I had made and needles I had sharpened. Imagine, a cripple who can work. At least Sister Mary Ellen didn't think that was so strange.

I also made friends with some of the other patients in the hospital. There was a girl about my age who was admitted with third-degree burns over 75 percent of her body. I was told she had been pretty, but when I saw her, it took a good imagination to believe it. Seeing her bandaged and disfigured, unable to move without it causing her excruciating pain, I thought less about my own problems and marveled at how this little girl could be so brave. Against hospital regulations, I organized a birthday party for her.

I sent out for cold cuts, salami, cheese, etc. forgetting it was meatless Friday. But for this girl, the nuns said that God certainly wouldn't mind and they joined in, too.

In the hospital, because everybody's problems were out in the open, people were usually more accepting of each other. On the outside, the common bonds were less apparent.

One day when my father came to visit, he brought a whirlpool bath unit and photographer, intending to use my picture in the new brochure he was working up.

Dad had always loved the promotion end of the business, especially television. The hearts of thirteen million women skipped a beat as emcee Jack Bailey pointed directly at the camera and said, "Do you want to be *Queen For a Day?*" If the Queen's list of torments included some kind of physical infirmity, she would receive a "Jacuzzi."

Now that the whirlpool had what was known in the business as "image identification," my father's new brochure would help clinch sales right and left. There was a picture of me sitting in front of a whirlpool unit smiling. Dad would be standing over me, with one arm partly around my shoulders, resting on the machine. The caption read, "BECAUSE OF A FATHER'S LOVE..."

After Dad and the photographer left, I told Kay about the brochure. "Why, that's wonderful!" Kay exclaimed. "It's a star you'll be, Kenny."

In my depressed mood, I glowered thinking of how my father was using me to get sales. "The son of a bitch. What does he know?" My father cast me in a role I did not like—a "handicapped" son for whom he invented a helpful device. It was a wonderful story and a great selling slogan. But it trapped me! I did not understand my reaction then, but now I know that I didn't like the limited role that Dad and everyone else created for me. Little did I know that my father's comments would also trap him, and make him forever think of the Jacuzzi as a medical invention and only secondarily as a luxury item. This was one description in the Jacuzzi brochures.

> Because of a father's love for his son, many sufferers of arthritis have been helped and many more will be!
>
> When Kenny Jacuzzi became a victim of painful rheumatoid arthritis, doctors prescribed a daily whirlpool bath...hydromassage...then available only at hospitals. Because his weakened condition made daily hospital trips impractical, Candido Jacuzzi, Kenny's father, put to work the facilities of the world-famous pump manufacturing organization of Jacuzzi Bros., Inc. to design a portable hydromassage unit for home use. Today Kenny is a high school student, leading a nearly normal life—thanks to regular hydromassage...
>
> Kenny's whole family enjoys daily whirlpool baths for relaxation and for keeping in top physical condition.
>
> And because of his father's love, today—in your own home—YOU can enjoy the convenience and advantages of the Jacuzzi Whirlpool Bath.

By the time I was to be discharged from the hospital, I was fairly excited about going home to the family again. During my six months at Santa Rosa Memorial, the hospital and Kay were like family to me. She was very quiet the morning I was to leave. As she was helping me pack, she mumbled something about writing to me from time to time, although she seemed to be talking to herself and did not even look at me when I spoke.

"Flynn!" I grumbled. "Where's my radio?"

She rummaged around in a pile of clothes, extracted the small but expensive device, and deposited it where I could reach it.

"I want you to keep it, Kay."

"What?" This time, our eyes met.

"Well, you're the only one who knows how to operate the damned thing."

She smiled, "You little bastard."

Kay was always my favorite, this small lady with dancing grey eyes, an elephant-sized heart, and a take-charge Irish soul. She could drink any self-respecting man under the table. But she took me under her wing and became, during my repeated pilgrimages, my surrogate mom and, eventually, lifelong confidant. Years later, less than a handful of people showed up at her funeral. My wife and I were two of them.

9

Adolescence

Tropical Disturbance: Weak and unorganized winds in an area usually hot, sultry and torrid.

The year before my hospitalization where I learned to do work, I had been excited about going to school for the first time so I could, among other things, make new friends. I was well liked by the guys but I wanted a girlfriend.

In junior high school, informal methods of achieving this end are slow and unreliable. And so it was that I went to my first school dance. Boys and girls in vastly diverse stages of biological development assembled to try on their new identities as adults. Some were better able to pull it off than others. On some of the girls, the spiked heels, nylon stockings, tight, mid-calf skirts, fire engine red lipstick and plucked eyebrows looked almost natural, even alluring. On the late bloomers, whose pyramidal bras clearly supported nothing but hope, the trappings of female maturity merely parodied the intended effect. The boys, in their padded-shoulder sport coats, hair slicked with globs of Brylcreme, were up against the same odds.

As Bill Haley and the Comets blared on the hi-fi, I sat in my wheelchair up against the wall checking out the girls, occasionally engaging in conversation with a friend who was too shy to ask a girl to dance. Dancing with a girl was a safe and acceptable way to investigate female sexuality.

I began to think that I was always in the shadow looking on, listening to the fall of dancing feet, like a voyeur. I shrank from involvement because I believed no girl would be interested in me. But I was interested in them. As I lusted after glances of anatomy that should have been totally covered, I understood that I should dismiss all expectations of going to Heaven. I began to realize that girls were going to be one of my first and lasting troubles, like teeth that never cease tormenting you from the time you cut them until they cut you.

Some of the girls would come dressed in a somewhat revealing manner and dancing with them, you could see more. In those days, a little shot of bra was really something! Of course, I did not dance. But at junior high dances, loneliness has lots of company. For this reason somebody invented what was known as the "snake dance," a ritual in which everybody in the place lined up single file, laying his or her hands on the person in front and in this manner, careened around the room like a lustful centipede. Everybody—ugly girls, gawky boys—everybody danced the snake dance but me.

I wanted to be up there dancing. But what could I do? I just sat there and felt lousy. Sitting down was not my favorite posture; it was my only posture! I had turned fourteen in the hospital, but I still could not dance. Neither could I dress or undress myself. Kay Flynn was worried about me. I would hardly talk to anyone and seemed to take no interest in what was going on around me, especially after being brought back from mysterious periods of isolation.

But I had been fortunate to have a real date. It was with Pat, the girl who was friendly to me at the dance so early on. She had a classy chassis and I took her to a nearby movie theater, chauffeured by my sister Irene's husband. I gave Pat a bottle of perfume. However, I became disenchanted when I found that my arms were too short to put across her shoulders and around her neck. The best part was the questioning by my buddies the next day to see how "far" I had gotten with Pat. She was a real beauty, with fair skin, medium build, soft blonde hair, and gray-blue eyes. I left others to romance her but we formed a friendship that exists until today.

My friend since the seventh grade, Pat, later stopped going to school because she'd become pregnant her last year of high school and didn't want "the bulge" to show. She had home tutoring during that period. Pat went on to have a child out of wedlock whom she raised to become a wonderful girl. Had Pat been around later, I probably would have talked to her at dances. But we sort of got out of touch for a time during those years with her child and my trips back and forth to the hospital.

Although I was just a young teenager, I realized that my family was becoming embroiled in problems far above my head.

Hating war as he did, my father tried to keep my brother, John, out of the country around draft age, just as his father had done with his boys. Dad had John learn Spanish and sent him to work in the Jacuzzi plant in Mexico. During the Korean War, when John received his draft notice, Dad asked Jacuzzi lawyer, Nathan Gray, whether a deferment or a restriction of duty might keep him from serving on the front lines. Nathan suggested he talk to high profile attorney, Joseph Alioto, who eventually became Mayor of San Francisco.

Joe and Dad exchanged pleasantries and Italian ancestry tales. Then Joe Alioto told my father to tell John to come back and serve but they would arrange something that kept him away from action.

Later, somehow the arrangement was considered "draft evasion" despite the fact that a lawyer advised Dad and John thusly. He was taken into immediate custody. The judge did not want John, he told others, to slip back into Mexico. At the same time, he ruled that John had lost his citizenship for leaving the country after he received his draft notice. It was reinstated by a higher court later on. My brother had to go to court and was sentenced to serve eight months in the federal penitentiary.

Our family saw it another way. John and his accountant were the only people in the Jacuzzi firm in Mexico. They had $150,000 of machinery there and couldn't exactly pack up and leave. John wrote them that he was willing to serve in the military but they ignored that letter and seemed to try him in absentia. Then suddenly they said for him to report back in the states. That's when Dad got in touch with Joe Alioto.

John described what happened:

> I was told I'd have to go back to California and report to Federal Court, then go into the military. Alioto arranged that I be brought from Tijuana, Mexico, to San Diego and was booked in San Diego. There was a bond established ($5,000) and I was released on my own recognizance.
>
> I took my wife with me and prepared to go into the Army.
>
> I flew to the Bay Area and set the trial date—two or three weeks later. Alioto had said there was no point in having a lengthy trial. They're never going to admit you wrote them a letter. Better go in with a nolo plea.
>
> I said, "Well, if that's what you recommend, that's what we'll do."
>
> Judge Murphy said it was okay to report to the service a week or ten days later.
>
> Grandmother died during that time. She was very dear to me. We had the funeral. It upset the family quite a bit. Articles started appearing in the newspaper. The draft board, for some reason, didn't want me any more.
>
> Cousins, etc. didn't like the publicity.
>
> The federal attorney petitioned the court to have me retried. It was almost double jeopardy. They dragged me back into court. This time, the judge said I'd have to do time. I had to go to Terminal Island. Eight months was reduced to six months and 20 days.
>
> Of course, I was bitter like hell. Here I had a young wife and a baby, and another soon due. I was in a bitter madness.

> When I was in Terminal Island, they stripped me of my citizenship. Immigration authorities visited me at Terminal Island. Stripped of citizenship got me more scandalized in the newspapers.
>
> Right after I got out, Alioto said they were litigating a case in the Supreme Court concerning a draft evader with a Spanish surname, born in the U.S. They had done the same thing to him. Alioto said wait and see what happens to him. The Supreme Court reversed his penalty and got back his citizenship. Immigration and Naturalization authorities reversed their stand on the issue.
>
> They said I could get my U.S. passport at the American Embassy in Monterrey. I couldn't get back to Mexico for several months because they held up my Mexican working papers, which were impounded when I went into the States.
>
> That was a harrowing experience.

This hit the newspapers and our relatives were very upset with my father for allowing the family name to be tarnished. It seems ironic because Alioto could have argued that since I was so severely disabled and probably couldn't father children, the family line could only be continued through my brother, or since John was nerve deaf in one ear, a medical deferment might have also been suggested.

John's wife, Margaret, was barely in her twenties, and was unable to speak much English. She rented a small apartment near Alba and Pete Kosta, to await her husband's parole, as well as the birth of her second child.

Alioto promised to take the case to the U.S. Supreme Court, but he never did. John was bitter. Mom was despondent. Dad was heartbroken. And I found myself constantly having to explain to friends who saw the newspapers why John had not served during the Korean War.

I'm happy to say, however, that after John served his time in jail, he went back to Mexico and continued to run the manufacturing plant very successfully. But it scarred him for life.

My father was doing good things for the business. In 1956, he signed an order with Pan American Airways to produce the largest machinery airlift in their history. Three tons of Jacuzzi pumps were transported from Mills Field to Panama to be installed.

But when it rains, sometimes it pours. Two years later, Dad got into trouble over creating a holding company. As I mentioned earlier, my father had been setting up opportunities for the relatives to work in other countries such as Canada, Brazil, Mexico, as well as the U.S. plants. He didn't want the company to be taxed both in the U.S. and the other countries; you know, double taxation. So Joe Alioto advised him to create a holding company. Alioto, like so many politicians, had a wall hung with plaques, pictures, mementos, bar association awards, courtroom honors, arranged to impress people, and my father was among those who were impressed. But the holding company ran into problems when my Aunt Stella's husband pursued a derivative action lawsuit, with a sort of anti-American framework. They argued that Dad was trying to avoid paying American taxes.

The case went to court. I was in the court room every day even though I was only 16. The trial was held in a judge's courtroom without a jury. In the back of the courtroom were two IRS agents. Joe Alioto was a good speaker but he patronized the judge and was rather flippant, as if he didn't think the issue was that important.

Dad was not a good advocate for himself. He had a strong Italian accent and looked nervous. He was nervous because he came from a country where people didn't trust their government. He thought the U.S. government was powerful, and he felt like a scapegoat. He'd seen his sister Stella taken from her home by the U.S. government during WWII, and he'd seen other immigrants and his own son go to jail. Here was Stella on the right side of the U.S. government now. Dad kept asking us, "What'll they do to me?"

I do have to wonder if my father had used his heart more than his head, would things have been different. During the trial, he commented that he had mainly learned from the people he met during his travels, as if he was innocent and was doing no more than what he learned others had done. That comment did not serve him well. In addition, he had become obsessed with the idea that the U.S. government was out to get Italians.

Interestingly, the IRS attorney was Nathan Gray, who had earlier been my father's Jacuzzi Company lawyer. At the end of the trial, the IRS agents said the holding company, Jacbros (Jacuzzi Brothers overseas) had to be dissolved and the taxes had to be paid.

After the trial was over, the shareholders and my father had to pay a lot of tax. He thought he was going to have to pay more. During this whole process, he made trips abroad and tried to stay out of the country, because he was afraid of being served papers.

Unbeknownst to me, my parent's life had started on a downward roll from which it would never recover. But it was 1958, the beginning of my last year of high school, and I was sitting on top of the world. My blind friend, Tom, came over to my house to study with me and tutor me. Tom recalled those times.

> Ken and I were inseparable. I was at his house 4–5 afternoons a week. His family had few people in but if people came, it was usually only family. Maybe

they didn't trust others or felt uncomfortable with non-family others. They built a wall around themselves. The business was a family and their social friends were family members.

I never met his brother John and never heard anyone refer to John, maybe because it was a shameful episode in the family history. I heard that Candido ordered John not to serve in the military, and nobody went against the patriarch's orders. I have to wonder if the U.S. government tried to make an example out of John during the Korean War when they arrested him for draft evasion, because I heard he was in pretty bad shape after he was paroled from serving jail time.

I understand that Candido built a cottage for him next to the family house and he stayed there for some time before returning to run the Mexican office.

I'll never know whether Tom's guesses about my father are accurate. At that time, of course, we didn't discuss such things together. My concern was my own progress or lack of it.

For the past six years, from the time I was eleven years old, I had undergone eight major reconstructive surgeries to my hips, knees, and ankles followed by one hell of a lot of in-hospital physical therapy. The goal of the surgeries and rehabilitation was to relieve at least some of the crippling effects of the Juvenile Rheumatoid Arthritis.

I later learned that nobody in the family expected me to live very long; not even my parents. Mom and Dad kept me away from family members, though I didn't realize it. As a result, I never knew my older cousins very well, nor even my own brother, John. What's more, my Dad became irritated when people asked about me and finally they stopped asking. My cousin, Silviano Marin, Aunt Stella's son, told me their reactions later on.

It was a very strong family. We were a lot closer than just cousins. We were almost like brothers and sisters, all of us. That was what was so difficult about Kenny, because he was the one who became ill and everybody was basically willing, strong and able, and none of us could understand that he wouldn't get well.

I think C.J. and Kenny's mother, my aunt, they started to shelter Kenny so that the family really didn't get to see Kenny that much except in the beginning when some of my girl cousins would go to help my aunt with Kenny.

At that time, the company was enjoying a considerable degree of success. Everything was succeeding except here was this youngest of cousins who showed us we were vulnerable to something. C. J. could handle all problems but this one.

My cousin had a good point. I was a reminder that money and success can't buy health and happiness. But finally, some progress came from the surgeries and rehabilitation. At the age of 17, for the first time in my life, I was able to walk about 100 yards with platform crutches, custom-built shoes with elevated heels, and a mind-set that focused beyond the pain.

With assistive devices and a custom shower my Dad had built for me, I also became able to bathe and, save for combing my hair and tying my shoes, dress myself, although my routine took me over two hours to complete each morning. Even though any run-of-the-mill tortoise would have beaten my walking speed, and I looked very much like a waddling penguin, especially from the rear, I was ecstatic with my newfound independence and freedom.

I also recall another time I decided to take a trip to Sacramento and stay in a motel, but returned home in about a week. I was a bit hard-headed or *testa dura*. In my condition, I really didn't know exactly how to be independent but kept taking *weak and unorganized* stabs at adulthood as I tried to handle my emerging new emotions and passions. The last thing I wanted was to live my life vicariously through others. I wanted to live it as fully and as personally as I could.

When I was 17, my father was instrumental in arranging a family reunion on August 16, 1958. The original seven brothers and six daughters had created, with second and third generation cousins, a total of 188 Jacuzzis.

I was the Master of Ceremonies introducing each event and each family group. It was held at the Colombo Club in Oakland, California, and included food and drinks, entertainment, dancing, singing, and photographs. A booklet was created from the photos with our family tree. In the booklet was this Family Creed written by Aunt Felicita:

> We believe in family unity. We must always believe in family unity. We believe the past has taught each and every one of us that strength is achieved through family unity.
>
> We believe that the world and each one of us has a purpose and that our lives are part of that purpose.
>
> We believe that spiritual things are greater than material things because Man cannot live by bread alone. He must have faith in his Creator.
>
> We believe that honesty and truth must guide our every action and that we must always be fair with our fellow men.
>
> We believe in that which is good, true and honest. Our parents taught us the fundamentals of clean, wholesome living—and we will remember them always.

I'll never forget the next and last family reunion on September 6, 2003, at the Cline Cellars in Sonoma Valley. Fred Cline, grandson of my uncle Valeriano Jacuzzi, hosted the party for 351 descendants of the Jacuzzi family. His special Jacuzzi Zinfandel was served to the group. Fred Cline welcomed everyone by explaining that his idea for the winery came to him while he was playing checkers with his grandfather Valeriano. Entertainment was provided, and the creed and a prayer written for the 1958 reunion was read. Group photos were taken and each of the 13 family groups distinguished themselves by wearing colored baseball hats, 13 colors divided among relatives of the 13 Jacuzzi siblings.

But to return to 1958, I have to admit that next to women, I had a love affair with cars. Ever since I can remember, I've been passionate about designing and building things—houses, cars, widgets, do-dads, thingamajigs, whatever. Take cars. Americans—especially young male Americans—have always been in love with the automobile and how the damn thing was built, ran, took you from here to the end of the rainbow, and, of course, how it looked, the *styling*. So, why should I, young American male boy that I was, be any different? Yes, I *loved* cars.

Back in the early 1950s, I'd always read the critical new-car assessments written by Tom McCahill for *Mechanics Illustrated*. Tom loved cars too, especially American cars. He loved our American mammoths so much that he'd never hesitate tearing them apart from one end to the other, hoping that Detroit would someday build excellent cars instead of just good ones.

Tom was unrelenting, criticizing with the vengeance of a Viking the American car's mushy, all-over-the-road suspensions, aim-challenging steering, pro-suicide brakes, and rattle-prone, ill-fitting bodies. McCahill's incessant jabs at America's road machines became even more bloody when he'd continually throw in Detroit's face such things as the superior braking and suspension systems and simple, classic styling of the European sports cars—the Porsches, MGs, Triumphs. These were being gobbled up by returning GIs from World War II and other middle-class American boys. McCahill would ask rhetorically why Dearborn couldn't build 'em just as good.

My juices really began flowing when McCahill would chop to pieces the go-for-cheap, planned-obsolescence styling cues tacked onto Detroit iron each year to distinguish the "new model" from one made the previous year. The styling silliness was almost sublime. I mean, gee, this year's Buick would be distinguishable from last year's model because it had four little chrome-plated, nonfunctional portholes on the front fender instead of three. The moronic creativity and added "value" of such changes literally boggled the mind.

I quickly began observing all cars with the eye of a critic on a personal mission. My mission was to revamp whatever vehicle I was beholding at the moment, from bumper to tail light, sculpting every detail in between, until the final, resulting entity would flow with the strength and beauty of Niagara Falls. Some said I had inherited my family's tendency to invent and reinvent. Maybe so.

I would think—should a car have to look "strong" as well as beautiful? I don't know except that my concept of an ideal car was that it should get you from here to wherever you want to get swiftly and unfailingly, with no hassles or bullshit.

I thought, too, the whole idea of a car—at least for a young, adolescence-transcending guy and maybe all guys—was this absolutely loyal, competent, hypnotically beautiful, pleasure-bestowing thing that was yours, totally. Its mission was—and still is—to be *your* baby and a glistening extension of that most important bodily part, your dick. It's enough to give even middle-aged bastards like me a hard-on. Usually, however, things and events got in the way, the baby never ended up yours; the hard-on didn't get satisfaction.

Nevertheless, whenever I'd begin my conceptualized remake of whatever car was before me, I would start at one end, usually aft, and move slowly, lovingly along the flanks, from bottom to top, all the way to the front. I wanted each piece, no matter how small or insignificant, to be perfectly shaped, balanced, and flow into adjacent body parts like Maine lobster into liquid butter.

Two additional criteria: the end result should look like it was going 80 mph while still parked on someone's driveway, and be so beautiful to behold that it would melt the most steadfast virgin as easily as immersing soft bread into hot soup. Sometimes the result of my redesign crusade would be spectacular and I'd ask myself why Detroit never got people like me to design their cars. As frequently, the passion behind the endeavor would be snuffed out by interruptions—homework, physical therapy, dinner time, the aches and pains of my stupid arthritis—sucking design inspiration into never-never land.

Even in those adolescent years, I wondered why big companies couldn't plainly see that crippled guys like me sitting in wheelchairs most of the day were able to *see* automobiles from a perspective that was fresh and more critical than most designers without physical disabilities.

Why? Well, first of all, I'd view them sitting down, not standing, and consequently my view contained almost as much of the underside of a vehicle as its top. I could see bumpers, kick panels, and wheel wells in more detail and more critically than someone just walking. The uniqueness of my design savvy sprang from somewhere deep within the passion-well that was integral to my soul, but filled to overflowing by my day-to-day limitations, frustrations unloaded on me by my disability.

My quest after design perfection undoubtedly stemmed from, partly, my need to overcompensate for what I thought was imperfect and/or lacking in me. By this time in my life, it was obvious that my growth would be permanently stunted and that I would end up being less than five feet tall. I soon developed this thing about my dick having to be bigger and better than the "average" dick so that, in my own eyes, I'd be as worthy of female affection as my ambulatory friends of normal height.

Likewise, I had this compulsion about wanting everything from the controls on a tabletop radio to those on an automobile's dashboard to work as smoothly, effortlessly as removing silk lingerie from a Latina in heat. So my quest for beauty and flawlessness was none other than an extension of Dickey-boy, just wanting to get laid. Uncultivated and simplistic as motivations go, but effective. A control freak with good taste?

One really good thing about living with a severe disability is that it forced me to learn all kinds of survival and coping skills. Everything I did throughout the day that required hands had to be done with malformed hands that were smaller and had a much weaker grasp than hands belonging to a kid without that physical disability. Adding to that the fact that my arms were short and couldn't straighten out at the elbow meant my overall reach was very limited.

Naturally, I quickly learned how to position the things I used often for easy access. Many times I'd modify stuff, such as the tools I used in making model cars and airplanes, to compensate for my lack of strength.

I used the workbench that Dad had built me to firmly hold the model I was working on, freeing both of my hands to use for cutting, assembling, gluing, or painting. I'd sometimes make the handles of knives, brushes, or other tools larger by wrapping them with adhesive or electrical tape. The more I did these things, the more adept I became at making things easier to use and positioning them for more convenient reach. I soon discovered that many of the modifications I did to accommodate my own needs frequently made things easier and better for most people too.

The bottom line was that if I ever intended to some day drive one of these beautiful, girl-capturing cars I loved designing, I'd better make sure that I could drive the damn thing too. Therefore, all of the car's controls had to be friendly to my limited physical capabilities. What existed at the time just wasn't good enough. Everything I could find or conjure up that would better respond to what I could do, physically, was, I decided, what good design was all about.

I became enamored with such things as the toggle switches on the dashboards of some European sports cars such as the Jaguar XKE. Why turn a funny misshaped knob when it's much easier to flick a switch? I already knew the answer, but at the time it didn't seem important to anyone but me. Nevertheless, I continued dreaming.

The coup-de-grace on the independence scale for me came in the celestial form of a limpid white, V-8 powered 1957 Thunderbird my Dad gave me for my seventeenth birthday. I wanted a real automobile. I ended up persuading my Dad on the idea; probably using that great sales ability which my brother-in-law Pete said I possessed. More *testa dura!*

Because of my four feet, five inch tall stature, the only way I could get into a car independently was to sit on the edge of the car seat and swing my legs in. The cars that were low enough to meet my butt height requirements included the Corvette, Thunderbird, and the newly imported French Citroen. My Dad didn't particularly like the Citroen and, because of its fiberglass body, neither one of us were enthused with the Corvette. The only modifications I had to make to the T-Bird to enable me to drive consisted of having a custom pillow made for my back and adding six-inch extensions to the brake and accelerator pedals.

In the high school parking lot strewn with heavy souped-up jalopies, my sleek, low, '57 T-Bird with a lift-off top, round side windows and chrome rims, was in a class by itself. Naturally, certain allowances were made for my disability. But it was a sexy car and fast. Its throaty, authoritative rumble drew admiring stares from the girls and had a humbling effect on the boys in their gravel-spraying hot rods.

I had to go through a special driver's training program, but I really learned to drive when I was thirteen, behind the wheel of a little electric car my Dad had designed for me.

Within less than two months after I first drove my T-Bird to school at the beginning of that fall semester, the owner of a manufacturer of swimming pool pumps and filters in competition with Jacuzzi bought his daughter, and senior classmate, a white T-Bird of her own. My parents, and especially my Mom, were somewhat miffed at this copycat one-upmanship of a fellow Bay Area entrepreneur.

This girl never shared any classes with me, so the only time I saw her was when I caught a glimpse of her in her T-Bird. I thought the entrepreneurial rivalry between our respective parents was ridiculous and actually preferred not being the only student with a T-Bird. As far as I was concerned, I didn't care if every kid at Acalanes High School had a T-Bird as long as I had mine and was travelin' down the road.

For better or worse, I took Latin my first two years of high school instead of a contemporary foreign language like French or Spanish. During my last two years of high school I switched to Spanish. "Mr. S.," a dark haired, well-groomed gentleman from Central America, who looked more like an Italian or Spanish movie director than a teacher, taught my Spanish class. The class was rather large and, because it was second-year Spanish, had a mixture of sophomores, juniors, and indecisive-about-their-future seniors like me.

Almost every girl in the class, except for one or two developmentally delayed eremites, thought Mr. S. to be handsome and charming. I learned some years after my high-school graduation that Mr. S was eventually let go because he had berthed his boat with a few too many of his female students.

Hormonal difficulties aside, Mr. S. was a very good Spanish teacher. He had the talent of bringing to life in a foreign language the everyday things teenagers are interested in, including music, sports, traveling, and important milestones like birthdays and graduating from high school. During one class, Mr. S. had each student give a brief, personal introduction in Spanish, stating one's birth date, place of birth, and desires, goals, or ambitions for the future.

"I'm called Julie and I was born here on April 22, 1944, and I just want to be happy," said the girl seated next to me in a musical Spanish voice. I turned to see who was speaking and saw a slender, but curvaceous female with ebony shoe-polish eyes, cascading hair, and vanilla skin. As Julie continued speaking in her lilting Spanish, my heart skipped as my eyes transfixed and drew into her delicate but petulant lips.

After school, I drove my buddy, Tom, home as I did every day since getting a car. Tom was legally blind and wore glasses that were about as thick as hunting binoculars. He had a wiry build and a shock of reddish-blond hair and was always fidgeting, rocking back and forth in his seat, and full of nervous energy. Tom was a voracious reader, Acalanes' in-house intellectual, and a treasured friend to this day.

Tom was insightful enough to know that I was still coming to terms with my own self worth and that I was miles away from becoming my own man. But he was fiercely determined to help me find my eventual destiny as much as I was committed to freeing Tom from the restraints imposed on him by his bad sight.

By the time we arrived at his house that day, poor Tom must have become thoroughly nauseous, hearing me talk about nothing but Julie from the time he got in the T-Bird. "Something tells me you really like this girl, Ken," said Tom as he got out of the car.

Yep, I sure think I do. "Bye, Tom, see ya' tomorrow."

Soon, the word spread among my other buddies about my apparent infatuation with Julie. After I had already been out with Julie a couple of times, one of the guys I knew casually came over to me and started talking to me about Julie. He said that Julie was "easy." I was still too insecure at the time to know to tell this bastard to keep his mouth shut and so I did the only logical thing: I said nothing. What a wimp I was.

Unfortunately, that son-of-a-bitch must have read my insecurities pretty well. His message did its number; reformulating in my brain the twisted notion that inferior, crippled Kenny might actually be permitted to mate with the likes of a secondhand, throwaway Julie. My old love for humanity kicked in once again. I respected people and I respected Julie and didn't want anyone badmouthing her. But I was torn because I still had too little respect for myself, and wondered how others could respect me.

Rather than focus on how wonderful Julie had been to me since we first met, the lyrical tenderness of our first kisses, and the fact that I was falling in love with her a little bit more each day, my love for her had been torn from its beauty, its innocence and tainted by society's worst taboos and fears.

I don't know why, but I never discussed this with Tom. Maybe my feelings of insecurity and lack of self worth went too deep, were too hurtful even to discuss with him. However, I felt that Tom was intuitively aware of some, if not all, of my inner battles. That was probably my biggest mistake: holding these emotions inside and not discussing them with Tom.

But I could not let Julie go. I wanted to love her, take her in my arms, and erase from my mind this daylight nightmare, making our love once again natural, pure. Several months later, Julie and I went for a drive through Sonoma's wine country with the Thunderbird Motor Club. Everyone stopped at the Mondavi Winery for a barbecue and wine tasting. Julie and I didn't drink, not because we were underage, we just didn't want to. After the barbecue, we got in the T-Bird and drove deep into the long, even rows of lush vineyards. We were far enough away from the winery to hear only the flittering of the grape leaves in the cooling breeze and serenading birds.

I held Julie's face in my hands like it was made of precious porcelain. She kissed me and began nibbling tenderly, alternating between my upper and lower lips. I reciprocated. Julie unbuttoned her blouse and removed her bra, revealing breasts that were like ripe pears. In my mouth she tasted of cream and honey and smelled of wild berries and grass after rain. She was panting. My erection was ferocious. I lay down across the seat and she saddled my thighs. As Julie started to remove the rest of her clothing, I reached up and begged her to stop.

The tapes had started playing in my brain. What if she became pregnant? How could I support this woman, any woman? Could I ever get a job? How could a cripple be worthy of such love? How could I be worthy of such love? Was I bad if I wanted to make love to her?

I was such a mess at that time. I just didn't feel ready to be self-supporting. I wanted to be my own man. I resented being taken care of by the family. I was denying myself a first sexual experience, but I didn't feel ready to be responsible for the consequences. I didn't feel capable. I was unsure if I would ever be capable. I had always been discouraged from trying to achieve. I wasn't afraid of trying; I just didn't feel there was much I could do in good conscience.

We left the winery in silence. Frustrated. Weeks later, I purchased condoms and tried again to consummate our love, but again pushed her away. My conscience proved to be stronger than my desires.

Then, several days later, almost as if fate wanted to punish me for being so indecisive and having such desires, I became ill with a high fever and boils on my thighs and groin. The next day I was hospitalized with an economy-sized relapse of my rheumatoid arthritis. A great deal more damage was done to my body. Even though I went through an intensive program of physical rehabilitation, I returned home from Providence hospital never again able to bathe and dress myself independently.

My sister Alba shared much of my travail during this period of my life. She knew my parents, my love of cars, my struggle for independence, and my weaknesses.

> Dad didn't let Kenny grow up like an invalid. If something was not available to him, Dad would make sure he got it. Like the car, made so he could drive it.
>
> I used to see him get mad at Dad, though. I didn't see much anger between the two. Though sometimes Kenny would get mad and throw books. Whenever Kenny got angry, everyone looked at it as Kenny being angry because of the way he was. There was always a lot of forgiving, compassion and love. I would even hear our parents say, "It's good to see him mad. He needs to get mad once in a while."

10

Dependent Forever!

Tsunami: A massive tidal wave produced by an underwater earthquake or volcanic eruption.

During the hospitalization when I was 18, one evening I decided I would make myself walk to the hospital chapel.

Ever since I put myself in the hands of Providence, the pain seemed to grow worse by the day, which meant little to me since I had spent most of my life in some degree of pain. The doctors told me that, by trying to do too much after my last surgery, I had put an extra strain on my already badly deteriorated cartilage. The first attack of arthritis destroyed most of the cartilage in my joints, leaving scar tissue which was strong enough to withstand some stress, although not as much as I gave it. They told me the second attack might weaken the joints to the point that I would never walk again, even with crutches. But arthritis is not the swiftest of diseases, so I was able to walk with great difficulty and pain to the hospital chapel.

In the hospital, I did not have to spend the usual two hours getting dressed. The endless hours of torturous exercises, the stretching of stiff tendons and strengthening of inadequate muscles was always accompanied by the painful grind of ruined joints. In the hospital, the "tricks" I had learned for getting shirtsleeves over arms weren't necessary. For the next several weeks, I would be wearing a hospital gown which, because of my deformities, was even more ill-fitting than most. The arms were too long, I could not reach the ties in the back which gaped open anyway, and the rest of it neatly dragged the ground, making me look like a poorly made hand puppet. If I could have seen myself in a mirror, I probably would have almost laughed.

When Julie came to visit me, she was completely unaware of what was happening to me and I did not attempt to explain. In those days, I thought if I discussed my physical problems or my fears with girls, I would seem less attractive to them. She was confused when I told her I thought it would be a good idea if we broke up. I was hoping beyond hope she would say no. It was a bit masochistic, saying to myself that I was not good enough.

I knew well what it was like to be dependent. Hadn't I spent the first half of my life being carried everywhere by my parents? It did not seem reasonable to me that a girlfriend would be glad to open doors for me, pick up things I dropped on the floor, or who knows, maybe even feed me. I didn't know what would be left of me after the virus was through gnawing away at me. If I could have a second attack at eighteen, why not a third attack at thirty? And with each attack, I would lose a little more function—perhaps a few degrees less mobility in my neck or maybe it would get my eyes. How could a woman depend upon me when I could not even depend upon myself?

It was like a slow-moving almost invisible tidal wave, engulfing me as I grasped a view of my future after my second major attack. My body was being broken down by a *deep earthquake* that made my hopes and dreams come tumbling down. I could see myself withdrawing from people.

Julie accepted my decree. If she was hurt, she did not show it. Perhaps she was out-martyring me but twenty-two years later when the subject of our breaking up came up again, she seemed to have no recollection of it. She was a free spirit and I loved her for it, but I wanted desperately to have her tell me she needed me, to tell me I was full of crap, that I was just feeling sorry for myself and, no, she would not let me roll over and play dead in the name of generosity. It was something she might have said and in those words. But she didn't.

I calculated it was between 200–300 feet from my room to the chapel, a distance that a few weeks before, I could have covered with effort, but little problem. In fact, for me to walk 200 feet would have been hardly worse than for the average teenager to run a brisk quarter-mile. Now things were different. Now 200 feet was a marathon. But in typical teenage macho fashion, maybe I had to see what I was made of.

Doctors were a lot more understanding back then. They understood how terrible suffering could be and how easy it was to alleviate it with medicine. After my second attack, they started giving me tranquilizers and Demerol, which they know now is a dangerous son-of-a-bitch. I was taking massive doses, not at first but later on.

When I was a tot, the doctors experimented on me with sulfa drugs, gold shots, cortisone and special serums. Now they were additionally trying out painkillers like Darvon and psychotropic drugs like chlorpromazine. The latter is an anti-psychotic drug that produces such side effects as nightmares, depression, impotence, confusion at night, and, ironically enough, even psychotic behavior if given to a person who isn't psychotic. I no longer remember why they chose that particular drug.

Chlorpromazine, better known by its trade name Thorazine, reacts dangerously with alcohol and, incidentally, with narcotics like Darvon. If I did not have enough cause to feel depressed about a second assault of arthritis, the prospect of being confined to a wheelchair the rest of my life and losing my first love, the drugs would make certain I did. I consoled myself with the thought that at least this was better than suffering pain. And if not, perhaps my care would make a contribution to medical science.

Ever since I was a child, I had a tendency toward slow, thoughtful planning, probably a result of having a severe mobility problem and having to frugally expend only as much energy as was absolutely necessary, for fear of overdrawing my limited reserve of physical strength. In fact, there is an old Italian proverb: "He who has no patience has nothing at all." But this made me quite different from others my age. This meant laying out my clothes and comb and toothbrush, each in its proper place, and putting things back exactly where they belonged. Most children are in the habit of leaving a large portion of their worldly goods on the floor, behind the couch, or wherever they happen to land.

If, even at the age of eight or nine, I had to exert the energy to collect toys from around the room, I would not have the strength left to play. Before I scooted my tricycle to the corner near our home, I had to consider whether or not I wanted to visit my friend that morning because I would not have the energy to do both.

Although I looked much younger than my years, I was always considered mature for my age because of the way I weighed several possibilities before making a decision and thought an idea through before speaking. When I did make a decision, people listened, even adults. And when I told Julie that we ought to break up, she probably assumed that I had thought about it from every angle and this was the best possible solution. She may also have believed me when I told her that we should not sleep together. What she did not see was that the hardest part for me was making a difficult decision. I was trying to think for both of us. I was too responsible, perhaps.

I often was so concerned with finding the best answer, and being fair to everyone involved, that, rather than take a step in the wrong direction, I would stop and agonize over the dilemma. This took more emotional and physical energy than making a hasty decision and dealing with whatever consequences came after.

The result was that it often unbalanced my energy budget, lowered my resistance, and invited illness.

I swung my legs over the side of the bed. My feet did not touch the floor. Abraham Lincoln, our tallest president was once asked how long a man's legs should be. He thought a minute and replied, "Long enough to reach the ground." My Dad always put it more colorfully, "Long enough to reach your butt."

I positioned my arms on the leather-covered, concave-shaped armrests of my crutches and eased off the stiff hospital bed. Because of my arthritis, short stature, limited strength, and range of motion, I found it harder to walk on smooth surfaces without losing my balance. Back in the 1950s and '60s, hospitals only had tile or linoleum floors and were never carpeted. In my present condition, if I slipped on the slick floor, I would not be able to get back up. If I fell and hospital personnel came to the rescue, they would tell me I should not have tried such a foolish stunt and send me back to my room. The thought was intolerable.

Maybe I was forcing myself to do this as punishment for not having the courage to accept what Julie offered or maybe it was just for not being able to make a real decision one way or the other. In any case, I needed to show myself I could still do something that took courage. And I needed to pray.

With considerable effort, I shifted most of my weight to the left side, threw my right crutch forward, and swung my right foot into position next to the crutch. It was sort of like the song, *Balling the Jack*, but not really!

I could hear the Rice Krispies squeak and sickening crackle of broken bits of cartilage in the joints of my hips and knees as I moved. I knew I could pray just as well in my own room, but I forced myself to put the left crutch forward and hoist my weight into position. Although I was eighteen, my body was the size of a six-year-old. The look of pain and anguish that was written on my face might have been that of a very old man who had lived through hard times. Breathing heavily, I noted I had progressed only about one foot.

As I was halfway through my next step, I realized that part of the reason I was so determined to walk to the chapel was anger. Why did I have to have arthritis? Why did I have to go through life short, twisted, crippled, and dependent upon normal people? All my friends seemed to want was money and new cars. I had a '57 T-bird and all the money I needed. I would gladly trade it all for a body that worked the way it was supposed to.

How could I enjoy what I had when I was in constant pain? Didn't those other guys realize how lucky they were to be able to take a girl to a movie and do a simple thing like put their arm around her? I would give anything even just for that. How much suffering was I supposed to endure? How much was too much?

My friend, Tom S., was already enrolled in junior college. Tom suffered, too, in his own way. He was almost blind, but his intellectual brilliance mostly compensated for his disability. His worst problem was that he tried to bury himself in his books because he believed all he really had was his mind. He was convinced no woman would have him, imagining that world was closed to him.

I wanted both worlds. I wanted and needed a woman desperately and I also wanted the chance to go to school. At least Tom could make it up the steps of the college and to the bathrooms without help. Without an attendant, almost all schools were closed to me. They might as well be posted NO HANDICAPPED PEOPLE ALLOWED. Without a certain degree of independence, I could not get through school and, without a university degree, I would never get a job, or so I thought.

Nobody could hire me, whether they wanted to or not. With my hands, I could never be a mechanic. I could not even pick up the tools. I could not be a janitor. I could not walk and carry anything at the same time. Assembly work? I could not even stand up long enough to do that. Even Tom did not appreciate how well off he was.

All my life, I saw how obsessed my father was with work and how obsessed both his parents were with raising a family. When my brother John went to work for the company, they were so proud. And when my sister, Alba, got married, they were very happy to see her start a family and anxious to have grandchildren. To me, it seemed these things assured my parents that they had raised their children well. What could I ever expect to do to win their approval?

I tried to be cheerful and positive, tried not to complain about the pain, and tried not to ask for help unless it was absolutely necessary. But that was not much of a contribution. How could they be proud of me if I spent the rest of my life living in their house, off their charity? My mother was an energetic woman and genuinely devoted to me. But she was no longer young and sometimes the strain of taking care of me showed. How easy would it be for her at sixty or seventy?

Everybody admired my father, even the people who hated him. They had to respect his drive and his will to succeed. When other businessmen were out playing golf on Sundays, Dad was working, making plans to expand overseas, thinking of ways to increase shareholders' dividends or how to use the talents of bright young men in the company. To Dad, Jacuzzi Brothers was more than a business. It was a means of expressing his generosity and love for the family. As long as he was alive, no Jacuzzi would have to pick oranges for a living. He would take care of them all.

And if one of the cousins or nephews were having trouble with his wife, Dad would try to straighten it out. He would keep the family together.

Candido was not universally loved, but he was respected. Everybody loved me, but who could respect me? Could anyone ever look up to me the way they looked up to my father? The earth did not tremble when I walked the way it did for my father. I did not make things happen. I was maintained like a finicky houseplant, existing, but doing little.

My slippers dragged softly on the linoleum as I laboriously made my way toward the hospital chapel. The temperature was kept a little high to accommodate some of the patients. Sweat ran from my forehead across my nose and chin. As it dried, it itched, but by this time, I was too weak to risk raising an arm to wipe it away for fear of losing my balance. The chapel door was now in sight. The dim glow from the altar cast a contrasting yellow into the corridor, lit by the harsh flickering fluorescent fixtures. A chill from exhaustion ran down my spine and I stopped to shiver.

A nurse bustled by in response to some patient's distress buzzer; a doctor, chart in hand, stalked past me without looking up. A night janitor, just come on duty, wheeled his mop bucket machine purposefully down the hall. Each of them had a job to do to keep the hospital organism functioning efficiently.

I thought if I decided to stay in bed tomorrow, it would not upset anybody's plans. Nobody was depending on me to do anything special the next day or the day after. Why was I beating my brains out? There was no work for me to do. There was physical therapy, of course. But it was not occupational therapy. As I pointed out earlier, the therapists were not concerned with a patient beyond extending certain physical capabilities. They wanted to get a patient up to the maximum efficiency with respect to the equipment they had to work with, and were not much concerned with anything beyond that. It would not make any difference to anybody if I didn't make it to the chapel. No one was expecting me anyway.

But then again, maybe Someone was.

I dragged myself forward again, first the right crutch, then the right foot, then the left crutch…It took me the better part of 20 minutes, but I had made it to the back row bench of the chapel. Prayer has always been a problem for me. It seemed so egocentric and selfish, asking God for anything. I did not know what to pray, so I said a Hail Mary and then I just asked God to help me survive, whatever the hell that might mean. I knew down deep that it was God who helped me bear up under adversities, not because of my disability but in spite of my disability. After that long walk, I was both exhausted and spent and didn't have the emotional strength left to desire anything. I asked a passing nurse to return me to my room with a wheelchair.

At 18, I lived through my last major "relapse" until near the end of 2003, when I was hospitalized the day before Thanksgiving for, among other things, a dangerously low sodium level and other electrolytes that had gone bonkers. But that is another story. With this 1959 siege, I had to reluctantly accept a settlement: even the occasional use of crutches for walking, except for very brief periods of regular exercise, was now verboten. I became a man mobile in a wheelchair, period! My ability to walk—and shower and dress myself, albeit a two plus hour project—was mysteriously gone, like my own youth. Unlike my own youth, some of my capabilities might come partially back down the road, but there was little rational promise of it. Juvenile Rheumatoid Arthritis tends to work in the opposite direction.

My sister Alba told me later the impact of those last hospitalizations on my father. She said: "There were a few more times in hospitals. I remember Dad just could not handle it. He always wanted everything perfect for you."

As I recovered from the relapse, I realized that I would be forever dependent. My hopes and dreams now shattered, I was suicidal and thought life wasn't worth living. I put a handful of pills in my mouth and was determined to do away with myself. To this day, I'm not sure why I spit them out. And sometimes, I wish I hadn't. But overall, I found a way to live with my "revised" self.

I was probably in no shape to start working toward my university degree but I could not endure the prospect of sitting around the house thinking about Julie and accomplishing nothing. I heard through the grapevine that she now had a new boyfriend. I had suggested she find someone else and she had done just that, never suspecting that the suggestion was a cry for help. I could hardly blame her for it, yet I could not help feeling sorry for myself. I had been expecting a miracle from Providence, hoping the rehabilitation would restore me to the same kind of independence I enjoyed before the second attack. But the doctors did not deliver.

Even if somehow I had gotten a complete return, it would have been foolhardy to attempt the same degree of physical activity, which, along with struggling over my relationship with Julie, led to my second attack. I began to think of more passive endeavors like investments. In 1958, the Brooklyn Dodgers and the New York Giants had moved to California, Los Angeles and San Francisco, respectively. In 1959, Willie Mayes became part of the Giant's roster, and almost instantly became a San Francisco icon; while the Dodgers went on to win the championship.

About this time, I had the good fortunate to meet and become friends with a young stockbroker who encouraged me to invest small amounts of money in the stock market. He was a great guy and during one visit, I shared my interest in broadcasting and asked about the prospects of investing in newer ventures in this industry. He became immediately animated and told me about a brand-new company that was about to burst upon the state of California.

The company was planning to string cables throughout the state, utilizing the existing telephone transmission network, to provide homes with television channels as well as a broad menu of unique programming. The company had already signed contracts with diverse entertainment venues like the San Francisco Opera Company, the Giants and Dodgers, and were lining up Hollywood studios for first-run movies.

The company had what would seem to be everything going for it, from the best in management talent to well-planned technology, diverse programming, and a bag full of financing. Definitely, the company was the equivalent of HBO, but more than a decade before HBO came into existence. But the company had not planned on the huge and well-organized opposition from theater owners. The media campaign did the trick and the company essentially was forced to close its doors before it even opened them. My $5,000, along with hundreds of thousands of dollars from other investors, went bye bye. Ah, my friends, the power of mass media disinformation and rumor-mongering; i.e., lying can never be underestimated.

So, I signed up for the fall semester at Diablo Valley College.

Dad did not want me to go to college. He felt that a university education was a waste of time because a lot of the people he dealt with, engineers and such, knew less than he did with his third grade education. This had something to do with his continuing battle with the people in the engineering department. He was right sometimes and he was wrong sometimes. But rather than admit he was wrong, he'd place the blame on the university degrees, which confirmed his doubts of their dubious value more often than not. What upset him the most about university training was how it seemed to stifle creativity and imagination in those who came out with degrees. To him, the world of work was the important thing. This attitude reduced my own options even more. It meant essentially that I had to compete on his level and, of course, I didn't have the physical means to do so.

The only university I knew of that was wheelchair accessible was the University of Illinois at Champaign Urbana, which I quickly ruled out because as an arthritic in a wheelchair, I did not think I would last long against the brutal midwestern winters. I might have investigated home study classes except that I was still looking for a miracle cure or solution that would get me out of the house and on my own. I didn't seek out the few existing progressive programs as much as I should have. If I had, I'd have been admitting there wasn't going to be any miracle. Sounds crazy to me now, but that's the way I saw things then.

Diablo Valley College was not then completely wheelchair accessible with its stairs and narrow bathroom stalls. But it did have one important thing going for it—it had Tom S. Tom had been my mentor in high school and was prepared to fill that role again in junior college. He understood my intense desire to get a university education. Tom also felt he would amount to nothing if he did not get a degree. But perhaps Tom's need was even greater since he had to work to make a living and never dared to develop a social life.

The plan was simple: I would have my push chair loaded into my car, and drive to the campus where Tom would meet me with the electric wheelchair which the college graciously allowed to be charged overnight in a storeroom. Since we took many of the same classes, Tom would also help me up carry books and maneuver obnoxious obstacles. Bathrooms remained a problem. There was just no way I could use the wall urinals in those bathrooms, so when I had to urinate, I would have to use a carry around urinal that Tom would hand to me.

In spite of all the logistic problems, I had a glorious time going to the college. I took four classes, including sociology. Part of the class involved sometimes rather heated debates of the kind that I had always studiously and wisely avoided at home, like a cat avoids water. However, when I discovered they could be a source of great intellectual stimulation as well as an instrument for strengthening one's power of conviction, I joined in, as John Kennedy used to say, with "vig-uh!"

Tom had always been a liberal and a champion of liberal causes and awakened this inclination in me. Neither of us had any love for the Republican candidate for president, Richard Nixon. We did not buy his plea of innocence concerning the bribery scandal and we certainly could not trust anybody who helped lead the witch hunt against communists along with that madman, Joe McCarthy. During the debate, one could see the instructor had his money on Nixon. When it came time for me to give my opinion, I surprised everybody by stating unequivocally that the next president of the United States would be John Kennedy. After the election, when I rolled into class, the instructor stopped what he was saying and made a low bow in my direction.

That semester, I made all A's and B's. Although I still felt inferior after my remission, and did not reach out to women for anything more than casual friendships, my confidence was building along with my physical strength. I began to wonder more and more what I would do with my life. In psychology class, I took an occupational aptitude test that showed I should be a banker, an artist or a priest. For some reason, this was not much help.

Shortly after I registered for the spring semester, I heard that Julie was pregnant. The father had run off. When her parents threw her out of the house, she came to me for help.

She had grown into a beautiful woman. But this only worried her parents more. They grew stricter with her, insisting she be home before ten o'clock every night. Years later, she explained, "They were more concerned with my being home at a certain time than about my welfare. When my mother threw me out, she was mostly worried about what her friends would think. Also, she was probably jealous of me. I guess all this made me even wilder."

When Julie came to see me she was almost frantic. That slow sarcastic wit and precociousness were gone. She was now just a scared little girl.

"You're the only one I can turn to!" she told me.

I needed her too. Now more than ever! By now I realized that part of the reason I got sick was that I needed her so badly that a sickness would not allow me to follow through with the relationship. At that time, I imagined that my emotional state had so much to do with my physical illness, that if I could remain calm, perhaps I could control my illness.

But things were not the same between us anymore. Our needs were different now and perhaps they always were. Of course, she could count on me. Weren't we still friends? I may not be worthy to be her lover, but I would try to be her friend. Also, I probably thought I deserved the punishment of helping her without touching her.

I negotiated with her mother, finally convincing her to take her daughter back for at least a few days. During this time, I arranged to have Julie admitted to the Florence Crittenden Home for unwed mothers in San Francisco. This suited Julie's mother just fine. With her daughter at what she called the "girl's club," her neighbors would not know of the terrible sin that was visited upon the family and the shame she suffered because of this wanton girl. After Julie had her baby, her mother refused to ever see her again. Maybe God forgave her, but Julie only would forgive her mother after many more years had passed.

I tried to shut Julie out of my mind. I was bitterly disappointed in her, first for not reading my mind and realizing that I didn't want our relationship to end. And second, I could not forgive her for becoming an object of pity. I wanted her to be stronger.

Barely into the second semester at Diablo Valley, I withdrew. Going to college alone (Tom was transferring to another college) was pushing my physical capabilities to the limit. The added strain of loneliness and seeing Julie in trouble was too much. I could feel myself draining quickly. The only thing for me to do was to check myself back into the hospital for more rehab and surgeries.

On April 12, 1961, Yuri Gagarin piloted Vostok I around the world in 108 minutes, running rings around Kennedy's Mercury space program. Even more than the launching of the satellite Sputnik, the fact that Russia produced the first manned space flight was a stunning blow to America's belief in its technical superiority. It was probably not until I read the story of the historic Russian flight that I began to doubt the United States had all the answers.

My father, a fiercely patriotic man, always believed there was no problem American science and technology could not solve, including my condition. He believed in inventions as some men believe in God. He had faith in the medical profession even though he had been fooled for many years by the hope for a miracle. He had so much faith that he could not understand how the medical profession could fail to cure me. But I was not sure anymore. At Providence Hospital all the king's horses and all the king's men could not put me back in the shape I was in before the second attack of arthritis.

It might have been partly due to my father's influence, but ever since I was very young, I had been very optimistic. I was always sure that a miraculous cure was just around the corner. However, with each operation, that possibility grew more remote. On one occasion, doctors cut my Achilles' tendons because they were shrinking up, making it impossible to put my foot flat on the floor. Maybe there was a way they could reattach them later when the time came. Another time, they cut my hip flexors so I could stand up straight. How would they reconnect my hip flexors? Then my wrists were fused to give them more strength. In a brilliant operation, Dr. J. D. Francis used a piece of a cow bone to fuse my left wrist. How could anybody reverse an operation like that? I began to realize that even if they ever did find a cure for arthritis, it would be too late for me. My body was mutilated. I would never walk again.

My old friend Kay Flynn was upset to see how my health was deteriorating but she didn't let me know. She also did not let me know that *she* was getting arthritis. In a few years, she would also be confined to a wheelchair. If I asked why she was limping, she would say, "It's the damned weather. Pay no attention to it."

With my knowledge of arthritis symptoms, I should have deduced what was wrong with Kay, but lately my thoughts had turned inward and became morbid.

Kay said, "He liked to scare me, sayin' he was goin' to die. He'd say, 'Flynn, we've all got to go sometime.'"

On one occasion, Kay was taking me for a walk and we happened to pass over a bridge. I had her stop my chair and said, "You know, I want to jump off this bridge."

"Such malarkey, Kenny! Let's be gettin' on. This wind is chillin' me to the bone."

"No, I think I will jump."

"Now just ya be waitin' a minute, Kenny. They aren't goin' to arrest you. They'll arrest me. Now mark my words. One day you'll meet somebody special and you'll be glad you did na' jump. Besides, I'd have ta throw ya in meself and I'm just not up to it today!"

I loved that woman. She was teaching me to love myself. The next day I put on my best clothes and diamond stud cuff links and asked Kay if she would take me to see my psychiatrist.

She said, "Kenny, I would na' go to those bastards. That's ridiculous."

I said, "Well, we'll go out and have dinner then."

Kay had lived in various stages of poverty all her life and, suspecting that my idea of a nice dinner would be an extravagant sumptuous affair, I guess she began to feel a bit uneasy.

"Not necessarily, Kenny. I don't want you spendin' all yer money on me."

"I know you, Flynn. You don't eat that much. Don't worry; I'll save enough for cab fare. Anyway, I promised you, so don't say no."

Kay told me later, "At this expensive restaurant all through the meal, I noticed you kept lookin' across the street. I knew yer every flutter by this time. Somethin' was up."

I said, "You know what? That place across the street! I've always wanted to go there."

Somehow, Kay failed to notice the neon lights above the establishment flashing: GIRLS, GIRLS, GIRLS. She did think it was odd that the windows were painted over but it was not until she stepped inside that she realized that I had dragged her into a striptease parlor.

"Now, listen," she said, "You've known about this place all along, haven't ye?"

I shrugged innocently. I knew she was the right person to accompany me to a den of iniquity safely.

She said, "Of course, I went in with ye. I could na' deny ya anythin'. It meant so much to ye."

A cloud of thick, gray smoke had settled on the predominantly male audience like a fog bank. It made rings around the footlights of the stage where a remarkably fit young woman was going through her bumps and grinds. I ordered a Martini and Kay, in keeping with her vow of abstinence from liquor, had a plain club soda.

We watched the show with enthusiasm, commenting on the relative merits of the performers. But after two or three drinks, all the girls reminded me of Julie and I suggested to Kay that it was time to head back. I suppose I wasn't the lounge lizard type. But, even so, as we were leaving, Kay said, "You know, Kenny, I bet ya got more out of this than you'd be getting' out of yer damned psychiatrist."

Perhaps she was right. I had wanted to lose myself for a while in the booze and the bacchanalian atmosphere but it only weakened my defenses and heightened my loneliness. I tried not to think about it, but my thoughts always returned to the same conclusion: if I had been "normal," Julie would never have left me and gotten in trouble. Now I was alone again with my futile desire for human contact. Logically, I felt there was no point in trying anymore.

Nevertheless, I showed up for physical therapy three times a week to see what could be done with what I had. Although I was beginning to resign myself to my condition, I could not accept the idea of being almost totally dependent upon other people. I wanted to be able to transfer from my bed to the wheelchair, but I simply did not have the strength. The orderly who usually helped me transfer on the therapy days was an amiable guy in his late forties. I did not know him well, but I was shocked to hear the morning after my therapy session that the orderly had suffered a heart attack.

I felt very guilty that I had caused the extra strain on his heart. They tried to explain to me it wasn't my fault, but I was convinced it happened because of me. I blamed myself for the orderly's heart attack, I blamed myself for not being able to get through school and I even blamed myself for Julie's problems. If I had stuck by her instead of playing the martyr, she would not have had to look for anybody else.

My sister, Alba, worked with the Florence Crittenden Home and kept me posted on how Julie was doing, since I was not allowed to visit the home. In fact,

Alba had arranged to throw a party for the girls at the house in Lafayette. Of course, I went.

As promised, I attended the Florence Crittenden party honoring the successful graduates of unwed motherhood. It was a very tasteful reception complete with tight security. Alba held it at our Jacuzzi home where the high fence provided a suitable degree of anonymity for the girls, most of whom were from "good" families and wanted to celebrate in private the end of their quarantine from "nice" society.

They were nervous and giggling. To look at them, you would think it was a debutante tea. And in a sense, that is what it was. It was a rite of passage, introducing young women into society, in this case, for a second time. This was to be their second chance to make a go of it within the rules of polite society. Since they all gave up their babies for adoption, no one need ever know of their transgression. This time, each of them could find a husband, raise a family, and be a credit to their parents instead of an embarrassment. I understood this ritual very well. I had reappeared into society several times, each time as a slightly different person.

I spotted Julie right away. She was off by herself, holding a cup of red punch. She saw me too, but made no move. I talked to Alba for a while and introduced myself to some of the girls to show Julie I was not as desperate to see her as she might have felt I was. In fact, I had begun to find a new role in life for myself. I wanted to make other people happy, and if I didn't always get what I wanted, so what!

Finally, I pointed my electric wheelchair in her direction, hummed up to her and offered to shake hands. I had to use my left hand since my right was still in a cast. Her slender hand engulfed mine like a child's and, as she withdrew it, I saw on her wrist the silver bracelet I have given her long ago engraved, "In Love For Life." Was this a sign that she still wanted me? We had both been taken down a notch since our high school romance, both too weather-beaten for puppy love. But when I looked into her eyes, there was sadness and confusion where once there had been vitality and defiance. She needed my help, but she had no room for my love. So my new role was confirmed: be a friend and helper.

She depended upon me as a friend, but she made no romantic overtures. That also confirmed in my mind that I was no longer worthy to make romantic overtures either. Ever since then, with women, it's always been more or less the same: I wanted them to make the initial move and it usually just didn't happen.

Months later during a return surgery sojourn, my window at Santa Rosa Memorial looked out onto a construction site where the hospital was building a new cardiac wing. I was seeing these guys working outdoors, taking off their shirts because it was hot. I remember being envious of them out there working. These carpenters and bricklayers were getting the sun and the nurses were ogling them. I'd hear comments like, "That guy's really cute!" I remember feeling that I'd like to be in that position. I thought it would be wonderful to have women lusting after me but probably equally wonderful to be useful, doing some kind of work.

While in the hospital in Santa Rosa, I read a lot. I was sitting upright on the edge of my bed, before me a book-strewn tray table. The torso of my four foot, four inch body was bowed over, elbows bent, forearms resting on it, mind obsessed with the words leaping out at me from James Baldwin's *A Fire Next Time*.

As I read, my arthritic and pain-racked body and soul became one with the black protagonist's blazing love and resentful hate for the white woman he was making love to. His unrestrained echoing cry from the New York slum apartment balcony where this irregular pair were coupling sent a river of lava flowing through me, flushing my face, burning my brain, turning my penis to stone, fogging over the white sheets and walls surrounding me.

A gentle touch to my shoulder jarred me back to the disinfectant-scented, asexual room that had been home for over four months. Barely moving, I glanced up and saw Sarah, the reserved, fragile nurse who recently started working graveyard. She was only about five feet tall and unassumingly pretty. She was about ten years older and the ring on her left hand warned me not to get too close. But she had been friendly and I was lonely so I had seen no harm in her coming to visit me some evenings.

It must already be well past eleven, I thought. Her raven eyes captured me, as they did from when I first saw her, but their usual crystalline sparkle was obscured, now sooty and melancholy.

Sarah moved the tray table over slightly, and stood almost directly in front of me. She took my left hand with her right one, reminded me that I needed sleep and asked if I required pain medication. As the word *pain* escaped from her exquisite lips, the jagged razor blades dancing in the arthritis-consumed joints of my shoulders, knees, and hips became magnified along with the relentless, aching harshness in my groin. The delicate rise and fall of Sarah's small, firm breasts as she spoke sent a second fierce dagger into my core.

She took a step and moved nearer. We were now inches apart, close enough for me to feel Sarah's warm breath on my chest. My autonomic reflexes succumbed to the crossbred pain of my joints, loneliness, and lust as my gaze avoided her, tears welling in my eyes.

At that instant, Sarah began to softly cry and speak in a halting whisper. Her words came hurtfully, remorsefully without pause. Sarah blurted out she was having a female surgical procedure tomorrow, and feared her husband's love, which had never been profound, would now disintegrate into nothingness. I realized how young women felt as vulnerable about their ability to interest men as I felt about my ability to interest women. Sarah said her femininity and sensuality felt as if they were vanishing and that she was afraid. Tears held back began their silent, ceaseless path down my face as her pain and my desire were drawn together.

I began to understand something more about these young women who gave themselves to their patients in nursing. They had a search for acceptance as strong as my own and that was probably why they devoted themselves to such a difficult profession. If they helped people live, surely they would be loved. I could understand that feeling because I shared the wish to help others and then surely I would be loved. I understood her—I was like her—and she wanted something from me.

Although I was in my early twenties and inexperienced, facing a beautiful woman at least ten years my senior, instinct born from some unknown source—perhaps the torment of living so long with a pain-racked body that also kept women my age at a distance—led me to pull Sarah towards me until air could no longer flow between us. We kissed, at first as tentatively as baby sparrows, then with the ferocity of giving birth in the midst of war. Sarah and I transformed into banyan tree, branches becoming roots becoming branches. We embraced, kissed, and held onto each other, my hand clasping her breast, her hand wrenching my chafing manhood, as life is held onto by the living when surrounded by sorrow and death.

Releasing her grip on me, Sarah began unbuttoning her uniform, revealing a body soft as ripe nectarine, heady as new wine. Everything was reeling, Sarah, me, the bed, the room and our inseparable, despairing heat. A chintzy noise suddenly violated our space and time, a crackling static, then the twice-repeated announcement: *code blue in ER, code blue in ER.*

Sarah, still flushed and panting, sprinted from the room, buttoning her uniform with one hand, blowing me a furtive kiss with the other. My desire to tunnel deep inside Sarah's perfection and become one with her surged through the three floors above and into the stratosphere. The ravishing pain of plummeting through shattering glass tortured my anus, testicles, and now scalding, cast-steel penis begging for release. Then the fog of despair draped me, making release hateful, reading futile, and mating me once again to loneliness.

I gradually recovered, only to come back again to the family cocoon where family arguments were consuming everyone.

In Julie's case, I thought I held back because we weren't married. My lack of courage about sex made me feel bad about my inability to take a risk. As a child, I was always encouraged to do the best I could but not to venture out too far.

Sex was just one example of inhibiting my natural urges. In addition, I believed I was too old to go back to school at 21. Tom S. would be leaving for Chico State the following semester so there would be nobody left at DVC that I knew and nobody to help me with my wheelchair. But I was hungry for learning and while at Santa Rosa, immersed myself in literature of all kinds, including Zen, Alan Watts, *The Thirteenth Apostle* and Henry Miller, who was considered pretty racy back then.

One day, one of the nuns happened to see the stack of books piled on my bedside table. She began surveying the titles until she came upon Henry Miller's *Tropic of Cancer*. She looked up, a little embarrassed, and said, "My, you read a variety of books!"

Even the nun was not immune. During my stay at the hospital, a young priest came to work there. He was a long-haired 60s radical and was very good-looking. Every time he walked by, the nuns looked up and the nurses sighed, "What a shame he's a priest!"

According to my occupational aptitude test, I would make a good priest. If only it were so. Sometimes I even felt like a priest, celibate, self-denying, and penitent.

One thing that helped me at the time was my wonderful car, the source of my independence. I had loved my white Thunderbird convertible and drove it, drove it, and drove it. It was a beauty. Then I traded it in for a newer model, a red Thunderbird. It was a nice car and of a new series but it didn't compare with the older, white Thunderbird, the white horse that I hoped to use to transport a damsel to my castle.

At that time in 1962, I remember the football season. I had spent a day in the push-button comforts of my parents' home, where I was "still living at 21," as I used to remind myself. Except for the housekeeper-aide who prepared my dinner, I was very much alone. It was late afternoon and I'd been watching the Cal-Stanford game on TV.

I waited a minute or two to watch the crowd reactions to victory as the cameras panned over a frieze of ecstatic faces, half hidden by clapping hands and swirling flags. There was an overlay of band music, trumpeting the winning college anthem. The crowd began to separate itself, and for a few seconds, the camera concentrated on the faces and forms of some very pretty cheerleaders. They left the stadium with men they must have chosen to match their own good looks and bodies.

I imagined the most incredible destinations for the chicks that were departing the stadium. On a tide of laughter, some would spill into the celebration rituals awaiting them in fraternity houses. Others would celebrate in other ways. I concluded that the tall girl with the blond, French braids and the small, but firm breasts would disdain the beer and buffet of a fraternity house.

Every man from every generation has seen a girl just like the one I saw at the televised football game. The person who wrote *The Sweetheart of Sigma Chi* must have known a girl like the one I was watching on television. "The blue of her eyes and the gold of her hair…" Or, the guy who created the movie "10." I turned off the television and thought about her.

If she were with me, instead of that jerk she walked off the football field with, I certainly wouldn't take her to a lousy frat house. We'd close out the day at this perfect beach I know about one-half hour drive north of San Francisco. I would serve her a picnic banquet of fresh crab, Italian cheeses, sourdough bread, and a fine California Merlot. I would pour the wine, seasoned to the colors of October in the valley of St. Helena. Then down between the white knees of sand dunes, I would be fully accepted…the cosmic lover of the television girl.

It was a long drop from this flight of fancy down to reality. I took the measure of where I was against the bounding life of the collegians of my own age. I was crowded back into my familiar corner of longing and anger until I came up with a plan.

I decided I was not going back to the life I'd been living. It was 1962 when I was released from Santa Rosa. Like a chronic criminal who just can't seem to learn his lesson, I was always going back to "prison." I kept landing back in the hospital, getting rehabilitated and turned loose for another try at the real world. The real world, in which things are accomplished and money is earned, the world in which C.J. was one of the ranking officers, did not invite me to join. And like the criminal newly released from prison, I was a marked man whom society maintained, but at arm's length, not wishing to have its weaknesses on display.

Yes, like Pinocchio, I had been created by Candido, my father, or Gepetto, the puppet maker. But I was not yet a real boy. I was wooden and stiff and could break limbs too easily. I wanted to be a guy of flesh and blood, like other guys. So what if I got hurt. That would be nothing new. But I had to break away from

Gepetto and find some friends. I had to leave my maker. Sure, I might leave but I was brought up too morally to stray very far. If I told a lie, people could tell it somehow. Maybe it was my nose! But I had to find my own new life. I had to remake myself still again.

11

The Disability "Cause"

Whirlpool: Water that begins with gentle swirling, caused by two meeting currents, which oscillates forming a central vacuum/eddy or turbulence until it collapses.

I had a plan. In fact, I had dozens of plans. I wanted to get involved with other people and do something productive. But I first got involved with a radio station to be run by people with disabilities.

The idea for this radio station concept started jelling in me sometime during my early mid-teens. It was during this time that my Dad purchased a rather decent stereo console and tape recorder made by Ampex. Ampex has an interesting history. It seems as though a GI returning from his stint in Germany during World War II went to see a famous crooner of the day, Bing Crosby, carrying with him a little gadget garnered from the spoils of war, the tape recorder.

Bing, ladies man and crooner extraordinaire, never got completely over his timidity and stage fright, even when recording a song for a record he was making. In fact, good old Bing was notorious for imbibing more than a few stiff ones before going on stage. With the tape recorder, however, he could now record a song and splice in retakes, should it become necessary. Bing had the savvy to realize that this little recording gadget could revolutionize the music industry, and Ampex was born.

My little 8-inch reel-to-reel Ampex recorder enabled me, assisted mostly by my buddy, Tom, to make rather good recordings of our favorite music tracks on LPs to audiotapes. A couple of years later, still in my teens, I designed a stereo system for our family room that filled one entire wall with great stuff, and made it maximally accessible to not only me but my nearly blind-as-a-bat friend, Tom. We could easily have recorded the Beatles right there on the premises, and with enough quality to produce a master recording that could stamp out LPs in the tens of thousands.

Besides recording music for my own pleasure as well as my close friends, I also made tapes for my parents who, like my grandparents, loved music and loved to dance. Naturally, they loved Italian music, including the latest pop songs from Italy, especially those that were big hits at the San Remo Festival each year.

And, because many of our housekeepers were Hispanics, and we had manufacturing operations in Mexico, I also became aware of some of the more popular Mexican music. So, I started recording and mixing all this stuff together on tapes that sounded not only professional in terms of quality, but also moved your Mojo forward at a nice rhythmic pace. About that time, I was 17 or 18, and my Mojo was also being prompted by the fairer sex and, specifically, Julie, a little light went on in my brain and the idea was born for a new concept in pop music for the FM stereo radio market: International Pops.

Although I had no specific training in the radio business, I soon developed a complete plan for a new kind of radio station featuring popular music from all over the world. The two people who helped the most in traveling around the Bay Area to gobble up information for this radio station were none other than my friend, Tom, and my nephew, Steve, my sister Alba's oldest son. I also visited big radio stations in San Francisco like KSFO and met my favorite deejays, like Don Sherwood. I saw their studios, record collections and transmission equipment.

I knew that I wanted MY radio station to be clear as crystal, which meant really good quality FM transmission antennas like those made at the time by RCA. FM transmission, unlike AM transmission, is line of sight. If there is something in the way like a big building or mountain, the FM signal will likely be interrupted or cause the signal to drift. To alleviate drifting signals, I wanted to operate at 100% of the transmission power and antenna height allowable by the FCC for that particular station frequency in our area. For the station I had zeroed in on in Walnut Creek, California, KDFM, at 91.1 of the FM dial; that meant I could take the station to 3,000 watts, with the possibility of upping it later to 10,000 watts, more than enough to cover the Contra Costa County and environs.

I designed a studio that would be completely accessible to and operable by persons with disabilities. Additionally, no one in the U.S. had ever launched a truly international pops station, and what better place to do so than in the urbane, sophisticated, multicultural San Francisco Bay Area? Pat, pat! That's me, patting myself on the back.

The music programmed during a typical hour, could have included the following songs: *In the Wee Small Hours, Around Midnight, Mr. Sandman, Earth Angel, Amami Se Vuoi, Got My Mojo Workin', Johnny B. Goode, La Bamba, Heartbreak Hotel, Shake Rattle and Roll, Take Five, Vaya Con Dios, Banana Boat (Day-O), I Got a Woman, Fever, Corde della Mia Chitarra, Sweeter Than Wine, Mack the Knife, Tequila, Kind of Blue, Chantilly Lacy, What'd I Say, Wake Up Little Suzie, Volare, Patricia, Chances Are, Django, Misty, Desafinado, Maybellene, Summertime Blues, Splish Splash, Bird Dog....*

Well, I think you get the idea. By the way, in case you are wondering why there is nothing from the Beatles, it's because they didn't really come together as a group until the early 1960s. In addition to the multinational pop music, I intended to insert throughout the day, spicy tidbits of international events, gossip, politics, latest fashions, weather and happenings such as music, food and wine festivals. It seemed to me that Bay Area ethnic restaurants, clubs, and upscale stores would not be all that difficult to enlist as sponsors and advertisers.

But, alas, my Dad turned down my request to finance the purchase price of $40,000 for KDFM, and my broadcasting enterprise came to an abrupt end before it even began. However, the dream died slowly and I attempted to resurrect it several times during my twenties. It was a bit ironic that some nine years later, in 1968, when I took my first trip to Europe, I accidentally tuned into, on the Volkswagen's radio, *Radio Monte Carlo*. I soon learned that this full wattage station broadcasting from Monaco featured European (multinational) top 40 tunes and was one of the most popular radio stations in Western Europe.

As I write this, no one has ever replicated my radio station concept in the United States. And today, with Neanderthal companies like Clear Channel near monopoly on today's North American radio broadcasting, the chances of a real top international station hitting the airwaves is practically nonexistent. But who knows, maybe someday on the latest broadcast venue, satellite radio, someone with guts will give it a try. Maybe Howard Stern...?

When I approached my father with the idea, he was skeptical. C.J. knew all about the pump business but he couldn't see much profit potential in an FM radio station. And besides I was being taken care of when he helped draw up the contract stipulating that I got a percentage of all *whirlpool* sales. The whole idea of creating a family business was to insure that all the men in the family would have a job if they wanted it, and all the women would be provided for.

My father reasoned that I would not be expected to work. Even though I went to a lot of trouble researching my idea for a radio station. In the end, it sounded to Dad more like a dream than a business proposition.

I understood my Dad's point of view. What did I know about business? I had no experience.

The station would have been an excellent outlet for my energies and an appropriate medium to touch all those I wanted to reach. If only I could get my chance! Then they would all respect me for my dedication and love me for my humanitarianism, not to mention creativity at developing a new, hip multinational radio format. Actually it was not the radio station itself that I so desperately needed; it was the contact with people. It was experience and respect as a doer in a world of doers.

The next year was the last year of the Kennedy administration, 1963. It found me a 22 year-old, still soaking in the whirlpool bath at my parent's luxurious estate in Lafayette, California. Deeply into James Bond books and world news, I drank martinis (which, I later learned, did not mix well with my meds, among them, Darvon), smoked cigarettes and followed avidly the movements of Martin Luther King and George "Segregation Forever" Wallace. It was my macho period. As I loosened and stretched my reluctant limbs, I thought that surely beyond the protective perimeters of my father's house a new world might unfold for me. With my current physical therapist, Bob M., I discussed the war in Viet Nam and the race riots in between therapy exercises.

He always said I was "very hip to what was happening." He'd see me and say; "Hey, Ken, what's going on?" and I'd tell him what I knew.

When we first met, Bob was teaching biology at Berkeley High, and moonlighting as a physical therapist. Three days a week, he would buzz over in his little Lambretta, sometimes coming a few minutes early to get in a hydro massage himself before going to work on me.

I learned that he used to tell people about our work. He'd say,

> That's a gorgeous setup! There was a swimming pool where we worked. It was an indoor pool, one of the first pools with a built-in Jacuzzi, with jets set in different levels of the wall. The pool had beautiful tile around it. They are a Catholic family and around the pool were statuettes of the saints. The pool had a little water-filled corridor with a Plexiglas partition, which you could open to go into the outside pool. They also had designed for Ken a hydraulic lift with a chair. Ken could go right up to the lift in his electric wheelchair and move himself into the chair that had a lever he could pull to let himself into the pool. Dr. No would have been envious.

Each session, we worked on strengthening and stretching exercises, loosening hamstrings and Achilles' tendons in the attempt to get me back on an ambulatory basis. The sessions took place in the pool because the buoyancy from the water allowed me to walk around in the pool without bearing my full weight on the arthritic joints, and without causing quite so much pain.

He'd have me straighten my knee and he'd give resistance to the lower leg. One advantage of having a therapist for a long time is that he gets a feel for how his patient is doing. "I can tell it's a good day if you're getting stronger," Bob used to say.

Throughout the session, my shoulder or knee would crackle and crunch horribly. Bob explained, "This sometimes happens with arthritics. Little bits of cartilaginous material get trapped in some of the capsules around the joints and tend to rattle around a bit."

I always called this my "joint mice." Having "joint mice" was at least better than having to wear a turtle shell, which was what Russ B.'s respirator looked like. I met Russ while conducting research on the radio station project.

My project sounded like a good idea to Russ, who was also interested in working with mass media, but he did not have much time to put into the project because running a service company for respirators kept him pretty busy. From a very early age, Russ worked almost continuously. He was always a compulsive achiever. People who know his story might think that was his undoing. He believes that trait saved his life.

During his late teens, Russ was working six days a week, raising hell all night and racing boats on the weekends. Even with all his energy, Russ admitted he had been tired most of the time. But he was young and what else was there to do but make money and have fun? By the time he was twenty he had won enough races to gain quite a reputation within the local racing circuit.

Russ said, "My racing sponsors were real good to me. They even dedicated a couple of races to me to help pay for my hospital bills when I came down with polio."

Part of that expense involved a forty-pound Fiberglass respirator that looks like a turtle shell with rubber at the hinges. The motorized contraption fit over the chest, contracting and expanding the chest cavity.

He said, "I'm totally paralyzed. I can't breathe on my own. This device makes your diaphragm bring air into your nose and mouth just like if there was somebody with a handle on your diaphragm pumping up and down."

Sometimes, such as when he was lying in bed, Russ was obliged to get additional air by blowing into a plastic tube, which further expanded the shell. I asked him, "What happens when you sleep?"

"Same thing." says Russ, "Sometimes I wake up thinking I'm chewing on a taco, but it's just the mouthpiece."

Many people in Russ' position would have considered that life was over and waited to die. But Russ wanted to get back to work. So in 1956 he started a respirator service company that he could operate over the telephone.

I was impressed with Russ' casual courage and the way he turned his disability into an asset for getting a new job. I knew there were not many people like Russ who are always ready to take on the world no matter what the terms. How many other people with disabilities were there who wanted to participate in the mainstream of life only to be blocked by stairs, and narrow doorways and curbs? If Russ could do this much against these odds, how much could he and others do with a little cooperation?

Russ later married one of his attendants, a Catholic nun who escaped Castro's Cuba, but his condition was just too hard on his wife. He said,

> It takes a special kind of person to be married to a someone with a major disability—both in understanding the needs, waiting on them, and what they have to do sexually. They have to do all the work, especially with people like myself. We're normal people, but we just don't move around. There's a mate for everybody. But you have to get out. They're not coming to you, that's for damn sure. You can't take your spouse for granted or make them think you're taking them for granted.

The next person I tried to enlist for my cause was Joanne W. When I met her, she was in County Hospital in Oakland getting her legs straightened. It was kind of nice to hear how she described our relationship to others years later. She recalled, "All the time I had gone to the therapy center, I'd never met Ken. I'd heard of him. He went to visit a friend of mine and she sent him over to cheer me up. I had this wonderful cast on—from the ankles to the thighs. Both legs were absolutely straight."

Joanne contracted arthritis at the age of fifteen. Seventeen years later, her tendons had shrunk so severely that she could no longer walk with crutches. To correct this problem, they made an incision behind each knee, wedging small pieces of wood behind the joints for the purpose of gradually stretching out the tendons and muscles. It was an effective treatment but it would just as effectively have brought confession from victims of the Spanish Inquisition. The worst of it was that there was nobody to talk to at County Hospital and the overworked staff was surly and careless.

She described our first outing years later. "Ken brought me a white orchid and his favorite candy, Almond Roca. That was the first time I ever had those. He came driving up in his red Thunderbird and said we were going to his house for dinner."

She quickly secured a pass from the hospital and with the help of a hospital attendant and my aide who spoke almost no English; we managed to pack Joanne, stiff legs and all, into the Thunderbird, which was no small task. Once this was accomplished, I glanced up at the sky and announced, "Looks like it's getting cloudy. I don't think I want to drive back here tonight. Why don't you just stay overnight?"

Joanne didn't know who this presumptuous little guy in the electric wheelchair was but she thought about the irritable staff in the hospital and about the prospect of being hoisted out of the car again and said, "All right, why not?"

The nurse ran back in and packed an overnight case.

Lo and behold, when we arrived, there were no parents at my house! Only a cook and a housekeeper who spoke only Spanish! She thought she'd been set up! It was so funny. Here she was with cement legs and I was tooling around in my electric wheelchair with my funny smile. We had a great dinner.

That evening the servants helped Joanne get ready for bed. She heard a faint knock at the door, and then the sprightly buzz of my wheelchair.

She asked, "What are you doing here?" We chatted a few minutes. I could tell she thought I was young and really cute. Finally, I said. "Good night."

The next day, we ate lunch by the pool. We had hamburgers and champagne. Since the clouds had all vanished from the night before, I drove her safely back to the hospital in the sunshine. I was coming to a new attitude about life. I wanted to bring some zest into my life by making a friend, falling in love, painting a picture, writing a poem, expressing my inner self, speaking sweetly, giving a party, taking someone out for a good time. Being a helper was my goal.

Others told me later how she described that experience. "Going to Ken's was the first time I had gone out from County. It reminded me that I was still a human being and could do normal things."

Of course, that was just what I wanted Joanne to realize!

What Joanne still could not do after her operation was secretarial work. That was just too physically demanding and she did not want to risk a relapse by becoming run down. Like me, she felt her best chance to enter the mainstream was to get a university degree. And like me, she was told that the only school that could accommodate her physical limitations was the University of Illinois where the cold weather and the cost of out-of-state tuition were prohibitive. At the age of thirty-two, she had never presumed to train for a career.

"Long-range planning has not been part of my life," she said.

She was reluctant to get married and have somebody depend on her because, at seventeen, when she asked her doctor what the prognosis for her arthritis was, he said, "In ten years, your arthritis will either be burned out and there will be some crippling you'll have to cope with, or you'll be dead."

She told me, "I've lived with that. It set me up for an existential attitude toward life. Experience has always been a high priority. Just living. If you're not sure there is going to be a tomorrow, you live from day to day. It's like being driven, like you have to do everything today. I go back to that day when you and I had champagne and burgers by the pool. We really enjoyed ourselves. We didn't do anything in particular. We talked. We were there together. It was nice. The sky was blue and the plants around us were growing, the whirlpool gurgling away. We sat there just enjoying it."

Unlike me, Joanne was not independently wealthy, but still she was under no pressure to get an education and a well-paying job. Social security benefits would keep her going. Did she want to work?

"Good Lord! I'm an American. Yes! When I was able to work and earn my own rent and pay my own bills, most of the time there wouldn't be much left at the end of the month, if anything. I didn't make a lot but it was such a sense of satisfaction to be contributing something and making my own way."

This sounded like something Russ might say if he ever took the time to stop and think about it. The difference between them was that after the 21 days when the polio virus ravaged his body, it disappeared leaving him paralyzed but essentially healthy. Joanne and I would have arthritis for life and any over-exertion was an invitation to a relapse. Of course, as I learned later, post-polio syndrome isn't milk and honey, either.

It was gratifying to know that I was not alone in my struggle for independence. There were a few heroes like Russ who managed to stay out of the hospital and make a contribution. There were many more, not so lucky or so brave, wasting away in nursing homes, or encumbering their parents. The more I thought about it, the angrier I became. Modern society could find ways of keeping people like me alive but after that, it turned its back on them. Eskimos who set their crippled fellow citizens loose on an ice floe seemed more humane.

With my money and family behind me, I was in a better position to do something about the situation than most people. President Kennedy was doing what he could for the blacks and other oppressed minorities. He had endured life-threatening diseases as a young man and had adopted a philosophy of living for the moment because he might be dead tomorrow. And, of course, he soon would be—from an assassin's bullet.

Why couldn't Kennedy be persuaded to help people with disabilities? The time of the 60's was becoming the decade of activism. Black people would no longer have to apologize for their existence and with a little luck and a lot of work, neither would people with disabilities.

I had a new idea. Bob, Russ, and Joanne were all interested in the rights of people with disabilities. They liked and respected me for what I was. Just having them around made me feel stronger and more competent. Why not gather them together to form an organization to promote the rights of those with disabilities? Together, we could try to give those with disabilities a sense of solidarity and a feeling of having some control over their lives and our lives. Whenever I attempted to take command of my life, it seemed to go out of control. But my friends could help me change all that. They would stick by me. They would not let me down, nor I them. But that plan could only go so far without help.

I wanted to create a foundation with the principal purpose of providing greater access to people with disabilities to government and public buildings and services, but especially schools at all levels—not unlike many of the provisions eventually set down by the Rehabilitation Act of the 1970s and the 1990 Americans with Disabilities Act, "ADA." Getting around and about, becoming a participating member of the general public, instead of isolated at home or an institution, was vital to ensuring one's integration into society and personal freedom.

Meanwhile, I developed another rather small plan for an outing with my niece. Candy, named after Candido, had, even in high school, some of my father's savvy, her mother Alba's motherliness, and a passion for experience all her own. Of all the grandchildren, she was most like my Mom, Inez. Candy was fearless in telling anyone exactly what she thought. She loved it when I would take her out on the town to expensive restaurants or nightclubs where we would sit talking for hours about politics or romance or philosophy.

I had always thought that I was a dull companion for my little niece. To her, I was probably a funny old uncle, perhaps with a bit of the polish and wealth upon me, but it was neither my looks nor polish that attracted her most. I think she caught a glimpse of my darker side and inner longings. She probably saw the look of a man whose keen eye, subtle smile and crippled body hid the wish to enjoy life and escape from loneliness. So many people with disabilities that I've known tend to put the natural demand for amusement out of sight, as some untidy housekeepers hide dust, and pretend that it was swept away. Not me!

One day, I came in carrying a pocketful of money, announcing that I was taking Candy to San Francisco and that we were not coming back until we had blown every cent of it. We had an elegant lunch at the Hotel St. Francis where vaulted ceilings echoed with million-dollar business deals and whose colossal chandelier quaked and shivered its crystal bones at the resolute steps of certain magnates, or whenever earthquakes threatened. I knew the maitre d' who immediately showed us to the best table. I gallantly escorted Candy to her seat, my wheelchair making slight furrows in the Persian carpet.

At twenty-three, I still had the face of a child, rounded, but pleasant and friendly. My sparse mustache tried to assert my maturity, but without much success. I smoked cigarettes then, an affectation of my James Bond image. Actually, Fleming's master spy was not nearly as urbane as I thought I was, but still he got the girls and an occasional nod from Her Majesty.

I hoped that Candy thought her Uncle Kenny had Bond beat all the way. I was the only adult she knew who did not make her feel silly and immature when she was silly and immature and the only one who was willing to try anything just to see what it was like. Candy was a bit overweight and quite a bit boy-crazy; she was impulsive and impatient. But I never judged her, perhaps because I did not feel equal to being judged myself.

Candy told someone how she saw me. "He's more like a brother than an uncle to me. He was never careful that he was fragile. I never felt sorry for him because he was so strong. I've seen him get angry at people who tried to cut his food for him. Even if it took hours to eat dinner, he felt he should be able to do this."

Always an idealist, my physical therapist, Bob M., would shake his head and say that I was resigned to the wheelchair. But I had not given up. I was only trying to be realistic. Lately I was trying hard to be realistic, imagining that since I was too old to go back to school I had better get down to business and make something of myself. My old classmates were now lawyers, junior executives or Ph.D. candidates while I was still living at home.

I was not really idle any more; I just wasn't making money. With Bob, Joanne and Russ, I had started the organization called the Physically Handicapped Memorial Foundation, based in my home in Lafayette, California. All my life, I had been grateful, like a welfare recipient, for the good things fortune had given me. I had a wonderful, loving family, good friends, and a serviceable intellect. I still used the word "handicapped" when referring to myself and others with disabilities.

I was and still am like many who feel that welfare programs kind of bribe recipients. They say, "Here, take it! We just want to forget about you!" But I needed more than that to live as an adult. I needed to be able to get into buildings without having to be helped up steps, to use a public restroom or an elevator without help.

After President John Kennedy's death, President Johnson had just signed into law a civil rights act that prevented a person from being denied access to a public place, regardless of his race, sex, or religion. They had to admit women to Yale and blacks into a Birmingham Woolworth's, but people in wheelchairs were still waiting to be set free.

On the day of my outing with niece Candy, I took a long pull on my Martini and carefully backed my chair away from the table. Candy and I had a big day ahead of us and there was a lot of money to spend before we could go home. Outside the opulent Hotel St. Francis, the streets climbed sharply to exclusive restaurants and luxury apartment buildings and beyond, to the tireless scurrying of Chinatown where descendants of railroad coolies struggled to make a living stocking shelves and working on the docks.

As Candy drove the big Thunderbird down Broadway, I sat on the passenger's side wondering whether I had taken my tranquilizer that morning. Going downhill at about a 45-degree angle, we started to pick up speed. Signs along the street warned drivers: "AVOID RUNAWAYS. TURN WHEELS TOWARD CURB." San Francisco was one of the few places in the country where this practice was observed. And no wonder. If a parking brake failed, an abandoned vehicle could be going fifty or sixty miles per hour by the time it reached the bottom of the hill. Candy and I were singing *A Hard Day's Night* when Candy tapped the power brakes and the pedal went to the floor.

"Oh, my God! No brakes! What do I do?"

Candy was desperately trying to pump some life back into the flaccid brakes, glancing frantically from the approaching cross streets to me and back again. I began laughing nervously. Candy's voluptuous figure shook as she cried, "No brakes!"

"Try the emergency brake," I suggested.

She did. Nothing! "Oh, my God!" she wailed, "Now what?"

"Run into something," I offered rather flippantly.

I think my composure had a calming effect on my niece. She later told the family, "He was laughing, so I figured there was nothing to worry about. I was never fearful that he was a cripple—that he was fragile. So what if the brakes failed? It was a joke. Everything was always a joke with Kenny."

Candy ran into a parked car and the Thunderbird stopped suddenly with a loud crunch, doing little damage to it and jostling us no more than a good trolley ride.

Since we had smashed into somebody's car, we set out to find a policeman, which on a Sunday was no simple task. Finally, we located a cop in a bar and explained the situation to him. After he left to write up his report, and we called the tow truck, there was nothing for us to do. So, we stayed in the bar, drinking Manhattans until the Thunderbird was roadworthy.

Several Manhattans later, as the sun sank slowly in the Bay, the mechanic returned with the car and a whopping bill. He mumbled something about it being Sunday and having to pay his people overtime, the upshot of it being that between the bar bill and the repairs, I was cleaned out. This wasn't the way I planned it, but sometimes goals are achieved through methods of their own. We had spent all my cash.

However, I had learned a secret that I wanted to share with my niece. With humor, you can soften some of the worst blows that life delivers. Once you laugh, no matter how bad things are, you can survive.

◆   ◆   ◆

Soon I drew the members of my foundation together, perhaps not carefully but lovingly. Bob became vice president, more out of friendship and mutual respect than out of a commitment to the cause. Bob, my physical therapist, claimed later, "I didn't really do much. I'd sign a few documents or maybe testify at a hearing. But I was working two jobs and didn't have a lot of time."

After a difficult day working on the foundation, we often had good times together in the evening. One time we went to a Greek restaurant in San Francisco with Bob M. and his wife, and Pat P., my friend of so many years who first spoke to me at the school dance. Bob remembered the incident as if it were yesterday.

> Right on Columbus and Broadway, there's a Greek restaurant called The Greek Taverna. Ken knew the headwaiter there who gave us a good seat. The men were dancing in a big twisty circle. We were sitting in a booth and Ken was sitting with Pat on the dance floor side. I had Ken's money because it was easier for me to pay the bill. (With his money, it was really easy!) He knew the people in the band. They were the people he was going to hire for his upcoming Fourth of July party. I think he even knew the belly dancer.
>
> Then the belly dancer started her routine. She had castanets and a stringy skirty thing and a G-string, and was dancing like crazy! She worked her way

around the room that was set in a semicircle. We were on one end of the horseshoe and she was starting on the other end. As she went along, the male customers would take a bill and tuck it right into the top of her G-string. Well, she was working her way through the crowd and, boy; there were a lot of bills tucked in there.

Ken said, 'Give me a five!' He was really into it and Pat was trying to give him dirty looks. The problem was that Ken's wheelchair was low and the girl was pretty tall. His reach was only about up to his head and the girl's G-string was a couple of inches higher than that.

So she came toward our table, shaking her stuff. Ken was really into it. It was a great show. We were clapping and having a good time. Finally she got to our place. I asked him, 'You want me to tuck it in for you?' He said 'Nope! I'll take care of it.'

He was trying to get into position to make his deposit and she was going like crazy and so was the band. Every time Ken reached up toward her G-string, the drummer did a roll and the band made a big crescendo. Every eye in the place was on our table. I was watching, thinking, 'Jeez, he's not going to be able to reach.' I asked him again. He said, 'No, no, no. I'll do it.' Ken would try to reach and the band would speed up.

I was really kind of getting nervous. I remember the sweat was just running off my chin. We were drinking ouzo and I was dripping right in my glass. Finally, the belly dancer made kind of a little dip and grabbed the money, making it look like he did it and went swirling away and, boy the people cheered and the band played a big finale!

Bob was very valuable to me and I enjoyed showing him my appreciation for his work with the foundation in such a way.

Joanne held the position of treasurer of the foundation, although she was devoting almost all her time to getting through school at Diablo Valley Junior College, physically confronting the very problems of accessibility that the foundation was trying to eliminate.

She told me, "My main goal is finishing school, becoming employable again. That's why I can't be much more than a sounding board for you most of the time."

The only salaried member of the organization was the secretary; a very attractive, dynamic, and somewhat naive young woman of nineteen. She had been working as a secretary for Atomic Laboratories, but wanted to go to school part time, eventually to become a teacher.

Answering my ad for the position, Diane D. knocked on the door of our elegant Jacuzzi home, the address given for the foundation. She had no idea who I was or what the foundation stood for. But she was certain it would be a job where she could learn a lot and people would like her. They always did. Her soft brown eyes widened when the housekeeper opened the door, revealing a scene of tasteful splendor, the kind she had only seen in her mother's decorating magazines. Then I entered. She could hear this buzz coming around the corner. She'd never seen an electric wheelchair before.

Diane was not expecting somebody who, first of all, had a major disability, and second, was so small and deformed. I, in turn, was not expecting anybody so beautiful. I later decided that Diane's beauty had made the world too simple for her. She just sort of drifted through life, aided by her good looks and sweet disposition. But it would take a while for me to learn about that. Meanwhile, we both tried to keep from staring while I explained the aims of the foundation and the duties of the secretary.

Diane was immediately enthralled with the prospect. She told me, "I'm really interested. I like learning. It will be a whole new world to me."

I hired her on the spot. Wheels were turning in my head. I could not help that. And she had seen the way I looked at her. Besides, she seemed quite capable. Her references were good, and she was free to travel with me when I went to lobby in Washington.

With the support of this "staff," I felt ready to take on the powers that controlled funding for schools and public buildings to convince them to remove architectural barriers, allowing people with disabilities to become independent and productive members of society. A climate of change was in the air. Martin Luther King was awarded the Nobel Peace Prize. Revolution was set to the sounds of the Beatles; the Rolling Stones and Bob Dylan promoted love, not war, and the rumbling of student activism on the Berkeley campus echoed throughout the country. In the complacent Eisenhower years, nobody would have listened to a little rich kid in a wheelchair, but now the time was right.

In one of several feature stories, my picture appeared along with that of my "able-bodied secretary." I talked about the millions of members of the "hidden population" who deserved a chance to participate in the mainstream of American society.

Contrary to my nature, I probably sounded a little stuffy and self important like an accountant at a board of directors' meeting. When asked why a person with a disability could not receive an education at home, I said, "Home courses are comparatively satisfactory at the grade-school level through home teachers, but the standards decline in the intermediate and high school years when one teacher has to teach many subjects. Besides this, confined to home, the student cannot adjust to social living, and there is more chance for mental depression since he feels the lack of personal contact considered mandatory in today's society."

I spoke in dignified generalities, trying to maintain a protective barrier around myself, wanting to draw attention to my work and away from myself. It was kind of like the *Wizard of Oz* who, upon being discovered, said, "Pay no attention to the little man behind the curtain." Perhaps my message would have had more impact if I had used myself as an example, explaining how, with the best of intentions, my parents deprived me of an adequate primary education by bringing in tutors instead of sending me to public school, and how as a child I desperately needed the experience of growing up and identifying with other children my age. But I did not want to reveal or even admit that I was also crying out for help myself.

People were taking me seriously. I spoke dispassionately to California Senator George Miller and Assemblyman Jerome Waldie about the manpower going to waste because most public and commercial buildings are not equipped to accommodate the hundreds or thousands of people with disabilities who are waiting for the chance to work and pay taxes. I explained that the amount collected in taxes would pay for the cost of the architectural improvements many times over. Unlike some other activist groups of that era, my cause did not organize sit-ins, strikes, or riots. My approach was calm, well-researched presentations delivered through the proper channels, observing every form of political protocol and social grace, which local moguls received with respect and no doubt relief.

Although I generally received no more than moral support from the other members, the foundation was gaining a reputation as a lobby group. My picture appeared in the newspaper; I was interviewed on television championing the cause of the "hidden population." The name "Kenneth A. Jacuzzi" was becoming known, not as a member of the family of hydrotherapy fame, but as an activist for the rights of those with various disabilities.

I was introduced to Ed Roberts by Russ. Ed, the "father of disability movement," despite polio completed an education for an M.A. from a bed at U.C. Berkeley where he attended classes by closed circuit TV. The university hesitated to admit Ed, as he was severely disabled. He had virtually no functional movement and was dependent upon a respirator to breathe. "We've tried cripples before and it didn't work," said the university. They reluctantly admitted Ed in 1962 and arranged for him to live in the campus medical facility, Cowell Hall. His brother, also a student, served as an on-campus personal assistant, often pushing Ed from class to class in an old manual wheelchair.

In the late 1960s and early 1970s, Berkeley students with severe disabilities organized into a group known as the Rolling Quads. Led by Ed, they began exerting pressure on the university to become more accessible and began seeking funding to develop a student organization to work for barrier removal and support services, including personal attendant services, for students with disabilities to live independently while attending school. This eventually led to the nation's first Center for Independent Living, "CIL," in Berkeley, California. One of the many ironies of Ed's life was that 14 years later, Gov. Jerry Brown appointed him to be the state director of the very same agency that denied him work because he was too severely disabled.

Ed said, "I'm tired of well-meaning non-cripples with their stereotypes of what I can and cannot do directing my life and my future. I want cripples to direct their own programs and to be able to train other cripples to direct new programs. This is the start of something big—cripple power."

Ed Roberts was featured on a variety of news shows, including *60 Minutes*. He invited us to be on his program at station KPIX, about getting monuments to be wheelchair accessible, such as the Washington monument.

Ed and I did collaborate on several things regarding disability access at that time, such as the TV show we did on the local CBS affiliate, KPIX, on expanding access to government monuments and buildings. However, I deeply regret not developing a long-term friendship with Ed. I've often thought that I should have become more involved with Ed's quest to complete his university education and his parallel efforts in expanding access opportunities to others with disabilities. There was much I could have learned from Ed Roberts, including, in all probability, a more timely completion of my own university studies. Ed was always an exemplary role model for people with disabilities, but especially during the all too brief time that I knew him.

I was establishing an image, part of which involved designing a logo that could evoke the aims of the Foundation, a symbol that on letterhead would demand priority even from the powerful, and, inscribed on stone or concrete, would be a sign of welcome to those with disabilities. All my life, I doodled and sketched almost compulsively. When lectures at school grew dull, I would draw caricatures in the margins. At home, I would devise prototype hydrotherapy components or draw up plans for futuristic wheelchair-accessible buildings. But I had no formal training in art and doubted my ability to do justice to the task of designing the logo by which the Foundation would be known.

The first artist I commissioned for the design project produced less than inspiring work. But I heard about another artist who lived across the street from my secretary, Diane D. Her name was Cecille and she did sensuous oil paintings of ethereally beautiful nude women. Her work was alluring without being vulgar. The lines were delicate, precise, and sensitive. I had to meet her, even if she would not do the logo.

When Cecille knocked on my door, the Mexican housekeeper let her in. The servant did not speak a word of English but smiled, motioning for her to wait. She was expected. Like Diane, Cecille heard the high-pitched whirr of the electric wheelchair approach and as the sound began to round the corner, it stopped. After some moments, an impish voice said, "Contrary to what you may believe, I am not a monster." The source of the whirr and the voice came into view.

Perhaps I had expected Cecille to look like her paintings or maybe like some Left Bank sylph that would glide across the room without disturbing the nap on the carpet and extend a long slender arm that I might kiss her hand. Actually, she looked a great deal more like one of Brueghel's fat, happy peasants. Her eyes shone with wit and there was something compassionate about her face. She was anything but mysterious or threatening. Cecille would probably have made a good spy because she had the kind of face that would enable her to extract the deepest secrets from total strangers. Instead, she worked for Dow Chemical as a technician. On the side, she baked magnificent cakes and painted some nudes.

This meeting marked the beginning of a long and powerful friendship. Cecille did draw the foundation's logo, but her association with me did not end when the project was done. I didn't work that way.

Cecille told a mutual friend, "I don't think Ken ever had a strictly-business relationship with an employee. He always loved people. He got involved with them."

I was always ready to share my good moods with friends, but my darker moments; I tried to keep to myself. My niece thought I was the happiest guy in the world, to whom everything was a joke. I had never told Julie or other close female friends when I was miserable or in despair. I was sure it would just frighten them away. Cecille was more understanding than she was beautiful. She did not pity me; thank heavens! She had to get by with art, brains and a good heart, and she never doubted that I could do the same. So I was willing to tell her anything without fear of rejection. With her as an honest critic and coach, I began to work more on my drawing as an outlet for the pent-up emotions I so desperately needed to express.

However, I was not the only man who found comfort in Cecille's candid, warm-hearted nature. Diane D. used to complain that men who came to take her out kept her waiting while they went over to visit Cecille. For a woman who was ungainly, overweight, and not terribly pretty otherwise, she found her company very much in demand.

She could also see that I was not interested in a casual relationship. In fact, I apparently was not prepared for any kind of relationship that would evolve slowly and naturally. After spending half my life in hospitals and a good deal of the other half recuperating, I was like a priest who just renounced a life of celibacy and wanted to make up for lost time. As a result, Cecille, in her kind and patient way, tried to gently pull back the reins of my galloping passions. But I was not willing to postpone life any longer.

◆ ◆ ◆

One day several months after John Kennedy's death, a story about the proposed John F. Kennedy Memorial appeared on television. I had always admired the young, eloquent Catholic president, and even identified with him in a way since both our fathers were founders of powerful dynasties. The news story discussed plans for the Kennedy Memorial, and at one point, the camera panned over the artist's conception of the finished product. It was loaded with steps. I wasted no time in phoning the Kennedy family.

In 1964, Mrs. Jacqueline Kennedy's secretary assured me that the late President's widow would want access for those with mobility disabilities fully considered in visiting the John F. Kennedy Memorial in Arlington Cemetery. The secretary put me in touch with Harold Adams, one of the San Francisco architects, who promised that consideration would be given to making the Memorial wheelchair accessible. I told him how to provide the ramp and they followed my suggestion. I even received a personal letter of thanks from Jacqueline Kennedy for my interest in the project.

At that time, the main goal of the Physically Handicapped Memorial Foundation, which I organized, was to campaign for the elimination of architectural barriers in high schools and colleges. I wanted to get design commitments by schools to be constructed in California so that wheelchair students could attend classes without difficulty.

Despite its success, my foundation did not grow. Any businessman could see that this was because the organization had no income. All the money and almost all the energy had been coming from me and I was determined to keep the organization true to itself by not soliciting donations. In one of the early newspaper interviews I gave, I announced, "We are not seeking contributions…If people have a passion for giving money, we ask them to go to their schools and have a look, then volunteer money to the school district." (*Oakland Tribune*, Thurs., Nov. 5, 1964).

Looking back on this stance, I realize it was one of my biggest mistakes. It kept the foundation from growing, although it also left no doubt that whatever the foundation accomplished, it was the doing of Ken Jacuzzi.

Diane D. greatly admired my altruism. It gave her the chance to express her boundless compassion for people she imagined less fortunate than herself more effusively than she could at the Atomic Laboratories. She was never just a secretary and not just another pretty face. She had that kind of defensive, frantic energy some beautiful women have when they suspect they are being patronized. This is not to say she was not bright and sincere, but perhaps she tried too hard to be accepted for what she was inside.

Diane and I would have made a good team. We were both energetic, both fighters. A true 60's liberal, Diane was ready to strike out against anything politically conservative, ecologically harmful, or suspiciously inhuman. Here I was, finding myself an adult but obliged to live like a child. I was angry about having severe disabilities and I determined to wage war on the world that kept me at arm's length.

Together I hoped we would charm the pants off politicians or storm off to an Easter Seals meeting, hoping to stir up some initiative in disheartened members. I played the "straight man," self-possessed, dignified, and very serious. Diane was officially the foundation's secretary but couldn't resist occasionally mounting the soapbox.

Once, at an Easter Seals meeting in Santa Clara, I was trying to rally support for legislation that would require all new buildings to be wheelchair-accessible. Diane began to urge some others with disabilities to start fighting for their rights. She may not have been a great speaker, but it was clear the spirit was in her and she commanded attention. Her dark eyes flashed, her perfectly made-up face was flushed with excitement, and her ample bosom heaved beneath the powder blue cashmere sweater.

"There is no reason you should not get a college education if you want one! It's your right. But you have to make yourself heard. You have to stand up and fight!" She paused a minute in slight confusion, realizing for the first time, perhaps, that there were certain expressions that might not serve well here. Somebody smirked so she pretended it was intentional. "That's right, stand up, and fight because you are not alone. You people of this hidden population have to make yourselves heard. And you have to stick to it!"

One of the girls in the group had been shifting restlessly in her chair as Diane spoke. She was blonde and pretty despite the fact that her neck was rather thick and her hands splayed and sinewy from a lifetime of walking with crutches. She had been near the boiling point all during the pep talk. Somehow, Diane hadn't noticed. The girl glared at her and in a voice half of controlled rage and half pity, she said, "You don't know what it's like."

My aide, Lolita, who traveled with us, had always tuned my wheelchair, assisted me in the bathroom, and handed me things I couldn't reach. So in a way, the woman was right. Diane didn't know some of the more intimate activities of daily living for persons with disabilities.

Diane said to me later, "All I saw was that you seemed to be getting along okay. I'd just go bouncing along forgetting you couldn't just jump up and do all this stuff."

Being an American from a fairly humble background, Diane found the idea of having a personal servant a strange phenomenon. Once, when my parents and I traveled to the plant in Little Rock for a couple of weeks, I asked her if she would like to stay at my house with the maid and the housekeeper until we all returned. Not only were the surroundings more luxurious than any she had ever encountered, but she discovered she suddenly had a great deal more free time.

She described her experience. "When I was home, I got up, fixed my breakfast, and drove to school. At Kenny's house when I got up, I'd find the table was already set, the newspaper would be on my left side, and on my right, fresh orange juice was being poured, breakfast was being made for me. I'd come strolling out and it would be all ready. I sat there and thought, 'You know, this way, you could afford to be intelligent. You've got time to read. Somebody's taking care of the basics for you. Your house is being cleaned so you can read a book. Your breakfast is being cooked so you can read the morning paper."

Some of her friends were already married, struggling with car payments and mortgages while Diane was still living at home so she could keep going to Diablo Valley College. Her clothes were nice but few were new and none as stylish as those of my sister Irene. (Irene became a socialite and wore only the best clothes. Once she married, Dad hired her husband but had to subsidize them. He wished she would learn to live on her husband's salary. Eventually she divorced, took their four children, and remarried).

Of course, Diane considered herself too young to get married but, living in that house, she could not help but fantasize what it would be like to be married to a man with my money.

Diane said,

It was fun. I liked it. But at the same time I realized I didn't have the personality for it. It hurt me. One night I had a friend over for dinner. An older man, just a friend. It got to be awfully lonely in that big house with just two servants who couldn't speak English. When dinner was served, I wanted the maids to sit down and eat with us. My God, there were only four of us! It wasn't a crowded table. But they refused. They wanted to eat in the maids' quarters.

I remember my friend saying to me, "You can't do that. You make them uncomfortable when you ask them to sit with you."

"Why?" I said, "I feel silly having them come and serve me while they stand there and wait to see if they can bring me any more food. This is ridiculous! I can get up and get my own food."

He said, "No, you have to understand. They know their place. They're hired here as maids. They've got rooms of their own, sleeping quarters of their own and when you ask them to sit at the table where the family sits, it's confusing for them."

Diane knew her place, too. As far as she was concerned, she was my secretary and that was it. Of course, I thought of her as more than that, just as I thought of Lolita D. as more than just my aide. Diane and Lolita were part of my particular corner of the world, dominated by my family, and I would not cheapen those experiences.

When not discussing the foundation's strategies, I wooed Diane with quotes from Gurdiev and ponderous passages from "The Great Books," some of which she still remembers and uses in the social studies classes she teaches. She was very attentive to me as a teacher and a boss. It wasn't until after our lobbying trip to Washington that she realized how deeply she hurt me with her indifference to me as a man.

Setting out for Washington to stir up some interest in the elimination of architectural barriers, we talked with every senator we could corner, which between my persistence and Diane's charm was not as difficult as it could have been. First on the list were the offices of Robert and Edward Kennedy. Both were extremely busy and in neither case were we able to get through to the head man. We did get through to Senator Dole who listened to us politely and had his wife send Diane a cookbook of recipes from Kansas.

We had a little better luck with the delegation from Arkansas where Jacuzzi Brothers had their headquarters. Senator J. William Fulbright, a very powerful man on Capitol Hill, was unable to see us but he had his assistant hear what we had to say. The other senator from Arkansas, McClellan, seemed interested in our case and so was his assistant—at least, the assistant was interested in Diane's case or Diane.

One of the most memorable meetings of the Washington trip was our interview with a representative from the office of Anthony J. Celebrezze, head of the Department of Health, Education and Welfare. It was the beginning of the hot, sticky, dog days of July. Lolita, stouthearted old trooper, panted slightly as she wheeled me into the stately office.

Until now everyone we talked to at least gave the impression they were interested in the foundation's cause, but the man from H.E.W. just loosened his tie and looked miserable as I began to tell him about the plight of the "hidden population" while Diane took notes.

"Well," he said leaning back in his sumptuous leather chair, looking out the window, "I've got my sons in college and I don't need anything new. How many people do you have backing you?"

Diane was stunned. As we walked out to the elevator, she said, "We were talking about human lives and this guy's doing a head count! We went there with what seemed the most reasonable requests in the world: ramps and a national monument—and to discuss the predicament of people with physically disabilities—and the only thing that matters to him is how many votes he can get out of the deal. I was almost literally sick! My God! Where do they get these people? The assistant to the head of H.E.W. and he said, 'Don't give me any new problems.' The problems are there. We were just trying to inform him about them."

Diane was surprised to see how calmly I received the whole matter. To me, it sounded like a thousand other conversations I'd heard my father relate at the dinner table, where some family member with a large number of shares in the company is given an easy job just because they need his vote. Dad would growl that this younger generation, his nephews, had lost the old values. Diane and I were seeing that someone at the top of government had lost the old values.

At this point, I could not afford any additional emotional strain. I knew what happened when I allowed myself to get agitated over something and I already felt myself cracking at the seams over my desire for Diane. I was so disappointed in myself—getting overwrought in my own personal desires once more.

The more I tried to gain her interest, the more distraught I became when she did not respond and the more I sank into my private misery, blunted by martinis and tranquilizers. James Bond would never fall apart if some woman failed to appreciate his finer qualities. If it ever did happen, he'd probably just toss off a couple of shaken-not-stirred martinis and say, "To hell with her!" I tried this approach but my heart was not in it. Neither was my stomach.

One time in Washington I got so sick I threw up right in the street. Lolita, poor thing, had to drive me to a little corner somewhere. It was just awful. I was trying to build a wall around myself. My self pity was compounded by the drugs. I was trying to "drown my sorrows," but it's not the sorrows that drown. The sorrows do fine! The more you feed them, the bigger they get. Reality is the best defense.

Diane did not suspect that I was having any problems, although she noticed I was strangely protective of her during the trip. She probably thought I was having a headache when I was really having a heartache. There is no silencing the voice of discontent. It has its own imperatives and will be heard. It spoke to and called me a sap. Diane said later,

> I wasn't going with anybody. I felt I could go out with whomever I wanted. I certainly would have if I were home. A couple of times I went out with the senators' assistants and it was obvious Ken frowned on it. He'd be really upset the next day. One time he got terribly sick and Lolita became angry. She took me aside and said. 'Kenny got sick because of what you did!'
>
> But I certainly wasn't his wife and he had no grounds to possess me. I think he had a lot more anticipation about what the trip was going to be like. I was going for the experience. It was exciting. I was going along to learn and we were doing some good things. I didn't think I was hired because of my looks. That may be how I projected myself but it was not how I perceived myself. I saw myself as a very bright and capable young lady.

Washington had been a strain on all three of us, so I extended our trip to Puerto Rico and Florida as a reward. In Puerto Rico, Lolita and I got to speak Spanish with the natives, and Diane developed a New York accent, which she affects to this day. It was not until we arrived in Miami with the trip nearly over that I made a move for Diane.

I rented a honeymoon suite in the Fontainebleau. It was as big as a house with connecting bedrooms separated by a common living room and a balcony. Diane and Lolita shared one of the bedrooms and I stayed, very properly, in the other.

During the past few days, with no senator's assistant or hot-blooded Puerto Ricans to monopolize her time, Diane had gotten in the habit of saying goodnight to me before turning in. She sat on the edge of my bed chattering excitedly about something she'd seen or thought of that day and listening with wide-eyed fascination to my replies. If she'd known what this was doing to me, she would probably have run terrified out of the room. But either I was very good at keeping it to myself or not good enough at communicating it to her. But one night the sexual tension became too much.

I was sitting there on the bed when Diane came in to say goodnight and somehow, we started necking. Then the usual thing happened; I got a huge hard-on. She said, "God, Ken! Where did you ever learn to kiss like that?"

I couldn't stand it any more! I made a move to continue and she pulled away and ran out of the room. I just sort of slid down the edge of the bed and landed on the floor. She had no idea that I was unable to support myself when she got up and was left in this fix until Lolita checked on me.

Diane recalled,

> It was really a passionate kiss. One of the warmest kisses I have ever had in my life. But I remember drawing away from him and being kind of shocked, wondering, "Why is he doing this? He's my boss."
>
> It made me think he was a more passionate person than I ever suspected. I had never really thought of him sexually. I didn't think he could actually do it, you know, although I admit I was curious at times, but at that time I wasn't sexually active myself. I was young and innocent.
>
> Ken didn't know it but one night, one of the senator's assistants made advances. We'd been drinking and he started to grab at me. My first reaction was just that I wanted to get back to the hotel and get away. At that time, girls played a teasing role. But just because you flirted didn't mean you were going to do anything.

On the plane back to California, Diane did not sit by me. Occasionally, she came bouncing up with stories of the things she'd done or the fun she'd had, then she'd vanish out of my line of vision to her window seat. Lolita was the first to notice that I was sick and upset. She knew me well enough to conclude that it was probably the result of a combination of factors. For one thing, Thorazine and martinis didn't mix. And Diane let me sit alone. Lolita coaxed Diane to sit with me but by then the damage was done.

After our return to California, I told Diane that her services would be no longer required. I had lost track of "the cause" in favor of my personal search for acceptance. She did not ask why I let her go until several weeks later when she stopped by to talk with my mother and the lady from across the street.

My mother could not come out and say, "Kenny loves you." She said simply, "Kenny's very hurt." In fact, I didn't want her to say that. I wanted nobody making any excuses for me. I got myself in that fix and I wanted to get myself out.

Diane said, "I knew he was attracted to me at the time. You know what you do at nineteen with that kind of power. You use it. It's an ego booster. Everybody was attracted to me. He was too. I think he fell in love with my energy. I remember one time he said he wished he had what I had—the vitality. He said, 'I'd trade all the money, all the luxuries, just to be able to turn my head to see a picture on the wall.'"

I was denied Diane's beauty and vitality so I sought solace in the ungainly, good-natured Cecille. This time, when I talked to her about love, I was desperate. She would either become my lover right away or I would never see her again. I don't know where this impatience came from. It was like I planned this thing all out in my head. I was saying, "I love you and you have to love me just the same way right now." I couldn't wait for things to develop naturally. I thought I had to do everything all at once. Again, I guess it was that old feeling of making up for lost time. I think I knew where it would end and was safe in revealing my urge to merge to such a good person.

Cecille stood her ground and said "No." This coincided with another ending. My work on the foundation trailed off without direction. Nobody else seemed interested enough to carry on. In my whirlpool, my *current* for a cause *met with a contrasting current* in a woman who cared *only* about the cause. This oscillated for a while before it collapsed as I realized the cause was less important to me than love at that young impressionable age. The Communists used to say, "Nobody cares about the communist cause when they are starving, so let us satisfy their hunger before we talk about the cause." I couldn't think about my cause until my hunger for acceptance was satisfied.

After Diane, I was getting sick again. I had been feeling ill since before the Washington trip, having trouble with my bladder and bowels, and even having trouble masturbating, taking forever to ejaculate. That seemed to tell me that my sexuality as a man was fading away without ever having been fulfilled. How much function would I lose during this relapse?

The MRI and myelogram were done and they found I had discs slipping in three places in my spine. I became depressed and stopped talking to my parents, which worried them to distraction. My mother, although she wasn't always able to understand my pain, seemed to feel it vicariously. My father, the great problem solver and optimist, could only watch helplessly. I began to see a "shrink" with this new attack.

Day after day, I wasted away, determined to punish myself for being unworthy to aspire to a normal life. I was going downhill fast and there was nothing I could do about it. Why try to fool myself? I was a 25-year-old crippled midget that no woman would want. I had no college degree and no job and no way to get either one. I was costing my parents a fortune just by being alive. They had given up the farm in Napa Valley so they could be near to take care of me. Today it would be worth millions. Then I began to change my outlook, and although it took nearly two years, I did it.

I was still an innocent, living in the Garden of Eden, not yet having tasted of the apple. Oh, how I wanted to sin. I wanted Eve to come along and tempt me so that Dad would kick me out of Eden and I could go and live among other sinners. But Dad and Mom didn't kick me out. And I only sinned in my heart like Jimmy Carter. So if anybody was going to change anything, it had to be me. It was time to leave. Gary Cooper would have said, "It's time to get out of Dodge."

12

Leaving Home

Typhoon: A violent cyclonic storm, which may last several days, and dies over land or cooler water where it loses power.

So a quarter of a century on this earth and what did I have to show for it? Most of my friends had already graduated from college and I had dropped out in my freshman year. After my second attack, I had become more—not less—dependent, and from all appearances, I would remain a virgin forever. It was a hell of a way for James Bond to end up; lacing my shaken-not-stirred martinis with Thorazine and wishing to God my parents would stop bitching at each other long enough for me to complete a thought.

When I was in my twenties, my life looked like a Dow Jones graph that was going down year by year. I was thinking back then that there was no time left. I hadn't finished college and I didn't really have a lifetime occupation. I wasn't really worth that much.

The second arthritis attack had been devastating. It had dropped me back into the wheelchair and all that went with it. True, I'd never been a Fred Astaire, but at least he had stood on his own two feet. With Ginger, too! How far away it seemed to me now as I sat alone with my pain under my father's roof wishing for bygone days of mobility.

Dad was worried about me. I remember that he described me to somebody in this way. "He was a lost soul. Days went by and he wouldn't talk. He could not do anything because we were perhaps too bossy, trying to help him too much. Maybe we were hurting him. We loved him too much."

Dad, of course, was a workaholic. He was constantly expanding and refining the business, setting up company branches overseas and filling management positions with nephews and the husbands of nieces. These positions were not gifts; they were all given to good, handpicked people. And he made them rich beyond their limited imaginations. This did not stop wives and mothers from complaining about how their boys were forced to leave their home and family to make new lives for themselves, sometimes in other countries. They never admitted that if they had stayed in the States, they would certainly never have attained the kind of wealth and influence they enjoyed overseas. And maybe, in the end, all that meant less to them than keeping their homes. After all, it had not been their dream. It was my Dad's because he wanted to help everybody and carry out his papa's dream of family unity.

Everybody wanted to do what they could for me, too. Alba had always said I was more like her son than her brother. She was always looking after me. She and her husband Pete worked with me day after day, stretching out my shrunken muscles, loosening my painful joints until I was able to walk with crutches. They had taken the initiative to give me the experience of public school that changed my life. It was not that she felt obligated. She loved me.

"Kenny," she told me one day, "you've got to move out of the house!"

She would later find me a nice apartment in San Francisco and a good attendant—not the Mexican kind that our parents always found—but somebody close to my own age who spoke good English, drove a car and knew how to keep the place clean. She was going to set it all up and do it right away. There was no reason for me to sit and mope in that big house while Mom and Dad had their "discussions." Watching me in my depressed condition made them feel bad and only worsened the situation.

I did not say no. I was in no shape to oppose Alba and I did not care one way or the other anyway. No, that was not true. I did care. I knew that I had to start the wheels rolling, to get involved again. There was no sense hiding out.

San Francisco was probably not the best place for me to live. Something near a university campus like Berkeley would have been better. But it was a step in some direction. So there I was, stuck in a nice apartment out in the middle of nowhere, with nothing to do, and two very strange aides, one of whom probably robbed old ladies on his days off, and the other one had been kicked out of Cuba for something and spoke only a little English. I had asked him where he was staying and was able to make out that he had an apartment he shared with some guy. I recall that I thought they were just two buddies. Jesus! I guess I was pretty naive.

It may have been an experience, but it was sure no way to meet girls. I got out of the house to regain my independence, to start up my life again and to continue the process of becoming a man and now I was stranded in suburbia with two gay weirdoes. Something was going wrong.

So I took my tranquilizers and tried to remain tranquil. I also took my Demerol and tried not to be demoralized. I got to know the nightlife in San Francisco, hitting the bars and jazz clubs, hoping to awaken myself by reaching out to people. I hoped others would reciprocate. They did not. Nothing succeeds like success and nothing guarantees loneliness like having someone see it in your eyes.

It wouldn't have been so bad if I could have been doing something. But I was living there and doing nothing. I get sick when I do nothing. Or, at least, I don't get well.

Doing "nothing" still included rigorous physical therapy, repeating the agonizing process of stretching out my arthritic limbs in the attempt to get back some mobility. I was also receiving counseling. I thought I had a grip on life and had accepted the role of being a helper, a doer, a giver but my infirmities were making me lose my grip.

I didn't stop to think, "Hold it, Jacuzzi! Just get your act together and take care of your physical and emotional problems, even if it takes a year, or even if it takes three years. Then start doing something like finishing college, so you can still earn a degree by the time you're thirty. That is still something many other people don't have." But I didn't think like that in those days.

After my second siege, I thought things like, "How many more of these attacks will I have? How much worse can I really become?" It was like people who get in an accident and become paralyzed. They can never adjust completely to the fact that they are no longer walking around, and they can't finally accept their new state of being.

The doctors told me the arthritis might stabilize, but then again I could get another attack at thirty. The mind-altering drugs the psychiatrist had prescribed seemed only to allow me to sink into darkest thoughts. What if I got another attack? Where would that leave me? Did I dare get married, ever? Was it even safe to fall in love again? I was more than half convinced that my second attack was related to my failure with Julie. I sent her away because I did not feel I was manly enough, as if to punish myself for being inadequate. I knew I needed somebody desperately, but wondered if it were in the stars.

In addition to everything else, it was after the spinal surgery that I developed retrograde ejaculation, during which semen was diverted back into the bladder instead of being expelled outside the body—a bummer from the sexual standpoint.

So who was my mate—my caretaker. "Do you want your bath now, Señor Jacuzzi?" said my aide.

"I think I'll grub it for today, thanks."

Actually, the Cuban was not a bad guy. He was more honest than the other guy and of all the gay aides I had in San Francisco (there were three or four) the Cuban was the most respectful of my heterosexuality. Only one of them ever tried to touch me. Even he could take "no" for an answer.

I stuck it out for a few months although I knew almost from the beginning it was hopeless. I wasn't making it. I was not making it with any of the women I met in bars, I was not making it with any occupation, and I was not making it living alone. I don't think I was homesick. I just felt like it didn't matter if I ever got anywhere. Between heaven and earth, I just felt erased, blotted out. I did not say my prayers one night; I felt what would be, would be. Que sera, sera!

My Dad was feeling bad about my moving away and he asked if I wanted to move back home. Much as I loved Dad, I hated that superior tone he took with me. Pete came to my apartment and spent six full hours trying to convince me to return back home. This was important to me. Pete had the gift of simple and moving expression. Because he talked so little, his words had a peculiar force; they were not worn dull from constant use.

Of course, I was still a little *testa dura!* You remember, hardheaded! But finally I decided it was the shits living in San Francisco so I returned home.

Everyone was polite and glad to have me back, but it was no joyous homecoming. They gave me back my old room. It was as if they had agreed that I was twelve years old again and not twenty-five.

Dad was no fool. He saw that I had inherited his passion for women and work. He also saw that I was well taken care of by signing over a percentage of the whirlpool patent royalties to me. He encouraged me to take an interest in the business, but he didn't really expect me to become very active. Not the way he had been. It wasn't necessary.

As far as women went, that was another matter. For one thing, a gentleman didn't talk about sex with his children. If Dad had not talked about it with John, how in the world could he with me? But maybe there was a solution.

When I moved back home, there was again the problem of finding a suitable attendant. It seems that most sensible, sensitive, sincere, sanitary, and "straight" people do not become attendants and the family sometimes had to literally kick them out the door when they proved unsuitable. Very few of them seemed to fit in well with Mom's house. Often they were less than meticulous in their housekeeping, and even more often they were less than reliable.

But one day, my parents hired a Mexican lady of about thirty who was sexy in a quiet, rural sort of way. This aspect did not go unnoticed by me, since I was ready for any break in the boredom. After a few days of watching her slow, sensuous movements as she bathed me and helped me get dressed, my imagination ran wild. Once or twice, our eyes met. I flushed, thinking, "She wants me. She wants me the way I am." What I did not notice was the way my father was watching us.

Dad always had an eye for the ladies, or at least that was the rumor Mom kept alive. He did a great deal of traveling for the company and loved it. He enjoyed going first class, eating in fine restaurants, staying in the best hotels. And there may have been women. I'll never know.

Amo, amas, amat! I love, you love, he loves! It was part of the image, practically expected. It was expected that Italian boys would be good Catholics, go to mass every Sunday and get their first piece of ass by the time they were eighteen. They would go to confession and if they said three "Hail Mary's" and two "Our Fathers" and managed not to knock up anybody from a good family they were considered to have successfully entered manhood.

I had my chance with Julie and blew it. Of course, that was different; I had been in love. I took the matter very seriously. I felt that I was unable to consummate the relationship sexually because I was not sure that was the right thing. Now somebody else had gotten her pregnant and abandoned her. I could not help but wonder how things might have been different if we had stayed together.

My trouble was that I was too circumspect. I tried to think a thing through from every possible angle before I acted. It came from years of having to carefully plan my every move, conserving my limited energy. I learned to put everything in its proper place. For an able-bodied person, looking for a misplaced object usually represents a few minutes of frustration. For me, it could be an exhausting ordeal that could take hours. My careful planning earned me the reputation of being mature for my age and later of being very considerate, even wise, but it sometimes robbed me of the spontaneous joys of life.

Now my choice seemed clear. The Mexican lady was interested in me and I was interested in her. What could be simpler? I still did not like the idea of starting something right in my parents' house. But still, that was where I lived for now and for the foreseeable future. It would mean I would have to go out and buy condoms again. I did not want to be irresponsible about this and yet I had been taught it would be sinful to interfere with the process of bringing a child into the world by using contraceptives. I was dying for affection, going mad watching that woman swish and sway around the house and consume me with the slow fire of those great, innocent eyes. I wondered if she knew what she was doing to me or what she could do for me.

One day, it all seemed to come together. Dad was out of town on one of his business trips and mother was making another go of it at the "fat farm" in North Carolina, hoping this time to stick with that awful rice diet long enough to shed a few pounds and maybe surprise Dad when he returned. It was unlikely that she could do it, or even that he would notice if she did, but it got her out of the house and gave her a vacation.

As the olive-skinned beauty glided past me in her flimsy cotton shirt, the morning light from the big bay windows caught her silhouette like an x-ray. She stopped there transfixed, letting the sun see through that first and only layer of clothes.

"Mr. Jacuzzi, do you want me to adjust your foot pedals?"

"Call me Ken, for Christ's sake. Mr. Jacuzzi is my father."

She bent over to straighten the pedals, confirming what the light suggested. "Your father?"

"Never mind. It was just a little joke."

She looked into my face with that calm, confident sensuality that women have when they know you've been staring at them with lust in your heart and the next move is theirs. "Kenny, if you want me, you can have me."

"Holy shit!" James Bond never had it any better. She was ready to crawl all over me and all I had to say was, "Okay."

I had even taken the initiative and had a few days earlier bought some condoms. But there had been a slight glitch. Behind the counter was a woman. "Can I help you?"

I swallowed. I coughed. I was stalling. "Uh, is there a man here I can talk to?"

"Sir, I would be more than happy to assist you with whatever you require."

I blushed. I hemmed and I hawed. "It's just that, uh, what I require is, uh…"

She smiled with a knowing smile. "Sir, all the men are either on break or otherwise occupied. Trust me; there is nothing you could possibly ask for that I have not furnished customers dozens of times."

I left with condoms, silently praising her for an angel.

Goodbye virginity! This lady knew what she wanted. She was not playing any games. It was like in the movies, almost too good to be true. And so convenient! After losing my girl, spending months in the hospital, then more months cooped up with those gays in San Francisco, here comes this angel of mercy just in time to save my sanity. Wouldn't the old man laugh if he knew what was going on!

I looked down at her working on the foot pedals, waiting patiently for me to say something. Suddenly I came to realize something as we come to know secret little facts about our family members. My jaw tightened. "My father?"

She rolled her huge, brown eyes and sighed. "To help you," she said. "It's okay." Oh my God! Dad had set it up! I exploded, "Get out of here!"

"But..."

"Just get out!"

I just wasn't that desperate, I guess. So I had a little self-respect after all.

◆ ◆ ◆

In 1967, the courts were still dealing with my father over trying to "save U.S. taxes on income derived from foreign sources." Judge Lyle E. Cook declared that the motive was not illegal, and "properly conceived, has the stamp of approval of our highest courts." But things had gotten worse within the family and the court now said that my father had created the holding company as his "alter ego" and did not properly consult other family directors and shareholders.

The court ordered that a Swiss firm become a trustee for the benefit of the Jacuzzi Bros. Inc., to restore all assets and property and that an accounting be rendered. The plaintiff group was made up of Rose Jacuzzi, widow of Gelindo; Rodolfo, a nephew of Stella Marin (Dad's sister); Rino, her husband; Silviano and George Marin, their children. The defendants were my father, nephews Dante and Giocondo, and Carmelo Jacuzzi Guarneri.

I saw the daily turmoil in my parents' faces and bodies resulting from this trial. The wish to get away from the chaos, give my parents some privacy for their miseries, plus my own quest for independence made me run an ad for a caregiver who might travel with me to Mexico. I felt like a Tom Sawyer or Don Quixote looking for a down-to-earth guide like Huck Finn or Sancho Panza so that I might learn to live like "normal people." What I found was Bruce C.

Bruce was not a bum. Not by his standards. In 1967, the term "hippie," though often synonymous with "bum" and conjuring up mental pictures of dirt, drugs, free love, communistic disregard for free enterprise and the American Way, still retained some of its original meaning of "one who is hip." Hippies were supposedly enlightened with a liberal, humanistic point of view and belonged to that cohesive brotherhood of those whose goal it was to conquer the world with love. "Hippie" was not a handle Bruce would have given himself, but one he would have accepted with a smile.

Mexico held a natural attraction for Bruce, first, because it was geographically alien to his home in Milwaukie, Oregon, and second, because it was the only place he knew where he could spend five or six months skin-diving and raising hell, and then pay for the entire trip with a few aromatic mementos. He never intended to get rich, and after a short stay in San Francisco, he found himself in serious need of the money. You could call Bruce a hippie, but you could not call him unrealistic. One Sunday morning, with a wistful sigh, he shaved off his burly beard and with want ads in hand, headed for Lafayette, California, prepared to tell whatever lies necessary to land himself a job.

Bruce circled several possibilities and, as is usually the case, the most attractive was also the most remote. It had everything he required in a job: adventure, honor, and a chance to learn something. It looked like there was money in it, too. It could be a great opportunity for him. He was not totally unqualified either. It called for somebody who could drive and swim, who liked to travel and was well-educated. He had the first three anyway. The problem was that the position also called for expertise in physical therapy with an emphasis on hydrotherapy.

On that day, Bruce, "The Beard," was totally clean-shaven and dressed in a shirt, slacks, and sports jacket. His stature was gaunt and wiry. Although he was about my age (late twenties), Bruce had a pronounced receding hairline. If you could imagine a balding, younger Clint Eastwood on speed, you'd start to get a picture of The Beard. His eyes were a penetrating blue, but darted about like a bird in search of prey throughout the "job interview."

"Why do you want this job wiping, washing, and dressing my butt?" I asked The Beard.

"Because I'm broke and need a job," he said.

What I had liked most, however, was how he responded: matter-of-factly, without hesitation or quiver in his voice. He was an honest guy. He could, I felt, go toe-to-toe with my parents if he had to. You see, when you're a cripple (I'm supposed to say "person with a disability," but I find that just too damn long for my taste, so you'll have to put up with *cripple*) and dependent on others—like your parents—to help you, you quickly learn you have to please *them* almost as much as you do yourself, especially when choosing relationships.

Nevertheless, I had long ago gotten used to it and learned how to work it to my liking...most of the time. Bruce also admitted that he needed wheels and wanted to earn enough money to buy himself a brand new Harley, about $3,500 at the time. Since he would be making about $500 a month, plus room and board, The Beard felt he could save up enough working with me for about a year.

I asked Bruce for a quick and dirty rundown of where he came from, his background and family and he quickly responded in his habitual, laid-back manner that satisfied me. The Beard's style worked its charm on almost everyone, but especially the women, as I later would come to learn.

Bruce was born and raised in Oregon, the son of Methodist ministers. Both his mom and dad were clergy. By the time I met him, he still would enter churches, admire their beauties, scrutinize the chapels, and might even flick flies off the paintings. But as he departed, he would then endeavor to run into some adventure, which, at the peril of his life, might supply a momentary thrill.

The Beard had spent the last several years bumming around the Pacific Northwest and working a variety of jobs, including a stint as a merchant seaman. Prior to these vagabond days, he had been asked to vacate a small, liberal arts Christian college he was attending in Oregon. Apparently, one starry night, he and a few other totally smashed buddies deposited at the tippy-top of the school's Bell Tower a rather large, live cow.

Following this singular event, The Beard made up his mind to live his rapidly evolving philosophy—before one dies, one should try everything at least once, but preferably three times. Since it was the '60s, "everything" included all alcoholic beverages and drugs known to man as well as those still unknown.

Several days later, by the time Bruce and I began living and working together, I had learned that he had already consumed in his lifetime rather significant quantities of hashish, heroin, and LSD, not to mention beer, wine, scotch, vodka, tequila; well, you get the idea. Did this knowledge of Bruce's past behavior give me any sense of trepidation? No, not really. I believed him when he said that he was off almost everything except an occasional joint or glass of wine, which, in Berkeley, in the '60s, was normal behavior for 90 percent of the population under 40. And I could see he was still a really good man underneath his experimentation with life.

I probably pictured Bruce as a guy like Bob Fosse in *All That Jazz* who takes chances and yet can still size himself up correctly when he looks in the mirror. Of course, I probably also pictured myself like Woody Allen in *Zelig*, a nebbish and chameleon who changed his personality to be accepted by those around him. These were both unfair characterizations because neither of us was really like that. In the end, we were much more like each other than I had any idea.

I was more like Tom Sawyer and he was more like Huck Finn, who would teach me about life. I had always fantasized living The Beard's philosophy of life and was determined that he would be my mentor and teacher over the coming months (minus the drugs because I had already been there, done that with the advice, consent and prescriptions of a myriad of physicians).

I had, at one time, begun to be afraid of the younger generation, but I desperately wanted to be one of them. Short, chubby, crippled, dependent body notwithstanding, I was, in the words of one of my favorite Vince Guaraldi numbers, going to *Cast My Fate to the Wind*—and live.

"I hate to admit it," Bruce told someone later, "but I was a fake. I told Ken I knew all about hydrotherapy. For some reason, I didn't associate the name 'Jacuzzi' with the company."

Bruce recalled an uncomfortable evening, having dinner with my family, and being grilled by my father about pumps and water massage. Somehow he managed to keep up a pretense until the next morning, when he was supposed to give me physical therapy. It became obvious that Bruce, as he said, "didn't know shit from Shinola" about it.

Perhaps I had the same attraction to Bruce that young actor Timothy Hutton had to the psychiatrist played by Judd Hirsch in the 1980 movie *Ordinary People*. Hutton entered the messy office of the psychiatrist, saw the doctor in a rather disheveled manner of dress, and heard him speak quite informally. It was appealing because it was such a contrast to his mother's orderly and sterile environment, and presented the authority figure as human and fallible. Not that my parents' home was so sterile, but I sought a very human and fallible helpmate.

I told Bruce, "I need your help." I explained there were certain goals I wanted to meet. I wanted to become physically stronger, which meant doing my exercises religiously; I wanted to get off my medication; and most importantly, I wanted to get out of my bathroom and out of my parents' house so I could meet people on my own and have my own experiences. If Bruce would help me achieve these goals, there was a $3,000 bonus in it for him.

Bruce swallowed hard and rubbed his pale, tender chin. Would it be all right if he grew his beard back? I said "Sure," although I knew how my conservative parents would take it.

"Working for Ken was the most intense thing I've ever done," Bruce said later. "I've done some intense things, like fish for crabs in the Bering Sea, but that was for a shorter period of time. Being with somebody like Ken every day is more exacting than being married. When you're married, somebody usually leaves to go to work."

For Bruce and I to maintain a polite sense of distance would have been impossible, given the fact that we were together almost 24 hours a day. For the past few years, Bruce had done what he damned well pleased, a condition I fiercely aspired to myself. Conflicts between us were inevitable. After Bruce's second week, we reached an understanding.

"Ken was fairly wealthy, used to having a lot of things his way and—I don't know if 'spoiled' is the right word—maybe protected from the real world in some ways. We had a blow-up about something—I don't remember what—and he gave me a ration of shit. At that time I was pretty independent. I just had to level with him. I said, 'Look, we have to be able to get along. If we can't, fuck it. You can just take this job and shove it.' I wasn't trying to be disrespectful, but on the other hand, I wasn't going to eat a bunch of bullshit either. It's very touchy. You go too far on one of these deals and that's the end of it."

I had found some redeeming quality behind Bruce's brassy, ungovernable exterior and decided to keep him on. I even sent him to the Easter Seals Society to get lessons in physical therapy from the head therapist.

Bruce admitted, "I was a bull shitter as far as the therapy went, so I figured I had to have something to offer him that was a reasonable exchange for my salary. My job as I saw it beginning to develop was not so much as a therapist, which he could find almost anybody else to do, but as a springboard to get him out of that scene he was in. He was shut up in that big house all the time, getting depressed by not being able to participate in life to the max."

I told Bruce that my main goal was to be liberated and especially liberated from my father. His observations of my Dad were very interesting to me.

> Ken's dad was a true lion in those days. He really dominated Ken's life in some major ways. I think he wanted to do some of the living for Ken that he couldn't do for himself. But his dad was a stumbling block to him. He interfered with his development.
>
> Sometimes I had to run interference between Ken and his father. Once I told Candido he couldn't run Ken's life for him. I mean I had to give him the respect he deserved. After all, he was the brains behind Jacuzzi Brothers. It wasn't easy to argue with him because he was so smart. He usually was right. He was the strongest-willed person I've ever met. In those days, he was such an impressive figure with the flowing white hair, strong and smart. But it was hard to communicate with him because he'd burn you down, consume you on the spot. If you contradicted him, he'd bury you.
>
> When I told him, 'You can't live Ken's life for him. You have to get out of his life,' he didn't want to hear that from anybody, least of all from this bearded young whipper-snapper.

Dad was painfully aware that I was having problems. I was still recovering from spinal surgery, and then he knew about my crush on Diane, the secretary of the foundation. Whenever I started putting too much stress on myself, pushing too hard toward some goal, I ran the risk of a relapse, and then the process would repeat itself. Dad thought I did not need some wild-eyed hippie stirring me up again with ideas of becoming superman. Whatever problems I had, the Jacuzzis could deal with it, thought Dad. Candido's philosophy was: "If you don't agree with me, it means you haven't been listening."

With a regimen of daily exercise, smaller doses of medication, and larger doses of self-confidence, I grew stronger. Bruce took me down to the seamy side of San Francisco to sate our appetites for good jazz and to Haight-Ashbury to indulge in some of the local smoke, and then with a case of the proverbial "munchies" we were off to some greasy spoon for a feast of fried eggs and bacon. It was an experience, but when Bruce wanted me to try more, I told him that I had been taking drugs all my life for arthritis and had no interest in recreational drugs.

Until now, my camping experiences had been limited to the paramilitary orchestrated chaos of Boy Scout campouts and the camping trip with Richard and his father. I never had a chance to reach out and touch the fingers of primordial nature. Our first trip was to the Mt. Lassen area 8,000 feet high, northeast of San Francisco where we awoke to find three deer standing over our sleeping bags, calmly nibbling leaves from the tree under which we slept to avoid the heavy dew.

I was first to open my eyes, and lay mesmerized by the animal's exquisitely fluid movements, innocent and grand, like something supernatural. Bruce lived in deer country and had often camped in the wild but he had to admit their visitation was a rare treat for him too. After the deer skipped away unstartled into the woods, Bruce boiled coffee in a tin pot over an open fire. The smells of breakfast cooking in the crisp morning air mixed with the scent of pine needles and the rich, moist earth around them gave us an appetite like we never had before.

Bruce recalled, "Ken was starving for experience. Camping in the mountains and hitting the jazz clubs in San Francisco—Ken didn't have these things in his life. We made an odd pair. I was up to go every minute and he was too, but he didn't want to look like a crazy fool to his family. I gave him that excuse. I was the catalyst."

One day, I decided I had been in the cocoon long enough and it was time to spread my wings. I announced to Bruce that I wanted to get out of the house and travel.

Bruce was shocked. "Here I was, this poor preacher's kid who would jump at the chance to go anywhere. And here Ken was able to travel, had the money, and was young enough to enjoy it. I was overwhelmed that we hadn't gone ten minutes ago!"

The first trip led us through the heart of Mexico down to Acapulco, the home of cliff divers, sumptuous resorts, wretched poverty, and some of the finest marijuana in the world. It was a place dear to Bruce's heart. One of the first things we did was to get me outfitted with a custom-made wet suit and head for the sea.

I had used swimming pools for years but never took on the ocean. In fact, my experiences in the water were much the same as my experience on land, conducted in a highly controlled, protected environment. And with good reason. As much as I might have wanted to be more adventurous in the water, there were dangers in allowing myself to become tired.

Because of the limited range of motion in my neck, it's difficult for me to roll over in the water if I get tired, just as it's hard sometimes to roll over in bed. So usually I swim on my back.

Part of the joy of swimming in Acapulco is seeing brilliantly colored fish dart through the crystal water, which I certainly could not do swimming on my back. The solution was simple—we would use a snorkel.

I thought that was a terrific idea and could hardly wait to try it out—that is until we were eye-level with the surf. Bruce could see I was having second thoughts, but this was part of my "liberation" and he would not hear of backing out.

"When you sit right down on the beach and look at the waves break, especially when you're as short as Ken is, the waves start looking a little bigger than when you're standing up on the terrace looking down. He changed his mind—he didn't want to go. I said, 'Come on, Ken. We've come this far, we've got to do it!'"

Bruce set me afloat in the shimmering water and dove in himself, keeping just a few feet ahead, in case of any trouble. We were only about 25 yards from shore when Bruce turned around in time to see me enveloped in a school of many-colored sardine-like fish. They lingered a moment, suspended, scintillating like a spirit and then, as if by common consent, they vanished. By now, Bruce was viewing the spectacle under water and remembered seeing my eyes suddenly grow huge within my facemask.

"I don't know what was going through his mind just then," Bruce said, "but he certainly was not scared, which was one of our goals—to get off all the fears and stuff."

Another major goal we had was to find me a woman, if only temporarily. It is one thing to be sweet sixteen and never been kissed, but a different ball game to be high and dry at twenty-six. I had gotten past my religiosity and was able to see myself as a human being seeking a mate, and needing experience in mating. I could forgive myself if I didn't follow every rule in the Bible.

As an adolescent, I was told by my doctor to forget ever having a woman. I prayed a little prayer that went, "Father, save me from the depression that comes from accepting every gloomy prediction as if it were the whole truth. Help me trust that I can cope with whatever comes as I try to find a possible road toward love and marriage."

Now that I was older, I longed for the sexual and emotional fulfillment a woman could give me in a relationship. I wanted a woman to share my life.

All the time I was growing up, I heard my father say that the most important thing in life is family. Money, power, work, even a person's self-interests come second. My mother's love literally kept me alive during my severe and frequent attacks. My brother, sisters, even cousins, uncles and aunts would do anything for me or for each other. My parents were beside themselves with joy when the other kids got married and started having children of their own. Raising a family was a good and natural thing to do. It was the best of what life had to offer and I wanted desperately to participate in it.

Bruce and I made a couple of clumsy attempts in Acapulco to get me some experience with women.

"In retrospect," Bruce said, "I can see how stupid it was for us to go to a whorehouse. I mean, here's a guy who's never been with a woman—we're trying to get him going and here we…, oh God! Well, I'm glad we did it anyway, although it must have been a stupid maneuver."

Finding a cathouse was no problem. We soon discovered that all the taxi drivers know where they are and are more than happy to escort their clients, not only to the door, but inside as well. By the way, our driver called the doorman and the bartender by their first names, and I suspected the driver was getting a cut of the action. While we went into the receiving room, the driver stayed to have a drink and chat with the staff.

I remember the place well. It was supposed to be really first class—out in the country. It looked like a big California ranch house. I think the girls actually lived there. It was classic. They had this big long bar and a little room adjacent to it where all the girls would gather. They had tequila, beer, American drinks like Coca-Cola, or even pot if you wanted it. The girls were waiting for us, scantily clad and smiling. When you picked out the one you wanted, you could slip into one of the rooms along the hall. Very luxurious. Each had a bed and a mirror, or so we were told. I was a little nervous. In fact, I didn't go to bed with any of them. Gosh, it's hard being a Catholic. Bruce didn't either but he wanted to. Mostly we stayed to do some drinking at the bar.

Another guy at the bar told us what happened when he went into one of the rooms with his lady. He asked the whore, who appeared to be American, "How much do you charge?"

She said, "I don't charge. I just take cash!"

So the guy said, "You know what I mean. How much do you get?"

She said, "I get all I can."

He got upset and said, "Goddammit, woman, I didn't come here to be made sport of. How much money do you want to give me a little?"

When he heard the price, he pulled out all the money in his pocket, which wasn't a lot, and said, "This is all I've got!"

She said, "That ain't enough!"

He said, "Well, how much would you charge me to get a slow hand job?"

She said, "Don't you know it says in the Bible it's a sin to cast your seed upon the ground?"

The guy said, "Hell, madam, I'm not tryin' to live at the foot of the cross!" Then he stamped out and spent his money at the bar with us.

We stayed on in Acapulco for a few days, getting a feel for the way the people lived. Bruce had great admiration for the simple, relaxed life the poor people lived. He took me to the open markets where the pale fly-blown carcasses of chickens hung in a row by their necks above the butcher's booth like a band of unremarkable desperados, and where haggard women in faded shawls haggled good-naturedly over the price of produce.

The people I paid the most attention to were the children. I always had an affinity for kids, partly because I was small enough to be a kid myself. Also because the arthritis stunting my growth, and the many long years of living at home or in hospitals had prevented me from fully developing an adult sense of life, I still had a child's fun-loving viewpoint.

Earlier when I represented the foundation, I appeared to take myself very seriously, perhaps too seriously. This should have given away the fact that I was not practiced in the art of projecting an image of stolid, authoritative maturity. It is true that as I grew older, I had built a protective wall around myself. I had been hurt too many times. But around my friends and especially around children, I bared my playful and inquisitive nature.

One thing that startled me in Acapulco was the serious and responsible way some children pursued a profession. The shoeshine boys especially seemed like professionals. They were persuasive, aggressive salesmen, quick to size up a customer and to establish the rapport necessary to land a sale. I thought Jacuzzi Brothers should recruit some of these guys. Marveling at the industriousness of the little tycoons, I asked Bruce what they did with the money. I was stunned to hear that they were probably supporting themselves and their families. Imagine, I thought, to be so young and already making it in the world!

The next trip was to Jamaica where we stayed in the Playboy Club, converted from a grand old hotel by magazine magnate Hugh Heffner, which retained a certain threadbare elegance. I was reminded that I was not the only man with disabilities who enjoyed the revelations of female flesh in *Playboy* and such magazines. Another person who uses a wheelchair is physicist Stephen Hawking, who had lost a bet about whether black holes existed, and awarded the physicist who won a subscription to *Penthouse* magazine. But lechers aside, soon after we arrived, as we were sitting around the pool, Bruce was sipping a tropical drink. I was drinking orange juice, attempting to abstain from alcohol and medication.

We met three Jewish girls from Canada. Eleanna was the superb-looking one. Born in Egypt, she had dark, smoldering eyes, olive skin, jet-black hair and a voluptuous body. Bruce made every effort to get her into bed, but failed. Irene was cute and slender with short, stylish hair and a self-assured manner. The other one, whose name I can't remember, seemed to be a young spinster-in-the-making who decided to have one last blow-out before settling down to an uneventful, extended old age. She was, perhaps, an example of Henry David Thoreau's comment that the masses "lead lives of quiet desperation."

We rented a car and took the girls to restaurants and to a little cove to go swimming. Eleanna and Irene expressed some dissatisfaction with life as secretaries in Montreal (although apparently the third girl liked it fine), which we took as our cue to plug the never-ending wonders of California.

They were so intrigued by our tales that Eleanna and Irene later went to California. They visited my sister, Alba, and my parents. Irene decided to stay in California and get a job. Several years later, she met a rabbi and when they were married, I painted their wedding portrait. Eleanna went to Europe and found a job in Florence where she met some married man and became his mistress. I saw her in 1971 when I was there. She had gained a lot of weight and aged a lot. Italians have a knack of making girlfriends believe they are going to leave their wives, but they never do. Why should they? They have the best of both worlds. The other girl went back to Montreal.

For being in Jamaica only five days, we covered a lot of ground. We hit some of the highest and lowest spots in the area, wining and dining attractive women. Every day overflowed with new experiences and challenges. I began to see just how much I was missing by sitting at home in Lafayette, feeling sorry for myself. After seeing how some people went not only without a college education and a job but without enough food or medical care or even hope, I started to realize how lucky I was. Visits to foreign parts usually convince Americans of how lucky they are.

The day we left for the States was hot and we were late leaving for the airport. The Playboy Club was on Montego Bay and the only road leading to the airport was mostly dirt and ran through some of the poorer districts. We said goodbye to the girls, Bruce put me in the car, and we were off.

Bruce had raced motorcycles in Oregon and there were just enough differences between a dirt bike and our subcompact car to make it a challenge. He described our ride later on.

> We had rented this Hillman and in Jamaica you have to drive on the wrong side of the road and shift with your left hand. It was so hot that I convinced Ken we needed some Red Stripe beer. So we started to drink this damned Jamaican stuff and actually started getting fairly tight. We stopped and picked up one of the natives who was hitchhiking and since they all drive like madmen there, I wasn't about to be outdone, so I started driving like mad. We drove through the marketplace on the way, just missing people and donkey carts, sliding around corners. Ken would start to fall over in the seat. I had to hold him up with one hand and steer with the other.

We were late but so was our flight. Bruce was drunk and trying to hurry our belongings through customs but the customs inspector was not about to bring disgrace upon the job by rushing through it. When she pulled out my old-fashioned metal urinal, the tourist behind us in line could not contain her jealousy and would not leave us in peace until I told her where she could pick up one just like it.

I couldn't believe it. She was saying, "Oooh, that's so cute. What is it? First she thought it was a Jamaican vase or artifact. A pee bottle? I've got to have one! Where can I get it? Is it pewter? What a conversation piece that would be!"

Arriving in the U.S., Bruce found that during the escapades in Mexico and Jamaica, he had accumulated a considerable amount of back pay. With swift calculations, he realized he had enough for a sizable down payment on a new Harley Davidson. So with a little help from my neighbor, who was president of a bank in Richmond, California, Bruce was able to plunk down the entire $1,800 for the gleaming machine. But Bruce's best-laid plans went awry. Wait, I'll let him tell what happened:

> It was a great thrill for me. I rode the thing across the Golden Gate Bridge and went into a coffee shop. When I came out three minutes later, it was gone! I was only in there long enough to grab my friend and chug a half a cup of coffee. It felt like somebody hit me in the solar plexus. I built a log cabin in Alaska years later, and it burned down. The loss of that cabin and all the stuff

in it and all the labor that went into building it didn't affect me as much as losing that motorcycle. I was planning to buy insurance the next day.

I felt for crestfallen Bruce. He couldn't even wait long enough to insure it before he had to take it for a cruise to the Haight-Ashbury district in San Francisco to show his motorcycle buddies. Bruce was heartbroken. He still had to pay off the loan, but left to his own devices, he was never able to save any money. The only way he was able to come up with the down payment was that during our trips, all his expenses were paid and everything he made was free and clear. Thus, it was partly my compassion for the plight of my Huck Finn companion that prompted me to begin an even more extensive leg of our adventure.

Bruce's influence had been just what I needed at this stage of my development. Bruce could not instill in me overnight the confidence that my disability, my doctors, my parents, and the public disallowed all my life. But he was a living example of how a person could cheerfully get by without any money, turn his back on successes and failures without a second thought, and regularly risk appearing foolish in pursuing new experiences. True, Bruce had no disability, but neither was I as "disabled" as I had once thought. Perhaps my greatest "disability" was my reluctance to take chances.

It wasn't part of our original "plan" for him to accompany me to Europe. I was supposed to hire someone else for this trek because, for some reason, Europe didn't appeal all that much to Bruce. The real reason, however, was that Bruce had a *chick* in Berkeley whom he didn't want to leave for three or four months. But fate in the form of a motorcycle thief stole the plan and gave The Beard no viable alternative except to do a 180-degree turnabout and insist on coming with me.

Bruce and I, along with the mommies and daddies with infants, were rushed to be pre-boarded on the 707 leaving JFK shortly for Lisbon, Portugal. After some nonsensical hassling, we were allowed to seat ourselves in the first row of economy class, right behind the bulkhead separating us from first-class, so that my legs wouldn't get squished during the planned nine-plus hour trans-Atlantic flight. It's ironic that a person like me, who's less than four feet four inches tall (yeah, my height kept changing as my condition changed) needs more leg room, but since I can only sit with my legs straight out in front of me, I really don't have any other alternative.

Of course, I could always fly first-class, where my feet would extend only about a foot or so beyond the edge of these much more commodious seats, but I choose, and chose then, not to. (In those days it was more for reasons of principle; today it's my economic reality).

As soon as we were seated, I got belted in. (Most airline hostesses/hosts seem to always want to belt in cripples immediately, as though we might fall out of our seats and start foaming at the mouth or something equally fearful). The other trans-ocean hopefuls are hustled in like a herd of over-packed camels. Even the smell emanating from some is camel-like.

Voila! The Beard and I were on our way to Portugal. The Beard was up and really with the program, snapping rhythmically his sinewy fingers to the beat of some surprisingly good jazz trickling from the plane's loudspeaker system. We had high expectations for this European jaunt. It would be the first for both of us.

After the usual demonstrations of how to buckle our seatbelts, place the pop-down oxygen masks over our faces, puke in the little paper bags, and use the flotation gear in case we decided to take a communal bath in the Atlantic, the 707 started rolling towards the assigned runway. Maybe 30 or 40 minutes passed before we got through the rigmarole of waiting our plane's turn in line and, of course, the Captain's pre-takeoff banter. Unbelievably, about an hour after we got on board, we actually took off for Lisbon. I've since come to learn that a one-hour wait is pretty damn good for today's international flights. Anyway, we get up there and everyone, including us, start stuffing liquid refreshments and appetizers—soft drinks, peanuts and pretzels for economy-class—down our guts in anticipation of the coming dinner and movie.

About an hour and a half into our flight, and just before the hostesses were supposed to start serving dinner, our captain announced that the airplane was experiencing "minor difficulties" and that we'd have to return to JFK. The lumbering 707 started slowly banking, making a turn to the right to retrace our flight path to Kennedy. None of us onboard seemed worried or concerned with our collective or individual fate. Hadn't it been grilled into us that flying is the safest form of travel? And, even though it's the 1960s and the Vietnam War is devastating our country, most Americans still believed what our government officials, institutions, and corporations told us. If they said that flying was the safest form of travel, then it must be. So if our Captain wasn't worried, why should we be?

Most of us continued sipping our drinks and munching our nuts. A few souls were overheard starting to complain about the delay and how this might screw up making their connections in Lisbon. I then noticed what appeared to be a momentary flash off to one side of the plane, but I couldn't figure out what it could have been. Maybe, since I couldn't turn my neck very well, I didn't see anything and it was just my imagination. The Beard didn't notice anything, but also started to grumble about the delay and how he was sacrificing by going to Europe because he had been too stupid to insure his bike before driving it on the street.

The Captain again broke into the canned music, this time indicating that we had lost power to one of our engines, but quickly adding that there was nothing to worry about since we still had three engines and the 707 was designed to fly just fine on only two. Almost everyone onboard began murmuring in a low, but obviously concerned voice to whomever was close by and would listen. A tinge of skittishness appeared somewhere in my belly, but I was still relatively unfazed. Even after the hostesses began removing all our drinks and snacks and had us stow our tray tables, I wasn't too concerned. About 10 to 15 minutes later, the Captain came on once more, announcing this time in a very subdued, monotone voice that another engine had been shutdown but that we were on our descent to land.

"Well," I thought, "isn't this plane designed to fly on two engines? We'll be okay," I told myself…more than once. A short time later, a hostess with an unexpected high-pitched shrill voice asked us to again direct our attention to the hostesses standing in the aisle, demonstrating the proper use of the flotation gear that was under our seats. We were firmly reminded that we were to leave the flotation gear in place unless and until directed otherwise by the crew. Assuring us again that there's nothing to worry about, the hostess firmly asked everyone to make certain that all of our possessions were properly stored in the overhead compartments and/or under our seats.

A sense of tension and nervousness vibrated throughout the cabin like a hushed, cutting winter wind, but no one said much. Except for intermittent sniffling, the remaining silence was pea soup thick. I made the sign of the cross and caught a glimpse of several other passengers doing the same. As we touched down smooth as silk on the runway at JFK, nothing seemed unusual except the dozen fire engines and emergency vehicles, made visible in the distance from their flashing orange, red, and blue lights, like incessant fireflies dancing for our pleasure and entertainment.

The Beard and I were among the last to disembark the 707 into the JFK terminal. As Bruce pushed my wheelchair into the people-filled terminal, we were both taken aback by the unnerving absence of noise and hushed speech between everyone we saw in this usually chaotic and bustling airport. Was it about our flight, our close call?

The Beard and I were directed to a holding area to await further instructions. I noticed an older black man seated on a bench facing me, holding a portable radio to his ear. He momentarily lifted his head, looked past me and said to no one in particular, "Martin Luther King has been shot. He's dead." I was flabbergasted. That was the cause of the silence.

Many hours later, Bruce and I finally boarded another plane for Lisbon. We never did learn what went wrong with our first plane. But it didn't seem to matter anymore. The death of a man of such significance dwarfed everything else.

We finally landed in Lisbon and checked into the Ritz, elegant cousin of the Paris Hotel of the same name. We went first class all the way, taking a trip to a casino on the coast, where we managed to break even at roulette, with Bruce doing most of the gambling while I fronted the money. We stopped at a nightclub and saw the flavas who danced and sang about alcohol dependency and unrequited love. We were so inspired that afterwards we looked for a whorehouse. We made a little more progress this time, although Bruce found himself at somewhat of a loss as to how far his duties as my aide should extend.

Bruce later described his version of what happened that night and what could have been a very devastating experience for me.

> We went up to this room—I'll never forget. I set him there in bed. Maybe I should have, it was hard to know what to do, undress him first or let the girl do it? It could easily have gotten to the embarrassing point. Maybe I should have stayed, but I went into the other room with my girl. When I came back it was all too much of an embarrassment for Ken. So he didn't consummate the deal. It was lucky he wasn't scarred by the experience but if he were the type who would be overcome by every little thing, he'd have been dead long ago. Besides, we were moving at a fast enough pace that there was no time to sit and mope about anything.

What actually happened has been long since forgotten in my brain but it went something like this. She said she spoke a little English and undressed me. I lay there waiting for something to happen but she was on a telephone. Finally she got off and I said, "It's chilly in here, isn't it?" She didn't understand. She said something like, "Is this your first time?" I said, "Yes, si, si."

She said in broken English, "When it you first time, it like me first time. Ven aqui a su madre (Come here to your mama)." Then I got kind of turned off, especially when I saw her undressing. I don't know what it was, but it wasn't natural. That just wasn't for me and I didn't know how to pretend or put on an act. I just stopped everything. I suppose I needed to have more of a relationship. Just having sex was not a sufficient drive for me.

After Portugal, we bought a used Volkswagen and installed hand controls hoping I would be able to use it. However, after my last few operations, I no longer had the strength to operate a car without power steering and power brakes. After blowing a big wad at the Ritz, we stayed in a real cockroach pit in Luxembourg. In Düsseldorf, we found out that the bars were outlets for different breweries, so we had to sample the distinctive qualities of every one. By the time we were done, we had to agree that we couldn't tell the difference. Or couldn't remember the difference. We drove through Switzerland and back through the Simplon Tunnel. When we arrived in Milan, Bruce announced he was leaving. As he said,

> I missed my old lady and I just worked for him long enough. Ten months was longer than I'd ever worked for anybody, and it was way beyond my threshold for staying with a job. I dug working for him right up to the end, when I realized I had to leave. Ken got a little mad, which was not unreasonable.

I told Bruce that I thought it was unfair for him to leave before all the goals we discussed were met. Furthermore, because the goals were not met, I didn't think he was entitled to the $3,000 bonus. This threw him into a temporary rage. When the dust settled, I had to admit the goals I'd set were pretty vague and Bruce had done a fine job as my aide. But I hated for him to abandon me just when things were starting to gel. So Bruce agreed to stay around long enough for me to find another aide, at which time I awarded him his bonus and we parted friends.

With Bruce gone, the last ties to home were cut. Now I was on my own in a foreign country whose language I could hardly speak with a wheelchair I could not push and a '66 Volkswagen I could not drive. I did not know how long I would be staying or even what I would do. But I was content...almost.

I had left home in a *storm* of independence, family members disapproving of my Bohemian aide, but now the storm was losing power as I reached a land of "cooler" waters.

13

I'm a Man!

Whirlwind: A current of air whirling violently in spiral form around a vertical axis that has a forward motion.

I had to find another aide before Bruce left. The first applicant was the son of a wealthy aristocrat who felt the experience of having to serve another human being would do him good. Although I did not hire him, I was impressed with the motive and wondered if such a thing could happen in the United States. The problem was that the man simply was unsuited for the job. Part of the interview involved helping me with my bath, which made the young aristocrat so nervous the shampoo bottle he held slipped through his fingers, exploding into a thousand slivers in the tile tub where his evaluator sat.

I eventually hired two aides, Egidio and Pasquale (Pat) who were to each work alternating shifts (one or two weeks on, one or two weeks off) to keep each other from burning out. Egidio was still in school at the time. He planned to join us in Spain. It was decided that Pat and I would drive to Yugoslavia for some gambling. Pat suggested that we go by way of Udine.

"Ken, Udine is full of good-looking women!"

Well, that was all I needed to hear and it convinced me that we must go to Udine. This proved that a woman is at the bottom of everything, whether in France or elsewhere. Cherchez la femme! Look for women, and you will find men.

When we arrived in Udine, I was surprised to see so many people on bicycles. When Bruce and I drove through France and Germany, it was mostly freeway, so we did not realize how popular biking was. At that time, the freeway stopped in Venice. The highway we took was called the Napoleon Highway and it was lined with trees on both sides so the fair-skinned Emperor would not be troubled to compete with the sun. The highway also was lined with bicycles, which I remember with particular fondness.

Jesus! I couldn't stand it. There were some good-looking women on those bicycles and naturally their skirts would slide up and give you just a beautiful shot of…everything! That was one of the neatest things I ever saw in my life. You could view things without committing a sin.

We stopped over in Trieste (my Grandpa's home earlier) on our way to the gambling town of Portorosé which, although it did not contain so many bicycles, was interesting in its own right. The city is like San Francisco in that it is built on hills and opens onto the ocean. It was a little windier than San Francisco, but I did not think anything of it until I asked a native why there were poles along the sidewalks with chains strung between them. I was told that when warm breezes from North Africa come up the Adriatic and meet the north winds from the Alps, hurricane-velocity winds called "La Bora" develop and if you do not hang onto the chains you can be blown away.

We were not blown away in Portorosé, but we were given a run for our money. We should have been suspicious when the casino doorman would not let us in until we showed him our passports. It seems the Yugoslav government did not want their citizens squandering precious dinars in the casino, but it did not mind taking dollars, lire or any other currency from foreigners. Gambling gives tourists something to do and it provides the country with a steady source of foreign exchange.

We went up to the roulette table, surrounded by grim gentlemen, probably losers, in evening clothes. There were also a few really stunning beauties of the Adriatic, listlessly watching as the little steel ball bearing attempted to defy the direction of the great, silent wheel, before succumbing to the inevitable, and tripping on one of the many-numbered slots falling firmly into place to a chorus of tired groans. Pat was getting wound up for a big evening. I knew little about gambling, and beautiful women almost always eluded me. Nevertheless, I could not wait to get started.

Pat's kidding never bothered me. "You can't win if you don't take chances," he explained. "Besides, it is not losing that's dishonorable, it's not making the attempt." He was not afraid to try his luck in Yugoslavia. So what if he made a fool of himself? He'd be gone in a week. And was he worried about losing a little money? Certainly not, as long as it was my money!

We each ordered vodka. No ice, no soda, no fruit, no straw, just a shot or so of room-temperature vodka in the bottom of a glass. I knew better than to order my usual Martini because all I would get would be a glass with some room-temperature dry vermouth. It would never occur to them to mix it with gin.

I did not intend to become Diamond Jim Jacuzzi. I simply wanted to have a good time. Of course, people noticed me. They always noticed the wheelchair. They gave me room while Pat placed a modest bet on black. The high rollers, betting on single numbers, were losing their ruffled shirts and sneered a bit at this conservatism. The Adriatic girls turned their attentions elsewhere, to the great dismay of Pat.

But we won. And we kept on winning. First we tried black/red, then odd/even, each time with an equal chance of winning or losing. After the high rollers were cleaned out, Pat and I were still placing bets, having built up our $10 stake to over $5,200. Now the girls were interested. They let Pat buy them drinks and gave approval with their eyes. They were openly impressed with me each time the croupier forked over the winnings. They tried to keep things in perspective. These girls were professional spectators. They would sleep with you for money or even just a place to stay for the night.

But mathematical certainty caught up with us. Our pile of chips dwindled to $10. The girls yawned. Some drifted away to wherever it is they drift off to on a bad night. The lights seemed to have halos like the moon, a presentiment of dog days. Pat was nearly frantic.

"Do something. But do it quick!"

"Look at it this way, Pat," I said. "Gambling has a lot of advantages over business. You can't lose more than you have."

He responded, "We did not have those girls, but we begin to lose them now!"

We settled down, betting only on odd numbers. Gradually, our winnings increased. Everybody loves an underdog. A crowd gathered around us again. The girls were skeptical, but watched and waited. The croupier shoved more chips at us. Pat gulped his warm vodka and howled.

"That's it," I said. "We're done."

Disbelief flooded Pat's face. "But we're winning."

"That's why we're done."

Pat looked hurt and so did the girls but we were up $400, which meant that our meals and hotel expenses for five days were free, courtesy of the Yugoslav government.

From Yugoslavia, we traveled to Rome, often called the birthplace of culture, the ancient vortex of power. After all, they said, "All roads lead to Rome." Two thousand years earlier, my ancestors had walked upon these stones, perhaps mulling over the engineering of a triumphal arch or marching on parade for Caesar with 200 pounds of weapons and armor on their backs.

Perhaps they even strolled with a senator discussing the disturbance of this man called Jesus of Nazareth. Although my contact with these historic stones was not with goatskin sandals or bare feet but with B. F. Goodrich wheelchair tires, I felt drawn to participate in the legacy of Rome.

I decided to paint. I always had been interested in art, and always carried a sketchpad for doodling. Some thought I showed talent, though I never studied formally. For me, art had been a way of joining with the physical world and preserving the magic of an encounter on canvas or paper.

Ever since I was an infant, I liked to look at and hold objects which to me possessed a certain beauty, warmth, or texture. Whether it was seeing the ocean crashing against the rocks at the beach, touching a giant redwood, or holding an apricot, I remember the great enjoyment I received from those experiences. When I was two years old and developed a disability, I felt the need to see, taste, feel, and grow even stronger, for the resulting physical limitations had shut me off almost entirely from that self-discovery.

Through the local Berlitz School where I began taking intensive Italian, I met Professor Cantini, a semi-retired painting master. Cantini was not one to waste time. He immediately asked the aspiring young artist before him, "What is it you want to do?"

"I want to paint portraits."

"Fine," he said, "then that's what we will do."

And so began a rigorous course in portrait painting, art history and the classics in general. With Pat piloting my chair, we would visit many of Rome's museums and art galleries where Cantini pointed out the first uses of perspective among the old masters and the color tones and combinations used in creating on canvas gold, flesh, silk, water, hair, eyes, sunshine and blood.

Before I met Cantini, I had bought paints and done a symbolic piece, which I showed him. It looked like a collection of rocks, stacked to form the shape of a sprinter getting ready to spring from the starting blocks. It was red on a blue background. The intention was to represent my struggle, the human struggle, to signify that it is hard to make a go of being human.

"It's interesting, this painting," Cantini mumbled, half to himself. "It's good, but it's very cold."

Cantini was extremely perceptive. I realized that what he said was true. Why had I used rocks? Was it because, as in the child's game, they are resistant to anything, incapable of damage? I probably had been too defensive, afraid of getting hurt.

Cantini told me, "The first portrait you paint will be yourself."

He had me mark off a mirror with equally spaced lines, three vertical and four horizontal, in a pattern developed by Leonardo Da Vinci. He also helped me make a small frame with equally spaced strings that looked like a sparsely strung tennis racket, serving the same purpose as the mirror. By holding this frame vertically, the artist could easily "measure" his subject for portraiture, even landscapes.

Cantini was adamant regarding the significance of observation in portraiture or painting of any kind. He also underlined the importance of continuing the observation process through every step, every moment of the painting. This proved to be an invaluable lesson, training me to glance frequently from the painting to the subject and to notice details and subtleties that I otherwise would have missed.

I came to realize that the slightest alteration of color or form could result in a totally different final picture. I also learned that observation is not easy to master. It requires more than simply looking at something. One must look for the purpose of seeing and understanding. During this time, I trained myself to keep in practice by disciplining myself to critically observe everything from the eye color of a new acquaintance to the floor plan of an apartment.

At first, Cantini was impressed that I could paint at all, considering that I could barely move my hands and fingers. All the standards seemed to apply only to other people. To be thought of as "doin' pretty well considering," was not good enough. But when Cantini suggested I could become professional if I applied myself, I realized I had an awesome responsibility.

Cantini deepened my knowledge of the physics of color, explaining that each color has its own wavelength and hits the eye at different times. Since red arrives at the eye a split second before blue, red appears to advance while blue seems to recede. He gave me a new understanding of how the juxtaposition of colors can create the effects of different colors, describing how to use "cold" colors like viridian green and cobalt blue and how colors could be used to give a subject greater warmth.

My self-portrait turned out well. Cantini was impressed, especially having gained some insight into me during our time together. The tones of the painting were dark, shadowy. It was as if an exorcism had taken place, leaving my withdrawn, timid, darker side behind in the painting, and releasing me from my fear of rejection.

Cantini looked up slowly from the portrait. "What you must do now is go somewhere and paint, paint, paint!"

I returned to my hotel in a state of mild elation. Like many European hotels, it seemed well worn by American standards, but it had a fine view from the terrace where I spent long hours painting or doing my exercises. I had heard about the place because the Australian couple who ran it had bought Jacuzzi pool equipment. Why else would I have checked into a hotel called The Boomerang? The couple took to me right away, perhaps partly because they felt a certain camaraderie with other English-speaking people. They were having a barbecue by the pool and I was invited. They had also invited an attractive English girl who had been living in South Africa.

Pat and I surveyed the party. The smell of spicy smoke wafted through the thin gathering of friends and neighbors, mostly older folks. Pat sighed, "If there is some way, maybe we could eat a little chicken and leave early?"

I was feeling pretty good and did not want to waste my mood on this dull crowd. Tonight we should celebrate, get drunk, and go find Caesar's ghost or something. I was about to suggest this when Pat made a low, prolonged whistle. "What do you think of that?" he said, indicating a lovely tall, dark lady standing beside the Australian couple.

"I think I'd like to meet her."

Pat was surprised at my sudden purposefulness. "I don't know, boss. You think you could handle it?"

"Well, what the hell. Let's find out."

I had Pat wheel me up to where she was standing. All eyes around her turned to me, and the crowd parted for my chair. I had long since given up trying to be anonymous. I accepted that wherever I went, people would stare, especially in Italy, where a person with a major physical disability is seldom seen on the street.

When I introduced myself, I felt that it was somebody else saying the words. Spontaneously leaning forward, I extended my small, shriveled hand for her to shake. I wondered briefly if perhaps this bold, easy-going person emerging from me now was the one Cantini said was hiding behind a mask. Cantini predicted that I would be a more expressive artist when I allowed myself to take chances.

Her dark eyes did not linger on my wheelchair or on my deformities. Neither did they avoid them. I knew immediately that I had found a friend.

I realized that I had been looking for a pair of eyes to portray in my painting. I had begun to work on painting a portrait of my father. Candido, after all, had dropped seeds into my soul! I had to paint him because I idolized, envied and struggled with him all at the same time. I had no trouble painting his eyes because they had seared me for so long.

But a woman's eyes! I knew what they should be. I saw them clearly in my imagination. But I could not paint them. I could not find a model to represent the aspect I desired. Yet, I could not describe it to anyone. Although I looked at every face I met, I could find no eyes that represented what I sought.

But I was in a curious mood that night, weary yet restless. I had the feeling that someone I did not see was looking at me, but I'd got used to that feeling. Then suddenly, just as I had concluded that I could never paint a woman for want of a pair of eyes, there they were. I scanned her countenance as I had never done a woman's face before. I forgot myself in her, feeling only a strong desire to draw nearer.

From the first day we met, she treated me as a man and not as someone to pity or someone "exceptional," which is almost impossible to live up to.

Her name was Marcia and she worked for Universal Studios in Rome. Her musical English accent and her huge dark eyes that projected an impression of innocence intrigued me. For all her vulnerability, Marcia was a survivor.

As a little girl, she was uprooted from an overly civilized section of London with its rainy weather, cobblestone streets, and polite "bobbies" and transplanted into South Africa's unrelenting heat and racial unrest. But she survived. A love of fast cars led to her racing in amateur rallies in South Africa, ending abruptly with a crash that ripped ligaments and shattered bones in her neck and back. She survived this, too, although she was left with stiffness and pain, especially in bad weather.

Marcia seemed to draw men to her. Her natural charm and unshakable confidence were irresistible. I found it disarming the way she opened her heart to me so easily. As the evening progressed, she told me she had a lover in Rome who had sworn by all that was holy he would marry her as soon as his wife agreed to a divorce. After months of waiting turned into years, the story grew thin and his motives transparent. They fought, but it seemed she always went back to him. Recently, during one of their rows, her Italian lover, sick of discussing his theoretical divorce, tore up all the clothes he had given her and stomped off. She did not hide the fact that she felt lonely and abandoned.

Marcia introduced me to her English friends, who impressed me almost as much as she did. One was an outrageous homosexual who wore designer clothes and spoke in poetic disjointed phrases. He seemed to have transformed his peculiarities into a style that was quite elegant. Another of Marcia's friends was a beautiful woman with whom I discussed my great love of music.

The band was playing something I really enjoyed and I mentioned to her how I always wanted to dance, although I couldn't. That's when Marcia's girlfriend taught me how to dance with my arms and hands; something called "hand jiving." It was great fun, and I recall dancing most of that evening with her.

After that night at the party, Marcia and I began seeing more of each other. Marcia spoke good Italian, but when we went out to eat she encouraged me to order for us, even if it meant ordering filet of army boot. She told me, "The only way to learn a language is to speak it, even if you have to bluff your way through 90 percent of it in the beginning."

Bluffing my way through even ten percent of something made me uncomfortable. My thinking may have been adventurous, but after years of having to conserve my energy, carefully engineering each move, my actions were cautious.

Marcia was openly impressed with my painting, giving me the courage to immerse myself in this work, to try new approaches, and not to hold anything back.

Meeting Marcia and enjoying my love of painting encouraged me to rethink how I wanted to live. At first, I recalled the wonderful words of the actress Ava Gardner, a kind of rebel, herself. She said, "When I'm old and gray, I want to have a house by the sea. And paint. With a lot of wonderful chums, good music, and booze around. And a damn good kitchen to cook in." Perhaps that was what I sought.

I was surprised to discover that I was not falling helplessly in love with Marcia. I don't think that she loved me, either. I thought only that I pleased her, and my passion flattered and enlarged her. It was exciting for me to be with a woman who really seemed to have the lowdown, who was so many different things to different people.

My only previous participation in love was as a hostage of love, a victim of my emotions. To me, love had been not unlike my illness: overwhelming, incapacitating, and requiring a long torturous period of recovery. I guess I did love Marcia, but it was a comfortable feeling that I thought I could control. I craved her and my release in her was all that I wanted.

From that evening on, our friendship flourished, just like what pestered my jockey shorts whenever Marcia was in my view. She knew my goal in life crested on parting her red sea. But, as I would gradually come to find out, she had definite ideas about how to "tutor" me for something so special.

"Dah'ling, sex is much like eating good Italian food. You must savor each course, every morsel, not skip anything. Take me to *pranzo*—lunch,—and I'll show you all about *eating*."

"When does the sex part come in?" I asked in a whisper.

"You're a horny little devil, aren't you? First Marcia teaches you to eat. Then we see."

Sitting under languid grapevines and a flower-and-spice-scented hilltop, Marcia at my side, drugged my senses. About ten minutes after we were seated, our waiter, built like a hunkered wrestler, but soft-spoken and shy in demeanor, brought us the menu. It was Rome; Marcia and I were together. That's all that mattered. In another ten minutes, our waiter came back, asking if we had decided what we wanted.

"I'll make you a deal, Marcia. You pick the meal and I'll order the wine."

"*Bene*. Fine, you pick the wine."

"*Est, Est, Est, per favore*," I said to the waiter. The wine's name translates literally to, This is it, this is it, this is it." Perhaps I was subliminally doing more than just choosing the wine. I picked it out, trusting that a local white would be the perfect accompaniment to whatever Marcia ordered.

Marcia then proceeded to order our *pranzo*. *Prosciutto con i fichi. Cozze gratinate. Cervella e zucchine fritte. Insalata di radicchio e rucola* (often called *arugula* in America). *Budino di ricotta*. Instruction began with the *antipasto*, the *prosciutto con i fichi*.

The appetizer was a thin ham with figs, a very sensual fruit, and what some call "sex on a plate."

> Kenny, aren't these large, green Roman figs just gorgeous? Before you even pick up a fork, behold what's before you. You see how they've peeled each fig, and then wrapped it gently with paper-thin prosciutto. Look at the way the pink and red center of the fig peeks at you. Breathe in its fragrance. Now, take some fig and prosciutto together and put them in your mouth. Don't start chewing, yet. Let the sweetness of the fruit and saltiness of the meat ooze and blend into your saliva. When you chew and swallow it, taste each moment. Let it linger. Sip some wine.

As Marcia coaxed me along each step, she'd occasionally brush her toe ever so lightly against my leg, sampling me with aesthetic glances. "Tell me, Kenny, can you think of some part of me you'd like to do that to?"

Marcia could talk seductively and raise my emotions to a fever pitch, and she loved doing it. Then, finally, one night in the Boomerang hotel, we made love as if it were the most easy and natural thing in the world.

I don't know how to describe it. In eighth grade, my friend Perry A. told me in precise detail how he thought people copulated. I was distressed to hear that the man is supposed to be on top, supporting himself with his arms, a feat I would never be able to perform. Even my doctors had told me to dismiss from my mind thoughts of having a normal sex life.

Maybe Marcia sensed uncertainty. But, as a superb dancer can make an inexperienced partner feel graceful on the dance floor, Marcia took my mind off the mechanics of sex and let me devote myself to making love.

She said things like, "Just let me take care of everything. Touch me here. That's it, you're doing fine. Now taste me here. Slow down, take your time. Oh, yes, yes, yes, that's great. You're doing fine. You did it, dear, you did it."

Simple words. Eve would have told them to Adam, as she held out the apple. Then the snake would have slithered up and said some of the same things like, "Yes, that's great. That's so good. That's the best. Oh, my God, yes! That's too damned good!"

For years, I had been obsessed with sex. It represented the ultimate communion with another human being, the ultimate contact with the physical world. I thought I would never get there. Throughout much of my childhood, I had been deprived of hugs and tickles and rides on shoulders because they would have caused me excruciating pain. I was separated from the earth by my wheelchair and, to a great extent, from society by my parents.

The act of making love came as an overdue assurance that I was all right, that I belonged and was needed. Sure, I'd been kicked out of the Garden of Eden and probably wouldn't go to Heaven because we weren't married. It did not bother me that I had to be "on the bottom" or that Marcia had to do most of the "work." Sex was even more wonderful than I thought it would be. What filled me with joy more than anything else was that Marcia could get pleasure from me. She was tall and beautiful and I was short and deformed. Yet she told me I was sexy and, for the first time, I felt sexy.

I leave the rest to your imagination. But this was not my imagination. Marcia was not only my first but was also my first "older woman." Sex was like a violent *whirlwind* between us, forming a unity that propelled us forward to completion and fulfillment. I truly was a man!

Another time we slept together, Marcia stayed with me all night since Francisco was not due to show up until mid morning. I was accustomed to waking up early, and I lay in bed watching the sun climb from the horizon, and using the time to think while Marcia slept. I watched her, perfectly still in the bed beside me, a barely discernible smudge of flesh-tone makeup on the freshly starched pillow. I wondered if this was what it was like to have a lover. For twenty-eight years, I had heard rumors but never really put them to the test.

Suddenly, another feeling swept over me. I looked at the lovely lady beside me and sighed. I had to take a crap. And bad. For most people this involves a simple, solitary exercise, but for me, even trying to get off the bed alone would be a death-defying feat. The stool softeners I was taking were doing their job and the inevitable could not be put off for long. Pat would not be back until 10 am. I looked at the clock. It was 7:15. I looked out the window. The sun did not seem to be moving. Only a few people were on the street. The clock said 7:18. Oh, well.

"Marcia? Sweetie, are you awake?"

A stupid question. She was obviously asleep. I shook her very gently. "Marcia?"

No response. I would either have to awaken her now or she would soon wake up by herself hearing me in a most embarrassing moment.

"Marcia, wake up!" I shook her again, gently but purposefully. She rolled over, groaning, luxuriously throwing her leg over me, snuggling closer. I thought I heard her say something in Italian. Was she dreaming about her old lover?

"Marcia, wake up. I've got a problem."

"Not that I could find. And I should know."

At least she was conscious.

"I've got to take a crap."

She rolled over, opening one eye.

"Now!"

She propped herself up on one elbow and smiled. "Why didn't you say so?"

She helped me into the bathroom and waited for me to take a shit. Then she helped clean me up. That was the first time any woman who wasn't a nurse or an attendant or a relative took me to the bathroom. Thanks to her I felt pretty good about it. To her, there was nothing to it. So nature calls; you have to take care of it. It was a good experience for me. It showed me it was not such a terrible thing to expect.

Reflecting on this period in my life, I know that Marcia did a lot for my confidence. To know you are accepted for what you are, no matter what, is the greatest thing in the world. It not only made me feel like a man. It also made me feel whole and complete, and made me believe I could really get out and do things; accomplish a lot with my life. It was the kind of inspiration I needed at the time. I wanted to shout what Mae West once said, "Too much of a good thing is…wonderful!"

Marcia was happy to serve as my inspiration. She encouraged my budding adventurousness and ambition. The only action she could not tolerate was inaction.

"Do something," she would tell me, "even if it's wrong."

It was in the late summer of 1968 that looming cold weather required my escape from central Italy to a warmer climate. Besides, I was burned out living in a motel, even though the Motel Boomerang was relatively inexpensive, and located on one of Rome's *circonvallazoni* (boulevards that circle the city). I wanted to be in my own apartment, condo, house or whatever.

It might have been wrong to leave when things were working so well for me, but I decided to set a course for Spain, where the winter would be warm enough that I could paint outside and where I could learn a new language and live within a new culture. Pat stayed in Italy. I and my other aide, Egidio, drove the Volkswagen down to Malaga, Spain. Looking at a map of the Mediterranean quickly reveals that one of the southern most points of Western Europe, where the winters are among the most mild and forgiving is the south of Spain. Malaga, in Andalusia, Spain, little more than a stone's throw from Gibraltar and Morocco, was where I decided to spend time in 1969.

Egidio and I stayed at a minimal, but still fairly luxurious, downtown hotel not far from the port and the bullring. The day after we arrived, an inquiry with the hotel's concierge resulted in the name of a local contact who worked for one of Spain's major real estate development companies. The concierge called and set up an appointment for us for later in the day.

The company's office was in an older, stately building about seven or eight blocks from the hotel, fronting on one of Malaga's elegant, flower-studded boulevards. Elegant wood paneling, oriental carpets, and modern Spanish art spelled money, big money. I thought, damn! I'll never find something I can afford in this joint. I guess Egidio had the same thought as we glanced at one another and our eyes rolled ceilingward in unison.

Before we had even been seated five minutes, the blonde, modelesque receptionist ushered us into an office where Senor Barros was seated with another gentleman. Senor Barros immediately got up and shook our hands, introducing both himself and Senor Peneda, his superior, and offered us an espresso, which we thanked him for, but declined.

Being in the habit of getting to the point when making an acquisition, or in this case renting an apartment, I explained that I was looking to rent for about a year, a two-bedroom, two-bathroom, wheelchair-friendly apartment somewhere in the downtown area. I then explained what I meant by "wheelchair-friendly" in terms of the reality of 1968 European construction: a building with access from the sidewalk via one or two stairs, equipped with an elevator that descends to lobby level and is large enough to accommodate my wheelchair without having to remove the footrests. Naturally, it also had to be furnished.

I then added that I didn't have a great deal to spend for rent each month. Senor Barros, who did practically all of the talking, was surprisingly candid, telling us that most of their furnished rentals were for one or two months during the summer tourist season and that by renting for a year we could get something very nice at a reasonable price.

The next day, Egidio and I were escorted several blocks from our hotel to a condominium just across the boulevard from the bullring. It was a nine-story apartment building with the terrace of each floor draped in pink and red geraniums and aptly called "La Casa de Las Flores." There was only one step up into the lobby and none into the elevator, which, thank God, also accommodated my wheelchair.

After introducing us briefly to the apartment's manager, everyman's helpful jolly uncle, we were shown a corner apartment on the eighth floor, directly overlooking the bullring and the area of Malaga's port where the cruise ships landed. It was a three-bedroom, two-bathroom luxopad with marble floors, classic Spanish furniture, a maid's quarters and even good china and silverware. The only thing I had to buy was sheets, towels, and soap and I was in business.

When I was told that my rental fee would be less than the equivalent of $200 U.S. per month, I accepted with as much restraint in my enthusiasm as I could muster, which wasn't a hell of a lot. In less than two days, we were totally moved in.

Life in Malaga was *fantastico!* Dinner (either in or out at one of the local family-style restaurants) was always Spanish style and usually didn't start until at least 9:00 p.m. After dinner, I'd hang out at a bar or flamenco club, sketching and sharing exaggerations with locals and finally get to bed between midnight and 3:00 a.m. the next morning. If I didn't get to bed until 3:00 a.m., I made the concession of not getting up until 8:00 a.m., instead of my usual 6:30 to 7:00 a.m.

Now if you think this routine was totally insane then you'd have to also question the sanity of most adult Spaniards who typically lived—and still live—this same lifestyle. You say that three to five hours of nightly sleep are insufficient and unhealthy? Well, maybe, unless you leave out of the equation God's gift to the civilized world, "la siesta." Yep, you'd be surprised at what 30 to 60 minutes of deep afternoon rest can do to one's body and mind, at least until you've tried it.

And if you really want to get charged up, try preceding—or following—your siesta with a nooner. But that's another story.

There were nights when I had more action, but that's another story, too, and not a pretty one. Being dependent upon someone, especially someone who can't be with you 24 hours a day, can be the shits! I'll just give you a little sample.

After my aide went home for bed, the only contact I had was a night watchman. One night I had to have a B.M. about 1 a.m. There was no phone in the room, but who would I call anyway. I calculated that if I slid down onto the marble floor, I could sleep on it if I threw a pillow and blanket. Not wanting to be near my planned defilement, I tossed a pillow on the other side of the bed and laid the blanket close enough to pull down once I got there. Then I rolled off the bed, plopped onto the floor, took care of matters, and crawled underneath the bed to the other side. There I got the pillow, pulled the blanket over me, and Francisco cleaned up when he came next day.

When he arrived, he said, "Did you feel the earthquake?" I didn't feel it. He said it was so severe that he and his wife went to sleep in the car for safety's sake. I was surprised. But, except for the occasional problem, I was enjoying my life in Spain.

I hired a housekeeper named Isabel, an earthy, good-hearted woman who was about forty years old, although she looked easily twenty years older. She had five children to support because her husband was in prison for selling contraband cigarettes. I suspected there was more to the story. All Isabel's stories about her husband were darkly incriminating and all ended with, "But he is a good man."

Isabel was not much to look at but she sure could cook. She made us fantastic soups and omelets. I have always thought that food is an important part of a balanced diet!

In Spain, I discovered that omelets are widely used as a first dish, unlike in Italy, where pasta is the first course. Isabella's omelets might contain anything from potatoes to shrimp and each one was a masterpiece. One day, she added baccala (codfish). Because the fish is so salty it has to be soaked overnight in water. It is an especial favorite of the Portuguese, who fished for cod extensively.

She and Egidio had taken to teasing each other about their respective sex lives. Egidio stuck his head into the kitchen.

"Hey, Isabel! Getting any lately?"

Her thick neck twisted toward him and she gave him a sour look, making her seem even more homely.

"Hey, Egidio! Come into the kitchen."

Egidio knew very well that she liked him and might, as she sometimes did, offer him a taste of one of her miracles-in-progress. She beckoned for him to come over to the large dish she cradled in her arms. He searched her face for some clue of mischief but, finding none, advanced cautiously.

"Close your eyes, lean over, and tell me if you recognize this smell."

As he bent down, Isabel uncovered the soaking cod.

"Oh, Jesus!" He choked, staggering back against the wall.

"I thought so. That reminds you of some of the women you've been with lately, eh?" she scolded, shaking her finger at him. "Why don't you go out and find yourself a nice girl for once." She burst into a belly laugh and flopped the fish onto the cutting board.

This was incredibly bad taste. However, I had learned something along the way. Since my youth, I recognized that the raw material of humor is painful. Jokes are about how dumb people are, how drunk they are, how broke they are, how sexually frustrated they are, greedy, lazy, etc. Humor is necessary to us; necessary to maintain our sanity.

Even though I ate like a gourmet while in Spain, I worked like a Spartan, getting in an hour and a half of exercise before breakfast. Three days a week I studied Spanish at the local Berlitz School and every day I painted. My first model was a lovely Eurasian girl on vacation. Then I painted the grandson of the night watchman. I even painted Isabel.

I was so involved with my work that I forgot Egidio had to go back to school in Italy. Egidio and I enjoyed each other so much that we have kept in touch and I heard from him just the other day, some three decades later. I was the first American he came to know and he was surprised by many things I did. For example, he pointed out the famous movie director Franco Zefferelli in Milan one day and was shocked that I had the audacity to say I'd like to meet him. After he met more Americans, he came to understand our character better. He said, "For you Americans, actors and politicians and all who live under popular consensus should always be prepared to stop, smile and respond to whomever because said person is part of his/her sustaining public."

He also thought it amazing that I wrote the President of the United States to ask that access ramps be installed in all public buildings. He later said, "Being together and climbing and descending the stairs of half of Europe, I noted then the importance of your request."

Egidio was astounded when I ordered a large number of roses for Marcia. He said, "Neither the florist nor I had ever seen someone order 30 or 40 roses at one time for one person."

He could hardly contain himself when he saw me smoke a large cigar one time. He said, "I had only seen these big cigars smoked in films and always by large people which certainly was not your case, making me want to explode in hilarity that I was barely able to restrain."

He claimed to have been inspired by my "steel will," as he called it, to exercise faithfully every morning and work so hard on the little details of things like my paintings. He later began to copy a Native American shout he heard me holler as I completed each achievement: HAHUUHA!

After Egidio, I needed another attendant and hired an accountant named Francisco, a reserved and diminutive young Spaniard who had recently married and lived nearby in the outskirts of Torremolinos, a trendy beach town where European celebrities and movie stars were more common than flies.

Every evening, after Francisco would help me to bed, he'd return home to be with his wife until I needed him the next morning. And just in case I had to wiz during the night, I had my trusty urinal sitting on the nightstand. During a typical day, my routine included an hour of morning exercises, followed by breakfast, both usually on the terrace. SS&S (shit, shower, and shave) were next, then painting in my makeshift studio (the third bedroom), a light lunch, walking with platform crutches from one end of the apartment to the other for more exercise, Spanish lessons at Berlitz with an occasional half hour siesta and more painting back at the apartment.

I also hired Jose, a schoolteacher who needed extra money and agreed to be my relief attendant. Perhaps like many teachers in this country, Jose felt his superior education entitled him to more money than he was making. He saw me as a rich American who could certainly afford to help out a fellow with a character as good as his. He began to casually mention that he had a little boy named Juanito who had a disability.

I couldn't really blame the guy. I thought, initially, he was just trying to figure a way to work a little extra money out of me by playing on my sympathy.

But I went out to see the boy one day. I brought him a model airplane which we worked on together, spreading the instructions, acetone, glue, and little bits of gray plastic, representing guns, wheels and engine parts all over the kitchen table, to the great dismay of the boy's mother, who fluttered around the perimeter of the activity, furtively checking to see that her table had not acquired any new and permanent engine parts. The child seemed happy enough and fairly healthy, but I could not help noticing how extremely pale he was. After the airplane was assembled, I took Jose aside.

"Jesus Christ! Here you are in this beautiful climate of Malaga and your son is so pale! Why doesn't he go outside more?"

Jose rolled his brown eyes woefully. "You know, the boy has a…" He lowered his voice, looking at his sandals, "He has a birth defect. Mama warned me. She said, 'Jose, my boy, do not marry that girl. She's too skinny.' But did I listen? Anyway, it can't be helped. It's done. You see, my boy cannot walk outside, so he stays in unless we carry him. He is too proud to be carried always. So proud. Therefore, he remains pale."

They were not sure what disease he had but it looked like cerebral palsy. He had trouble with coordination but there was nothing wrong with him mentally.

I saw this as the classic lame excuse. Having been used as a design consultant for Jacuzzi, I knew how to go about constructing a prototype. After some thought and a few sketches, I came up with a design for a walker using modified platform crutches attached to a tubular frame with a built-in seat that could be flipped up when not in use.

This triggered something in me, something that had disappeared when I lost interest in "the cause" of disability. I regained this interest on this little child.

I had a lot of fun working on this project! I found a little machine shop. Just a little hole, the size of a one-car garage. The owner welded the frame together, then I had rubber crutch pads put under the arms and had those along with the seat upholstered in a kind of red Naugahyde. Finally, I took it out and had it all chrome-plated so it would be really nice looking. And when I took it over to the house, Jose's kid went crazy. He really enjoyed it.

The boy, who was about nine years old, had never walked independently in his life. Now he was able to stand up inside this frame and scoot around outside.

The main thing I was trying to accomplish was to point out to his folks that he ought to be out in the world a little bit, among people, not stashed away in the house.

I did not expect miracles. They kind of saw the light, but you've got to work with people on a regular basis over a period of years to really get anywhere. I think they appreciated it. We remained in contact for quite a while after that. They would call us when we went back to Italy. Collect of course.

While working with little Juanito, I thought back to the looks of surprise on people's faces when they saw me in the streets. I began to notice that the only people with disabilities one would see on the streets were men, mostly war veterans, who got around on three-wheel vehicles that were a cross between a large wheelchair and an even larger tricycle. There were very few women and children with visible disabilities on the streets. I was puzzled about this until I talked further with Juanito's parents.

They felt their son's condition was punishment from God, but they didn't seem to know the reasons why God had done this. Other Spaniards also felt that when disabilities occurred years after a child's birth, some form of illicit sexual behavior or excessive drinking must have been the root cause of such a cursed problem.

I began to appreciate why families chose to keep their children at home. One doesn't usually advertise one's mistakes or sins. I began to realize that this attitude permeated all of the southern European countries. I offered to pay for a side entrance ramp for wheelchairs in a Catholic church where I belonged, and the church found a thousand excuses for why it couldn't be done. The church is an accurate mirror of the society's deep inner feelings in southern Europe.

While working on Juanito's walker, I heard about a home for orphans with disabilities that was run by nuns. By this time, I was something of an expert on children's hospitals and the kind of care children with disabilities received in the U.S. The facilities at the orphanage were humble compared with our counterparts in America. It looked more like barracks than a home. However, I was profoundly impressed by it. Not only was it spotlessly clean, but the children seemed quite happy. Perhaps "fulfilled" would be more accurate.

Depending on each child's particular ability, he was given the responsibility of certain chores. Some would help with the dishes, some made the beds, and some helped others eat. They understood they were in the home because they were missing one or both of their parents or that their parents simply could not take care of them. Yet they were happy because they were useful and felt needed.

Marcia got a couple of months off from the studio and decided to come down to Malaga. They were in the middle of filming *Those Daring Young Men and Their Jaunty Jalopies* and she had the honor of being Tony Curtis's secretary. She filled me in on how nice Mr. Curtis was to work for and how Englishman Terry Thomas had to have his Rolls-Royce brought in or he would not come to work. Dudley Moore and Peter Cook were also in this 1969 comedy about a motley bunch of racers competing in a 1920s auto rally.

Marcia and I enjoyed ourselves and went for drives in the country and ate at some of my favorite restaurants.

She, Francisco and I went to the bullfights in a small town one day. The bullfight was my idea. This gory but proud tradition is not to everyone's taste. The picnic lunch was Marcia's idea. It turned out to be to everyone's taste. Poor Francisco at first tried to pretend he did not know us but after a while the chicken smelled so good, he thought, "What the hell?" and dove in.

A few days later, Marcia had to go back to Rome and Tony Curtis. A few months later she wrote to tell me she was going back to her married lover. My search for the "pair of eyes" was over but new searches began.

I spotted Ted Kennedy's picture on the cover of a magazine in Spain. I used it to paint his picture but he looked very sad. I suppose I was thinking of the loss of his brothers, Joseph, John and Bobby, so I thought that he must be sad. I painted it in one day. Strangely, the next day I heard the news about Chappaquiddick. In later years I met him in Washington, D.C. and told him of the painting. I explained its sadness and offered to send it to him as a sort of exorcism. He kindly accepted my offer.

Not long after Marcia left, I began looking for a new model; somebody really unusual. Like Michelangelo, I searched the streets for faces with character. Like Toulouse-Lautrec, I hunted lowly bars for that special fallen angel. I studied people's faces, their colors and shapes, trying to really see, the way Cantini showed me. I would notice an old sailor with a face like leather, deep creases around the stern mouth and cobalt-blue eyes. How would I paint him? With vivid, unblended oils applied not with a brush but a knife? A little girl, ethereally beautiful, passed me by, eye-level, smiling a distant secretive smile. Would I paint her in pastels or watercolors?

I ended by choosing a prostitute, one of the few women who would do something for hire by a fellow like me. I never was able to determine her age, although I was certain that she was no longer young. We first met in a bar in Torremolinos. She was a truly striking beauty. For me, it was fascination at first sight. Every day I saw women as beautiful as she was, but there was something special in the ease with which she moved, slowly, luxuriously, as if feeling the air move around her. She could return a smile with a steady confidence without shame or invitation. She could look desirable without being cheap.

Of course, for money, she would sleep with anybody. She had a couple of kids and no husband. A girl has to make a living.

My proposition was the best she had had in a long time. I would pay her standard rate and all she had to do was pose for me. I did not even ask her to take off her clothes.

She turned out to be an excellent model, sitting patiently for hours while I attempted to capture that quality that captivated me. She never seemed to grow cross or moody, but held her pose tirelessly, apparently enjoying every minute of it.

As I studied her, mentally disassembling the components of her color, the combination of lines that composed her smile, and trying to faithfully reconstruct them on canvas, I could not help but be attracted to her. If she was aware of this, it did not show. She would talk candidly to me about her life, never hesitating to discuss any detail that might interest me. She mentioned that one of her sons had a disability, the nature of which she did not describe in any detail.

I volunteered to take her and her two boys on a drive one afternoon. I sat in the back of the car with the model and her younger son. Francisco did the driving and next to him in the front seat sat the boy with the "handicap." He seemed to get around fine and was bright enough, although he was very nervous and the slightest distraction irritated him. The boy shifted in his seat, whining to himself. His mother was nervous, too.

Gradually, I was coming to terms with what kind of person I was going to be. I was to be a kind, generous, helpful person. I could bring happiness to those who had none, and my money didn't hurt in achieving that goal.

Most of the men who came to see her did not care much for her children and although she loved her kids, bringing them along sometimes made her feel self-conscious, as if she were afraid of being judged a bad mother for producing a child who was not normal.

Perhaps she felt a little out of her element. Here I was, this young artist from America, probably very rich, who treated her with dignity, paying her only to sit while he painted her portrait, and was even kind enough to invite her and her children for a ride in the country.

The boy in the front seat jabbered some nonsense to nobody in particular. His mother patted him on the shoulder, asking him to be still. Immediately, he began squalling at the top of his lungs, furiously beating the back of his seat with fat little fists. Francisco glanced at the model in the rear-view mirror, checking for any sign of rescue. The other boy, no doubt familiar with but not indifferent to the caterwaul, began to set up his own version from the back seat and, although they were both ordered to hush, neither seemed to be so inclined.

The model shut her eyes tight against the scene. Then I did a curious thing. I leaned forward, placing my hands on the head of the screaming child in the front seat. Despite the mother's look of astonishment, I kept my hand on the child, hands no bigger than those of the child himself, and gently massaged his temples. I don't know what possessed me to do it, except that I could identify with this little fellow and his discomfort.

Very shortly, the boy stopped crying and sat still. The mother stared, marveling at my little miracle, as if Saint Francis were charming the animals of the woods. She moved closer to me and whispered words of admiration.

Two evenings later, I invited her to my apartment and we went to bed. I had fantasized about what it would be like to sleep with her. Would the secret of her fascination that I sought to uncover on canvas now become clear to me in the sheets? But my fantasy was interrupted by thoughts of Marcia. Although I was never actually in love with her, I still felt loyal to her as my first and only lover thus far in my life. I was much more of a faithful fellow than I had any idea.

I couldn't get an erection. I was still thinking about Marcia. Well, actually I got an erection but it went away. Life, the mind, and religion are so strange.

The model became terribly upset. She blamed herself that she failed to please me. Usually, men came to her and whether or not they paid her, they had to somehow convince her to sleep with them. But this time, she made the first move. This time, she tried to give herself to a man and it did not work. I didn't feel too good about it either, but mostly because the beautiful creature next to me was so miserable.

When I tried to explain, it only made matters worse. My words failed to communicate. I was silent. The model and would-be lover turned away from me, crying softly into the pillow. Suddenly, hardly realizing what I was doing, I began stroking her long, black hair. Gradually she relaxed and fell asleep. I knew my role. I was to comfort people as they had comforted me early on. I was to fulfill them as I had been and still often wished to be fulfilled.

Weeks later, when I dropped in to see her before I left for France, I found her with a big lunk who had been her lover on and off for some time. Apparently, she had confessed something of her relationship with me because when the burly character saw me, he seemed to bristle.

The guy looked at me like, "So you're the bastard!" I thought it was pretty funny.

14

The Bathing Suit

Eddy: A current of air or water, moving against the main current, with a circular motion.

I had never known my father to be bored. He could be overbearing, tyrannical and hyperactive. But he was never bored. When I left for Europe, he acted hurt that I would leave home but I knew Dad would be too busy conquering the world to worry about me. However, he was forced to leave the company to save its reputation and forced to leave the U.S. to save himself from indictment on charges of income-tax evasion, I sensed a change in him. (This will be explained later.)

We had agreed to meet in Paris, France, before heading on to Mexico for a family reunion. At that time, he had gone with Mom to live in Italy in the old family farmhouse. My mother told how they had adapted it and what it had meant to everyone. She said:

> His family didn't want to sell the farmhouse in Casarsa. When Candido and I went to visit, we redid it. Had to put in electric, new tiles for floors, each room had its own toilet. We put in Jacuzzis. Added porch to house, turned barn into party room. Put in bocce ball court. Divided house into two apartments.
>
> They (Candido's parents) went with wagon and took stones from river, 20 miles away. Famous in story and song, that river. Tagliamento. Blood flowing down into the river. Fighting there with Austrians, Germans.
>
> Candido's parents raised their own chickens. Made their own salamis. Raised pigs. Later I converted pig trough into flower container. Made smokehouse into gardening shed. Had fruit trees, peaches.
>
> I lived there (Casarsa) with Candido for one year. I went back and forth a couple times to U.S. The house was within walking distance of the factory.

I think my father was under considerable stress despite living in the old family home. I could not help but notice how much older he suddenly looked. He was still physically active and quick-witted. He could still roar like the lion he had been, but his roar seemed to have lost some of its conviction since he had been de-clawed.

He took me to a fashionable restaurant to discuss a matter he said he had been working on for some time. I assumed it would be an investment proposition or a business strategy. However, the pressing matter he wished to discuss was bathing suits. He explained that for a long time he had watched the women of the Italian Adriatic lie on the beach with their bras and bikini strings untied, trying to eliminate strap marks while getting a tan.

His idea was to design a bathing suit without straps or strings.

Like a fool, I told him I liked the idea and said that only yesterday in the paper I had seen there was a big fashion show coming up in Nice. I think the role I had chosen to play, an aide, a comforter, a facilitator, kicked in as I talked with my dear old papa.

"Do you think you could get us in it?" he wanted to know.

The entire idea sounded absurd. Neither of us knew the first thing about fashion design, yet we thought we were ready to enter a prestigious fashion show. Somehow, in time for the show, our revolutionary prototype was ready. The top was conventional but the "untied" effect of the bottom half of the swimsuit was achieved by means of a wire sewn into the edge of the fabric, allowing the piece to stay in place although it did not come together at the sides. It looked somewhat like a clamshell, hinged at the crotch. Thus I named it the "coquilini" a combination of the French word, "coquillage" meaning shellfish, and "bikini".

We secured a booth and a voluptuous model and we were on our way. Coquilini became the hit of the show. The fashion magazine *Marie Claire* presented us with an award for the best new item of the year and the event was covered by national television.

The show went on for several days and one day I was obliged to man the booth alone, because Dad had left for Italy before flying back to Mexico for the winter. My new aide, Joseph, a part-time writer from Africa, was on the other side of Nice getting some work done to the Volkswagen. The place was teeming with fashion designers from all over Europe as well as manufacturers' representatives and beautiful, wealthy members of the beau monde.

I did not want to seem out of place in this gallery of rarefied taste but *Marie Claire's* latest discovery had to take a crap. Here I had wanted to be the helper and I needed help, myself.

Not only did the act itself require assistance, but because the only restroom in the area was at the bottom of a long flight of stairs, I needed two strong men to carry me. Excusing myself from the booth, I wheeled up to a doorman and was able to convey to him my predicament. The doorman listened thoughtfully while I explained and although, from his expression, I could see that this was highly irregular, he summoned another doorman and proceeded to carry my wheelchair and me down the long flight of stairs.

The doormen in their dashing fitted uniforms with gold brocade and white gloves waited politely, though somewhat impatiently, outside while I did my business. When I was through, I called to them to help clean me up and get me off the toilet. When they finally comprehended what I was saying, they were astounded.

"Oh, no, monsieur! We are doormen! We could not do such a thing as that!"

My French was not terribly fluent, but I told them as best I could that I would be willing to pay a nurse to help if they would make the call for me. Relieved at the prospect of passing on this responsibility, they dashed off to make the call.

In just a few minutes, I heard sirens, the slamming of car doors and the scuffling of heavy feet. I was afraid some old dowager had fainted over a particularly fetching outfit. Soon, I realized the feet were heading in my direction. They were coming for me!

A few days after my "rescue," some Japanese manufacturers who were interested in the Coquilini approached me. However, I was unwilling to let such a hot item out of my control and refused to sell them the rights to produce it. Before the end of the fair, I naively lent the prototype to one interested party who never came back or returned it. I later saw our creation in a mail-order novelty underwear ad.

I felt that this little episode or *eddy* with my father showed our similar good instincts. We both loved creating a new product but neither of us had any knowledge of the fashion industry nor realized all of its potential. No matter what the product, it can die if you don't know enough about the industry. Even so, I was glad we could share this moment together.

It was one of the only times I can remember being able to actually help my father, who had helped me so very much during my life.

15

My First Real Job

Thunderstorm Supercell: Rotates like a living breathing creature, creating winds that spin and spiral and can become tornadoes.

I decided it was time to return to the North American continent. I thought I'd travel about Mexico with Joseph, the personal care assistant I had hired in Nice during the fashion show, before returning to California.

Before I left for Mexico, I contacted Tom S., agreeing to meet him in Tijuana, where Tom's folks had a little one-room beach house. I had so much to tell my old school friend. It was a warm reunion. We sat up far into the night talking about old times and catching up on how our lives were progressing. We spoke of our old selves as though our old selves were dead and gone, and indeed they were—dead and gone.

With no city lights to compete with the evening sky, the stars blazed in the heavens, their reflections dancing on the Pacific tide. The night was hot and we were drinking cognac. I told Tom with great relish how I traveled through the cultural high spots of Europe and how I studied painting in Italy. I described my adventures with women. With each episode, Tom filled my glass. Later, he admitted getting me drunk on purpose to get me to talk about myself.

Yes, I had had a wonderful time in Europe. But the drunker I became with my old friend, the more my thoughts returned to the unfinished business I left in the States. Tom had finished his bachelor's degree and was now planning to go on for a Ph.D. or J.D. I had only one year of junior college under my belt with no practical skill or experience that could land me a respectable job.

Tom has always been one of those men who lived for details. He had always placed his faith in particulars. I had too few and he had so many. I had little to show for my time while he had much. I thought about how yesterday was my past, tomorrow was my future, but today was the present—a gift? I had to do something with this gift, this present.

Who was I that I should be disturbed by my old friend's changes, when I myself had come back, so changed in my own way? By the time I went to bed, I was gloomy and drunk, but still sober enough to be dismayed by my lack of achievement. I wondered if I should have had the courage to stay in the States and finish my degree, and, if so, where?

I was so exhilarated landing in Mexico, almost triumphant. But now, I was afraid that, having spent my youth in hospitals, I was now spending my adulthood playing instead of working. How could I have any self-respect if I did not work? I must, however, contrast my friend Tom's viewpoint of my life with my own view. Here is what he said about me and my father.

> In those days, I think Candido thought the only acceptable thing for a man to do was to go into the family business. Business was a cutthroat competitive game. Maybe he should have stressed using one's intellect more.
>
> In my family, we had college graduates. It was so much easier for me to go that direction. But Candido told Ken that the best education was travel and experience. He had pride in his own cleverness. He was intelligent, well-traveled, experienced, but had no understanding of what a college education could do for you. This corporation needed managerial talent. Selling and improving pumps wasn't enough. They needed tax people, accountants, and other kinds of expertise.
>
> Ken was only supposed to have enough college to prepare him to work in the company. I believe that Candido saw me as an interference or competitor. So I sort of got fired when Ken told me to move on. I had tried to encourage Ken to go on with college. I was a bookworm.
>
> Roy, his younger cousin, had gotten a two-year college degree, and went on to become a major force in the company. Roy had turned the Jacuzzi into a luxury product rather than a medical device, a form of entertainment that became a status symbol.
>
> This must have rankled Candido. Roy took his whirlpool bath invention and the "child ate the parent," the whirlpool idea ate the pump technology.

I know that Tom felt he was "fired" but the truth is that I wanted him to move on and not be held back worrying about me. However, after my meeting with Tom, I began to change my life and prepare myself for work.

Then, unexpectedly, my father experienced a violent *thunderstorm*, in which fear of prosecution rotated and spun him around like a creature that got hold of prey and wouldn't let go.

But it was less violent for me. The opportunity to renovate and rebuild a "dream house" fell into my lap. The "dream house" was our family business in Italy on my grandparents' property.

In 1963, Jacuzzi had moved its international headquarters to a more centralized location in Little Rock, Arkansas. In 1965 a second modern, highly sophisticated manufacturing facility was put into operation at nearby Lonoke, Arkansas. The following year, a movie called *The Fortune Cookie* helped build the Jacuzzi name even more. The movie starred Jack Lemmon and, in one scene, he planted a microphone in the air intake nozzle of a Jacuzzi as a spy mechanism.

During 1965, Mermaid Fountains contracted with our company to provide the spectacular fountains in front of Caesar's Palace, which opened in Las Vegas in August, 1966. The *Jacuzzi Injector* house organ of fall, 1966, described the opening of Caesar's.

> Fountains of water in infinite variations are a special attraction at Las Vegas' 25 million dollar Caesar's Palace. Mermaid Fountains used 30 Jacuzzi pumps of various capacities to create the breathtaking Caesar's fountains. The spectacular water displays at Caesar's Palace are flooded with 180,000 watts of light.

Eventually new offices were opened in Walnut Creek, California, to provide sufficient office space for Jacuzzi Whirlpool Bath headquarters. Plants in Canada; Monterrey, Mexico; Brazil; Chile; and Italy served foreign customers.

But the biggest thrill for our family was when we opened the plant in Italy on land that was owned by Grandma and Grandpa Jacuzzi. The cycle had been completed. The Jacuzzis had come back to where they started. Our grandparents would have been so happy if they had been able to see this.

The Italian San Vito on Tagliamento manufacturing plant was built in the late 1960s on the Jacuzzi family property. During the Jacuzzi family's absence from Italy, Grandpa Jacuzzi leased his land to local farmers and charged them the equivalent current going price of X number of bundles of hay for every hector of land. This way he cleverly protected himself from the ravages of inflation and currency devaluation over the years.

It was thanks largely to my father that this company expansion had taken place. Dad had, in addition, acquired 31 U.S. patents under his own name between 1933 and 1971, in addition to 20 other patents of eight other Jacuzzi family members.

Dad was the General Manager of the Jacuzzi Brothers Company for 25 years. After the deaths of Giocondo and Rachele, Valeriano grew less interested in the company and more interested in his ranch. Giuseppe died in 1965 and the brothers who were left (Frank, Joseph, and Gelindo) took on various functions in the company allowing my father to head up the operation as president. Not only had he found places for most family members somewhere in the company structure, but he even set up pension plans for them and their widows.

I should mention that other family and non-family members alike played important roles in Jacuzzi Brothers' growth and evolution during and post World War II through the 1970s. These included Louis "Lou" Ansani, Nathan Gray, John Armstrong, Dick Silva, Rino Marin, Ray Horan, Bill Hartmann, Pete Kosta, Ray Schwartz and Joe Alioto, to name a few.

I must also include my cousins, Rudy, Giocondo and Virgil Jacuzzi, Harold Benassini, and my brother, John. I think my father's main error was in not grooming relatives to head up the parent company in the United States, preferring instead to send them to other countries.

Nathan Gray was a fascinating man. He worked as a machinist while studying law via a correspondence course. He completed the course, became a lawyer and passed the California bar exam. From the late 1930s through the 1950s he was one of Dad's earliest confidantes. He was later hired by a family member to oppose my father in a lawsuit, as I mentioned earlier.

Rino Marin was married to Stella, Dad's sister. Rino, like Dad had a strong personality, but more often than not he was a thorn in Dad's side. He chose to adamantly protest most of the changes and innovations proposed by my father, his own brother-in-law. It was one of those provocations which ultimately resulted in a schism between Nathan Gray and Dad and the first intra-family company lawsuit. The lawsuit was brought for future wages because Dad fired Rino after having made an oral promise to employ him for the rest of his life no matter what.

My father said, "They all (the 13 Jacuzzis) wanted to be ahead of the other. Maybe I created that, I don't know. For years, the family of Joseph and Valeriano were not very friendly because Joseph was the president of the company and Valeriano was not, although he was the oldest. It wasn't love {that kept the family talking to each other}; it was because we had more or less shares. It's different when five large shareholders control the company."

I believed in the Biblical saying, "Love thy neighbor as thyself." Nevertheless, there weren't two people in our family that were speaking to each other at that time.

Lou Ansani was another brother-in-law to Dad. Lou's wife, Zita, was my mother's sister. Lou was a numbers man and worked closely with Joseph and Dad on the accounting and administrative end of the business.

John Armstrong was one of Jacuzzi's most innovative engineers and shared with Dad some of the first patents obtained on the Jacuzzi Whirlpool Bath. I remember my Dad telling me from the time I was a boy that one of the things he didn't like about most engineers was that they were unwilling to stretch, go out on a limb and really invent something radical and new. However, John Armstrong didn't fit that mold and was willing to take risks.

Ray Schwartz was the sports writer I mentioned earlier who helped promote the Jacuzzi Whirlpool Bath. He died only a few years after joining the team, but not only succeeded in his assignment in spades, he made the Jacuzzi name a household word.

When Dad retired as President and CEO from Jacuzzi Bros. in the late 1960s, Giocondo Jacuzzi, Frank's eldest son and savvy, skilled manager, probably should have been appointed CEO. However, intra-familial politics and conflicts kept that from happening. My Dad always admired Giocondo's communication skills and thought that he should be the one to succeed him when he retired. Instead, Ray Horan, another one of the company's respected engineers, was selected CEO by the Board of Directors.

While he was president, Dad returned to northern Italy to set up a factory for sales throughout Europe. While there, he learned about viniculture and produced an Italian wine called Picolit, made from a rare white grape. He didn't market it but gave Picolit vino to family members, friends and business associates.

My father was already in hot water over the Swiss holding company when he moved to Italy. The problem was that, although U.S. authorities were satisfied that Jacuzzi Brothers had met the tax requirements; they still contended that Candido personally owed the government over $60,000 in back taxes for income he received from the Mexican company.

The local papers all carried the story, much to the embarrassment and perhaps the secret delight of other family members who did not hesitate to twist the old man's tail, imploring him to pay his taxes. Alioto firmly maintained Dad's innocence, but a summons to appear in court scared him so badly that he voluntarily surrendered his United States citizenship and took refuge in Italy.

When the second generation of Jacuzzis started to find jobs in the company, they had been obedient followers of Dad's commands. But after years of enduring his mandates and dictatorial reign, they now may have wondered if they could do things a little better. Without him, the board of directors concluded that his status with the Internal Revenue Service was injurious to the company and it would be better for all involved if he took his retirement at this time.

Dad had seen something like this coming for some time, but he still felt betrayed by the very people he helped make successful. He was in a poor bargaining position. His only leverage was the fact that he held the office of president. But they were anxious to be rid of him, I think. As a condition for his retirement, Dad insisted on a pension contract, complete with full cost-of-living increases, similar to the contracts held by the other founding members.

In addition, he renegotiated my royalty contract to also include royalties not just from sales of the original hydro-massage, but all products of Jacuzzi Whirlpool Bath. They ground their teeth, but some of them may have been contemplating "going public" to cash in their shares while the market was good and they did not want the company president having problems with the I.R.S. And besides, Dad was 66 years old.

But then I was 28 and felt it was time to begin my career. I had acted as a consultant for the company off and on for a couple of years, offering my advice on whirlpool products, hanging around the production line and talking over policy with my brother-in-law, Peter Kosta, the Whirlpool Bath president.

I had tried to make my contributions but they were not really accepted. The hydro-massage itself was originally invented as a medical product, and for years the company had toyed with the idea of expanding its medical products line, including a line of wheelchairs. When I came back from Europe, Jacuzzi Research requested that I start working for them full time, devoting most of my energies to developing new products.

The trouble was that I did not have a great deal of autonomy. Most of my suggestions had to be filtered through my cousin, Roy, who had studied design at a college of arts and crafts in Oakland, and was largely responsible for most of the stylistic changes in the design of the spas. He would design the basic exteriors of the bathtubs and I would test them out. I did not always care for Roy's design and Roy usually did not care for my opinion. After all, I didn't have the formal training he did. My instincts told me that Roy's designs could stand improvement, but without an education, I did not have the strength of my convictions.

One of Roy's projects was to redesign the spa. His idea was to create a unit that was low to the ground. I insisted that he had a "sports car mentality," and when he thought of jazzing up the "bathtub," he thought "sports car." Roy had about as much tolerance for me in the shop as a football coach would have for his mascot on the field during a game.

My field was the medical products line, an area in which I had developed considerable expertise over the years, so when Roy came up with a design for a three-wheeled wheelchair, I had to tell him it would never work.

This time I knew where I was coming from. It was a bad design because it could turn over easily. But it was a good-looking piece of equipment so I lost my case. I was generally treated like an asshole, but a friendly little asshole. Somebody to be nice to but somebody you could get by with ignoring because he didn't know shit. They thought of me as C.J.'s son; poor little crippled Kenny who's getting all these royalties and doesn't know how lucky he is. I didn't have the self-confidence to sell my ideas convincingly.

My Dad was a salesman at heart. When he wanted to sell an idea, it was as if God came down from Heaven and visited him with this idea. He was an old-time salesman who'd convince you that the product would do everything: give you a million dollars, a three-foot erection, happiness forever—no matter what he was selling. When he was trying to sell a concept, he would go to that same extreme.

I, of course, wasn't like Dad in those ways. I grew up very dependent upon other people. It's difficult to get into a knock-down drag-out argument with somebody if you are dependent upon that person to bring you a cup of coffee or clean you up. Naturally, this frame of mind carries over to other personal interactions.

I think Dad would have liked for one of his sons to put himself on the line and take a chance; to say he had taken up where Dad left off and had taken the ball farther. Dad didn't have much respect for people with college educations or for me getting an education. But he must have secretly wished for more education because he often said, "If I'd gone to college, I'd be dangerous!"

I knew where I was when it came to wheelchairs. I knew Roy's three-wheeler wasn't good. A prototype was completed and sure enough, it kept tipping over, so I set to work on a four-wheel model with a rigid folding seat. Also, during this time, I secured a patent on a disposable urinal which might have provided long-awaited relief for people with disabilities in a non-accessible world, except for the fact that no material yet existed that was, at the same time, waterproof and environmentally flushable.

Roy and I filed patents in 1969 for the disposable urinal bag and in 1970 for the foldable wheel chair.

If things were tough at work, they were not much better at home. Upon returning to California, I found a shabby little apartment in Lafayette. By the European standards I was used to, it seemed perfectly adequate. I had hired a new PCA named Manuel. He meant well but had no talent for housekeeping.

One day I ran into my old friend, Pat, the little gal I met at the dance who spoke to me, whom I invited to my place in Lafayette. She was appalled to see me living in such a place and convinced me to move into her apartment complex where I found a room on the first floor under hers. Manuel went back to Mexico, which worked out all right because he was a little crazy, and Alba did not like the way he looked at her youngest daughter.

I replaced Manuel with a young man named Wayne who, as it turned out, was twice as crazy as his predecessor in some ways, but a nicer guy. Once while Wayne was my aide, I checked into the hospital to have hemorrhoids removed. On the way home, Wayne and I stopped by Alba's house.

We were having a nice chat when the subject of my apartment came up and I was carrying on about how sloppy my place was. Alba began to say how terrible my aide was for not taking better care of it. I was still recovering from the hemorrhoidectomy and was not quite up to dealing with my sister's energetic criticism. I felt sorry for Wayne who was no housekeeper but a nice guy. He got very upset about how Alba had laid into him. I've always appreciated my aides more than others because they are my lifeline and I can forgive them so much.

When I went to bed that night, I started hemorrhaging. By the time Wayne brought me back to the hospital, I had lost a lot of blood and my blood pressure had dropped dangerously. The doctor had to stick a "cut-down" into my heart and give me a transfusion to get my blood pressure back to normal.

Wayne went a little crazy over the incident and criticism. He started writing weird letters to Alba, threatening her with unspeakable forms of retribution, and telling her what an evil person she was. But I loved my sister, and I didn't know who to defend more—Alba or Wayne.

Sometimes Alba's criticisms were quite accurate, even though hard to take. For example, she described me to someone saying, "My brother was more independent than our own children. He was able to do a lot of things and make a lot of decisions and be involved in things that were very expensive for my parents. Almost nobody gets those kinds of experiences. Was he spoiled? Oh, yes! Ken became kind of spoiled like his mother, expecting people to do for him. He's bossy, demanding, and fastidious."

Well, nobody's perfect.

Back at Pat's apartment complex, she used to worry about the way I drove my wheelchair to the middle of the street because there were no curb cuts. Also, I had developed the habit of being a night owl after my time in Europe.

She said, "I'd lie there awake because I lived right above the driveway and, at two o'clock in the morning, I'd hear bzzzzzz down the driveway and think, 'God! He's going downtown.' So I lay there until I'd hear bzzzzzz coming back home."

It was at that apartment that I threw my famous Fourth of July party, ostensibly to celebrate handing my money from the foundation over to Easter Seals. I invited everybody I knew and they all came. It's a wonder we didn't get evicted. Fortunately, I had the foresight to invite everyone in the entire apartment complex and there were none left to complain about our commotion."

That was the proper part of the party. The proper people left before midnight and the rest stayed until dawn. There were doctors, lawyers, and people from Haight-Ashbury. The intensity of the party bordered on frenzy most of the night and, much to the distress of my sister, Alba, the champagne flowed as long as there was a soul left standing.

Joanne W., who had worked with me in my "cause," managed to hang on until the end. She recalled, "The last of the guests went home about 5 o'clock in the morning. Dawn was just breaking and Ken was in his electric wheelchair. He went out to the street where the cars were parked, out to the middle of the street and he was so happy that he made circles around and around and around. It was so neat! I don't think I ever saw him so happy."

Even then, I was operating under the principle of the cosmic economy, which holds that, "What goes around comes around." If there seems to be something lacking in your life, it means you need to give more. In my case, I felt that since people had been taking care of me all my life, this was a good opportunity to start giving to others.

Pat and I had been friends since the eighth grade. There was never any real romance between us, but we felt comfortable together. We knew each other's histories. She was with me through my many operations and prolonged hospital stays. I was with her through her short, unhappy marriage. I thought we might be good for each other. I needed a woman in my life and she needed a husband and father for the little girl she was struggling to support.

Pat never seemed to occupy the center of my life or me hers, but for those months that we lived at the same complex, it was almost as if we were married. Our relationship had settled amiably into assumed affection and domestic tranquility. Pat, who always thought of me as a special friend, began to realize she cared for me, not passionately, but deeply. When I asked her to marry me, she refused. But later, I asked her again and she accepted. I bought her a ring.

I must admit that I wasn't living an exactly sterile life at that time. Things would occasionally occur in a most unexpected way. For example, it was a day that wasn't at all different from most others. As an almost dwarf-sized man in a wheelchair, I thought I would stop at the library at almost 7:00 p.m. Inside, I was surprised to notice so few people; but then I realized it was dinner time in the suburbs and only hard-core library patrons would be hanging around.

As I rounded one of the long rows of shelves in the Social Science section, I came face-to-face with a bearded, scrawny-faced, dressed in green and beige, tattered, homeless person, commanded by two manipulating bluestone eyes and slice-of-cantaloupe smile. "I can change your fortune and make you walk, if you believe," he said, regurgitating warmed-over, backyard-brewery vapors as he spoke. "Give me ten dollars and I'll pray the Great Jehovah lift the evil eye crucifying your body and soul," he continued, his face almost up against mine.

"Ken, is there anything I can help you find this evening?" announced Jackie, one of the librarians, as she walked towards us, accompanied by the on-duty guard. The grifter-savior still didn't back off, but remained squarely in my face. "I must save this man from the devil, from burning in hell for all eternity," he continued, keeping his eyes on mine, but aware of their presence.

"John, you know the rules, you mustn't disturb the library's patrons. If you don't let this man alone, the guard will have to escort you outside."

"Don't worry," interjected the grifter-cum-savior, "I was just leaving!" and with that he stomped out in a droll goose-step.

"Thanks, Jackie, for coming to my rescue!" I said, transfixed by the way the setting-sun's rays streaming through a west-facing window irradiated her firm torso as it played peekaboo against her wispy jersey dress.

"No problem, Ken. Anything for you. Can I help you take these books to our back room to give you some privacy and peace to work?"

"Jackie, that'd be just great. If I don't finish this damn research, my presentation will never get done."

Although I'd used the combination conference-staff-lounge-research room before, I let Jackie lead the way, mainly so that I could drink in the slow jazzy sway of her up-turned ass as she walked. *Research, hell*, I thought, as Jackie unlocked the door with her master key. I positioned myself at one of the two small tables in the room while Jackie knowingly placed the books within my easy reach.

"Hey, Ken, how about a little special research atmosphere?" Jackie queried. "I bought this delightful candelabra today for my apartment, but I just got the urge to light it now. For you. What do ya' think?"

This was probably the fifth or sixth time over the past several months that Jackie had assisted me. Certainly, there wasn't anything extraordinary about any one of her body parts or, at first glance, her overall physical beauty. Yes, her espresso-colored eyes and hair, ripe apricot mouth, freckled porcelain skin, and tall, slender body were assembled quite nicely. But there was a bewitching magic in the way she enchanted rather than presented herself, granny-glasses and all.

I had learned that she'd moved here from Pennsylvania three years ago with a degree in anthropology, was an agnostic, and had lost a brother, a Vietnam War veteran, to suicide. And with each time I'd see her, I would get turned on as quickly and loyally as my morning alarm clock radio awakens me to Morning Edition on NPR. No words exited my mouth.

Jackie slipped over to the small corner table where the candelabra had been placed. She lit the candles with a single match, snuffing out the flame between tongue-moistened fingertips. Keeping her eyes on me, she strode back to the door, lowered the window shade, and turned the lock. Jackie then stood motionless, but without lifting her warming scrutiny of me.

Heaters were turned up in my face, chest, and thighs, but I still couldn't figure out what I should do, if anything. Finally, something told me to move my wheelchair back from the table several feet and, as soon as I did, Jackie started slowly walking towards me. About halfway between the door and me, she stopped again.

She then came over to me and as I started to mumble something, Jackie touched my mouth with her index finger, motioning me not to speak a word. Cradling my face in her hands, Jackie kissed me. Ambrosian feasts were only foretastes of that smoldering kiss.

She then reached down and expertly removed my wheelchair's armrests, laying them aside on the floor. Her magnificent legs straddled my knees as she kissed me again…then again. Tiny beads of perspiration were beginning to dance down both our brows. I wanted desperately to caress her neck, arms, breasts, but Jackie simply motioned me again to stay perfectly still. It was impossible for me to know the crescent moment I became entrenched and one in Jackie's paradise. The carnation and dandelion aroma of her sweat, her bottomless, murmuring moans capturing all other sounds, drenched my senses. The fecund alchemist's fusion of obsidian obelisk and molten slough bathed loins, turning our groins inside out, making us one.

I don't know how such things happen—these surprises of life. We don't expect them and we don't deserve them. We only realize that others want to offer something and who are we to decline the offer?

◆ ◆ ◆

After my return to California in 1970, following my extended sojourn in Western Europe from 1968 through late 1969, I spent a good part of my days at Jacuzzi Research in Berkeley, the company which manufactured and marketed the Jacuzzi Whirlpool Bath. In addition to the individual Whirlpool Bath units, the company was now aggressively marketing its first series of fiberglass bathtubs with built-in Jacuzzi Whirlpool Bath Jets, introduced in the late 60s, just prior to when I left for Europe.

About a year or so prior to that, my cousin, Roy, was hired by my dad, CJ, and my brother-in-law, Pete, to transfer over to Jacuzzi Research from Jacuzzi Brothers, Inc., for the purpose of heading up the design efforts of the company's first bathtubs with built-in Jacuzzi Whirlpool Jets. Roy saw the move to Berkeley as an opportunity to show his stuff, unfettered by multiple bosses except for, of course, Pete Kosta, who managed Jacuzzi Research. But Roy was also honored by the apparent respect and trust he had just received from his uncle Candido, "CJ."

Even prior to the move to Jacuzzi Research, Roy had remarked on various occasions to me and others that he had always wished uncle Candido had been his father. Roy's father, Aldo, was a very nice guy and smartly accumulated a nice pile of loot for his family by buying and accumulating stock in Wal-Mart from the late 1970s/early 80s, even if he wasn't the inventive type.

As the sale of Jacuzzi Whirlpool Baths *bathtubs* began taking off, Pete, had also been contemplating starting a division of Jacuzzi Research to focus on the healthcare industry. From the very beginning I had managed to weasel in my two cents worth regarding the medical use of whirlpool jets. I thought we needed to add one or two jets for the neck and shoulders, adjust the rear angle slope of the tub, and integrate grab handles, for example. Roy was never impressed with anything I had to share and didn't shy away from letting others know how he felt.

Hey, what did I know? I was the guy with only a few college courses under my belt and little, ongoing day-to-day experience with the products being produced and marketed by Jacuzzi Brothers. So what if I had learned to speak a few languages and paint portraits while I was in Europe; what relevance to the company's current endeavors did that have?

Roy, on the other hand, had a two-year fine-arts degree from the College of Arts and Crafts in Oakland, and already a number of years of hands-on experience working in the company. As my Dad said, "Roy knows how to make things pretty." Roy's stuff was wonderful. Gosh, I was jealous.

The bathtubs became Roy's baby. It was kind of interesting to see my little two cents worth eventually incorporated into later editions of whirlpool bath tubs. But, of course, that's what the marketplace wanted. However, when Roy and I did work together on the design of a wheelchair prototype, I first did some research on the pluses and minuses of current wheelchair design at the library of the University of California Medical Center in San Francisco. One of the things I learned was that people who ended up spending a lot of time in wheelchairs usually developed kyphosis (curvature) of the spine and/or hips due to the fact that the seats and backs of most wheelchairs were of a sling-type fabric design, not unlike that of a hammock, which permitted wheelchairs to be easily folded and thrown in the back seat or trunk of one's car. So we had to design a new folding wheelchair with solid seat and backrest.

I also thought there were a lot of other things that needed improvement in wheelchairs, such as brakes, adjustability to a person's size, ruggedness and, of course, aesthetics. I came up with a brake design that looked not unlike that of a bicycle, but employed new features, such as a lock toggle, that were needed in a wheelchair. We worked together on other items such as the flip up, adjustable armrests and the frame adjustments, but it was Roy who conceived the three-wheel design. When the boxed, brushed aluminum frame, lightweight wheels, and canary yellow fiberglass seat were all assembled, it made for one damn good-looking wheelchair.

There was just one little, itty bitty problem: if the person sitting in the wheelchair were to lean over a wee bit, the whole damn thing would topple over and said person would be making intimacies with the floor. Not a good thing.

Not long afterwards I was visiting with Pete and he said that he was still interested in getting a wheelchair into production, but obviously not this one. I wanted to try a free hand at coming up with some alternative concept, but I could only do it if I didn't have the shadow of Roy looming over me. I knew that at the Jacuzzi factory my brother, John, managed in Monterrey, Mexico, there were a slew of engineers and technicians who could potentially assist me. Additionally, they had the materials and machinery available to fabricate relatively quickly a working prototype. John agreed to me coming down and Pete wished me luck, but also reminded me that a Jacuzzi Brothers' Board of Directors meeting was coming up in less than a month and it might be helpful to have something "that works" to show them.

Wayne, my PCA at the time and a great guy from my perspective at least, and I packed our suitcases and flew down to Monterrey shortly thereafter. Wayne and I spent most of our time at the factory, working with a couple of technicians and fabricators John let me borrow. In coming up with the new wheelchair design, I wanted to preserve the solid seating, but knew that we needed to go back to the more traditional four-wheel configuration. Of course, the wheelchair had to be able to fold up into a package that was smaller than the one I was sitting in.

From my description of what I wanted the wheelchair to look like, the draftsman quickly put the drawings together. I decided to fabricate a prototype using more traditional lightweight steel, chrome-plated tubing. Because there were some glitches in the frame's first design attempt, we ended up with less than a week left to finish the prototype, get on a plane and attend the board meeting.

For three days straight, Wayne and I were putting in much more than the 10-hour working days we had been doing previously. But now we only had two days to go before flight time. One of the technicians and two of the fabricators agreed to work with me round-the-clock to get the wheelchair prototype built in time. The incredible performance of a handful of men during the four or five days would put to rest for all time the stereotype of the Mexican being either slow or lazy.

Just as the prototype was being polished and readied for the flight, I remember going with Wayne into my brother's office bathroom to shave, wash my face and hands, and change clothes. Less than an hour later we were driven to the airport for our flight to Little Rock via Houston.

A few hours later that same day, during the Board meeting, a non-tipping, attractive (if I do say so myself) chrome plated, paisley upholstered new wheelchair prototype was rolled onto the top of the board of directors table.

All those present at the board meeting (except, maybe, Roy) truly liked what they saw. However, the decision was made not long thereafter to postpone indefinitely the company's expansion into the field of durable medical products. Later I brought them before the Veteran's Administration in Washington, D.C. and they were well received there, too. But for now, Jacuzzi Research was to focus its resources on expanding the development, manufacture and marketing of Jacuzzi Whirlpool Bath tubs and spas.

I once again felt that my value to and relationship with the Jacuzzi family business was a questionable element lolling around somewhere in the twilight zone.

My brother-in-law, Pete Kosta, God bless him, could see that I'd become a floundering soul with nothing to do who couldn't wait to get on a plane back to Europe. I didn't know what I was going to do this time, I had some vague notion that I wanted to complete my university education abroad, but I didn't know where. Pete offered me a ray of hope when he said that Jacuzzi Research was soon going to launch a full-fledged expansion program in Europe and that I could probably play a major role in the project, if I was interested and ready to commit. I wanted and needed some more time to think, but I soon began preparing for my next trip over the Atlantic.

In 1971, I left for Italy to visit my father, who was still in the sanctuary of the family home in Friuli, to discuss with him the possibility of expanding the Italian operation. Wayne, however, refused to make the trip but offered to introduce me to his 18-year-old cousin, Helen, who agreed to act as my attendant, at least until we arrived in Italy.

Of course, my imagination ran wild but that's as far as I got. I wanted to screw this lovely girl so bad! She'd screw every guy she met except me! Her reasoning was like this: since I paid her to be my aide, it could be construed that I was paying her to have sex with me. But any man she would meet: a waiter, a guy she would meet on the street in Rome, she'd drop her pants for them. It's my life story. We had connecting rooms in Udine. I'd hear her going at it with some guy in the next room! If you don't think that was frustrating!

Then just before she was supposed to leave for the States she said, "Well, Ken, if you really want me to screw you before I leave…I will." It was so anticlimactic.

I said, "No, not under those circumstances." Like she was doing me a very big favor, a charitable act. I sent her home.

I don't know how or why but sometimes I felt like there was some little voice in me saying, "Live so that the priest won't have to lie at your funeral."

After spending Christmas with my parents in Italy, I was about to fly back to California when my brother called. John asked if I would stay in Italy and help find ways to reduce the cost of materials at the plant in Pordenone. I agreed. And so I began my first real job.

16

Italian Businessman

Tempest: A violent and extensive calamity caused by wind, but may include rain, hail or snow.

After serving as company president until 1971, my father retired and Giuseppe's son, Aldo Jacuzzi (1921–1989), took over as president. But he was quickly succeeded by Ray Horan, as I mentioned before.

I arrived in Italy and began my new job. My dream of working and being productive, and in the place of my dreams, was coming true. I wanted to do a good job so I set to work, although I was not sure about where to start. Almost immediately I began finding large discrepancies between the market price of raw materials and the price being paid by our company.

I began going around to the various foundries and discovered we could get components at a lower price. That's when I began to suspect that either the purchasing was being done badly or someone was creaming off the top. I sent a couple of letters to John at the factory in Mexico, which was Italy's parent company at the time.

John and Candido reasoned that because of my knowledge of both Italian and basic company operations, I might be useful in communicating the problems the Italian company was having back to the U.S. and Mexican offices. They were probably not expecting much and paid me a consultant's fee of only $300 per month in the beginning. That was only about enough to pay my personal attendant, Bruno.

I spent several weeks checking out the marketplace and buzzing around the plant evaluating the production line and the quality control. I had no official position, but because I was a Jacuzzi, I had free run of the plant. At first they weren't very worried about this little guy buzzing around, watching them, asking questions, and not even writing anything down. Being unable to make notes all my life, I had acquired an exceptional memory.

I soon became concerned with the quality of the pump castings, which often turned out to be porous and had to be rejected. One reason was that they were still using the old-fashioned sand casting method, which was cheaper than the shell molding process used in the rest of Europe and the U.S., but was less reliable and could not stand up to higher volume production. I concluded after research that new molds would be expensive, but would more than pay for themselves in the long run, allowing for greater output and automation.

Jacuzzi Europe was still in the Iron Age and the Bronze Age, selling iron and bronze pumps, which, although high in quality, were also very high in price, compared to the plastic models that competitors were selling.

The executives in the company were starting to worry because they realized I was sending letters out to the parent company. John also became worried, and requested more detailed information on the company's operational problems.

Something told me I'd better start learning the ins and outs of pump manufacturing, or I would forever lack credibility in the workplace. Unfortunately, my self-confidence was about at the same level as a pimply-faced adolescent about to get laid for the first time. So, even though I began to rapidly accumulate knowledge about this business, I still ended up listening to advice givers more often than to my own gut. I later learned, the hard way of course, that ignoring one's gut is one of the biggest mistakes that any savvy business person or entrepreneur can make. But I'm jumping ahead of myself as usual. In retrospect, I'm amazed at how much I did right, especially with respect to educating myself about the business.

Also, my father had given me a piece of valuable advice using an old Italian adage. He said, "Don't talk in the wind!" He meant don't talk unless you know that you are being heard by everybody at the table, and then they will hear you out. He had attended my business meetings and he told people, "Kenny has the *word*. When you hear Kenny, you hear positive words. They mean something." But I still had to learn the business, beginning with pumps.

A water pump is essentially a casting enclosing an impeller and connected to a motor, via a shaft. At the beginning of my self-education process, I was told in the "shop" (what everyone called the manufacturing facility) that the castings coming in from our suppliers were pieces of porous, cardboard shit. About 50 percent of the castings dissolved like sawdust before they could be completely machined. Many of the others were so porous they'd leak water like a sieve, not exactly what a pump is supposed to do. When pressed for a reason why the castings were so bad, a few of the suppliers indicated that up until now, the kick-back commission paid to the company employee(s) ordering the castings was more important than the quality of the product delivered to Jacuzzi. I almost couldn't believe what I was hearing.

There was also the problem of whom to ask, whom to listen to, whom to believe, and why some would rat on others. I had learned that the appeal of secretiveness was irresistible. I would simply float a notion, ask a question, and flit from fact to fact, like some pest nibbling at fruit. It was my purpose to learn the truth without revealing what I already knew. The young had great zeal and wanted to smite evil and soar above the common lot. The old knew it was often wiser to stoop than to soar. My information-gathering techniques began to work. Words came tumbling out of mouths, and I learned some Italian cuss words I'd never heard before.

I've always loved languages. I spoke English, Spanish, was becoming more fluent in Italian by the day, and was fair to middling in French. I'm reminded of what the Holy Roman Emperor Charles V is supposed to have said: "I speak Spanish to God, Italian to women, French to men and German to my horse." Well, I didn't have a horse so I didn't need to learn German.

The shop itself was another example of instituted chaos. The normal manufacturing process—inventory to machining—assembly—testing—painting—packaging to shipping—was about as far from reality as one could imagine. Instead of a logical, progressive flow, the Italian factory's manufacturing process zigzagged, hiccupped and stumbled worse than a drunken sailor on shore leave for the first time.

The more I asked questions of the factory workers putting together our pumps, the more "by the way" information was poured into my skull. I learned that some critical inventory components were in short supply or lacking totally while other parts were so numerous they couldn't have been used up in five years. I found that crucial production lathes and machines were in disrepair and/or operated by untrained personnel. Then I was told that jigs and fixtures vital to production accuracy and consistency were glaringly nonexistent. Even the paint facility was in violation of environmental laws and dangerous to the health of those working in and around it; product testing was inconsistent. Haphazard packaging often didn't protect the integrity of the products and on and on.

Naive and inexperienced in the ways of business, I continued to worry people as I sent steady reports of my findings to the parent company and openly shared them with the management of the Italian operation. I just didn't like the idea that shitty products with my name on them were being continually manufactured and returned by justly unhappy customers. Appearance-wise, I'd long ago reconciled myself to never being a James Dean or Elvis, but being known for making nothing but crap was a little too much for even me to handle. What I didn't appreciate at the time was that I was actually learning by doing, as I did in learning how to paint portraits.

My gut told me that these problems could be solved and I even began suggesting ways to go about doing so. Little did I realize how much my reports were shaking up the universe around me. However, the caca soon hit the fan. My critical letters to the home office and their stern admonitions to management eventually caused all of Jacuzzi Europe's administrators, including the manager himself, to resign en masse.

The next month, March 1972, I received a request from both my brother and Ray Horan, the new president of the American parent company, to consider becoming the new general manager of the Italian company. As thrilled as I was about the prospect of being a manager and getting the chance to prove myself in business, I was under no delusions about my importance. For some time there had been rumblings to the effect that because Jacuzzi Europe was not pulling its weight it should be closed down. It was no great honor to be named captain of a sinking ship. The rats had already gone overboard.

Even after that, no one took my role very seriously, including me. For one thing, my "jobs" up until this time involved primarily discussions of my design theories with respect to the evolving whirlpool baths and spas with my father and other immediate relatives, and part-time at that. Secondly, my formal education hadn't progressed beyond a high-school diploma and several semesters of community college. Third, and probably most importantly from everyone's perspective including my own, I was a person requiring assistance from others just to survive day-to-day; therefore, how could *I* be expected to run anything?

My instincts told me to first think this over for a while, while my starved-for-recognition ego told me to grab the bull by the horns and accept the offer.

Boy, that was a groin-centered decision if ever there was one. In spite of everything, I accepted the position. Not that the decision to accept being the company's manager was in itself wrong—it wasn't—it's just that I rushed to say yes without first thinking everything through. What I should have done was first determine what priorities lay before the company, what kind of manager I was, how I would get people to do what I wanted, what needed to be done, etc. I needed to devise my personal management strategy and values for turning around Jacuzzi Europe and anchor myself to them so that I wouldn't appear fickle or unsure.

As I quickly came to realize, not having a strategic plan anchored to clear priorities and proven methods of building teams and relationships makes it nearly impossible to successfully turn around any company, particularly one that would soon prove to be not just in major disarray, but also financially bankrupt.

In my Professor 'enry 'iggins mood, I wondered why couldn't these employees be more like Americans, be more like bosses and entrepreneurs, be more like Jacuzzis, be more like me? I could speak their language but could I get them to work with me to accomplish Jacuzzi company goals? And, in a *tempestuous* sea like this, the captain had better be a rock-solid son-of-a-bitch if the ship is to have a decent chance of making it.

I strongly suspected the company was in bad financial shape, but I didn't know the half of it. The books were so badly scrambled that it took the accounting firm, Touche-Ross, a year to uncover just how bad things were.

I learned that in Italy, many of the small and medium-sized companies had two sets of books, called the "white" and the "black." The white set had all the accounts in order for the fiscal authorities and tax authorities, and the black set had records of all the business they did on the side for cash, thereby allowing them to skim off profit without paying taxes on it.

Then there was the problem of the social security payments. In Italy, social security encompasses medical coverage, pensions, and the unemployment system. Included in social security is a bonus system whereby an employee is given a month's salary at the end of the year as a bonus. Upon retirement, an employee is pensioned at 80 percent of his salary. Needless to say, the social security payments, made entirely by the employer, are not insignificant. Jacuzzi Europe was between six and eight months behind on its payments and at least that far behind in recording the debt.

Other drains on the company assets were the extravagant expense accounts and luxurious company cars for the executives. The list went on and on. For a company on the brink of collapse, the management had been living pretty well. They even kept a manufacturing operations office in Milan.

They maintained an office in Milan because management had girlfriends (mistresses) there. It was a nice place, the economic center of Italy. With the small operation of Jacuzzi Europe, we couldn't justify a separate office in Milan. It was nice for the manager because he could go there and entertain foreign clients while getting his rocks off and so on. Milan is a sophisticated environment, too. It has a much larger range of restaurants and nightclubs. You could whiz up to Switzerland and go gambling. It's where the action is, not like little conservative, laid-back Friuli.

The Jacuzzi Europe manufacturing operation was a young company, only about two years old, and as long as it was acting as a distribution point for the U.S. headquarters, it seemed to function effectively under its own direction. It's one thing to sell a product that's already made, but it's another thing to make *and* sell it. When it became involved with manufacturing, additional competency was required in the upper echelon, but people with the necessary skills were not hired. Instead, the choices reflected cronyism. Dad was accused of cronyism because he chose family members to fill positions, but usually he tried to put relatives into the jobs they were best suited for.

One of the reasons the manager hired the man in charge of production was that he was a champion marksman and they liked to go out target practicing. They had a lot of fun, these guys, but they were not necessarily getting the job done.

Another problem I had was with my own father. Unfortunately, Dad, who was living there, was partially blinded by his own problems with the I.R.S. and with his cousins, nieces and nephews. He was more concerned with his own self-esteem and it was difficult for him to see the writing on the wall. Besides, at this stage, he was not consulted much for these things. He might go out and give advice on problems with a casting or machining, and sometimes he would be very emphatic, but he never made a detailed study.

The manager would listen intently to Dad's suggestions, hanging on every word. Then he went out of his way to see that the old man was wined and dined in a manner befitting his station. At the time, Dad felt betrayed by the family and, forced to live as an expatriate, he was in no position to be critical of somebody who treated him as a friend.

I could see that the factory layout itself was a mess. There was inventory, finished and unfinished, piled together all over the floor, making it easy for any enterprising freelancer to start his own pump business on the side without much chance of getting caught. Internal theft by employees usually accounts for a 5–10% loss from your bottom line. But here it was likely to be much higher. Inventory and quality control were impossible because they never knew how many of anything they had, or whether it had passed inspection. A pump would be in production and they would not be able to find the screws to put it together. At first, I could not figure out where the assembly line started and where it was supposed to end.

It was incredible! You'd think you'd have a layout where the stuff comes in one door and goes out the other, right? That sounds like the logical thing. The assembly line should begin where you have your components. You have them machined, assembled, tested, painted, finished, tagged, recorded and put in finished product inventory to get shipped. There's nothing transcendental about that. Any dunce could figure it out. But we didn't.

The work area was filthy and there were fire and health hazards everywhere. The paint booth was so poorly ventilated, it is a wonder there were not sit-down and sympathy strikes just over that. Morale was certainly low enough. Not only was it a poor work environment but inefficient and costly. I won't even get into punctuality and absenteeism. Why hadn't these people seen the proverb, God gives the nuts but he doesn't crack them? I wanted to crack some nuts, but that's another story.

I argued that good manufacturing operations would increase our productivity and quality, which would decrease cost in the long run. If it costs less to make something, and you make it good enough that people continually want to buy it, you price it right and make more profit. This was so elementary. I instituted all these changes during the first year-and-a-half and we had a really trim operation. I had to design the layout, but I had no production experience. We had this guy brought in from Jacuzzi Canada who turned against me in the end. He was the one who really got the production moving. I designed the layout. I like to see orderliness and flow. Maybe because of my disability, and my need for well-planned steps to get anything done, flow comes naturally.

Another thing that came as naturally to me as it did to my father was to build the company from the top down, and find topnotch people to fill the recently vacated division manager positions. However, the board of directors for the U.S. Company told me to go slow and not rock the boat. They said I should fill the positions from within and if I could handle any obstacles that arose, I was worthy of my position.

After this "vote of confidence," one of the same directors is recorded in the minutes of a subsequent meeting saying, "I don't see how a handicapped person could ever be the manager of anything!"

My brother, John, who was on the board of directors, reported this remark, which added to my suspicion that some people in the family might not want to see me succeed.

My father wanted very much to see me succeed, but we had very great differences about how Jacuzzi Europe ought to be run. He thought my meetings were too long, which was probably true. However, I was trying to get all the information I could get about the company and about business in general. Those meetings would have to serve for the time being as my business education. Dad also did not like it when I sold the expensive Mercedes, Opal and Citroens purchased by the previous management as company cars and refused to allow the company to pay for Dad's own Mercedes as part of his pension plan.

To pay off some of the bills and keep the company from closing, I even sold the company house in Casarsa known as the Jacuzzi Library, where my father and his brothers and sisters were born. Convincing my father that the $100,000 the house would bring was more important than preserving a family legacy was no easy matter, but finally the old man gave in. Dad always believed in allowing the manager to manage the company, even if it meant sometimes letting him make his own mistakes, a responsibility he had rarely offered me.

The bottom line in determining the success or failure of any business is cash flow and Jacuzzi Europe's was terrible. Part of the reason seemed to lie in the company's choice of clients. Jacuzzi Europe was turning out pumps, water systems, swimming pool equipment, and filters. Their customers were usually large firms, either major distributors or dealers, or manufacturers in the same line, who purchased from Jacuzzi what they did not have or did not bother to make themselves.

A product Jacuzzi was famous for in the U.S. was the submersible pump, but because of poor quality control and high prices, they lost most of the European market. Thus, their customers rarely wanted the whole product, requesting only pieces, or a pump housing without the motor. Since most of them were manufacturers and large distributors, they could get pumps as cheaply as Jacuzzi could. When I saw this, I was astounded. Why were we supplying our competitors?

They were buying the pump ends and not the motor. Then they got to the point that they wanted just components. They were going to buy their own shells and cast their own pump housings for the shell. Really what they wanted was the shaft and the impellers. They didn't want to go through the hassle of paying for the molding equipment for making plastic impellers. In order to be profitable selling components, you had to sell millions of them, while you only needed to sell several hundred pumps to be profitable.

The only reason for serving these customers was that they were large accounts so they would only have to be contacted two or three times a year at the trade shows, or by visiting them on special trips. Naturally, these trips were juiced by their lavish expense accounts, wining and dining these clients while management enjoyed themselves in the process.

Although I did manage to turn this company around after four years of exceptional struggle and countless, stupid mistakes, I could have done it in a shorter period of time and much better if I had listened to my gut and prepared better in the first place.

My cousin, Harold Benassini, faced many similar problems during his tenure managing the Brazilian operation. It took him the better part of seven years to turn things completely around, and I had begun to do the same in four years.

Of course, I could be sarcastic and/or bitter by saying that with Candido out of the way, you can get away with giving his son, the cripple, a shorter leash, but then, what would that say about the family?

There is more to be told about rebuilding this family "dream house" after I describe my wife and marriage in Part Three.

Mom, Inez

Dad, Candido

Ted Kennedy

Ronald Reagan

Aurelia, Daniela's friend

Rachele Jacuzzi, Ken's uncle
(unfinished)

Spanish boy, Málaga, Spain

Cady, Pat Janzen's daughter

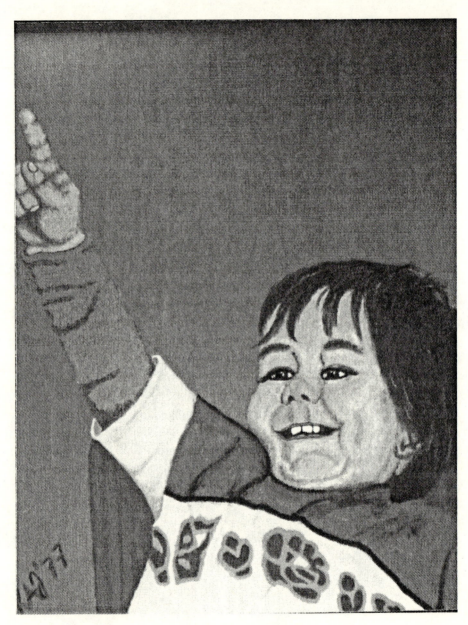

Mattia, Daniela's nephew

Rabbi and bride, David and Irene

Kenny at one year, Berkeley, California

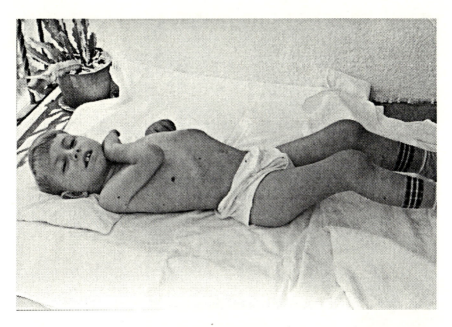

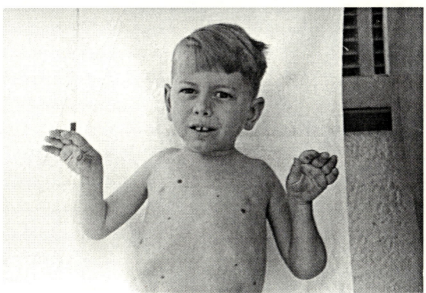

Kenny, age 3 approximately, following onset of systemic juvenile rheumatoid arthritis (2 photos)

Kenny with his family: Alba and John standing; Irene, Kenny, Candido and Inez in Berkeley, California

Kenny mobile on tricycle, 1950, Lafayette, California

Jacuzzi 7-Passenger Cabin Monoplane, 1921, Yosemite, California
(Passengers: uncle, Giocondo Jacuzzi; aviation consultant and writer,
John H. Kauke; a visiting aviator from England, A. Duncan McLeish;
and pilot, Harold L. "Bud" Coffee).

5 Jacuzzi brothers, Candido, Gelindo, Frank, Joseph, Valeriano, 1958, Richmond, California

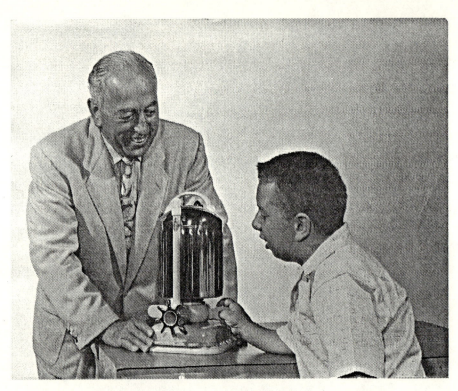
Kenny, his dad, Candido, and first Jacuzzi Whirlpool Bath

Inez, Candido and Kenny meet Jack Bailey, host for TV's "Queen for a Day"

Ken's brother-in-law, Peter Kosta with children and Jacuzzi Whirlpool Bath

Ken's cousin, Virgil Jacuzzi, inside Jacuzzi Canada manufacturing plant

Jacuzzi brothers, nephews and managers at entrance to Jacuzzi Canada in Toronto

Ken's friend and caregiver, Bruce "The Beard," near Lassen Volcanic National Park, California

Ken skin-diving, Acapulco, Mexico

Ken's friends: Tom, Peggy, Wayne and Ray, in Ashland, Wisconsin

Ken's friends and caregivers, Wayne and Helen,
near Seattle, Washington

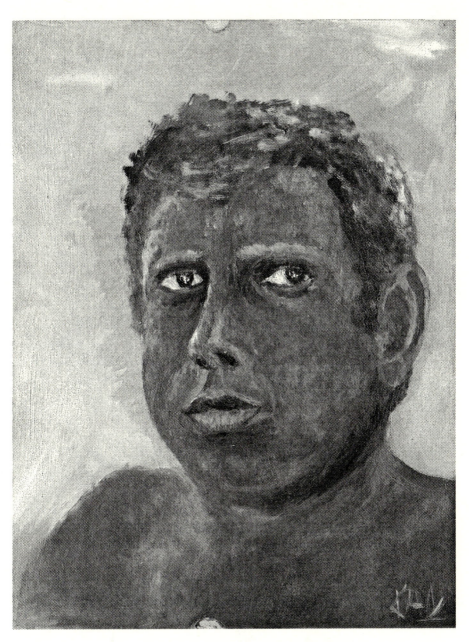
Ken's self-portrait, 1968, Rome, Italy

Ken's friend and caregiver, Pasquale "Pat," St. Peter's Basilica, Rome, Italy

Ken's friend, Marcia, Hotel Boomerang, Rome, Italy

Kenny riding a camel with Francisco, Marrakesh, Morocco

Ken's friend and caregiver, Egidio, Málaga, Spain

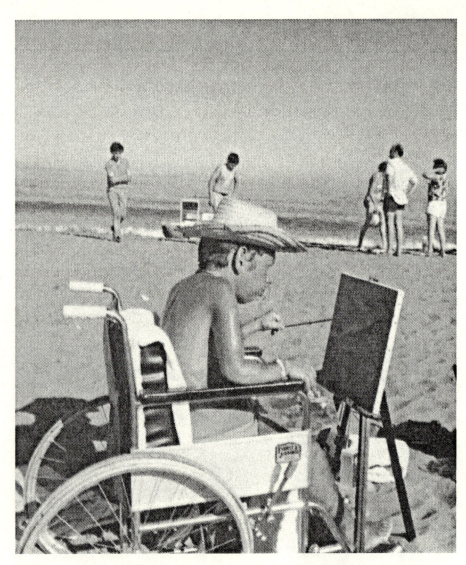
Ken painting at the beach, Torremolinos, Spain

Ken's friend and caregiver, Francisco,
countryside near Torremolinos, Spain

Ken's wife, Daniela, Pordenone, Italy

Coquilini, created by Ken's dad, Candido,
awarded "1968 Fashion Innovation" by *Marie Claire* magazine

Author, Tom Robbins and friend, Kitty Wiesenthal, in Jacuzzi Spa, 1985

Charlton Heston in Jacuzzi Spa, 1986

Ken's grandparents, Teresa and Giovanni,
with Ken's dad, Candido, age 8

Dad's house, Casarsa della Delizia, Italy

Mom's house, Rapallo, Italy

Ken with friend and caregiver, Dave Carr, 1983, Beijing, China

Ken's management training class, Computer Ministry employees, 1983, Beijing, China

Ken skydiving for 60th birthday, Eloy, Arizona

Kenny sail planing for his 60th birthday, Lake Pleasant, Arizona

2003 Jacuzzi Family Reunion, Sonoma, California

Kenny with aunts, Stella Marin and Gilia Peruzzo,
2003, Sonoma, California

Ken with wife, Daniela, 2003, Phoenix, Arizona

Part III
Learning, Marriage, and Stuff

17

Meeting My Future Wife

Tornado: A violent whirling wind, accompanied by a rapidly rotating funnel-shaped cloud that usually destroys everything along its narrow path.

As if my work was not putting enough demands on me, I found myself obliged to look after my brother's son, Johnny. He was attending Bertoni, a prestigious Catholic boarding school not far from the factory in Italy. Johnny had been a difficult child and was having problems at school in Mexico, so Dad, who was living in Italy, said to John, "You send Johnny to me! Let me take care of him."

I should explain that life had gotten very serious for John's family when Johnny suffered a health tragedy himself. He was in the garden helping to light smudge pots when fuel spilled on him and caught fire. He had first and second degree burns and after considerable treatment and scars, was left with recurring problems on both feet and most of one leg. This trauma may have contributed to being "difficult."

Johnny lived with Grandpa Candido for nearly a year, which was probably a character-building experience for both of them, after which time Johnny went to live at Bertoni. In addition, since I was now nearby and spoke Italian, Spanish, and English, it was only natural that I should help Johnny settle in at the school and maybe show him around on the weekends.

Johnny never liked school. He liked adventure. He liked learning things from other people, like his dad's gardener in Mexico who showed him how to grab a rattlesnake right behind the head with his hand without being bitten. Although he was only thirteen, he had already learned a lot about drinking and women from other Mexican kids before coming to Italy.

Despite his mischief, Johnny and I got along well and I was glad to accept the role of guardian. On weekends, Johnny would stay with me and my personal care assistant (PCA) at the Astoria Hotel where I lived.

Sometimes I would visit with Johnny's school principal to discuss his progress. Although he spoke English and Spanish fluently, Johnny was having a great deal of trouble with Italian and French. Studying wasn't something Johnny liked doing, so he didn't. One day, the principal, a surprisingly youthful, tough-minded priest, told me that if Johnny didn't get some hard-nosed tutoring soon he wouldn't be able to pass and complete his courses.

He recommended I hire a university student who would also be capable of keeping Johnny in line. When I asked him if he knew anyone who might be up to the challenge, he suggested a university French major, Sandra. Soon after hiring Sandra, Johnny's grades turned around and I came to appreciate how well she could get him to hustle. She certainly reflected the hard-headedness that's notorious in the people of Friuli. Maybe the tough-mindedness becomes inbred in people who have been invaded and pillaged by dozens of races and cultures over the span of hundreds of years.

Some weeks later, when two accountants from the Mexican parent company came to help out at the Italian plant, I suggested they go to Venice along with my father, Johnny and his tutor, Sandra. Somehow, around the middle of the afternoon, they were separated, Dad and the accountants in one group and Bruno, Johnny, the attractive tutor and I in the other. We went for a gondola ride and saw the sights of Venice, drinking wine and looking for the other group, although not looking very hard. After experiencing Venice, I knew why my grandparents had honeymooned there. As Truman Capote said, "Venice is like eating an entire box of chocolate liqueurs in one go."

Later that night, Bruno insisted we all go to his mother's house for homemade salami, and about two o'clock in the morning, we converged upon an all-night pizzeria. While Bruno and Johnny finished the last of the pizza, Sandra and I fooled around in the back seat. As another Italian female, Sandra wasn't only sharp as a tack; she was pretty, vivacious, and just plain irresistible. However, with Bruno's occasional returns to inquire if "we needed anything" the fooling around stage was as far as we got.

When we rolled into Pordenone, it was 4:30 in the morning and Dad was livid. "Where the hell were you?" he shouted. "I called the police. I thought you were kidnapped. What's the matter? You trying to give me a heart attack in my old age?" The bawling out he gave us was nothing compared to what Sandra received from her brother, Paolo, when she got home.

Sandra and I saw each other from time to time, usually to review Johnny's progress. One day when we were talking about our families, she mentioned she had a sister. I asked her to bring the sister along and we would all go out to a restaurant. We went to a rustic little place in Trieste, world famous for their bean soup.

Daniela, the sister, wore a white Angora turtleneck sweater. She was very quiet and reserved, seemingly the opposite of her boisterous, fun-loving sister. Something about her intrigued me. She didn't talk much, except for the brief necessities of life, but when she spoke, it was usually something perceptive and subtly funny. I recall that as we talked, sometimes she didn't say the words but looked at me with a "yes." Her face and body were very expressive, even if she said little.

I recall how I first had the chance to contemplate Daniela as we sat across the table from each other in the hilltop restaurant in Trieste. As we chatted over menus, I couldn't help but notice how her chestnut hair, cut rather short, and her brown, mysterious eyes gave her an aura quite different from that of her blond and flirtatious sister. Sandra was an expansive, talkative person while Daniela was reserved, but noticeably observant of everything and everyone.

With Sandra occupying center stage in all their lives, Daniela had developed a more refined style. She was poised, tactful, and elegant.

As the dinner meal progressed, I became intrigued with Daniela's unaffected smile and pink cheeks. Her cheeks gave off that girl-from-the-mountains glow that commanded me to think of those other soft and most tender places of female flesh that lie hidden and unknown, under the breasts and where the thighs meet the buttocks, and make all grown men grovel. Daniela's reserved manner and puzzling mystique only helped further fuel the slow heat building in my face and other bodily parts.

That evening, after we had taken the girls home, Bruno and I were comparing the two sisters. Bruno was the type of man who would ignore an unfamiliar side dish because he was intent on sirloin steak.

"Well, I think Sandra is the hot one," Bruno insisted.

"Daniela just has to be tapped," I said. "Still water runs deep."

The first time we went out, I took Daniela to a nightclub with a restaurant on one end and a disco on the other. Some of the tables had overstuffed couches covered with animal hide. It was a dark, sexy place. We seemed to get along well.

I remember the dress she had on, a flowered dress, the same one she wore two years later when we were married. I bought her an orchid, the first she'd ever received.

My former aide, Egidio, took time off from his studies to visit me. Somehow, Daniela, Sandra, Egidio, and I ended up on a double date in the back seat of a taxi. True to form, Egidio wasted no time moving in on Sandra. I looked at Daniela who was pretending not to notice what her sister was doing with this strange young man. When I tried to kiss her, she stiffened and said, "No!" It took a while for my ego to recover.

◆ ◆ ◆

It was a bone-chilling, melancholy winter Sunday morning in Udine, characteristic for this part of northeastern Italy, which bordered to the east, Yugoslavia, now Slovenia. The year was 1972 and I had arrived at mass early at *Il Duomo d'Udine,* the beautiful fourteenth century cathedral of Udine. I purposely came early, expecting to see Daniela. I was hoping that she might join me for lunch at *Siora Rosa,* so I could get to know her better and her elusive, but captivating aura might begin to unfold.

Siora Rosa, "Signora Rose," a favorite local restaurant or *trattoria,* was located on a cobble-stoned street just across the piazza from the cathedral. Its specialty was *bollito,* a boiled and slowly simmered mixture of meat and vegetables, including carrots, celery, potatoes, beef, chicken, tongue, and a fat Italian pork sausage called *cotechino.* Plainly, it's what my soul needed on this dreary winter day, especially when combined with *Merlot,* a robust, aromatic local red wine. What could best complete my quest for cheer, even if only momentary, would be the nearness and leisurely company of this lovely, intricate female.

My newfound career as a turnaround manager of a company in financial and manufacturing crisis had been battering me incessantly, testing my wits, within weeks of my return to Italy in late 1971. The only thing that made sense to me now, over a year later, was trying to establish some equilibrium and wholeness in my life. My age and state of existence left me with a profound emptiness and need for a woman to share my life with, not just to make love to.

I had no idea if this speculative lunch date would even materialize, let alone if she would ever be that woman. I only knew intuitively that some one-on-one contact was now desired. At least by me! I had asked her if she would meet me after this morning's mass and she said she would. Lunch, maybe.

Although I had been working in Italy for a year, I was still living in a small two-bedroom suite at the *Hotel Astoria Italia* on *Piazza XX Settembre,* named for the date of the final unification of Italy (September 20, 1870). The hotel was not far from Il Duomo and the geographic center of Udine. The Astoria was a recently renovated, well-maintained old hotel, but then almost everything was old in Udine, a cosmopolitan city of 100,000 citizens, established over a thousand years ago. Besides being one of the best hotels in town, and one of *the* places to go and be seen by the local movers and shakers, the Astoria had two worthy accoutrements: an exceptional restaurant and intimate, fun bar. It was a home away from home that provided me with a warm place to sleep and bodily nutrients, but little nourishment of my spirit or soul.

After a typical workday, my evening would start at the Astoria's *American Bar*, called that because the lights were dimmed and the ambience was dark—*as are all bars in American movies*—in stark contrast to most Italian bars which are illuminated as well as a Sun City, Arizona, retirement community's self-serve cafeteria. The tables were small and few and I always felt lucky to get one to sit at with my wheelchair, even during this time of day when the bar wasn't normally full.

I would choose either a *Campari, Cinar,* or *Rabarbaro con Selz*, all Italian *apperitivi*, the latter very bitter. I'd exchange local gossip or a few jokes with the bartender, Stefano, maybe catch a glimpse of the news on TV, and then head for dinner. Sometimes before leaving, Stefano would tell me if this was the night *belle donne*—very attractive, liberal-minded women—were expected at the bar.

The subtle nuances in the Italian language demand that an expatriate bachelor like me, interested in the opposite sex, know the difference between *belle donne* and *le belle donne*. *Belle donne,* as usually used between guys, generally meant women who were quite attractive, but not opposed to hopping in the sack with the right man. Whereas *le belle donne,* emphasis on the *"le,"* usually referred to women of varying degrees of attractiveness who make their livelihood by sleeping with you. An even more unequivocal term for women who market their love services is *le belle di notte*.

Every now and then, one or two *belle di notte* would grace the Astoria's bar in search of an appropriate client, but I never succumbed. Not that I didn't want to, but it seemed that whenever I had enough time and energy to perhaps indulge my horniness, *le belle donne* were never there. Besides, the more isolated and entrenched I became in trying to save the family's Italian enterprise, the less appealing sex for money waxed between my brain and groin.

After a diversional half hour at the bar, my personal care assistant and I would go to the Astoria's restaurant for dinner. The restaurant's proprietor and host, Giovanni, slender and jaunty in his white dinner jacket and personally attentive to each customer, made me always feel welcome (no matter how many times I'd been there before).

While in Italy, I'd really gotten into the gusto of a multi-course meal—not for the quantity, since all portions were half of what is normally served in American restaurants, but for the food's unending variety and goodness. But it was the virtuosity of the tableside service, provided nearly always by male waiters that made a meal in an Italian restaurant an excellent stress time-out. It was quite a treat after dining in some American restaurants where waiters are not always glad to see you.

I'm sure most people have dined in the kind of restaurant where the waiters would much rather you didn't come. Sometimes a waiter standing around looks at you with an air of evaluation and curiosity, as if it had occurred to him that you are rather like his brother. Then he shifts a leg and takes a new view of you, as if he had rejected the resemblance to his brother, and had begun to think of you more like his aunt, or uncle, or grandmother. Finally, your own waiter brings some food, pitifully unlike your expectations. Meanwhile the idle waiter still looks at you, but suspiciously now, as if you were the party who made off without paying last month. When finally I leave such a restaurant, I don't doubt that the waiters say to each other, "I hope we never see him here again."

This was not the case at Giovanni's. However, I still had to remind myself that I had to get up early the next morning and go to work, so I would keep my meal sizes contained, especially during the week. A typical evening meal for me at Giovanni's would be three moderate courses, antipasto or pasta to start, followed by the main course of either fish or meat with selected vegetables and a side salad that was made to order and tossed at tableside from a wheeled cart, and fresh fruit and/or cheese for dessert, always accompanied by a glass or so of wine. As was the custom then for guests staying more than several days, the hotel's restaurant would keep your wine in storage so that you could enjoy it over more than one meal if you drank little.

Once inside Giovanni's restaurant, it was knife-through-warm-butter easy to momentarily forget my other, bleaker reality: the frigid weather, the unending survival problems of the business, even my arthritis and disability. It was this juxtaposition of agony and ecstasy that my life in Italy—and later with my wife-to-be, Daniela—would stick most in my mind.

No matter how tired I was, my assistant and I would inevitably gravitate back to the bar for an after-dinner espresso and/or *digestivo*, usually *Rabarbaro* or *grappa*. By this time of night, about ten o'clock, the bar was full of people and cigarette smoke. Italians smoked too damned much. I think they got that from watching too many Humphrey Bogart movies.

The patrons were either businessmen or young men or women not unlike America's '80s yuppies. Most of the latter were from the Friuli aristocracy or moneyed class. Apart from the fact that essentially all northern Italian men and women, regardless of class or economic status, dressed very well, these *figli di papa* were always chic, especially the women. There's quite a lot of merit in being able to sit back after a long day and good meal, sip leisurely on a glass of *grappa*, while feasting one's eyes on women as beautiful as super models, dressed exquisitely, but still sharing generous amounts of their flesh from the shortest of skirts and sans bras. Occasionally, the sight alone was almost enough to make me want to get out of my wheelchair and walk. Instead, the *grappa* was soon finished and only my lonely bed called out to me.

That was my daily routine, but it was about to change. Here I was awaiting Daniela's arrival and mass. The Cathedral of Udine was started in 1335, from a design based on a Latin cross-shaped plan with three naves and chapels along the sides. In the 18th century, the Manin family, at their sole behest and expense, initiated a radical project of transforming the Cathedral into its present day Baroque interior of monumental dimensions, containing priceless works of art by Tiepolo, Amalteo, and Dorigny. The bell tower's ground floor was embellished with frescoes by Vitale da Bologna. A contemporary family, the Cledes, had recently installed the wheelchair ramp along the side of the Cathedral's front entrance steps for use by their son, but it now facilitated my access.

Finally, I saw Daniela, dressed in a wool overcoat and leather gloves, enter the church and take a seat not far from the aisle where I was seated in my wheelchair. She looked very quiet, reserved, and composed. She did not see me. At that instant I flashed that she would someday be my wife and that our life together would be as rich, intense and sometimes as volatile as the Friulani people in whose capital we were both residing. I don't know why I thought that. I was still trying to make out with her. It just kind of came to me. In fact, it seemed inevitable.

The lunch went well. In fact, it was divine. I think I was already in love with her without realizing it. There was no doubt about that and everyone else sensed it. I learned that she was born in Eraclea, a province of Venice, in 1948. She had an older brother, Paolo, who was born in 1939 and there was, of course, her sister Alessandra (Sandra), born in 1949. Her family came to Udine after her father retired in the early '70s from a career managing farms.

She had completed high school and had specialized in secretarial training. First, she worked in a regional agricultural office, and followed that by working for an older gentleman lawyer, answering the phone, filing, and doing general secretarial duties. However, she had this way about her, a caring way. She said her aunt used to think she would make a fine nurse. Perhaps I was her destiny, the man she was born to care for?

I learned that she had seen me on the city street a couple of times before her sister introduced us to each other. Later she told me that it was funny to see little me in that big silver Mercedes going to work. After all, it's pretty hard not to notice me. I had not turned her off. In fact, I wanted to turn her on. Suddenly her character became clear to me. She was kind. She cared more for kindness than wealth, class, polish, and status. Moreover, she has remained kind unceasingly, committedly, and eternally.

Daniela had been in love in high school. She told me how she had to meet her boyfriend secretly because in Italy, girls are not to date without a chaperone. Then there was another boy that she loved but her parents disapproved because he was a poor boy from the mountains.

Daniela told someone about her early dating, "That fellow, he liked me before I liked him. He was a little pushy. I didn't want to rush. Then I started kind of liking him. He was a nice person." But that was long before I met Daniela.

Then it began to happen. During the day, I was no good at all. Several men came to see me at my office, but I got all muddled up in trying to talk with them. They kidded about my inamorata, laughed, and walked away. I didn't laugh. Tears came into my eyes. I was so happy that I wanted to shout.

She was always composed; always compact. Oh, look at her frills, her edges, her gloves, and her hair, at everything about her. How does she do it? What does she do to be so neat? How is it that everything she wears belongs to her, and cannot choose but to be a part of her? She does such miracles on her own behalf, that, one of these days, when she dies, they'll be amazed to find an old woman in her bed, distantly like her.

I was almost afraid to think she was "my woman." I was even afraid to look at her sometimes, as if she might disappear before my very eyes. Often I would think about her, and wonder what her life had been, that life she never shared with me. I made nothing of it, of course. In fact, I was ashamed of my curiosity. I wanted to bestow a kingdom upon my lady. A knight-errant without a mistress was like a tree without fruit or leaves, or a body without a soul. She made me feel like Sir Lancelot.

◆ ◆ ◆

My friend, Pat, and I were briefly engaged in between my trips to Italy. We'd celebrate special occasions like our birthdays together. To this day, Pat has never tired of reminding me that I'm nearly 5 ½ months OLDER than she is. Although despite our strong feelings and my great love for Pat, I realized I loved her as a friend. I was not sure I was ready to get married earlier anyway, at least not until my life stabilized a little. I wrote Pat a letter, trying to explain my feelings as gently as possible. My intentions were good, but my timing was lousy. Pat's father had just died and she was taking it very hard. My letter made her feel even more deserted. I felt terribly guilty about it, but there was no use pretending. I knew I was not going to marry her after I met Daniela.

However, Daniela was slow to make a decision and took a long time to think over our engagement and whether she would accept a ring. She was not suited to surprise, and lived in a world where people set out long-lasting intentions and shunned change and abruptness.

She worried about her family's reaction. There are so many things to consider when a family believes that a "normal" person wants to marry an "abnormal" person. She told someone about us later.

> My parents said, 'You don't want to be in that situation.' I tried to think of all that work he had done, everybody else accepting him, and I realized 'you've got to start somewhere and then go from there.' Nevertheless, I worried about how long my family would be against me. Even my sister got mad and ripped a dress that Kenny bought for me. He has a gift for figuring out perfect things. He bought a strange but most perfect brown and black dress, and she (Sandra) tore out the seams.

Daniela wanted time to work with her family and perhaps to work with herself. But I needed her. I wondered whether she necessarily had to be a wife. I was out there alone, dealing with the company, with Johnny, with my Dad, and trying to deal with the lifestyle he had developed. I was living partially off the Italian company as if it were a large profit-making organization. I was trying to deal with external and internal family politics. Therefore, I needed a mate like her beside me. I needed to feel complete and know that someone could love me so that I could give to others and could try to save the family business. I felt empty, a brittle shell, vulnerable.

In October 1972, I had to go back to the United States on company business and asked Daniela to come with me. I thought it would be good to get her to see how it is to be alone with me, to travel with me, help me with my bath, help me get dressed and undressed.

She refused. I was not deterred. While I was in the States, I bought her an investment-quality diamond ring, designated "VVS," meaning it was the most perfect diamond available—with one lone flaw, to represent the imperfection in anything human. It was a beautiful ring. I could not contain my excitement about it and about Daniela. I wanted to tell everybody. Instead, I told my niece, Candy. I invited her to join me and my aide Glauco at Scoma's Restaurant on Fisherman's Wharf in San Francisco.

Candy had exciting news of her own. Finally, after extensive and diligent searching, she found Mr. Right: bells, fireworks, choirs of angels, the works. There was no doubt in her mind they would get married. She seemed almost as thrilled to hear I found the woman I wanted to marry and she was awestruck by the ring.

She told a friend:

> He had just bought it and let me wear it the whole evening. I was so proud! Without having to say to anybody that this is my uncle, I would have been so proud to sit there and show this ring off and say, "Yes, he just gave it to me." And that was all I would say. He let me wear this ring the whole evening; even before Daniela did, and that was really special to me that he felt I should wear it. I could have gotten drunk and just lost it, but he trusted me with it.

Actually, she did get drunk and dropped it on the floor where it rolled under a table. It was so dark in there that, for a couple of minutes, we couldn't find it.

The next thing that happened would cast a pall upon my life. On the way back to Italy, I stopped in Denmark for a medical examination. The specialists there could not give me a positive answer to my question. Since my spine surgery, I had been unable to ejaculate. I could get an erection; that was not the problem. It was a "dry" ejaculation, because the semen went back into the bladder instead of out the penis. The doctors in Denmark could not determine whether the dysfunction was just physical and/or psychological, too. Would I ever be able to father children naturally? They did not know. I had to tell Lady Daniela that I was Sir Lancelot without the ideal lance, but still ready to ride up on my steed or wheelchair and carry her off.

It was then that I wrote to Daniela, relating the problem to her and what the doctors had told me. I suggested that if the problem was physical, we might still have children through artificial insemination. Somehow, Daniela's sister got hold of the letter and passed it on to their parents with disastrous results.

Daniela's parents loved me at first, until they discovered I intended to marry their daughter. The final straw was the letter I wrote to Daniela describing my sexual dysfunction. I wrote her telling her that I could not ejaculate outwardly during sex, the sperm retreating to my urethra to be peed out. But doctors could take urine specimens and cull out the sperm, implanting them if the couple wanted to have a child. The condition, retrograde ejaculation, is seen in spinal cord injuries and prostatectomy patients. I also told her I wanted to have sex with her before we wed, so she could appreciate the differences, to help her decide about marriage with a crip.

Her parents wanted Daniela to have children and, being good Catholics, they abhorred anything as unnatural as artificial insemination. When I returned to Italy, it was early November. I gave her the ring, but she would not accept it.

"I can't," she said. "It's my father. I've got to convince him. It's going to take time."

I soon learned that this was Daniela's personality. She takes time to do everything. She's very insecure and reserved. She was very nervous about getting a driver's license until I convinced her she could do it. She failed the test twice and became very uptight about it. She couldn't sleep the night before the test. Nevertheless, she passed. I had something to offer her, I thought—encouragement and love.

This indecision about marrying upset me greatly, however. I had to fight the battle for her heart and mind while I fought a battle to overhaul the company, doubtful that I was making the right decisions because I was uneducated and inexperienced. In both cases, I should have followed my instincts more closely.

I was keeping a diary during my time in Italy. I wrote the following passage during this period. "Is my fate written already? Will this love I have to give ever be received and given back to me in return? Probably not, if my fate is written! The only problem is how to adjust to such a situation, permanently. How to adjust and rationalize—if one can call it that—an equally or sufficiently equal reason for sustaining all the negative things in life. I'd really like to go on living as long as possible, but I'd like a reason to give such an existence sense and meaning."

We were finally engaged on Daniela's birthday, January 4th. I had taken her to a seafood restaurant where the owner had a couple of fishing boats. They served the classic dishes of fish and rice and fish and pasta. There was, of course, fried fish, squid, strong white wine, and a special fragrant yellow bread made in the town of Cividale.

The owner's wife worked in the kitchen and his mistress, who had borne him a daughter, waited on tables. Years later, he had a stroke and had to walk with a cane. His wife and his mistress worked side by side, managing the restaurant together. Their arrangement was no secret to the townspeople who saw the old man hobble from his house to the cottage next door, where his mistress lived, just as he had done for years. They simply spoiled us and helped create the wonderful mood that I often had when I was around Daniela.

I wanted to do more for her and her family. Still looking for good people to fill the top company positions, I hired a production man recommended through Daniela's family. He had a good record as an engineer with Fiat, but it seems that, when working in Fiat's factory in Yugoslavia, he had become enamored of Marxist doctrine.

He felt the best thing in the world to do was to create jobs. He became our production manager and really loaded up the shop with employees. It was true that we needed larger production runs to get the kind of quality we were after (to justify the expense of new molds) but it could have been done more slowly.

The sales manager I found changed his mind and went elsewhere. The parent company was not willing to spend the kind of money necessary to get quality managers, as long as the Italian company's cash flow was so poor. Of course, the cash flow could not improve dramatically until good managers could be hired. I moved a salesman up to the managerial level. He was a good salesman, but certainly not managerial material.

All the while, I struggled to cut back on expenses, trying to set an example by taking for myself a minimal salary of $1,000 a month and buying my own car for business.

Meeting and falling in love with Daniela was the most extraordinary event of my life. Like a *tornado*, it blew away reason, patience, and planning by the very nature of its violent force. It was almost the only thing I could focus on, but she was not easily won. Her rejections were destructive to my ego. I will always regret what I did in that state of turmoil. I made her go to war with her own family.

I eventually learned that the business of a lover is to sense what will please his sweetheart's relatives, to tread on no one's toes, to break no glasses as they say in the Mediterranean, and to square the circle. However, since I could not change my body, the square remained in a square "wheelchair" no matter how much I tried to change it into a circle. I wanted to run capers around her whenever I saw her, but I have always been kept apart from others by my metal vinyl "chariot."

18

Marriage

Extratropical Cyclone: A storm caused when warm and cold air masses meet.

Early in December, I took out an ad for an aide, not another attendant, but somebody to take care of the house. I had been putting this off because I thought Daniela and I might be getting married soon, but that was not to be the case. I found a quiet, unassuming girl named Ada who moved in right away. Daniela was jealous. Christmas came, and then Daniela's birthday. Her sister Sandra was planning her own wedding. Again I asked Daniela to marry me.

"If you can just wait until my sister gets married," she begged, "then I'm sure I can convince my parents!"

I said, "Look, you've kept me waiting for over a year now. It's always been later, later, later. That's it! Either you want to marry me or you don't!"

When I asked for my ring back, Daniela cried but she surrendered it.

Probably every person, with or without a disability, fears that they won't be loved for themselves. When Daniela resisted me with arguments about her parents' acceptance, I probably worried that she really couldn't accept me. I, having a famous name and some amount of wealth, couldn't help but wonder if those were the things that attracted her.

I've seen women study our Jacuzzi possessions and house with an envy that was all too apparent. I've also seen women change their affections when money is no longer a drawing card. But I learned that Daniela was not like that. Sometimes the things that go with money like prestige, power, and security can be attractive, but that is true for almost everyone.

Dad, who lived nearby, learned that Daniela's parents were dead-set against me, thought their attitude unreasonable, and set out to change it in typical salesman-like fashion.

He said, "Kenny, don't you go see Daniela out at her house?"

Then I told him, "Dad, they don't want me at the house. They prohibited me from coming to their house."

"Why?"

"Oh, maybe they think I'm some kind of a freak. They don't want me."

He said, "Kenny, I'll go see them."

So he went to see them, and both Daniela's father and mother were very cold towards him. It was a strange meeting, like a *cyclone or storm* of warm air clashing with cold air.

He said, "Listen, you're kind folks. Let's have a little chat together. I have a boy who is what he is…as you see, he is smaller. He is not as big as a normal man. And, of course, nobody asked me to come here. I would just like to see that Kenny is not rejected. He's a nice boy."

They said, "Well, we don't want our daughter to marry him!"

"Why not?"

"Well," the father said, "he's not normal."

My father said, "What's normal?"

So they had some words. My father reported these conversations to me later.

Daniela's father was sitting there and said to his wife, "Maria, why don't you open a bottle of wine?"

Dad continued, "Because there were two opinions there, you know. The wife was more against you than was the husband. We drank a little wine."

"You know," Maria said to me, "my daughter and Kenny, if they get married, they may not be able to have children? And she may cheat on Kenny. Because she may want to have a regular man."

Dad said, "Don't you think that's their business?" She didn't know what to say.

Then Dad said, "I don't want to predict what's going to happen. I'd just like to be your friend. And our children and God will settle that. Let them do what they want."

Dad couldn't work it out and I couldn't go over to the house again. But Daniela came to see me. She told me that even though my father was extremely friendly and everybody seemed to like him, it didn't really help much for Dad to go and talk with her parents.

Dad said, "Kenny, you and Daniela have to decide what you want to do."

My father had to take a trip through Europe and in the meantime, two days later, Daniela and I gathered some friends and relatives together for witnesses and got married at a nice church near San Vito on March 10, 1974. We were married in a historic old church that Dad knew well as a boy. In fact, the church was very important to Dad and he had dreamed about it just after World War I. After Dad's recent arrival in America, he was awakened from a sound sleep by a dream that San Vito was bombed. Later he found out the Church had been bombed on the very night of his dream, leaving nothing standing but the steeple. It was rebuilt exactly like the original.

My landlord and his wife were witness to the wedding, as was Daniela's cousin. Her sister, Sandra, attended the wedding but not the reception. Since her parents were not going to attend the wedding, I did not invite my parents, which displeased them very much. Another disappointment for Daniela was that she did not wear a proper wedding dress, at least not in her eyes. I don't know why I was so insistent to rush our wedding. I only know that I could hardly eat or sleep or rest. I felt as if I was struggling in the water and someone was telling me to rest. You can't tell someone who is struggling for fear of drowning not to drown but to rest within an arm's length of the shore. I felt I must reach it first, and then I'd rest.

The next morning, I lay on the bed looking at the woman who was now wholly mine. She looked unchanged. This astonished me because I felt as though the night had changed me, yet here was this woman arising as she had arisen every day of her life. I wanted her to like me. But I satisfied myself, for the time, that if she married me, she must like me well enough.

We took our honeymoon in Rhodes, Greece and Cortina, an Italian city in the Dolomites, famous for their wonderful dish called Sarmale. This dish of several meats, cabbage, and vegetables takes three days to prepare, and has been a closely guarded secret for 2,000 years. But we had our own closely guarded secrets. I'll jump ahead and say that the second time we went to Cortina, things had improved with her parents so much that they went with us. But that took many months.

When her sister Sandra was married, Daniela was invited but I was not. But the two weddings had only been separated by several weeks. We were glad to be married finally, but I worried that I had created disharmony with Daniela's family by forcing her to make a decision too soon.

Dad returned to find that we had married but he learned how Daniela's family still resisted. He went to see her folks again and said, "Look! The kids are married now. Don't you think it's time you forgave them and gave them your blessing?"

Her father, Francesco, said, "I'll never forgive Daniela for what she's done to us, for not being obedient to us!"

Dad said, "Daniela's over twenty-one. She's her own boss. See?"

They responded, "But she didn't tell us anything! They ran out and got married without telling us nothing!"

"Don't you think it's time that you forgive them now?" my father continued. Then Dad said to Francesco, "Why don't you open a bottle of wine and at least the three of us can have a drink together in peace, because we have nothing against each other."

He said, "You're right." So he went down to the basement and opened a nice bottle of wine. Dad raised his glass and said, "Here's to our children! And to you, Francesco! Maria!" And he got them to smile.

My parents then threw a nice party in our honor with many relatives and friends. Daniela loved my father. She said, "Candido's white hair made him look like a father figure. He was very friendly with everybody. He loved to be in Italy and he loved speaking Italian. I always spoke Italian with him but I usually spoke English with Kenny's mother, Inez."

In retrospect, I realize now that I should have given Daniela more time. It got our relationship off to a bad start and I've always wondered if it made her too angry with me. We might have been able to bring her parents around. But I had known and dated her for two years! I felt I needed her then. In fact, I needed her a year before. If I had her living with me at that time, instead of the harried dating, I think I would have been much more secure.

I guess we are all possessed and haunted by our own needs, insecurities and demands of those we care about. To have a mind is to be haunted by the voices of everyone who is important to us—mother, father, brother, sister, spouse, priest, friend, and countless others. I had pushed Daniela into doing something that made her uncomfortable. I could feel her resistance and arguments haunting me. I didn't know what price I would have to pay later if she became unhappy because of my impatience and pressure. All I know is that it seemed so important then for me to have somebody to listen to me and love me. It became especially important a short time later.

In October, 1973, the Arab Oil Embargo hit and the bottom dropped out of Europe's economy. Jacuzzi Europe had been balancing between life and death and now the plug was pulled. There would be no help from the U.S. Company, still trying to recover from the hit on the economy caused by the devastation of the break-in at Watergate during the summer of 1972. They wanted Jacuzzi Europe closed immediately. In protest, I resigned. They would not accept my resignation, but they would also not agree to pour any more money or expert personnel into the factory. They had recently received the financial report from

Touche-Ross, outlining in gruesome detail exactly how unsound the company was and how unlikely it was that it could ever recover.

It was an emergency. The company was dying, they told me, and "for Christ's sake, you've got to fix it." It needs blood; in this case, the blood was money. It not only needed transfusions but it needed the wounds closed and a complete rehabilitation program, getting it back exercising, taking care of itself, and then running. The poor bastard company was lying there, dying! I wanted to keep it alive. I felt terribly sorry for the people there who were workers in the factory and in the office. I felt sorry for the fact that they might all lose their jobs. There were not that many jobs available and Italy was going through some hard times.

If Jacuzzi Europe was going to keep its doors open, I knew we would have to lay off 15 or 20 employees, a dangerous thing to attempt and, with the power of labor in Italy, virtually impossible.

After I took command of Jacuzzi Europe, we had corrected the product defects and the product line manufacturing problems. But the oil embargo resulted in a recession that delivered a crushing blow to prices and business.

We had to bring in German motors and translate the lire into marks. The lire kept going down and the mark kept going up. Business was falling off. It couldn't have happened at a worse time.

The people in the U.S. Company could not be made to understand what it meant to try to lay off employees in Italy. It was not like the United States. Labor was more powerful than business. When Italian labor heard about this American capitalist pig who was trying to throw Italian laborers into the street because he could not manage his company, they sent down the biggest labor leader in the region, a communist, to take on the case.

The Catholic-Socialist-Communist Labor Federation was a strongly unified group at the time. The Catholics were as militant and leftwing as the communists or socialists. This was done, of course, for political reasons. They were all trying to outdo one another in militancy to keep membership. They did not want a Catholic member to switch to communism or vice versa. I knew the company had to lay off those workers. On that we could not afford to compromise.

I called a spade a spade. I said, "These guys in the States are going to close this factory. I'm on your side but that's the way it is."

The company attorney said, "You know factory closure has not been done peacefully in the North in the last ten years. I can tell you right now, they're going to occupy the factory. They're going to stop all products from going in or out of the factory; they're going to stop production."

Such action would not be exactly legal, but it was not a matter of legality. Who in the government or in the courts was going to argue? Even if the police charged in on a business or factory, before anything could be done about it, firebombs would be set off and the inventory would be destroyed. Jacuzzi Europe had to be prepared for occupation by police or government, and they were not going to challenge it. Nobody challenges it.

The labor hearings went on for two weeks, sometimes lasting until after midnight. Whatever the labor leader expected, he must certainly have been surprised to encounter something quite different. His opponent was not a capitalistic corporate bulldog, totally ignorant of European labor practices and built like an All-American, but a sympathetic little man in a wheelchair who spoke Italian and seemed interested mainly in keeping his factory open and his workers employed.

I had a lot of credibility by that time. I had gotten rid of the luxury cars and the big expense account. I had sold the family house. When I told them I wanted to keep the factory open, they believed me.

After a flurry of telexes to and from the United States, an agreement was reached and sealed with wine. Each of the employees to be laid off was to be paid a year's salary and turned loose. There was no raid, occupation, or interruption of work, and Jacuzzi Europe gained some respect from European labor. This saved the company from being ostracized by the European market, which does not like doing business with enterprises that have a reputation for being inconsiderate of the aims of labor.

19

My Father's Disability

Tropical storm: Winds are 39–74mph in a usually hot, sultry area.

During the year after I married, the company was improving steadily. New clients were being developed; we had updated the tooling and converted to the metric system. We even straightened out some seemingly impossible accounts like the deal the previous manager had made with Yugoslavia.

Eastern European countries like to avoid paying cash for products because it upsets their foreign exchange. They prefer to barter. For example, if a company sells them pumps, they sell the company hogs. Yep, I said hogs. Of course, the company probably has no need for hogs, and they do not actually take possession of them. The transaction goes through an intermediary usually located near the border who finds a buyer for the hogs and pays the company for the pumps with the hog money and ships the pumps, getting a commission in the bargain.

Jacuzzi Europe, under the previous administration, was to sell the government of Yugoslavia pump ends, pumps without motors, and in turn they were to send Jacuzzi electric motors. It was known that they were pretty good motors, not excellent but decent, serviceable equipment that Jacuzzi could use in their pumps. It sounded like a perfect trade, except that when Jacuzzi sent Yugoslavia the pump ends, they sent back fewer motors than Jacuzzi expected. And those were monstrous things, 300 horsepower, totally unsuitable for the pumps we manufactured.

As it turned out, Yugoslavia was just getting into the production of the smaller motors and they needed all they produced for the Jacuzzi pumps they were importing. Thus they sent their big motors, which were higher priced so they could send fewer and could get a good number of pumps in exchange. When I saw the shipment, I could hardly believe it.

I said, "We can't take this stuff!" But we had to. We had this intermediary who was supposedly going to sell them for us, and he took months and months to do it. In the meantime, we had this huge cash flow problem because we had to pay for the components to make the pumps for Yugoslavia, the workmen had to be paid and we had no income for the motors. When we finally did sell them, it was at such a discount that with the commission, we really lost our asses. But we negotiated another contract, which was another one of my better accomplishments, so we eventually did trade with them for smaller motors.

I cultivated an account with a well-driller in Norway. In the first year, the well-driller was responsible for over $100,000 in sales. I entertained him at the plant and made a trip to Norway. I remembered the contractor liked Parmesan cheese, so when I went to Norway, I brought him a wheel of Parmesan. The contractor had certain engineering problems, so I flew in one of our technicians and solved the problem. The word was beginning to spread that Jacuzzi was producing quality and was serious about satisfying its customers.

As I said earlier, I was able to turn the Italian company around but there were problems and I made errors. It wasn't so much that my first error precipitated all the subsequent ones, only that it became a kind of building-block of insecurity or self doubt, amplifying with each of my successive "blunders." I put blunders into quotes because although they often were "stupid mistakes" in the literal sense, they were actually, in the broader sense, lessons I needed to learn to give this company the wherewithal to eventually survive on its own.

One of my very first inklings, for example, was to immediately search for and hire decisive, technically competent individuals to head up the company's major sectors—engineering, production, finance, and marketing. I was advised, instead, to hire a "general manager" who would report to me.

What a bloody disaster. Ironically, the advice I heeded came from none other than my own father. To this day, however, I can't really blame him for his lack of confidence in my take-charge capability. I had never really proven myself in the trenches of business and, although I had already done a lot of gutsy things in my life, I still now and then relapsed into indecisiveness and vacillation. Yeah, I too was guilty of buying into the incompetent, crippled, disabled, handicapped, useful-as-garbage stereotype.

I don't know if being crippled (i.e., dependent on others and feeling less capable) influences how people ultimately judge their own abilities, strengths and weaknesses, but I can't help believing it does—and usually for the worse. Take the example of Franklin Delano Roosevelt. Here was the President who led the United States out of the Great Depression and to victory in World War II against Hitler and the mighty Nazi war machine. He also happened to be crippled from polio and mobile only in a wheelchair. However, FDR's disability has most often been associated not with his courage and achievements, but rather with the ill health he suffered at the end of his life and some of the less than satisfactory geopolitical arrangements he made with Stalin near the conclusion of World War II. In other words, his disability produced his mistakes. What the hell, it's an easy answer and humans like easy. You know, "the Devil made me do it!"

By logical extension, then, a significant disability most likely affects not only one's physical prowess, but also one's ultimate ability to lead the proverbial country or company to uncompromising victory. Not that being a person without a visible disability would necessarily ensure better geopolitical agreements, but associating "crippled" with "undesirable result" is a nice, easy-to-grasp hypothesis and fits neatly most people's views of the world. If I bought it then—and I'm the cripple—why shouldn't others, including my Dad? How could you run a company if you might need assistance taking a pee or crap?

Finally, I redid the floor plan so that production flowed from one end of the shop, the "in" door, out the other end of the shop, the "out" door. Production quality improved and we finally got the operation to comply with governmental environmental rules. Also, we had to promise customers that we would improve quality by using better stainless steel tanks. Some of these improvements further drained the company funds.

Our biggest seller was submersible pumps. The motors used with them were made in Germany by an American subsidiary. At that time, the mid 1970s, following OPEC's first oil embargo, the Italian government wanted Italy to export, but not to import. The European Common Market was only being talked about then, so the Central Bank of Italy required that we put down a 50% deposit for six months on anything imported like motors from Germany, since we imported and exported. That was a terrible financial burden. We were just regaining customers with our improved quality, and now we had to deposit so much in banks that cash flow was again a major issue.

My brother was already forced out of the Mexican company with the nationalization of the branch in Monterrey. Jacuzzi Brothers was obliged to sell much of its stock to Mexican nationals, which left the company in new hands and left John out of a job.

All his life, Dad had worked to make sure everybody in his family would have a job with the company if they wanted it. Now, he and his two sons were all forced to resign from the company and his son-in-law, Pete Kosta, was accused of improprieties and fired. They claimed that Pete was having company employees repair the fence in his back yard. If he did, it fit my father's theory that a person in management had to spend his time managing, and couldn't afford to be worried about his house springing a leak. It was cheaper for the company to go out and repair it than to have the manager, at his higher salary, take time away from his job to seek out people to get the job done. In addition, the company was making a profit thanks to Pete, but they said it wasn't growing at the rate the board thought it should be growing.

A totally baseless witch hunt against Pete was brought on by the remaining ruling family's desire to rid the Jacuzzi Company of all remnants of influence of Candido's family—now that Dad was retired and out of the way—over a choice Pete had to make as manager that infuriated a cousin, Anna Liotta.

Anna's son was working for the company and he had been warned about his inappropriate conduct (harassing female employees) by Pete. He brought a gun into the office one day and brandished it about to employees. Pete called him into his office and ended up firing him. Anna was insulted and wanted to get even. She had shareholder votes and told the others that she agreed with the removal of Pete. She had gotten the shares because of my Dad. She had taken care of Rachele's wife and Dad thought she should get a nice share of votes. Gordon, Rachele's adopted son, got mad that Anna had gotten so many shares, believing he should have gotten all of them.

The monstrous ingratitude of it was too much for Dad. But as Aristotle said, of all human qualities, gratitude stales the soonest.

"Why I have been so attached to the whole family, I don't know," Dad said, years after he retired. "Because I don't see it in anybody else."

Of course, it had been his father Giovanni's dream for the whole family, all seven brothers and six sisters, to emigrate to America, to live together and prosper together. The propeller business had done well, and might have eventually become, with the inspiration of the brilliant Rachele, one of the greatest aviation companies in the United States, if the sons had opposed their father's wishes and continued after the plane crash. Everyone in the family, including Rachele, knew he was wasting his talents on the small-time family pump business. He could have become chief engineer for any airplane manufacturing business if he had been willing to break away from the family to seek his own destiny.

Grandpa Giovanni ruled his sons and daughters with a firm and loving hand, insisting on only one thing, that they stay together. He understood there were few things in life a man could count on. Foreign troops could invade the land you sacrificed to own and slaved to keep, reducing it to rubble or stealing it outright. Your country's currency might someday be declared worthless. Neighbors could move away and friends could turn against you. Therefore, one man alone is weak and at the mercy of a merciless world. But in family solidarity there is strength. This simple truth Giovanni passed on to his youngest son, who lived by it faithfully and tried until the very end to share it with the family.

As the organizing force behind Jacuzzi Brothers, Dad attempted to place every family member where he or she could do the most good for the company. With the geometric growth of the family, sometimes there would be a member who was not able to fill a key position in the company or did not care to. This person was still encouraged to find work in the business, but when that was impossible, he was encouraged to buy stock in the company. The founders were determined that Jacuzzi Brothers would never become a public corporation.

It was not always easy for Dad to find the talent he needed within the company. How much easier it would have been to hire "outsiders" sometimes, without straining to fill the position from within, than straining to assuage the feelings of other family members who might have felt they were passed over. The latter was something my father often neglected to do and was, in fact, his undoing in the end.

Relatively early on, Dad assumed the position of patriarch of Jacuzzi Brothers and he did it in the Old World tradition. I think he was stubborn, arbitrary, dictatorial, sometimes abrasive, always generous, and usually right, the combination of which made him feared over the years and often hated. If the plant in Brazil needed a new manager, Dad uprooted a cousin or nephew who had proven himself, and sent him to Brazil. In most cases, the appointment was to everyone's mutual benefit. But nobody likes to be pushed around, even if they get rich in the process.

In 1958, Dad organized a huge family reunion that was the beginning of the end. Jacuzzi Brothers was largely a democratic company, based on competition. As a result, some of the family members had larger salaries than others, and some had more shares than others. Some of the women had more furs than others. At the reunion, cousins and nephews, brothers and aunts all began comparing notes.

Some wondered why they, who were born with the name "Jacuzzi," were given inferior jobs with inferior pay in comparison with some who only married into the family. Or why a production manager in California should make less than a production manager in Arkansas. The answer to all these questions was painfully obvious: because they were being paid what they were worth to the company or what the going wage was in their area. After all, Jacuzzi Brothers was a business, not a relief program. Perhaps they could have lived with this reality in relative peace if not for the reunion, but, standing like Jacob and Esau at their father's bedside, their jealousy and resentment grew, and rather than looking to their own inadequacies, they chose to blame my father.

Eleven years passed from the time of the reunion in 1958 to 1969, when Dad was age 66 and family rivalries got out of hand. Dad, always pushing toward new horizons for the greater glory of the company (and himself), was at this time trying to set up a branch office in Switzerland for tax purposes. His Swiss attorney advised him against it but his American lawyer, the pushy and arrogant Joseph Alioto, a man not unlike my own Dad, convinced him of what he wanted to hear. Alioto said that Jacuzzi shareholders would make a fortune from a Swiss corporation.

Dad was surprised to discover opposition to his plan. In some cases, as with his sister, Stella, their vision was less international than his. Stella was afraid of investing outside the United States because she had seen the economic disintegration brought about by war. Also, she been removed from her home in Richmond, California by the government for appearing to be un-American and wanted no more such trouble.

She argued, "Why own something in Switzerland?"

Dad told her, "It is the same thing. You own in Mexico and Canada and Brazil. Except it gives you a better chance for a tax reduction, see?"

But she did not see. Some of the others, however, did see. They saw that my father was sticking his neck out, and it was their chance to get even after being under his paternal thumb all those years. It might even be their chance to separate him from his power. Those who controlled small percentages were not content with inching their way up the ladder.

But Dad was still the boss, still the patriarch of Jacuzzi Brothers. He felt he knew what was best for the company and the shareholders. But suddenly, Dad and the Jacuzzi Brothers were in trouble with the Internal Revenue Service. We will never know whether the families of Dad's six sisters and six brothers had planned to remove him and his immediate family from the vortex of power earlier.

True, he was sixty-six years old, and maybe it was time for him to step down. Still, he never expected to be forced out of office by the very people he helped make successful, his own cousins and nephews! They argued that, since they were contemplating going public, they did not want the president having trouble with the I.R.S. So they engaged the best attorneys they could find and pushed Dad out.

Before Dad agreed to resign, he wanted to be sure a royalty was set up for me because of my disability. I would have preferred a guaranteed annual income with a simple cost of living adjustment for the rest of my life. If it had been set up in 1969 at perhaps $3,500 per month, with medical coverage and COLA, it would have been more acceptable to the family and more equitable, because inflation happens.

But the family members went to lawyers and the whole situation became more inflamed. I felt personally that they didn't have the individual guts to fight my Dad. They only had the collective guts to hire some big guns.

It was not a graceful retirement. Not only was he forced to resign, but the I.R.S. had a summons waiting for him should he ever set foot on American soil. He was in Italy when the indictment came down. Since Italy did not recognize him as an American, he had to have an Italian passport. Later, a notice from Memphis stated he would lose his U.S. citizenship because he had an Italian passport.

Dad was known as a man who could roll with the punches, but now it seemed everything he worked for was slipping through his fingers. Even his own family turned against him and he was no longer welcome in his own country. Months before, he was an iron-fisted general. Now Dad felt like an old man. He was so tired. How had he kept it up for so long?

My father could stand toe-to-toe and fight it out with any corporate executive, but he was not so sure of his ground with my mother, though they loved each other. They never really got along well, and when things got bad, he would find a reason to inspect one of the foreign companies. Now his excuses would be more transparent, and he was not certain he could bear to be challenged at home.

Still, his exile was not without its compensations. They had built a beautiful home in Busarias near Puerto Vallarta, Mexico. It was grand even by Dad's standards, built right next to the huge round house Richard Burton and Elizabeth Taylor were building until they closed the curtain on their marriage. And like their marriage, their house, extravagant in appearances and lavishly begun, was just a shell, never completed. It was somewhat ironic that my folks and the Burtons were building homes next door to each other, since the volatility of their respective marriages likewise paralleled. Since foreigners could not own beach property, the Jacuzzi home was put into the name of their daughter-in-law, a Mexican citizen. The Burtons' home, such as it was, remained in their names, theirs being a special case.

My parents had just finished moving the furniture from their Italian home to Mexico when one day, as Dad was adjusting the hands on the grandfather clock, he felt a tremendous pain in his stomach and crumpled to the floor. Mom was terrified that he'd had a heart attack but it turned out he'd had an aneurysm of the descending aorta.

Like a ruptured inner tube in a tire, the inner wall of Dad's aorta punctured, allowing blood to rush out, forcing the outer wall to expand like a balloon to the size of an orange, crimping the tributary vessels and interrupting blood flow to his spinal cord. He was rushed to a hospital in Monterrey, Mexico. Physicians there said they could do a by-pass operation, but the real experts were in Houston. It took valuable time but I called my lawyer friend, Tom S., to see if we could take him to the "real experts."

Tom said that I should bring Dad back to the U.S. and pay whatever the fine was to get him the medical care he needed. Alba's involvement was critical when she got Dr. Michael DeBakey and his associate Dr. Noon to operate. Dad was then flown to Houston where a successful by-pass was performed the next day. Nerve cells are the only cells that do not regenerate and some take longer to die than others. Two days without adequate blood supply to the spinal cord resulted in Dad's permanent paralysis from the waist down.

Tom recalled the conversation about my father's health and legal problems:

> I told Ken, "Pay them (I.R.S.) off to get the medical care that he needs." It amounted to about $600,000. I hated that the time for these conversations resulted in so much paralysis for his father. I never saw him after 1962. After Candido got rehabilitated, Ken's older sister Alba looked after him until he got into the nursing home, and then Ken and Daniela saw him through to the end. I hated that his active mind got trapped in this hulk of a body. The power was gone but there was enough money to ease him to his end.
>
> He set himself above the system. But the family wanted him out. He was the last of the first generation of Jacuzzis. Roy probably saw him as the last of the old-country bumpkins, considering him old-fashioned. Roy probably thought they could do better without him. It all began with family togetherness and ended with lawsuits.

Tom was right about many things but I'm not sure Roy saw Dad as an "old-country bumpkin" because I think he looked up to the old man.

Even under heavy anesthetic, Dad could tell something terrible had happened to him. Why had they all betrayed him? Even his own body betrayed him. Now that he was back in the States for treatment, he would be served with a summons. That is, if he lived. This raging *storm* of events attacked him relentlessly from within and without, and in his usual area of Mexican hot, *sultry* respite. His weariness and the drugs beckoned his consciousness away from the recovery room.

He drifted back to Italy during the German invasion when he was thirteen years old. Everybody was hungry, even the German soldiers. The Germans and hunger drove Italians from the North away from their homes. Whole villages wandered through the fields like herds of animals, looking for food. Sometimes, a Southern family was fortunate enough to have a little more than they needed and could adopt a family from the North. Giovanni had six hard-working boys and a good piece of land. He took on a family, among them, two beautiful girls. One of the brothers (Valeriano) fell in love with Josephina, who was then fifteen, and married her secretly so the Germans would not interfere.

Soon after the wedding, Dad and a friend went out for a walk. They had long since grown accustomed to the bitterness of war and were not overly disturbed by the destruction that surrounded them, only inconvenienced by having to walk across the fields because most of the bridges were blown up. As they were returning home by way of a wheat field, they saw a soldier lying on the ground.

"That's a dead man," Dad told his friend with certainty.

"Let's run!"

"Why? Let's go see."

Dad walked up boldly to where the man lay. A few feet away, he stopped short. His friend gasped and turned his head. It was an older man. My father could determine that much from the streaks of gray in his hair. At this stage of the war, the Germans were drafting anybody who could carry a rifle. Beyond that, they could only guess what manner of man he was. His face and hands were completely blown away.

Looking around, Dad found next to the dead man what looked like a chunk of mutton, partially wrapped in newspaper. The other boy ran away but Dad stayed long enough to pick up the soldier's treasure and brought it home to his mother.

"Where did you get this meat?" she said.

"I found it."

"Where did you find it?"

But my father wouldn't say.

His mama smelled it. "It's good! It's fresh meat." The family, including their adopted family, ate it, his mama having made a fine stew out of the mutton. Meat was a rare commodity and they needed it.

Mama Jacuzzi was always proud of her cooking. She said, "What's the matter with you, Candido? Why don't you eat?"

He explained he had a stomachache. But he was hungry, too. He had to admit to himself that he was just as terrified and sickened as his friend by the sight of the dead soldier, but his family could use the meat so he had brought it home to them.

Dad lay in his bed, half asleep, wondering why the aged infantryman who had fresh mutton was apparently killed by opening up a can of meat rigged with a bomb. Such post-op and bypass operation dreams are not unusual, as people dream of death or being herded about by others against their will. Did he sense some parallel with himself—a man who had enough but wanted more, or a man who had a share and perhaps wanted another share for someone else? My Dad, old soldier, lay back in his hospital bed, waiting for sleep to come.

My father's aneurysm was some months after my marriage in 1974, just as I was bringing my new wife Daniela, her parents and her brother to Mexico for Christmas. Daniela and I flew on to Houston to be with my Dad but her brother and parents stayed in Mexico for the holiday.

Suddenly Dad had a major disability in common with me as we were both in wheelchairs. His treatment, ironically, included whirlpool baths to help his blood circulation. But I had had many years to accept my condition. My father never really accepted that he had a disability like paralysis and had to depend upon a wheelchair for mobility. As a result, he was not very interested in any recommendations I gave him. He turned to my sister Alba for more direction, and turned less to me. Yep! He had the *testa dura* that I had developed so long ago. Hard-headed!

During his recovery in Houston, he finally went before the judge and got the tax issues settled. The company had already paid its share, but then my father had to pay a lot of tax, about $200,000. Although he was relieved that the worst was over, he was a different man in so many ways.

At some time after this, there was a big news story that Joe Alioto was supporting rice-growers in California and getting rich as their lobbyist. Alioto found himself being accused of Mafia connections. He sued *Life Magazine* over a story alleging that he had underworld ties and won. Joe did a better job of defending himself than he did defending others.

A friend of ours, Al B., said that when Alioto became Mayor he was a millionaire, but by the time he left office he was a billionaire, what with oil tanker deals and the Arab oil embargo. I always felt that lawyers were supposed to keep you out of trouble, but Alioto encouraged my father to take shortcuts. Dad was susceptible because Alioto was a charming, eloquent, prominent Italian. But, perhaps Dad knew he was running risks.

My friend Tom had another point of view about my father and Alioto. He said, "Candido might have chosen to get legal advice from a man whom he knew was not exactly a straight arrow. I don't know but what Alioto had a reputation for hoodwinking the government."

Perhaps Dad's choice of Alioto deserves consideration. One thing is crystal clear and will go with me to my grave: after my dad became paralyzed, Alioto never went once to see him or even called him on the telephone.

When my father became paralyzed from the waist down due to his aneurysm, he thought it was only a temporary problem and that he would soon be back on his feet. But I noticed a change in his relationship with my mother. Now he was no longer the lion, he could no longer be the boss, call the shots, care and provide for her. My sister, Alba, noticed it too. She had this to say about those years and about me, even though it stings.

> I'm certain my father cared for my mother. He was very good about giving her things. He always came home from trips with beautiful pieces of jewelry. I can remember her saying, "Ugh, I don't really like this" or "I don't know why you brought me this." One time he brought a necklace and mother said, "This belongs on a young neck" and wanted to give it to my daughter, Candy, but I didn't let her accept it.
>
> I don't think Dad had affairs. I think he was friendly and like all Italian men, embraced girls. So did my uncles. Northern Italians are good looking. But after the aneurysm, Mom and Dad were together too much.
>
> I think my mother needed him to take care of her. She didn't take care of him, even when he was in the wheelchair. She would get angry some days and go and have dinner in her room. Dad would call me and say, "Come and keep me company." My children couldn't believe that even at my adult age, I would still drop everything and go, obeying my father as I had always done.
>
> My mother was never one to baby sit for grandchildren or take care of you when you came home from the hospital. She always felt she was sicker than the next person. If you came home from the hospital with a new baby, her legs were bothering her. She didn't understand that other people had responsibilities, hopes, desires and wants.
>
> Sometimes the aunts criticized my father for bringing nice things home to my mother or for taking her on trips. There were lots of perks that they enjoyed. I tried not to have the company pay for me to do things with my husband, Pete, like go to openings, so they wouldn't say the company spent money on me.
>
> Sometimes Kenny doesn't realize how lucky he is. He's had more stock than we, and lots of perks. Sure, he was too trusting, kind of in a fantasy world. He'd pick aides who were hippies and probably took advantage of him, but he wanted experiences of real life. He got them. And he even gave them to others like my kids. That naughty Kenny took my kids to their first bar and my boys to their first topless bar.
>
> Kenny did a good job in pursuing his destiny, experiencing so many things in life. He's had tremendous opportunities and has grown from his experience. I never had those experiences. He lived on his own, had his own apart-

ments, was a free spirit, and was able to live in Spain, go to France, the Orient. He's been in and out of various businesses and had the ability, fortitude and guts to do it. Oh, God! To have that kind of nerve!

20

Return to America: Fast vs. Slow

Bermuda Triangle: Area of unpredictable wind and tidal currents associated with unusual events involving airplanes and sea crafts.

This bird is a giant, glistening needle, menacingly bending its piercing beak whenever it begins to descend. Its 205 feet length, 186 tons weight, and cruising altitude of eleven miles make it a peremptory creature. As the titanium and steel animal bursts into its natural pace, it releases a wail that can shatter the windows of skyscrapers and all but stop the human heart. It's a natural-born, take-no-prisoner glutton which must consume a disproportionate share of nutrients to achieve the skin friction heat of 266 degrees Fahrenheit it generates in flight. But it's the brute's rifle-bullet speed of *1,330 miles per hour* that sanctifies and cements my devotion and love.

Upon what other body could one sail nearly 2,000 feet per second while sipping the world's finest champagne? The time was the late '70s. I had a window of a chance and couldn't deny the supreme *mammita*—flying the Concorde.

◆ ◆ ◆

It's interesting to me to contrast the fastest moving thing I ever experienced with the slowest moving. The Chinese Astrological Calendar operates on a twelve-year cycle. I was born the Year of the Snake, but I have no idea what year P.J. was born. It was twelve years post-Concorde when P.J. showed up.

The antithesis of the Concorde, P.J. lumbered along hypnotically as if perpetually dieting on lithium and Valium, instead of the lettuce, apples, and moist whole-wheat bread he actually consumed. Hard shelled and rotund, P.J. casts the same-sized shadow as a computer monitor and has the aspect of a miniature armored tank on stubby legs. His adoptive relatives soon learned from a zoological expert that P.J. was about 35 years old, still youthful for a desert tortoise. He also especially liked to rub up against his own reflection on the Arcadia doors. Alone, vigorous, and 35, P.J. was undoubtedly horny.

◆　◆　◆

My wife Daniela and I had been living and working in Italy during the '70s and we were about to move our lives from the rain-drenched, rolling hillsides of the province of Friuli to the burning flatlands of Phoenix, Arizona.

Why not travel to the USA *first class?* The money might not be there later on what with my job gone. So I contacted British Airways and reserved a flight for two from Venice to London and then London to Washington, D.C. via the Concorde. The money was shown; no problem. I told the person at the other end of the telephone that I traveled at least four or five times a year across the Atlantic on business and wanted to make sure British Airways would treat me at least as courteously as other airlines. Absolutely! Specifically, I asked for assurance that I would have my own wheelchair waiting for me at the gate shortly after arrival at Dulles. A long pause and hushed, muffled speech ensued.

"Mr. Jacuzzi, we are delighted that you chose to fly British Airways, but we *deeply* regret that the Concorde *doesn't have the safety features* required to transport someone handicapped like yourself. But we would be certainly able to accommodate you and your wife in first class in any of our 747s to Dulles or JFK."

"Let me talk it over with my wife and I'll call back in a day or two."

About 45 seconds after relaying the details of the conversation to Daniela, I flashed on something I learned in sociology in college. The British were the only slave owners and traders in the new world who had absolutely no compunction in splitting up the black families they brought over from Africa. In South America, the Catholic hierarchy let the Spanish and Portuguese aristocracy have their slaves, but on the condition that the children and their parents would be kept together. I smelled some good ol' British aristocratic prejudice peeking through the Concorde turndown.

◆　◆　◆

In 1985, P.J. has been living with Daniela and me for the past five years. Following the Labor Day weekend, Daniela mentioned that P.J. hadn't materialized to eat for several days. "I'm worried he's missing. When I came back from bringing your Mom home from the barbecue, the back gate was open. I closed it, but P.J. could have gotten out before, without me knowing it," Daniela fretted.

On Wednesday, not knowing what else to do, I sketched a "P.J. Missing & Wanted" flier on a sheet of paper and made six dozen copies. I gave a kid who lived next door ten bucks to shove the flier in the mailboxes in our neighborhood. When I got home from work on Friday, the very first thing Daniela said was, "Guess what? The lady who lives at the end of our street called and thinks she knows where P.J. is. A couple of days ago, P.J. was walking around her front lawn, but she didn't know who he belonged to so she took him to the vet at Scottsdale and Shea. She thought someone might claim him. I called the vet, but the girl that answered said she'd have to speak with the veterinarian and couldn't do that 'til Monday."

"What?" I said, "Wait until Monday? You've got to be kidding; what's her number? After all we've already done to track him down? If I can help it, I want P.J. back this weekend!"

"Okay," Daniela humored me, "but she said the vet couldn't be reached 'til Monday."

I called the office and explained that P.J. was important to us and that I needed to contact the vet right away, not Monday. The young woman appreciated the concern for P.J., and the fact that I wanted to speak to the vet now, but said it was impossible because the vet was on his way back home to Las Vegas. He was only a visiting vet, filling in for two weeks while an old friend of his from Scottsdale went on vacation. The regular Scottsdale vet wouldn't be back until Monday, either. However, I wouldn't give in, and upped the pressure on the hapless receptionist a few more notches. She promised that she would do everything possible to track him down and have him call me.

Several hours later the phone rang; "Hello, Ken Jacuzzi here."

"Hi, Mr. Jacuzzi, I'm Ron Smith (not his real name). I think I have your tortoise. A lady brought him to the shop where I was subbing a couple of days ago, but no one asked after him. So I decided to bring him back home to my kids. They like tortoises and already have a couple, although theirs are tiny compared to P.J. At this point, I don't know what else to do 'cause I won't be back to Scottsdale until next year. Also, it cools off in Vegas sooner than in Phoenix, so P.J. will probably be hibernating by next week."

After more chat with Mr. Smith, I asked if he could meet us somewhere if one of us flew to Vegas to pick P.J. up. He said that would be a piece of cake and he'd even meet us at the airport so that we could fly back the same day. Perfect. As soon as I'd find out the day and flight times, I'd call back and we could synchronize our timepieces.

And I thought transporting a cripple on a Concorde was tough! The story of the tortoise (P.J.) and the hare (Concorde) continued.

Southwest, America West, United, airline after airline didn't transport *accompanied animals*, unless advanced permissions was sought, preparations made, etc. Finally, after my umpteenth recounting of the *P.J. Incident*, Northwest Airlines said they'd take him, providing we'd procure a special cage that would stow under the airline seat. This cage had to fit in a space approximately nine inches high, 14 inches deep, and 22 inches wide. Monday reservations were made for Daniela's round trip to Las Vegas. I was hoping I could find a suitable cage at some pet store on Saturday. I called Ron and gave him the news. The next day I lucked out and found the perfect, high-impact plastic cage at pet store number four.

Daniela reported that the exchange of P.J. with Ron at the Las Vegas airport went smoothly, but drew more interest from onlookers than the C.I.A. subduing an international terrorist. By the end of the short flight from Vegas to Phoenix, there wasn't a single passenger who hadn't heard about the *P.J.Incident* and come up to pay his or her personal respects to P.J. Meanwhile, P.J. nibbled on his lettuce and seemed to have enjoyed the flight. Later on, whenever friends would inquire, we'd tell them that P.J.'s lack of a suitable companion made him melancholy, so he decided to take a break and do a little gambling, see a few shows. Very healthy.

◆ ◆ ◆

In the late seventies, only two airlines flew the Concorde between Europe and the USA: British Airways and Air France. After my problem with the Brits, I called number two. Reservations were no problem. Handling the wheelchair was no problem. Concorde's safety for cripples wasn't even brought up. Gee...silk doesn't get any smoother, I thought. Since I had nothing more to worry about, I got even more pissed off at the British. But, enough of that. Daniela and I would finally fly the Concorde!

The day of our departure arrived. Daniela's dad, Francesco, drove us to the Venice airport to get our connection to Charles de Gaulle, Paris. Except, the day before I hurriedly read the departure time from Venice as "3:00 p.m." instead of the 1300 hours (1:00 p.m.) actually written on the ticket. We missed our flight.

But we were flying the Concorde. All stops were pulled out by the airline to get us to the plane. There was another flight immediately leaving Venice for Milan, Italy, where we could make an immediate connection to Paris. No questions were asked. It was just done. Connecting flights to Paris were a time-warped blur that seemed to take no more time than making a cup of instant coffee. At Charles de Gaulle, we were given barely a minute to empty our bladders before being the last two passengers to take our seats.

The French, like the Italians, know about two of life's most important things: food and love. About three minutes after we were seated on the Concorde, before the great bird even began taxiing to the runway, Daniela and I were given a flute of Brut champagne. In minutes we were poised at the end of the runway. We felt a slight lurch, and 24 seconds later we were surpassing 200 miles per hour and airborne. Time of departure—exactly on schedule. A digital screen above our seats informed us of our velocity relative to Mach 1—the speed of sound (which is 605 mph, ground speed). The Mach meter read 0.6 and was climbing.

Smoked salmon, Beluga caviar, and other delights were brought to savor with the flowing champagne as the blue of the sky outside began to deepen and an extravagance of tiny, brilliant lights awakened. Mach 1, we've broken the sound barrier. The inside of the small, three-pane porthole we viewed the outside world from was sizzling hot to the touch. The filet mignon, vegetables, salad, and desserts were as close to perfection as we almost were to the stars.

I looked out and never before now had seen pitch-black sky, nor the brilliance of a trillion stars. At 11 miles altitude, we're beyond all weather and into astronaut territory. Mach: 2.2. We were now flying at more than twice the speed of sound—all enhanced by fine wines and/or champagne. An after-dinner cognac, perhaps? Madam was given complimentary French perfume, and I was offered a fine Cuban cigar.

Ten minutes later our bird softly caressed the Dulles runway, a wee bit shy of three and one half hours after our departure from Charles de Gaulle. Life is good. Of course, I welcomed every reassurance that America stood where I had left it. As we made our triumphal entry into Washington, D.C., and one of the Dulles passenger transfer buses wheeled up to our Concorde, I couldn't help but wonder if I would ever make it to a real space flight?

I'm glad I flew the Concorde since it's been retired from commercial service. Recalling the flight, I muse, if a healthy 77-year-old like John Glenn can fly into space, is a crip in a wheelchair far behind? In pursuit of *salud, pesetas, amour y tiempo para gastarlos*, (health, money and love and time to enjoy them) one never quits. Champagne, Madame?

21

Another Slant on Things

Monsoon: A wind that reverses direction seasonally, characterized by heavy rains.

For about a year after Jacuzzi Brothers, Inc. was sold to Kidde (the fire extinguisher manufacturer) in the fall of 1979, the second-generation Jacuzzi family members either immediately or soon thereafter went into retirement. So did many of the third generation as well. However, Roy stayed on to manage Jacuzzi Research and was subsequently elevated to manager of the entire Jacuzzi organization upon the retirement of Ray Horan several years later. Roy was even retained in his position of CEO of Jacuzzi after Kidde was sold to Hanson, the British conglomerate, in the mid 1980s.

Unfortunately, Roy let himself be sucked in by that darker side of American corporate culture which apparently has come to require that CEOs not just have super salaries and super perks, but be positioned in the media as Supermen as well. So Roy's resume was rewritten to state that he had obtained an engineering degree from UC Berkeley, instead of the quite respectable two year degree in the arts he earned from a technical college in Oakland, California. His resume also stated that he was the inventor and/or innovator of everything of any value having to do with either the Jacuzzi Whirlpool Bath or the Jacuzzi family company itself. Talk about miraculous conception! Some of the things claimed or insinuated by the Jacuzzi public relations press releases at the time, would have been done by him, in some instances, before he was born. How's that for miracles? It was regrettable, too, because Roy always possessed the savvy and design sense that made the exaggerations of his accomplishments unnecessary and the minimizing of the role of other family members ultimately degrading to him and the entire family.

I know I could have left this as some kind of dark, inside-the-Jacuzzi-family bad joke, but I had to say something to honor those who really created the Jacuzzi company: my father, uncles and aunts, and Roy's grandfather, uncles and aunts, the original seven Jacuzzi brothers and six Jacuzzi sisters. It's a shame, too, that Jacuzzi Research chose to ignore the development of a whole spectrum of products relating to the Whirlpool Bath, including those that could be used in rehabilitation and medicine, as well as more popular consumer products targeted to meet the needs of middle and lower income households. What saddens me most, however, is that the disability community's contribution to the creation and development of the Jacuzzi Whirlpool Bath has never been recognized in any tangible way by the company that bears its name and/or its stockholders, past or present.

What did I do after the 1979 sale to Kidde? First of all, when I was let go in 1976, Daniela and I left for California where I participated in 13 days of depositions involving litigation with the company. During the flight over, I had investigated attending Thunderbird, the Garvin Graduate School of International Management in Glendale, Arizona. Before I could attend, I had to complete my B.A. Since we would be living in the San Francisco Bay area for awhile, Thunderbird recommended St. Mary's College in Moraga, California, where I obtained a B.A. in management in 1977, the same year an out-of-court settlement was reached with the company. We then moved to Paradise Valley, Arizona, where I earned an MBA in international management from Thunderbird in 1979.

Jacuzzi Bros., Inc., was also sold in 1979, by the Jacuzzi family which numbered close to 200 persons at the time. I spent a lot of time and effort investing my proceeds from the sale of my stock, as well as beginning in earnest several other projects. I was doing quite well, but I still had a lot to do to prove myself...to myself. I figured that with my transcontinental experience, foreign language skills and international management MBA, I was highly employable. With a local job placement firm, I set about looking for employment.

After more than a decade hiatus, I also resumed activities within the disability community and helped some friends finance and start a local independent living center, now known as ABIL (Arizona Bridge to Independent Living). And, no sooner had I assisted the local Cerebral Palsy chapter to finance acquisition of a group home, than I was invited to enter the door of volunteerism.

As days turned into weeks and months—then many months—I reluctantly came to the conclusion that my perceived potential value to employers was exuberantly exaggerated at best and somewhere south of a dry well at worst.

During this same end-of-70s, beginning-80s time period, one of the Chinese language professors at Thunderbird, Jane Kuo, introduced me to her brother, Sunny. Sunny, who lived in the San Francisco Bay Area, was in the process of putting together a business to produce a personal computer created by him and a couple of his Chinese-American buddies. The Personal Computer (PC) was similar to, but potentially more flexible than the Apple, first introduced at the end of the 1970s. Jane explained that Sunny and his partners wanted to ultimately produce the PC in China, not only for that market, but to have a PC production source that would be very cost competitive worldwide. Sunny, his partners, and I met shortly thereafter in San Francisco and after several days of getting to know each other well, we negotiated my investment in their startup company, a sum of a bit less than $50,000.

This was all the money that Sunny and his partners needed to move the company, Digital World, forward full steam ahead. Sunny Kuo asked me to serve on the Board of Directors of Digital World.

As was and still is common in the Chinese-American culture, money, regardless of the available amount, is to be spent most sparingly. In fact, this startup capital was used strictly for expenses—which were kept to a minimum—and no one took any salaries. The hopes and dreams of building a better Apple PC were soon dashed when Apple made the decision to not license its operating system to other PC manufacturers, a decision that Apple came to regret years later.

However, Digital World wasn't about to give up and throw in the towel, especially since some initial, positive contacts had already been made with several individuals and government officials within the People's Republic of China regarding some type of commercial venture. Over several years, Digital World evolved into a manufacturer, within China, of PC components, such as power supplies, in a joint venture arrangement with a Chinese partner that was essentially a government-owned enterprise.

Although I could only strike the keys of their PC's keyboard with either one finger or the eraser end of a pencil I held in my hand, I immediately saw that the PC had great technological potential in the areas of work productivity, learning, and entertainment. Almost as soon as I had completed my first and only investment in Digital World, I came to the conclusion that this new technology—the PC—needed what turntables and tape recorders needed decades earlier: "stuff," like music, to play on them. But because contact or the relationship between the user of the PC and the PC itself was so interactive and continuous, I began visualizing what a neat learning tool a PC could be, especially for people with disabilities. Physically, I could not do many things, like assemble an automobile engine or climb a mountain, but perhaps a PC's keyboard could someday give me—and others—the "virtual" experience of doing these things. So, I decided to build a company that would design, produce and market PC learning software.

I began an exhaustive search to put together a top-notch software development team that was to be headed up by a software design engineer who was proficient in interactive, learning software. I contracted with the nation's top headhunters to find qualified design engineer candidates. As my company, which eventually became known as KJ Software, was gradually evolving, Sunny had asked me if I could put together a one-week, management training seminar and come to China to deliver it to the Computer Ministry. He said that China's new openness to enterprise had made Chinese leadership realize how starved for information they were regarding modern management systems and techniques.

I jumped at the opportunity Sunny had presented to me. I decided to put together a one-week seminar with one underlying, primary message or theme: the need to be customer focused and market-driven if an enterprise is to be successful and profitable. Whether examining finance, research and development, production, or distribution, the central focus of the seminar always went back to the customer, the person who needed and wanted your product or service. I contracted with someone locally to write up the seminar and assemble transparencies for an overhead projector. Regrettably, I didn't allow enough time before my departure for China to thoroughly go over and doublecheck the prepared text for typos or similar.

Daniela and I were having a difficult time with each other and she saw my efforts in some areas as trifling. Her long, astringent silences and moodiness were tough for me. I'm not vain, but as I worked on some plans for a house in Italy to satisfy her wish to be near her family, I didn't enjoy putting my own light under a bushel with the person I wished most to value it.

Unspoken, I began to question her feelings for me. I allowed myself to indulge in a replay of the unpleasant reactions of her mother and, especially, her father, when Daniela and I had made the decision to get married. It was all like taking a long drink of bitter brew and my body responded with an acute gastrointestinal hemorrhage. As I recovered, I had less than enough time to make clear plans for my first business trip to China.

I don't think there would have been a better person on earth to have with me on this trip to China than Dave. Dave was a member of our parish and was a jack of all trades for the church. He was retired after having worked many years for and on the Santa Fe railroad. His thought processes were crystal clear, insightful and he had a great sense of humor. Mostly, Dave was just a neat guy who was deeply respected by everyone who came to know him. Dave, who became over time like a second father to me, liked to chide me about working too hard. He'd say stuff like, "Ken, you work too damn hard. One of these days, you're going to kick the bucket and end up leaving Daniela with a whole barrel of loot. Then she'll marry some guy who'll end up smokin' fine cigars and drinkin' good whiskey with that dough."

With the exception of my wheelchair, which was folded and stashed within easy reach, the next most important item on the plane with me was my briefcase. As we went along in the usual, monotonous way of a long flight, I found myself asking Dave to repeatedly open the case, so I could reread portions of the prepared text and double-check for any missing materials.

I'll just add a note of explanation about computers and software. Since my fingers are not capable of typing on a keyboard, I have come to use the latest technology of speaking into a computer microphone which then types what I say. It is possible to correct typing errors and to make the auditory component familiar with one's particular regional accent. This technology—that had its origin at about the same time Dave and I went to China—is another example of PC software fairly commonplace today, but initially developed to help people with severe disabilities.

It was late afternoon. The grey chroma of sea far below had taken life from the sun and was throwing bright yellow glints up to the cabin window. Clouds were nowhere to be seen. Dave and I quickly conjured up and gave the flight hostess an ETA—*estimated time of arrival*—for our flight's halfway mark between Honolulu and Narita (the town near Tokyo where Japan's main international airport is located). On the flight over to Beijing, I won a bottle of champagne by coming the closest to picking the time we'd cross the international date line. Dave and I thought it was rather auspicious since the event also occurred on my birthday, April 22, 1983.

Sunny Kuo met us in Beijing and was very helpful in getting us registered and settled in at the Beijing Hotel. From there, Dave and I were on our own, at least for a couple of days.

I had looked into Asian history, which helped me appreciate their culture all the more and improved my ability to do business with them. Even today, a visit to the Peoples' Republic of China, for the purpose of conducting serious business, is considered exotic to the usual business person with their rare stratagems of the marketplace.

When we woke up our first morning in Beijing, we found waiting outside our door our shined shoes plus a tray with a couple of cups and a thermos of piping hot tea. Very nice. After breakfast, Dave and I decided to take a walk around the streets of Beijing. You couldn't help but notice the Chinese who were wearing more westernized, modern attire that contrasted against the traditional Mao suits which were still worn by most. We got a kick out of the one to three-year-old toddlers, dressed in outfits that covered almost everything, but left exposed their little bottoms so they could do what comes naturally without soiling their clothes. Very practical!

Near our hotel, Dave and I came upon a residential district made up of small, attached homes, many with interior courtyards. Some of the residents were sitting out on the sidewalk, selling all manner of things from stuff to eat to live baby chicks.

After a couple of days of exploring, bright and early Monday morning, about 7 a.m., our host from the Computer Ministry picked us up with a very official Red Flag limousine. Dave was able to put me in the limo, seated in my portable wheelchair. We were then taken on a 45-minute drive into the countryside on the outskirts of Beijing. Along our route we witnessed China starting its day, with cars, bicycles and office buildings melding into cultivated fields and orchards, and men and women of all ages doing their morning Tai Chi exercises.

As we pulled up to at our destination, it had the feel of a school-like courtyard with a large, old-world style two-story building in its center. The minute Dave helped me descend from the limo, we were introduced to a young man who was to be my English-to-Chinese translator during the five days of the seminar. I soon learned that this was such an honor for him, that he and his fiancée postponed their wedding so he could be my translator. Wow, no pressure here I thought!

After Dave and I did the "urinal thing" in the building's first-floor bathroom, we learned that the only way to get up to the second-floor classroom was via a very long, rather steep staircase. No problem, however, because about four of the students just proceeded to pick me and my wheelchair up, carry us up the stairs and deposit us behind a table desk at the head of the class. Dave was seated a little behind and to my left where he manned the overhead projector. And every day, on our desks, two items were placed for our comfort and enjoyment: a bottle of Coca-Cola and a pack of Chinese cigarettes.

The seminar turned out to be rather well received and I was surprised at how many rather candid questions I received during the last hour of the fifth day of the seminar which was reserved for questions and answers. I was told that the Chinese people were rather reticent about questioning those in authoritative positions and especially teachers, so I should expect few questions at the end. It became obvious, however, that many of those present, including higher up officers and middle managers, became rather enthusiastic about the whole concept of consumer-focused marketing and manufacturing. Our host also made sure that our last several days in Beijing were memorable, too. With Sunny along in some cases, we were treated to several large banquets where we were served more than a dozen dishes, including two to three different soups, thousand year-old eggs, a liquidy white mushroom they called "fungus" and fowl baked in clay.

The most incredible experience of all, however, was when we were taken to visit the Great Wall of China. Here again, wheelchair and me were taken up a very long flight of stairs to the top of the wall where Dave and I were able to meander along, potentially as far as the eye could see. We only went the equivalent of a city block or two, but the vistas of the rolling hills and country sites below were truly exceptional. Experiencing firsthand the Great Wall, I understood why it's the only man-made object that astronauts can see unaided from Earth orbit.

In the late afternoon, we drove to the airport in a hesitant spring rain. David rolled down the window of the limousine so that we could catch a last, clear look at the city. The freshets of damp air that came into the car told me more than I could see. The fires had been banked in the brass foundry we had visited a few days before; and the tendril of white smoke surrounding the well-aged building was acrid. The powdery odor of gypsum and mortar had settled around the day's work at a prefab project and in passing the urban parks, I caught the spicy drafts of pine needles and wet moss. At intervals, there was an overlay of the smell of food cooking; almost like pan-frying vegetables and pork or beef. Then it turned into a broth-like aroma. It seemed a blend of cabbage, soy, and meats, boiling on a stove of charcoals or wood. It told me that many people were keeping their personal lives privately to themselves behind the shops and public buildings of Beijing.

While waiting with David for our pre-boarding seating to occur, I caught a glimpse of our flight crew in the vestibule of the plane's access ramp. The pilot and co-pilot looked boyish. One was tall, gangly, with crow-black unruly hair, while the other was rotund and almost as small as me. They were intent on an animated, clattering preflight exchange with the tower. The Chinese language, especially when spoken by younger adults, always sounds quite excited anyway and I entertained the floating hope that all was well between us, our plane, and the takeoff business with the tower.

From where Dave and I were sitting, I was able to watch some of the passengers who were settling into our section of the plane. As far as my view would permit, they appeared to be all businessmen. Judging by their attire and the quality of their carry-on luggage and briefcases, I made some theoretical conclusions on which of them lived on the mainland and which were citizens of Hong Kong.

Four gentlemen directly across the aisle from us sat facing one another, enjoying the beer that was being passed around as soon as we took off. One of them acknowledged us with a raised beer bottle and we responded. Then, each of them got around to opening his briefcase. They exchanged sheets of computer printouts and shared these with a continuous flow of animated comments and grunts, frequently interspersed with beer. When the youngest fellow in their group began circulating a handful of floppy discs, I was no longer the slightly nosey, passive observer.

With Dave as my aisle-side emissary, I was finally able to learn from them that the discs they were tossing about were made in Czechoslovakia. Dave managed to get across to them that I was developing PC software in the United States. This brought on a shower of fraternal salutes and smiles from my Chinese brothers in the business of computer software.

After a while, the congenial men across from us closed their briefcases. Almost like children, tired and weary of the playing, they had scattered into the silence of their own thoughts and I into mine. My thoughts were lingering over China.

I pulled my mind away from these musings long enough to rescue David from his noisy struggle with a map of downtown Hong Kong. He was trying to refold the map for his collection of Asian souvenirs.

"Give me that damn thing. I'll show you the knack of it. Dave, take a look for a moment at those blank, snoozing faces across from us. They are the stuff of the new Cathay. Anyone working international trade these days must ask himself if China will really come out and play the game of laws and profits with the West and the rest of the world. I think China will be sought out and the quest will be made from worldwide data, collected electronically."

I did visit China again with my wife in 1985 with the intention of offering the services of my KJ Software firm. I met Deng Pufang, the oldest son of Deng Xiaoping. Xiaoping succeeded Chairman Mao Zedong and was the de facto ruler of China from 1976 to 1997. Xiaoping was one of the military leaders who accompanied Mao on the "Long March," and was also a close associate of Chou En Lai.

However, Mao was on the outs with Xiaoping during the 1960s. During this time, Xiaoping's son was studying to be a physicist at the University of Peking.

Pufang, a paraplegic, told us through an interpreter that when his father was alienated from Mao, Red Guards at the University surrounded him in 1968. When he resisted them, they threw him out of the fourth floor window and he broke his spine. He was at the time of our visit the chairman of the China Disabled Person's Federation and in 2003 was awarded the United Nations Human Rights Prize. I learned from him that the word "handicap" means "garbage" or "useless" in several Asian languages. Of course, our word handicap means someone who defers to others, "cap in hand" or beggar. He, like so many others and I, still wrestle with our self worth in various ways.

Back to my first trip to Beijing, after a couple of stopover days in Hong Kong with Sunny, Dave and I took off for our return home via Honolulu and several days of R&R to visit his son, a naval officer, who was stationed there with his family. When we got off the plane in Honolulu, we were met by a driver and an electric cart to take us to the main terminal to go through customs.

As we were riding to the terminal, the driver, who was a tall, olive-skinned, raven-haired beauty, proceeded to inform me that she was off tomorrow, had access to a handicap van and was wondering if I might be interested in her showing me around the island. *Joseph, Mary and Jesus, I'd have to be long dead and buried not to be.* Just because I'm a married cripple doesn't mean I'm less of a potential Casanova slimeball than any other guy walking around.

Anyway, notwithstanding Dave's gung ho encouragement that I see the sights with the lovely lass, fate decided otherwise when, the following morning, I woke up in the Honolulu Hilton with a humdinger of a cold. Other than Dave, the only person I saw that day was an old doctor, sporting an Albert Einstein hairdo, who sent me back to my hotel room with a fistful of antibiotics.

Two days after our arrival and just before leaving for San Francisco, Dave and I spent a wonderful day with his son, daughter-in-law and grandchildren at their home. They were a neat family and almost as cool as Dave himself. Dave is no longer with us, but I shall never forget him nor this precious time in my life.

On the flight back across the Pacific Ocean, I read an article in one of those airline in-flight magazines about an investment banking firm in San Francisco by the name of Hambrecht & Quist that financed the startup of a lot of high-tech companies. I knew that I would be staying in the San Francisco Bay Area for several days to visit my sisters, Alba and Irene, so I set up a meeting with Bill Hambrecht at his office.

The next day I met with Bill Hambrecht and shared with him the kind of software development company I envisioned and was in the process of putting together. I told him about my idea to develop highly interactive, software learning programs that would be based on skill principles espoused and taught by best-selling authors and/or recognized authorities in those areas of learning most in demand by the general public. It would include subject skill areas like writing, mathematics, financial savvy (work and personal) verbal communications, relationships (work and personal), stress management and so on. Mr. Hambrecht was quite positive about the concept and expressed his personal interest by assisting me to finance my company.

Soon after I got back to Phoenix, I set up a meeting with my accountant from Price Waterhouse to discuss my meeting with Hambrecht & Quist and what I wanted to accomplish with KJ Software. I had already been building KJ Software for more than a year. I rented office space near my home and hired Lisa, a recent, top-of-class graduate from a local technical college. Even though Lisa was one very smart lady, she still wasn't of the caliber or experience needed for the position of Product Development Director. But, most of the people who were brought to me by the head hunting firms couldn't even fill Lisa's shoes.

I fired them all and went on my own in-depth quest to find the caliber person I was looking for. Eventually, after many months of search and interviews, I found David, a software development engineer who specialized in interactive learning software. At the time, David was working in Washington, D.C. on learning/teaching software used by the National Security Administration (NSA) in the training of operatives and troops.

Meanwhile, Price Waterhouse (PW) suggested that I finance the startup of KJ Software and only go to Hambrecht & Quist for subsequent financing after we had a completed prototype software program to show them. PW said that I would have to give up 80% or more of KJ Software from the get-go if H&Q financed my company from startup, whereas once the company was on its way and we had a viable product to show them, maybe they would settle for as little as 50%.

This argument really resonated with me because my own family's company, Jacuzzi Brothers, in 1979, was left little choice but to "go public" by selling all of its stock to a publicly traded company. The sale of Jacuzzi Brothers was necessitated because all those Jacuzzi family offspring had diluted individual stock ownership to the point that the company could no longer be successfully managed by family coalition—there were too many of us. And, I certainly didn't want to end up in a minority position with my own company. So I listened to Price Waterhouse and used my own money to finance the startup and beginning phases of KJ Software.

David came on board and proved to be not only a brilliant software development engineer, but a person of great integrity and a true gentleman. David confirmed that Lisa was a winner, so he kept her on and added two other full-time computer-savvy employees to our team. We also brought on board a marketing director with extensive experience working with major publishers and selling learning/teaching materials, including books, audio and video media. His initial task was to bring on board to KJ Software well-known author/experts in the various fields we were targeting.

As the company evolved in the early-mid-1980s, however, we came to the realization that there still wasn't enough PC ownership among individuals and very small businesses in the United States to sustain multiple learning/teaching software companies like KJ Software. In fact, at the time, the bulk of PC sales was going to large businesses and organizations in the private and public sectors. Also, although we didn't have the multimedia tools available in the mid-1980s that we do today, our software was still quite sophisticated and required an upper tier PC, the kind that were normally sold to larger businesses, but not normally to individuals, at least not then.

Market projections showed us that the home market wouldn't really be ready for our kind of software until the late 80s, early 90s and those projections proved correct. So we shifted gears and changed our target market from the home user to big business, the consumers who were dominating the PC market. Many of the same subject areas were retained—writing, selling, financial planning skills—but a new marketing approach had to be developed. You just don't stick your software on the shelf of a retail outlet and expect a corporation to come in and buy it.

In most large companies there are human resource personnel who are in charge of employee training and development. These are the people that purchase training materials and services for the purpose of enhancing the skills of their company's employees. We had to market and sell our software to these human resource people. Fortunately, there were plenty of ways to reach these customers, such as human resource publications and trade shows, so it wasn't difficult getting good-quality sales leads. Making the sale to these companies, however, involved considerable cost.

Usually, we had to meet with the training and human resource personnel before the sale would be consummated. Our initial set of five programs, covering the following skill sets: management, finance, writing, selling/marketing, and handling stress, sold for approximately $400 a program or $2000 for the set. Even large corporations would only need to purchase several sets of KJ Software programs to keep in their training library for use in employing training as necessary. A typical sale of $4000–$6000 to a big company like AT&T would barely cover the cost of making that sale.

In contrast, productivity software programs—such as word processing (Word-Perfect or Microsoft Word)—when sold to a corporation, had to be licensed for use by each employee, which translated into sales worth tens of thousands of dollars, making one-on-one sales contact still cost-effective for the software publisher. Obviously, we had to do something to keep KJ Software alive until the individual consumer market would be large enough to give us a marketplace that could make up in volume what we lacked in margin. In the mid 1980s, a sufficiently developed consumer market was still three to five years away, even with conservative projections.

Several options were available to us. The entire KJ Software team made a valiant effort at realizing those options. One of the first things we did was to re-contact Hambrecht & Quist and solicit their assistance to obtain long-term financing for KJ Software.

In the several years that had transpired since my original contact, Hambrecht & Quist, as was the case with the majority of investment banking companies wanting to get a piece of the burgeoning PC software industry, literally threw money at almost any fairly decently conceived software venture, including interactive, computer-based training/learning software. Qualitatively, even though our software was heads and shoulders above almost anything on the market at the time (we had received numerous industry awards for the effectiveness and quality of our software) and we got there with about 10% to 15% of the expenditures of our would-be competitors, Hambrecht & Quist were no longer interested in financing training/learning software. The large amounts they had invested in other similar software firms produced only money-losing enterprises.

We quickly learned that the response from other investment banking firms would be the same: "unless you have the next productivity blockbuster like WordPerfect or Lotus 1-2-3, don't come back to us until the consumer market can support sufficient sales of your software programs."

David, KJ Software's Director of Product Development, wisely chose to maintain his top-secret security clearance and government contacts when he became part of our company. Ronald Reagan was deep into his first term as President and initial prototype development of the anti-ballistic missile system shield he advocated—which came to be known as "Star Wars"—was underway. David became aware of a RFP (Request for Proposal) that involved developing software that he thought the KJ Software team would be exceptionally good at. The contract, if awarded to KJ Software, would certainly have been sufficient to keep the company solvent. As a serious contender for such an RFP, we required, of course, a fine-tooth-comb check by the FBI of our company's operating environment and systems as well as each and every one of our employees.

About a decade earlier, I had painted a picture of Ronald Reagan, believing he would eventually be the Republican nominee to go head-to-head for president, with Ted Kennedy. The Democratic nominee, instead, was Jimmy Carter. After Reagan won, I was extremely happy that he was forthright in dealing with Russia but I was sorry that he closed down so many helpful social agencies. I was particularly impressed with his brave reaction when he was shot in 1981 and Americans later learned how close he came to death.

As CEO of KJ Software, I was on the top of the FBI checklist, which included not only extensive personal interviews with me and all those close to me, but extended fact-finding with almost everyone who ever knew me. The FBI wanted to know everything so I told them everything, including that I had slept with a lady of the evening or two and smoked marijuana on several occasions in the 1960s (for which I shall always thank good old Bruce the Beard). During their fact-finding process, the FBI did manage to commit a bit of a faux pas, however.

Two agents, one quite tall, one quite short (kind of a Mutt and Jeff pair) showed up at our house and rang the front doorbell. Upon opening the door, my wife, Daniela, asked these two gentlemen what they wanted. They proceeded to show her their FBI identification and inquire as to what she can tell them about their neighbor across the street, "Mr. Jacuzzi." My wife, doing everything she could not to burst into laughter, went on to inform them that Mr. Jacuzzi was her husband and lives in this house, not the one across the street. The FBI agents faces turned about as red as an Arizona sunset.

Although we passed our FBI top-secret security clearance with flying colors, we came in second to a competing company based in Colorado. David felt strongly that they chose our competitor because they were based in the same locale where that part of the Star Wars project was being developed and those in charge preferred their proximity. By this time, the money from a bridge loan I had obtained from the Small Business Administration was starting to run out and my own personal financial resources were running low. I didn't want to give up, nor did anyone else involved in KJ Software. But the employees, starting with David, had their own lives, and in many cases families, to support. Thankfully, I was able to make sure that every one of KJ Software's employees received wages until they were able to find suitable employment elsewhere.

With the sale of 90% of the stock I held in a community bank in Yuma, Arizona, I was able to pay off the $250,000 SBA loan. I paid off the accounts KJ Software owed money to. Probably, when all was said and done, I could have conserved anywhere from $350,000 to $450,000 of my own financial resources if I opted to have KJ Software file for bankruptcy instead of personally paying its bills. Maybe it was my macho cripple hardheadedness or the fact that KJ Software was something I had created, given life to, that didn't let me abandon it on its deathbed. I don't know, probably both. The reality of my personal, nearly 5-year-long quest to cut out a niche in the burgeoning PC software market—and pay the freight myself—translated into a price tag amounting to about 80% of my total net worth.

To this day, when people hear my name is Jacuzzi and that my father invented the Whirlpool Bath of the same name, they often think I'm the Italian-American version of Donald Trump. I'm sorry to disappoint you, guys, but I didn't follow the Donald's cash-conserving savvy path of bankruptcy and instead paid those damn bills. As Forest Gump would say, "stupid is as stupid does."

Go figure, I'd probably do it again.

22

Identity Crisis

Stationary Front: A potential storm threat as two masses of air of different densities co-mingle.

One day not long ago I woke up feeling depressed. There's a stomach full of ambivalence about where I've been the past 60+ years and a brain-plaguing uncertainty fogging the minutes, days and possibly years ahead.

I'm reminded of actor Dustin Hoffman's joke about turning 60. He grew up with a guy and after high school, they went their separate ways but agreed to meet every ten years. At their first ten-year reunion, Dustin's friend said he had married and all they did was have sex and eat for 24 hours on their honeymoon. At their 20th reunion, Dustin's friend described how he'd been married many years but still loved going out with his wife, having a great meal, dancing till 3:00 a.m., and making love all night long. Hoffman met his friend when they were both 60. His friend told how he had celebrated a milestone wedding anniversary with his wife. They went out, had a nice dinner, came home and he took a nice crap.

"Think positive, pleasant thoughts," I say to myself. "Relax, you need to relax. I try to coax myself into recalling those times—now fewer and fewer—when my body worked as it should." Stupidly, I think of Scarlet O'Hara's words, *"Tomorrow will be a better day."*

You see, physical and/or emotional "relaxing" for me is complicated a bit by the body I live in. Not that I'm necessarily totally dissatisfied with the fact that I've had Juvenile Rheumatoid Arthritis since the age of two and have had to get around with a motorized wheelchair—I'm not, because I know it could have been worse. Trust me.

Now, if you place your ass in a wheelchair after your shower in the morning, like I do, chances are that it will stay there until you get into bed at night. So, all day you're sitting with your thighs at a 90 degree right angle to your body, crimping and scrunching up your insides and their contents even more.

But, what makes you feel like S-H-I-T when you're loaded with it and, at the same time, its yellow liquid brethren, is that an unexpected bump in the pavement may cause a corresponding jump of your wheelchair and, yep, wet pants. Not a big wet, mind you, just an unexpected spurt or two, but, nonetheless, enough to probably cause a one or two inch damp area to form around the lower part of the pants' zipper.

My mind, playing with me as it so often does, instantly transforms that damp area from a couple of tablespoons of pee (which, itself, is nothing more than water and waste minerals) into an evil nemesis that physically and psychologically hammers on my body and soul. Day after day. Why? Simple. Rheumatoid arthritis, like multiple sclerosis and other similarly disabling diseases, is degenerative AND progressive. It means that today is not only, "as good as it gets," but that tomorrow, maybe next year, if I'm lucky, definitely won't be as good.

◆ ◆ ◆

Here it comes again. My never-ending interaction with the medical profession.

"Okay, Connie, Tom, grab the draw sheet and at the count of three, lift and pull Mr. J onto the gurney. Ready—one—two—three—pull! Smooth as a New York City pickpocket. Are we good, Mr. J, or are we good?"

"You guys are damned good," I managed to mumble through the approaching Twilight-Zone shot of Demerol I'd just been given. *Nothing like science-through-chemistry to calm me ol' nerves and get me ready for the possibility I may not be back from this one.*

"Hi, Ken, my name is Sally and I'll be with you from here to O.R. Are you comfortable on the gurney?"

"Yeah, Sally, I'm fine. Let's get the hell out of here."

"Getting some work done on your cervical spine, I see. You've got Dr. Sonntag, one of the best cutups around."

"Cute, Sally. You doing anything after surgery?"

"I'll be there when you wake up. How's that?"

Before my Demerol-delayed brain can figure out something appropriate for a diehard ladies' man to say, Sally wheels me into the operating room, illuminated like a summer's day on a white sandy beach. Blinking computers, gurgling chrome and stainless steel machines, and hypnotic lights surround the room, staring at me. Milling about are a half dozen green-masked men and women. A woman with faraway tornado-grey eyes comes and stands beside me.

"I'm going to start an intravenous drip, Mr. Jacuzzi. Just a little prick on the back of your hand. There. That didn't hurt a bit, did it?"

Of course, if I asked the nurse, "Will it hurt?" she'd never say, "Yes, very much!" So I play the game and say: "I can't believe it. You hit the vein right away. You're good."

"Why do ya think I'm in O.R.? Because of my looks?"

"From what I can see, you look even better than you stick."

"Thanks, but you can't see enough to say *that*."

The anesthesiologist's assistant with his white mask and hair covering was next. "Well, well, Mr. Jacuzzi, always a fan with the ladies, eh? We're going to intubate you shortly. But first I'm going to give you something in your IV to relax you. If you drift off, that's all right, just sleep. Because your neck is short and constricted, I've put something else in my concoction to give you momentary amnesia should the anesthesiologist encounter problems getting the tube down your throat."

He doesn't explain and I don't want to know, that he's going to use Versed, a medicine that will relax my breathing muscles, prevent a gag reflex, give me amnesia for the procedure of getting the tube down my throat, unknowingly allow me to comply with their requests and kill me if not carefully monitored.

"If I wake up from this, am I going to be nauseous and sick like a dying dog?"

"You shouldn't be. This stuff is nowhere near like the anesthesia we once used. It's really good shit. You'll see. Now, just close your eyes and start counting backwards from ten."

Before reaching seven, the medicine did what it was supposed to do, blocking my memory of this procedure and inserting in its place recollections from the past. And I began to ruminate about my life, marriage, and identity crisis. I continued during that hospitalization to dwell on the peaks, but often valleys, in my life.

I went back through all the sins I'd committed over a lifetime and all the lacks I could think of—quite a sum, I might add. I don't know how long I was "out" but it seemed like minutes, even though it was many hours. I must live with these truths and go on with my life. But there are longings that are hard to mask. We all long for passion and love and other things. But unfulfilled passion is a tough taskmaster.

The surgery went as expected and I soon returned home to continue to struggle with my "identity crisis."

◆   ◆   ◆

Home again, at last!

A few feet away from me now is the woman whom I have loved for decades, making her best efforts to ignore my passion but attend to me physically. I understand that at moments she feels disappointed. But I can only be who I can be. I have my own history, memories, problems and questions about who and what I am. I hear and understand her needs, I think. But I can only answer with quiet and regret. So much of me is being used for the major job of being Ken.

Most of my coping difficulties have always been amplified by an insecurity crisis. With me, feelings of insecurity usually breed a kind of loneliness that can be as confusing, menacing and profound as a deep depression.

The more I wanted to get out of this funk, the further away I traveled from my lifelong quest to internalize the "impression" that I had the right stuff within me to make the craved breakthrough beyond despondency. I sometimes felt that I had become an outcast who could not get a decent job despite my experience and education. Desperately I promised everyone, my wife, my family, my friends, my God, that I would do better. Better than I have. I made a plea as urgent as any deathbed wish.

Why was I letting these feelings cave in on me, a guy who had, at one time, a sack of money put away, a very sweet, giving wife and a whole lot to look forward to? Primarily, it's because I've never completely gotten over my sense of inferiority and insecurity. Even now, although my moments of depression are minimal and infrequent, I'm still rather doubtful about my own self worth.

I can't judge if you or others are like me or not, but with respect to yours truly, time and experience have only fostered the capability of better dealing with my emotional problems, making them seem less significant and more "ordinary." As far as solving them is concerned, no such luck. At 63, I'm still searching for many answers. But what is that one thing I'm seeking the most? I'm not sure. But perhaps it's what Marcia sought many years ago when she entered my life: peace.

Years have passed since Daniela and I married and, although I lavished tender names upon her, I often received no sweet sound in reply, no answering caress. I looked at her with yearning glances, but saw no gleam of recognition to warm her haunting eyes. Yet her fair body was molded by the Great Sculptor with gentle grace and was always there before me. This was the visible punishment for my sins.

When I completed graduate school at age 38, about 15 years later than usual, I had one hell of a time getting anyone in Phoenix (or elsewhere) to seriously look at me as a potential employee. Here I was with this degree in international management and all this experience abroad, and the rebuff ruled.

Although I was managing to do rather well with my investments, the multiplying employment rebukes and the growing distance of my wife were managing to take control of my thinking and bring up old "you're a failure" tapes. I was starting to experience a vacillation of purpose and progressively became less and less focused.

Even though some of my lovemaking endeavors prior to marriage were with women of questionable virtue, the number of affairs with them was limited (as was the sum total of my love life). In fact, immediately after my first "experience," while some were very kind to me, I became painfully aware that liaisons with such women were often unsatisfying and usually rather dispiriting. And, most importantly, the emptiness and loneliness in my heart that drove me to seek such warm, inviting flesh in the first place, never, ever improved after our encounter.

Maybe I sought those brief feelings I had experienced before marriage where a woman's passion for me seemed so fierce. It brought out in me a wildness, a blindness, an abandon, a love with no sense of the future, bent on experiencing only the present. No one in my life had been so openly desirous of my company, so appreciative of everything about me but a rare few had come close. They had nudged ajar a door that I wanted to fling open with Daniela. I wanted to hold and be held, to kiss and be kissed willfully in return and to breathe in the fragrance of, and exchange the breath of, a female.

Why not now with my wife? Because we had developed, as many couples do, an invisible barrier of isolation between ourselves. We were living together under the same roof, but were both more in our own worlds than in each other's. It reminded me of a "*stationary front*" where we each had different "densities."

Daniela was never one to be hastened. I began to see that words, to her, were things to be carefully caught one by one and released with much difficulty. Our words had become so routine that they created more distance between us than closeness. The freshness was evaporating.

As my loneliness worsened, I instinctively knew that I needed to do something, but I became less sure of what I should do. You see, I am in love with my wife. If you were to say that my marriage is not a happy one, I would call you a liar. When I think of some other woman for a few minutes, I may think that I was closer to that person than I have ever been to anyone else. Then I will think of the time when I will be as close as that to my wife. Daniela is, to me, an awakening woman. For a moment I will close my eyes and the eyes of some other woman may look into mine. Then I will quickly open my eyes and see again the dear woman with whom I have undertaken to live out my life. Then I will sleep and when I awaken, the other woman will be utterly gone.

But I felt and feel depressed. What else do you do when you reach this age and feel you haven't made any meaningful contribution to this planet? My mind drifted and my thoughts turned to many years ago, in a place far away. I was remembering many of the lost opportunities to make money and achieve true financial wealth that I totally pissed away. It hurts a lot realizing that I've been such a dope! I wonder if I've since learned anything about listening to my gut more and others less. Maybe.

There are several examples of unprofitable investments in this book, including the cable company, software company, etc. Back in the early '80s, I had the chance to double the amount of shares I was purchasing in a community bank in Yuma, Arizona, but I declined. Those were the good ol' days when I still had a small fortune in liquid assets—M-O-N-E-Y—to invest in sound projects and make even more money and real wealth. Instead, I only bought $50,000 worth of the Yuma bank's shares, rather than $100,000. That $50,000 grew into over $250,000 in less than five years.

People more well-known than I have missed opportunities. One of my favorite Mark Twain lines is "The first time I ever saw St. Louis, I could have bought it for six million dollars and it was the mistake of my life that I did not do it." Of course, he was a teenager at the time with probably ten dollars sewn into his coat.

I was not the only one in the family who had money troubles. As I described earlier, my sister Irene and her husband had invested in a winery. She wanted it to grow quickly and poured so much into it that it failed and was taken over. Perhaps the stress of it got to her because soon thereafter, she developed cancer and died in 1986. She thought she failed because she always compared herself to our father. Compared to him, we all failed. It's impossible to feel you have achieved anything when using that kind of yardstick.

How can the children of famous and successful people cope with the overarching level of achievement looming over them? How can any one of us ever measure ourselves against the great achievers—Olympic gold medalists, zillionaire entrepreneurs, Hollywood superstars, heads of State, Nobel laureates, fallen soldiers defending their country? How can the individual mind and body withstand the never-ending onslaught of a society and culture that relegates everyone who is not the cream of the crop to inferior status? We must recall that we are all part of the human race and, as such, each one of us is here for a purpose.

So where have I gotten to after all our years in Arizona? As I looked about for work, the Americans With Disabilities Act, the landmark civil rights act for people with disabilities attracted my attention. Until the ADA legislation was created and signed into law, cripples like me did our best to shuffle through each day, educating others if we could that we weren't really hexed or contagious, but most often just putting up with misconceived, stereotypical concepts of non-cripples.

The ADA has started to make an impact on our society by requiring companies like airlines to educate their staff to treat us more like human beings and less like stereotypes. But, as with blacks and other minorities, ingrained fears are hard to let go of and shit still happens. In his autobiography, John Hockenberry, the TV journalist who also happens to get around in a wheelchair, recounts the time (in the late 1990s) when an airline hostess asked him, as soon as he got on the plane, if he had contemplated committing suicide. Like, if you're a cripple, it's the end of the world and, therefore, only logical that you'd prefer doing yourself in.

I liked what the ADA was doing and thought it was going to be a worthwhile "cause" like my foundation. But here, I might get paid. So I took a job with the state to get the ADA program going. The *Phoenix Gazette* covered the story on July 18, 1991 which read as follows:

> A new state Office for Americans with Disabilities was unveiled Wednesday, with Gov. Fife Symington naming Paradise Valley businessman Ken Jacuzzi as its first director.
>
> Symington created the office to oversee "quality, long-term implementation" in Arizona of the Americans with Disabilities Act signed into law last summer by President Bush.
>
> The federal act, patterned after previous landmark civil rights legislation, is intended to outlaw discrimination against the disabled, and promote equality in services and treatment.
>
> Symington said the state office will help guide his administration, the courts and the attorney general on matters pertaining to the state's treatment of the disabled, and in putting the federal act into practice in Arizona.
>
> It will be a part of the Department of Economic Security.
>
> "The task is very large," said Jacuzzi, 50, who has been severely disabled with rheumatoid arthritis since the age of 2, and has been a wheelchair user for many years.
>
> He has been active in a drive to make public facilities and events more accessible for the disabled. Among his targets are the Iceberg Phoenix Grand Prix and the America West Arena.

Jacuzzi said university accessibility is an immediate goal.

He said the state's track record is "mixed" but improving in making the 8,000 plus buildings it owns or leases accessible to disabled people.

Jacuzzi initially will work in the office with a clerical assistant, administration officials said. His salary will be $61,000.

The office's budget has not been completed. Symington said extra money was not budgeted for it. Instead, it will be funded through a combination of federal grants and money reallocated from the budgets of DES and the Department of Administration.

"This is an area where we will play catch-up after years of neglect." Symington said.

The governor said he selected Jacuzzi because of Jacuzzi's "first-line experience as a disabled person, his bright and articulate approach to problems, and his background working on issues confronting the disabled."

Jacuzzi since last year has been a principal partner with Peterson, Jacuzzi and Green, which specializes in strategic planning, marketing and research.

This appointment was, for me, a tremendous responsibility and honor as well. Almost instinctively, I knew I wanted to establish something that would not only implement the ADA federal legislation, but have a long-term, positive impact on people with disabilities and the state of Arizona. My hope was despite a relatively small budget and a modest team of exceptional people, we could create something that could serve as a model for other states and the country. What was needed, first, was a roadmap or implementation outline of goals, strategies, people and timeline required to accomplish what needed to be done.

From experience, I have learned that the best way to put together such a plan is by utilizing a small group of two or three people, preferably from diverse backgrounds and essentially live together for two or three days until you get the job done. At the time, I knew of no better person to work with on this plan than Dan Green, a former Thunderbird professor and all-around great guy.

Of course, the mission of our department—and the plan—was to implement the law created by the ADA. But the word and spirit of the law sought to ensure access to public and private sector facilities and services by people with disabilities. My principal charge was to do this for the state of Arizona, but I strongly felt that our department needed to also serve as a facilitator and helping hand in implementing the ADA with the private sector as well.

I also wanted to create an entity which would resolve access problems to facilities and/or services long before they could ever reach litigation stage. One way, was to develop simple guidelines and visual aids to ensuring access for use by public and private entities. I envisioned a department which would maintain close, ongoing communications with businesses and the private sector, people representing a broad spectrum of disabilities, including the impaired elderly and the State's administrative and Attorney General's offices.

In relatively few pages—Dan has the added gift of being parsimonious and on point—a plan was written incorporating all of these objectives and strategies to achieve them. When the plan was completed I shared it with the Directors of similar offices in other states and their feedback was universally enthusiastic. We were on our way, I thought. But I made a few faux pas on the way. First, I let myself be ensnarled in bureaucratic overkill and spent far too much initial time distributing copies of the federal law and regulations to state agencies working with us. In retrospect, I should have held back on 80% of the paperwork and spent the time, instead, on listening to their thoughts and concerns regarding implementation of the ADA. I should have been, too, more patient regarding getting things done. Government, indeed, doesn't move swiftly. The big knot, though, came at budget time.

I had put together a budget for an ADA office which had the people (a team of four including myself) and resources to successfully execute our entire plan. The team included a troubleshooting, problem-solving ombudsman and resources adequate to ensuring ongoing participation in the ADA's implementation process by people from throughout the state, representing a wide range of disabilities. The price tag? About $500,000 a year. Well, Governor Symington's right hand man and budget czar thought that what I had proposed was ridiculous and something south of $250,000 would be all that would be acceptable. I protested vehemently and began to think that the only reason I was appointed in the first place was because of my name, Jacuzzi, and the desire to have someone in that office as more of a figurehead than anything else.

Regrettably, I resigned rather than preparing alternatives if they didn't accept my budget. Wisdom happens too late. So, after having served for something less than seven months, I sent the governor a written resignation, suggesting as well three candidates who I felt were qualified for the position and perhaps could be more adept at dealing with day-to-day politics and the machinations of bureaucracy. Interestingly, one of my suggestions was chosen to head up the office. Ironically, within less than a year, their budget had far exceeded my original proposal.

And here's a little footnote for all my brothers and sisters out there who have disabilities. As soon as the news hit—thanks in this case to our local and state media—that I had resigned my office out of protest, almost everyone that was anyone in the disability community clamored to take my place. Hey, I'm not knocking that; the job paid $63,000 a year! What was interesting was that barely a murmur was heard from the disability community in my defense. See, guys, when all is said and done, we're not any purer than non-disabled folks. We are all that same species called humanity.

Well, work and income have been sporadic since then. As I've grown older, I've considered whether to cut my expenses by selling my rather expensive house, designed by the Taliesin students of Frank Lloyd Wright. My wife views our house sentimentally and doesn't want to leave. She said:

> The American mentality advocates change. People want a bigger house, so they move. In Italy, a home remains with you forever. My father was moved from one place to another to manage farms. It was a tragedy each time, leaving friends, starting all over. I don't like to change. That's why I don't want to leave it. To me, the word "house" is a building and "home" means the people inside. To say "home" doesn't come easy. This house is my home—my everything. I've worked so much inside and outside. Yes, I know it's a big property and I'm getting older, but I'm used to it.

Daniela prefers, she says, to think of today and maybe tomorrow, but not too far ahead. But I keep trying to think ahead for the future. I try to give her breaks from caring for me by using personal care givers when she visits her family in Italy once or twice a year.

She tells me that after a few weeks or a month of seeing her family and having a rest, she doesn't mind taking it up again when she returns. Sometimes I don't know how she does it, day in and day out without complaining. She tells me that if I were grumpy, she would get grumpy too and be tired of it.

Along the way, we keep rediscovering what it takes for a couple to develop an enjoyable life when one person has a major disability. Daniela tells people that it's not difficult to live with a person with a major disability. She said, "You've got to love the person and have the right attitude or you won't survive. And the person with the disability has to have the right attitude, too!"

My dear wife may not be perfect, nor have all the same ideas that I have, nor express her love for me in the way that I want. But we love each other and I may have to be resigned to the lacks like most couples. We continue to work together and compromise with each other but I sometimes long for more intimate contact. I begin to wonder if anyone has the kind of relationship that I seek. If truth be known, perhaps my wife feels likewise.

I am reminded of Woody Allen's funny lines. Women say, "We have sex all the time—three times a week." Men say, "We hardly ever have sex—three times a week."

I've learned that the reason my wife loves me is that I am full of ideas, I'm positive and not negative, I don't get down and depressed for long and, as she says, "Kenny doesn't sit around and watch TV; he's always doing something. He's always busy."

Daniela admits some problems in living with me. She says, "When he was younger and stronger, he could be more independent. He went on trips here and there, some with me and some with personal care assistants. I was free of his care at times. But those times are gone now, just as his strength is going. We would need another person to travel with us."

She has told others her attitudes about people with disabilities. She said,

> They're human beings but have a wheelchair between you and them. I need to have a lot of understanding and caring. It's not easy. He gets depressed because he doesn't like the situation he's in. I try to talk a little but he doesn't want to talk or bother me with a problem. He doesn't stay depressed long. He bounces back.
>
> Sometimes I think about others who are having fun, but I'm not jealous of them. We have fun, friends, and I am happy because I'm a house person. The young people now are not. We have fun together, good laughs, and it's nice to be together. He's understanding and has a good sense of humor.
>
> If I hadn't married Kenny, I'm not sure that I would have married. I might have worked or raised kids or had a home and traveled a little. But I would have lived a simple life like here.
>
> I think it helps to show people that they aren't the only ones going through difficulties and that while nothing is super perfect, it can be beautiful. This book that Kenny is writing can show him how much he has done in his life. Others might get some examples from him. He's helped a lot of people. Maybe in this book, he can help more.

Other changes that I made as time passed were to turn my work around and become a business and career coach. I have found that if you direct your energies toward areas that are important to you, it will be easier to find success. So I encourage people to strive in the areas most important to them. To my amazement, some of my clients have stayed with me over the long haul. Some say that I am an example to them.

In the same way, when I get "down and out in Beverly Hills" so to speak, I call up or go visit someone with even more problems than I have and they are an example to me. If they can't feed themselves, and I still can, I take heart and think that if they continue coping with life's problems, so can I. It's a good "wake up call." Then I say to myself, "I've got better things to do than worry that I can't cut my meat as well as I used to, or I hurt more than I used to."

I know that I keep learning about what I need to do to make it in the business world. I've learned in these last years that sometimes you have to "go with the flow" and keep your mouth shut if you're working with people who see things differently. They may cause you problems, but Phoenix or Rome wasn't built in a day and neither are good worthwhile projects. I've learned that I must be patient, even when I find out that people are working against me in some way, so that my goals can be achieved in the long run. My impatience and tendency to make decisions too quickly have become personal goals that I still work on and help others work on.

When I feel good, I can be a little manic. I want to do too much at once. That's when I can lose focus. It's like being served a ten course meal and wanting to do it all at once. I've got to do one course or thing at a time. I guess age has given me more perspective but it also slows me down.

Since people have to help me, I try to help them help me. I try to create assistive devices. Sure, I get into a mood of "what's the use?" It usually follows having figured how to manage something, but as I lose more function, my old solutions don't work any more. Then I finally decide, "It ain't goin' to happen the way I want it to," so I readjust how to keep on functioning, but not the way I did before. Older people can understand this as they get more Rice Krispies in their knees and more pain and loss of function. With me, the volume is turned up and it's a multi-speaker system so I have more noticeable discomfort from more different angles.

It gets most disheartening when I'm being bombarded both physically and emotionally, especially when I feel my self worth is in question. When I come up with good ideas and nothing happens, I figure I don't have much value. It's like pain. Sometimes when I feel more pain, I think, "God must not like me."

But Daniela knows I have recovery power. I'm so happy that Daniela still wants me to work and achieve something. It gives me the drive to keep on trying to make my mark in this world. I've heard that Sigmund Freud was still asking at the end of his life, "What do women want?" I'm still asking that question about my wife. What does Daniela want? Is it possible she only wants me?

23

Being Different

Squall: Brief but violent windstorm, usually with rain or snow.

I am frequently reminded of what many in our world still think of me and others with disabilities or people who are considered "different." There are train loads and plane loads of people who are fearful and even hateful of people with disabilities, especially those with severe, deforming disabilities. While some of this pathological fear has gradually subsided over the last half-century, it still exists more predominantly than you might think. It parallels very nicely how many of these same people feel about homosexuals, people of color, etc. Well, you get the idea.

Like when all I want to do is have a simple dinner at Marilyn's, a nearby Mexican restaurant in Phoenix, that's, ironically, no longer in business. Karma? But back to the story.

Unfortunately, I couldn't go there because I felt that I and others like me were not welcome. You see, Marilyn's owner consistently set up benches and umbrellas in the handicapped parking spaces for the convenience of customers who were enjoying their Coronas and margaritas while waiting to be seated. Nice touch for his customers that did not otherwise need handicapped spaces.

But there are others, like me, who are "different" that our society rejects and shuns outright. Who are the different ones? Who should we hate?

I turn to an event of recent years that was in the news and my Bible for possible insight into reasons for this insanity about the great dislike—and even hatred—for those who are different.

One day in Casper, Wyoming, on October 17, 1977, a boy named Matthew Shepard was born. But at 12:53 a.m., October 12, 1998, at the age of 21, Matthew died. His heart failed.

Being Different 379

> *You are the light of the world. A city set on a mountain cannot be hidden.*

Matthew was small in stature, just five feet, two inches tall, 105 pounds, and I can identify with that short stature. He was still a handsome, rather dashing young man. He had the boyish charm and good looks that girls go for and guys admire. His friends were captivated by his gregarious, sometimes feisty personality and openness. Matt was a respected comrade and a loved son who was studying political science and aspired to a career in international affairs. Matt was openly gay, but never obtrusively so.

The end for Matthew began at the *Fireside Lounge,* a favorite bar among young adults and students attending the University of Wyoming in Laramie. During the course of the evening, Matthew began flirting with another young man who, with his friends, later lured Matt outside. Russell Arthur Henderson, 21; Aaron James McKinney, 22; Chastity Vera Pasley, 20; and Kristen Leann Price, 18; were the individuals who persuaded Matthew to leave the *Fireside Lounge* and go off with them to be eventually tortured and killed.

Matthew was brutally pistol-whipped and tied to a fence—crucifixion style—just outside Laramie, Wyoming. Matt was left unconscious, bleeding, shoes removed and crucified. The place where Matthew was left to die is a rather lovely, wind-swept, high bluff. At the foot of the snow-capped Rockies, Matt lived a frigid night. Hypothermic, comatose, and severely brain damaged, Matt was finally found and brought to hospital eighteen hours after his beating. Rescue might have occurred sooner, but a passerby mistook Matthew for a scarecrow. Soon after the story broke in the media, letters came pouring in from people all over the world decrying this horrible murder and all acts of hate. Letter after letter said that the time to stop hate crimes is *now.*

Miles away in New York, Catholic and other Christian clergy and believers were marching and demonstrating in front of a theater that was showing the stage play, *Corpus Christi,* by Terrence McNally, depicting a Christ-like figure, *Joshua,* and some of the Disciples as gay. Such a stage play was an abomination and the work of Satan according to the demonstrators. Most of the demonstrators had never even seen or read the play.

> *But I say to you, whoever is angry with his brother will be liable to judgment, and whoever says to his brother, 'Raqa,' will be answerable to the Sanhedrin, and whoever says, 'You fool,' will be liable to fiery Gehenna.*

The weapon used to pistol-whip Matthew Shepard was a .357-caliber magnum. When it was found in the back of McKinney's pickup, it was covered with blood. Matthew wasn't just robbed and threatened before finally passing out, he was also beaten incessantly. Matt's wallet was found by police in McKinney's home. McKinney and Henderson were each released on $100,000 bail.

Philip Dubois, President of the University of Wyoming, later said, "I think we will all join together in trying to express our support to the Shepard family and to express our commitment to an open and diverse university community. I hope and I pray that this was an isolated event that was motivated by whatever motivates those individuals."

Normally, many of the religious right would have contended that Matthew Shepard could have escaped this assault *if* he had successfully gone through an "ex-gay" program. However, they have admitted that even if Matthew had never "come out"—or had been a heterosexual—as a *small man* he was too close to popular typical stereotypes and would have been targeted by homophobes.

Such an isolated event, or *squall*, can be extremely violent but, unfortunately, such events continue to occur. The F.B.I.'s statistics on hate crimes show that 1,000 attacks occurred in 1996 against people because of their "different" sexual orientation.

Congressman J. D. Hayworth, U.S. Representative from Arizona, met not long ago with a few individuals from a retirement community in Mesa, Arizona, who were concerned that some of their fellow retirees were advocating that their community's transit buses—used to transport residents to grocery stores, shopping malls, cinemas—be made accessible to wheelchairs. According to the individuals visiting Mr. Hayworth—which included people from the company owning the transit concession—this would represent an undue economic hardship on the company running this bus service and might threaten the continuation of the service for everyone else. (Actually, the owner of the contracting transit service was already willing to equip at least one of the seven buses with a wheelchair lift, prior to this meeting).

"As far as I can see," Hayworth said, "this service is like a private club and, as such, doesn't have to make *any* of its buses accessible if it doesn't want to." Thus far, none of the buses have been made accessible to people using wheelchairs, who are, of course, different from the majority of people who don't require wheelchairs.

Two people went up to the temple area to pray; one was a Pharisee and the other was a tax collector. The Pharisee took up his position and spoke this prayer to him-

self, "O God, I thank you that I am not like the rest of humanity—greedy, dishonest, adulterous—or even like this tax collector. I fast twice a week, and I pay tithes on my whole income." But the tax collector stood off at a distance and would not even raise his eyes to heaven but beat his breast and prayed, "O God, be merciful to me a sinner." I tell you, the latter went home justified, not the former; for everyone who exalts himself will be humbled, and the one who humbles himself will be exalted.

Matt's skull had been crushed in the beating. In the four days preceding Matt's death, his body temperature fluctuated wildly due to the damage inflicted on his brain stem. Matt remained comatose and was only able to breathe by the grace of a ventilator. Judy and Dennis Shepard, Matt's mother and father, said in a joint statement, "Life has often been a struggle in one way or another (for Matt) including a premature birth and ailments during childhood. He is physically short in stature, but we believe he is a giant when it comes to respecting the worth of others." Dennis, who works for an oil company and was in Saudi Arabia when he learned of his son's beating, admitted that even he harbored one "intolerance." He hated "when people don't accept others as they are."

A friend of Matthew, Phil LaBrie, shared that it was Shepard's goal to end injustice. Phil stated, "One thing he (Matt) said was that he would sacrifice his happiness to help just one human being who was suffering. It's so ironic that something like this would happen because he spoke of it only a week ago."

Fred Phelps, a man from Topeka, Kansas, who has gained notoriety for demonstrating at funerals of people who have died from AIDS by marching outside the funeral chapel, holding signs such as: "God Hates Fags," planned to demonstrate at Matthew's funeral in his birthplace of Casper.

Matthew's funeral service was held on Friday, October 16, at St. Mark's Episcopal Church in Casper, Wyoming. A broadcast of the service was fed to overflow crowds at the First Presbyterian Church nearby. Matthew's cousin, Anne Kitch, pastor of St. Peter's Episcopal Church in Peekskill, New York, gave a homily. Pastor Kitch said, in part,

> I believe Matt has shown us the way out of the abyss into which his murder has plunged us. Matt has shown us the way, away from violence, hate, and despair.
>
> How can we not let our hearts be deeply, deeply troubled? How can we not be immersed in despair? How can we not cry out against this? This is not the way it is supposed to be. A son has died, a brother has been lost, a child has been broken, torn, abandoned. We become engulfed in a turbulent stream of grief, anger, guilt, fear, shame, outrage.

The answer, Pastor Kitch said, was in Matt's love for others, his faith, and God's love.

Shortly before Pastor Kitch spoke, angry anti-gay demonstrators from Texas and Kansas staged a demonstration across the street from St. Mark's, carrying signs which read, "No Fags in Heaven" and "No Tears for Queers." A young girl in the group held a sign saying, "Fag =Anal Sex."

Earlier, in their first appearance before the media, Shepard's parents, Dennis and Judy Shepard, thanked "the citizens of the United States and the people of the world who have expressed their deepest sympathy and condolences to our family during these trying times."

Many in Washington believed that the federal hate crimes bill, proposed by Senator Ted Kennedy, had little chance of becoming law. The gay community's fierce push for this bill—following Matthew Shepard's death—prompted the religious right to oppose this legislation with fiery fervor. Kennedy's legislation would have made it a federal crime to attack someone because of *gender, disability, and sexual orientation*. (All three were grouped together as being "different," you see, from male able-bodied heterosexual beings). The inclusion of sexual orientation in this bill galvanized the opposition, making legislators fearful of not being re-elected if they voted for its passage.

> *You have heard that it was said, "An eye for an eye and a tooth for a tooth." But I say to you, offer no resistance to one who is evil. When someone strikes you on your right cheek, turn the other one to him as well.*
>
> *But I say to you, love your enemies, and pray for those who persecute you, that you may be children of your heavenly Father, for he makes his sun rise on the bad and the good, and the just.*

In a remark given to the news media, Matthew's mother, Judy, said, "Go home, give your kids a hug and don't let a day go by without telling them you love them." Shepard's parents were grateful that the last words they heard from Matt while he was alive were, "I love you."

As I said elsewhere in this book, because of the severe physical disability I acquired as an infant, I require a personal caregiver for assistance with activities of daily living such as bathing and dressing. Several years ago, my wife, who's normally my caregiver, was about to go out of town for four weeks to visit her family. I thought about advertising in our church bulletin for someone to assist me during her absence. I was told that to run an ad in the bulletin, I had to do so for one entire year. That was the requirement of the bulletin's publisher in California. Regrettably, my church told me, they also couldn't put in a simple announcement in the bulletin because if they did it for me they'd have to do it for other parishioners. They didn't want me to be *different* from other parishioners. My parish is the *Community of the Blessed Sacrament Catholic Church*, Scottsdale, Arizona.

Years later, our parish established a caregiver's ministry. God is, indeed, mysterious.

I recall another person who did not like people to be different. He was an admitted and convicted hate-crime murderer: Sgt. Kenneth Junior French. He was born January 15, 1971, and on August 6, 1993, murdered Ethel Parrous, 65, Pete Parrous, 73, James Kidd, 46, and Wesley Cover, 26, in Fayetteville, North Carolina. He was convicted on four counts and sentenced to four consecutive life terms plus 35 years.

Kenneth Junior French was an Army sergeant for the 18th Airborne Corps stationed at Fort Bragg in Fayetteville, North Carolina. He didn't specifically murder a homosexual, but his crime was integral to his feelings towards them.

Sergeant French was vehemently opposed to President Bill Clinton's 1993 plans to eliminate the ban on gays and lesbians in the military services. He said, "If you're introducing a minority group that's frowned upon and looked upon as being weak and your commander's saying it's fine for him to be here, guys are saying, 'Guess the military isn't really as tough and bad as we thought it was.' Everybody's wanting acceptance. It's a one-world system—global unity. Well, at what cost? Our military's going down the drain?"

On the evening of August 6, 1993, Sgt. French claimed he blanked out after drinking a fifth of whisky while watching a Clint Eastwood film, *Unforgiven*. He then went to Luigi's, a local family restaurant, and ambushed clients, killing four persons and wounding seven. During Sgt. French's trial, witnesses testified that while shooting randomly, he shouted, "I'll show you, Clinton, about letting gays into the army!"

French told the jury, "I'm not gonna apologize for the views that I hold towards gays or homosexuals but...I don't think that I went in with the intention of just singling out any certain group of people, be it black, white, male, female, gay, or straight. I was just angry at the world I guess at the time, I don't know. I was just taking out aggression and hatred on whoever was there." How can it be that someone can believe the only acceptable people in the world are white heterosexual males, like Sgt. French?

The week following Matt Shepard's death, Dr. Slepian, a gynecologist in Baltimore, Maryland, was shot in his home by a sniper's rifle. During his lengthy career as a physician, he saved the lives of hundreds of infants and mothers. However, some people, including the sniper, didn't like Dr. Slepian because he also performed legal abortions. He died less than two hours after being shot. Dr. Slepian was seen as being different from the sniper, who believed that everyone who did not look at life the same way should die.

This last summer, James Byrd, a black man living in Texas, was accosted by white men, beaten, and physically dragged behind a motor vehicle until he perished from decapitation. He was different, his skin was black, through no fault of his own, so he was sentenced to die by white men.

Miles away in Moscow, two young Mormon men, about Matt Shepard's age, were beaten by thugs. They were in Russia to proselytize the Mormon faith. One young man sustained many injuries, but is still alive. His companion wasn't so lucky. He died from his wounds. Russian white men saw the American evangelists as different from themselves and decided that they should die for that difference.

Fifty years ago, among the very first people to be exterminated by Hitler were his society's misfits: the severely disabled and very old—the holocaust followed. Hitler, like all these other people, was threatened by the differences he saw in people.

Frank Caruso, Jr., 19, was recently sentenced in Chicago for the barbaric beating of a then 13-year-old youth, leaving him permanently and severely brain-damaged because he was black. Caruso decided that he could not live in a world with people different than himself, a white male.

Not too many years ago, a little girl named Cindy was almost drowned when her angry baby sitter forced her head into the toilet bowl in punishment for "being different" and having wet the bed. The trauma scars Cindy emotionally even today.

> *Postscript: The italicized remarks of Jesus Christ are from the gospels of Mark and Luke, The New American Bible, Catholic Book Publishing Company.*

I have a nephew who was diagnosed with Bipolar Manic Depressive Affective Psychosis. He is very different. When I visited him during one of his more severe breakdowns, I realized that my life could have been much worse than it was. After I saw his living quarters in Arizona, I was haunted by his misery and loss of reality, which eclipsed my own by a very large measure. He has not chosen to be different, any more than I or others did. But many view his differences and his sickness with hostility and prejudices that I wish I could dispel.

I do not wish to minimize the bad choices any of us, including my nephew, have made that may have disrespected or dishonored others, or ourselves. However, I wrote the following poem to celebrate him, including his times of despair, and others with mental disabilities.

Eclipsed

Did you know it's a clear cold Sunday
Morning 7:30 a.m. in
Phoenix and tomorrow's
Valentine's Day?
Were you
aware that a brother-in-law
aunt uncle
had begun a Prescott pilgrimage and were on
their way…to you?

Your bearded big-daddy physique
confused and receding hairline
greet your kinsman as you pace,
smiling sickness without will, the Guidance Clinic's
parking lot hugging your bloodline in the freezing
mountain air
dressed only in T-shirt, sweating.

You're 35 now and have loved
your guns your knives since
your boyhood but you
dust us absentminded permission and keys
to your house, gun safes
to take away a piece of your root.

Your bewildered squiggly map to your house
on barren earth, surrounded by life-giving
air, cleansed by puffing winds, sweeping
the embankment overlooking

Chino Valley is
boggled bipolar like your
eyes today.

Your acre your doublewide abode your desert adopts
five parked cars in lonely repair
by your
tenant, Bubba his house-framing
sister, Stacy asleep inside
the mess
you call
your home.

Guns in your broken truck
killing rifles in your gun safe
pistols in your closet in a hidden
compartment beside your bed, the
arsenal of reload ammunition, knives, swords…
and the collection of empty toilet
paper rolls.

But you no longer need a nose to smell the rancid smoke
of stale cigarettes nor eyes to see the jumbled life
your house reflects nor
fingers to feel the closeness longed for that's not
there nor mirror
to echo the desperation your medications don't dispel
all you need to
do is
look at us.

24

Being Small

Sandstorm: A windstorm in which large quantities of sand are blown about in clouds, reducing visibility, pelting and infiltrating structures and windows.

A Phoenix College class assignment to write *my last letter before dying* stimulated me to write a Self Portrait, as I saw myself in my late fifties. I am different and while some don't like me because of that, I would be in trouble if I couldn't like myself. But it's not always easy to see oneself clearly when the storms of life have *pelted and infiltrated* your very being.

What are the things I notice about myself while looking in the mirror? I have an average-sized, oval-shaped head covered with medium-short, dirty-blond and gray hair that's parted on the right, fairly short, but with longer sideburns more in keeping with the '60s than the '90s. The most notable thing about my head is that it tilts to the left, the result of two cervical surgeries and multiple fusions performed in 1966 and 1991. Fortunately, the surgeries were done by competent, albeit liberally creative neurosurgeons.

My head is attached to a thick, very short, almost totally immobile neck, which, in turn, is connected to a small, stocky torso, stooped over from the Juvenile Rheumatoid Arthritis I've lived with since I was two. The other telltale sign of my JRA is my receding chin. The full face, however, comes more from genetics and a wee bit too much pasta and other goodies rather than the arthritis. Rather large ears with detached ear lobes flank my face. The furrows across my forehead give way to two widow's peaks nestled between my eyebrows.

Experienced, intuitive, hazel-brown eyes are the crown jewels of my face. I don't know what I would have done without the gift of vision these eyes have given—and continue to give me. But although I'm still learning to live with my body as you now know it, you will appreciate that contemplating my own death, particularly from the perspective of near-term certainty, has never been on my top ten list of pleasurable things to do.

Teetering on the Edge and Trapped: A Self Portrait

I'm madder than
hell and I just don't
want to take it…
I won't
take it…anymore.
(But I must, there's
no choice when there's
no one else to help
me but me).

Living silently, repressed
battered incessantly by
the drone of amputated
nourishment, restricted
breathing, somewhere deep
within my
life's soul.
(A bad ass neighborhood).

It might be
nice to curl
and uncurl fingers, stand
and sit and walk
around and take
a solo shit.
(And, sometimes, I'd
just walk out).

If I could leave
you, even for
awhile, I'd cry tears
of joy, freedom.
(And, sometimes, I'd
just walk out).

Is your silence, suppressed
existence, supposed
to be as golden
as they say?
(Hell, no, but
just keep your stupid mouth shut)!

You're mad, angry
and pissed off, sometimes
enraged at your
unlockable cage.
(It's part of
you, too, so grow
up and live with it).

I was in my early forties when I first felt as though my death could come at any time. Before then, I had come close to death several times on the operating table, but somehow the possibility that I could die never registered emotionally, never caused me to gasp for breath or stirred fear in my heart. Convulsions were occurring in my forties that I had ignored and chosen to be deaf, dumb, and blind to for too long.

Unlike the unrelenting sights and sounds of war, which shove massacres and mutilations, explosions and wailing in your face, forcing you to react, the nemesis arranging my first date with the grim reaper did so with cunning stealth. It's like being stuck at the bottom of the path of slow-moving, white-hot lava, but not turning your head to see your fate until the volcano's molten vomit is inches from your feet. It isn't death which turns the heart to fear, it's not being ready. It's about not knowing and living one's destiny.

I wasn't ready in my forties because I chose to not turn my head and see what was coming. All my life I had quested after making something of myself and being loved for myself. While I still had a measure of financial resources and time to change, I chose, instead, to hide my head in the suffocating sand of the Arizona desert until, starving for air, I heaved up, took breath and saw my loathsome kismet laughing at me. I thought I was neither productive nor lovable. That's when I first feared death. I wondered, "Who would care?"

In another sense, I share with all men who've been in war the fear that I might be a coward when faced with the inevitable. As battle comes closer, men fear they will run away from the enemy. What keeps them in place is the greater fear of being embarrassed in front of their buddies. What keeps me still when faced with absolutely certain piercing pain from a giant syringe seeking large amounts of blood from my femoral artery near my precious parts? It's the same thing, I guess; the fear of being embarrassed in front of medical personnel, who have become the buddies in my life.

I guess I learned that with each reoccurrence, I know I'm going to live. I have to put up with it. I try to grit my teeth. I've called God every name in the book, which I'm sure He doesn't appreciate. Sometimes I talk to Him and say, "What did I do to deserve this? I thought I'd had that lesson already!" But I get this feeling that it's supposed to happen, so live with it. Usually pain and discomfort do finally subside so I say to myself, "This too shall pass."

In my late fifties, death appeared even more fearful and inevitable than in my forties. The reason behind the fear is the same for my quests, still unchanged, still unrealized. The difference now is that I'm 63 and feel I'm much nearer death's door. My destiny in this life still mirrors my short stature, making Lilliputian sense. I guess it's why I've always been crazy about my other second personal theme song, Randy Newman's "Short People." Here are a few of my favorite lines:

Short People

> Short people got no reason to live.
> They got little hands, little eyes
> They walk around tellin' great big lies,
> They got little noses and tiny little teeth
> They wear platform shoes on their nasty little feet.
> They got little baby legs that stand so low

You got to pick 'em up just to say hello.
They got little cars that go beep, beep, beep
They got little voices goin' peep, peep, peep.
They got grubby little fingers and dirty little minds
Don't want no short people 'round here.

◆ ◆ ◆

This obsession with being Lilliputian reminds me of a dream drive.

The canary yellow Mustang is driving east on the south side of town and from the car the driver suddenly notices that the street dead ends ahead with only a vast, rolling, grazing field beyond. The driver turns left onto a paved two-lane street that seems like all other city streets except that it's somewhat curved and meandering. Something tells him that he's never seen this part of town before.

Then, to his right, his eyes begin to digest a most incredible sight: from almost the edge of the road to as far as he can see out over the rolling hills, large animals are lounging, grazing, and pacing to and fro. At first the driver thinks he's looking at large tigers and other felines grazing in a special area on the periphery of the Phoenix zoo, but rapidly grasps that the land area seems far too vast to be part of the zoo. More importantly, the animals are much larger than he's ever seen at a zoo before. In fact, they're huge, maybe two or three times as big as normal tigers and other wild felines.

As he drives and looks more intently, he sees that their heads are also disproportionately larger and longer, shaped, in some cases, like those of giant rodents. The driver pulls the car over to the side of the road and makes a U-turn to go back when he notices a prefabricated house in the distance where the road he's on dead ends. He decides to stop at the house and ask about the large animals he's just seen.

Driving onto the gravel-paved driveway, the driver observes a few potted plants and flowers, but no lawn or formal landscaping. Drew—that's the name of the driver—yanks his Ultra-Lite folding wheelchair out from the backseat, snaps it open and slides onto it in one swift move.

Now out of the car, Drew wheels along a bumpy brick walkway to the house's front door and knocks. There's no answer. Drew knocks again and again; no answer.

For some unfathomable reason, Drew decides to try the door handle, which yields smoothly to his touch, releasing the door from its sole constraint. The door swings wide open invitingly. The door's threshold is only about one half inch high so entering with the wheelchair is relatively easy. Inside, the house looks more like an office with several desks, computers, and a table strewn with books and papers. Drew decides to investigate further and starts wheeling from room to room.

The first room is rather long, with a desk on one end and a single bed on the other. High above the bed on the side wall there's a window overlooking the vast fields beyond. Because it's so high, Drew cannot see much out of the window, save for a smattering of rolling hills and mostly sky. Except for a lone chair and unused clothes rack, there was nothing else in the room.

Why he suddenly decided to flip up his wheelchair's armrest, slide onto the bed, and take a nap in this quasi-surreal house worried and confused Drew even as his eyelids were getting heavy and he drifted away.

A gentle, but persistent nudging of his left shoulder brought Drew quickly back to the now, eyes focusing on a tall, middle-aged man with a quizzical, but not unfriendly look on his face, standing alongside the bed. "What are you doing here; are you alright?" the man asked, genuinely concerned.

"Oh, hi…. Yes, I'm okay. My name is Drew; Drew Segno. I don't know what happened, I got sleepy…. I guess I'm kind of like *Goldilocks and the Three Bears* when she fell asleep in their house where she had trespassed."

"I am very relieved nothing's wrong, what with the wheelchair and all. I was concerned. Forgive my rudeness, Drew. I'm Adamo Crain. May I be of any assistance to you?"

"No, thank you, Mr. Crain. I can manage by myself. But I'm the one who's been rude. I came into your house, uninvited. Got into your bed. Forgive me. I can't figure out what…."

"Don't be concerned, there's nothing to forgive, Drew, and please call me Adamo. Why don't you join me in our backyard for some coffee?"

"Thanks, Adamo. I could use something to wake me up."

Drew followed Adamo back into the living room, out through the back door. Adamo picked up a small, dusty table and placed it to the side of Drew's wheelchair, then walked back into the house. Adamo came out carrying a tray with an old percolator coffeepot filled to the brim, two mugs, a sugar bowl, and cookies, setting the tray down on the table. He pulled up a chair and sat down. The acute angles of Adamo's knees when he was sitting brought into focus his considerable height. Drew thought, "He must be more than six feet eight inches."

"You like your coffee black or sweet?"

"Black is fine." While sipping the strong, hot liquid, a bell somewhere rang and Drew noticed something wasn't right. "Adamo, where are all the big tiger-like animals I saw out here before?"

"Excuse me. I'll be right back." With those words Adamo quickly got up and went into the house. Moments later he came out accompanied by a younger, heavyset man. "Drew, I'd like you to meet Chris. Chris, this is Drew."

As Drew set his coffee mug on the table to shake Chris' hand, Adamo stepped behind his wheelchair, grabbing Drew's arms in an iron-vice grip. Chris moved forward placing a hockey-like mask over Drew's head. Despite the cutouts for viewing, Drew could see nothing beyond his own nose. He tried speaking, calling out, but no sounds left his throat. Everything went blank.

Everything was as in a dream...

When you're little, everyone and everything seems awfully big...and strong... and scary.

My surgeries, therapy, education, travel, work, relationships, marriage, and grotesque efforts just to survive seem to have resulted in a being whose only "destiny" seems to be one without recognized profession, appreciative remuneration, consummated love, inner music, or meaning. The incredible thing is that there remains in the darkest recesses of my viscera a pin dot of life refusing to extinguish against this missile-barrage of pain, pestilence of loneliness, quicksand of despair. With every new attempt to make my own way, connect in love, be my own person, I fail, my body defaults, spirit breaks, death creeps closer, keener. But the pin dot of light always there wants me to fight, live my dream even though it too is static-plagued, receding into an ever weaker, but recurring fog.

Is death all about knocking you down, plummeting your body, breaking your spirit until you feel lower than shit, devoid of self worth, ready to be the nothing you've become, forever extinguishing the light? Perhaps. What I've come to know is that that smidgen of light, though rendered faint and shadowed by my war, will be part of me until the day I breathe that last breath, combating desolation's destruction, holding out for absolute victory.

25

This Is Your Life, Ken Jacuzzi!

Thunderstorm Multicell: Storms accompanied by thunder and lightning, lasting longer with squall lines and flash floods.

It's 5:55 a.m. I've been semi-awake 30 minutes or more, called by my body's stiffness and aches, while Morning Edition rattles off the latest pains of the nation and world. My caregiver soon comes to my bedside to assist me in rising. A urinal to urinate, sweat pants slipped on legs, back and limbs stretched, a few minutes of exercises, perched on bed's edge, I'm transferred to the wheelchair. Two extra strength Tylenols swallowed, then coffee and sitting a short while to try dulling the pain.

Nix to anti-inflammatories, a bleeding duodenal ulcer and emergency hospitalization years earlier took care of that. While growing up, doctors prescribed 24–36 aspirins per day, so when some later suggested long-term steroids, I objected.

At 6:45 to 7 a.m. the shave, shower, dressing routine comes next. If it weren't for a caregiver, I'd rot and die in my own accumulated filth. As it is, I can shave myself, once helped with the shaving cream. These hands and arms have neither the strength nor reach to lather or rinse, nor dry, dress or transfer me to the powered wheelchair I remain in 'til nightfall. For someone with some income like me, personal care assistants—PCAs—start at $50 for a good slice of the day. While with you, their food and such is usually also your responsibility.

Oh, yes, while up and about, I can urinate in the urinal unassisted, but it takes 10 to 15 minutes or more: if I don't drop the pliers I carry in a pouch at the side of my wheelchair and use to unfasten the Velcro closure of my $200 a pair, custom-made pants; if I've remembered to remind my caregiver to wax my trousers' zipper when they've just returned from the cleaners; if I don't drop my urinal, whether from fatigue, or the weight of up to a half liter of urine or more accumulated from holding it until the time and place were convenient.

Of course, I may not even make it out of the $50,000, custom-equipped van I drive to business meetings in the first place if, per chance, a limit switch or relay should fail on the van's wheelchair lift. A prospective or existing client sometimes understands, sometimes doesn't. That's not half as bad as half entering a men's room, then having to back out when I realize that I won't be able to leave once I'm inside and the door closes behind me. And that's not half as bad as finding out after it's too late and the door has already shut.

Meeting with clients at their offices, attending workshops I facilitate at hotels, or getting to business luncheons at restaurants is frequently frustrated by access aisles at disabled parking spaces that are blocked or nonexistent, sidewalks without curb cuts or made impassable because of tabloid stands or garbage cans, doors that have to wait to be opened until a walking person strolls by and helps, elevator buttons that can't be reached because of ill-placed, floor-standing ashtrays.

At restaurants I try to be patient when waiters ask others I am with in what section I would like to sit or what I would care to eat or drink. Despite my greeting, they seem to think I cannot speak or think. But I burn and seethe inside when building or restaurant managers pretend to be totally unaware of accessibility problems with their facilities or patronizing when they tell me everything has been done "according to the law" and choose not to treat me as a client, customer, or patron. Instead, their speech and body language broadcasts to me in 50,000 watts that, for them, I'm a pain in the ass they'd like to get rid of as soon as humanly possible.

Then I must have someone cut some of my food for me, another embarrassment. So I ask waiters to cut it up on the plate before they bring it to me in restaurants. I used to cut an apple pretty well, but that was 30 years ago. To go backwards in progress is quite depressing to me, but anyone with a progressive degenerative disorder has the same problem.

Near bedtime, about 10 p.m. or so, I sit on the pot. My "routine" is at night so as to shorten the morning get readies and start work on time. Sometimes the p.m. pot routine is successful, sometimes not. I can only blame myself, of course, when the big event doesn't occur. I need to drink more water during the day. I wonder why I don't. I must be stupid, too, or maybe I don't want to pee more frequently. Maybe both.

Sleep comes quickly most of the time. Most deep dreams wander in around 2 or 3 a.m. Last night, I was striking out, a huge cattail whip in my hand, beating furiously, relentlessly at walls, giant boulders, and convention product displays until their remnants lay in shambles and dust. I awoke sweating, wrung out and alone.

Where am I and where have I been the last six plus decades? I gyrate! Is it jaybird or jail? I often think it's Einstein's theory of relativity gone amuck, reconstituting itself onto me like an irremovable tumor. Like some super-intelligent alien has decided to amuse herself by delivering unto me this schizoid chair, making it a partner in my existence, regardless of my opinion in the matter.

It's not as though there aren't any more attractive alternatives. In fact, I remember one such distant time when my ass actually could make prolonged contact with cotton, wool, or velvet, rather than a cheap synthetic. Or, I ask, why not stretch out on a backyard chaise lounge, James Bond paperback in hand, in the midst of the watered grass while my nostrils fill with mossy dewdrops, making me feel free? Yeah, sure, but where else could I meander with a chaise lounge? Maybe the alien-bequeathed Jekyll and Hyde freakish mate is okay after all. Maybe I have Hemingway's "movable feast" right under my butt. But it moves, therein lies the *rub!*

Bounce like a bear, buzz like a bee, where oh where is my privacy? But then, how many of us actually live private lives? Can't we all hear each other coming, I inquire to/of myself, wishing to whitewash my own brain cells. Forget the telltale noises of my mobility; doesn't every environment have them? The sound, the smell. What does this alien gift, or is it really me, smell like? Lordy, go figure. Let's see. Try taking a bit of worn rubber, adding splatterings of men's cologne, sweat, piss or semen, depending on mood and age, street dust and grass and then stir. Voila, my doohickey's *Alice in Wonderland* hummingbird aroma. Is it getting smaller or getting bigger? The aimless man-vapor wafting around me, silly; not what YOU were thinking—dirty old man/woman!

But then, there must be some redeeming social value in mobility? After all, there are a few chic aspects to this zone of mine, like its facade of metal cross beams and gadgets, some shiny, many black, perplexing to the unbaptized, but not to me. Would you believe slings, arrows, downy plastic, callous rubber, zinging electricity, and tidy tools surround me? Or, have all these goodies become part of who I am, not just inseparable but soldered to my soul?

Zoom, zoom around the room into the wild blue beyond. My eyes, ass-high to the world, drink in, like 70 mm cinemascope, the passing mall stores and kiosks with their enticing wares and chic-looking, clueless sales girls. Hippity-hop, bumpity-bop sidewalks serve up bumper-to-bumper cars to my left, skyscrapers mixed with derelict buildings to my right. Rolling grasses of city parks and manicured meadows for rich old codgers playing with their balls and sticks all blur through my brain cells, unremembered except for an occasional quacking duck or happy child.

Then, too, there's ever present the corrupt, spiteful, Judas side, ready, willing, and always able to lock me up and throw away the key. With the finesse and expertise of a great king's most favored courtesan, she's whisked me over hill and dale, taken me to beaches and speeches and has given me a glimpse of the Promised Land. In an obscure little café in Marrakech, we drank Coca-cola from a bottle labeled in Arabic as we watched in awe with everyone else the lone TV and American astronauts walk for the first time on the moon.

From a casino at Porterose, Yugoslavia, to a patio-blessed trattoria near Ponte Vecchio, to the smell of mother earth atop the Great Wall of China we've been, peas in a pod, my alter-ego and I.

Through Copenhagen's walking street we gobbled wieners while gorgeous, carefree Danes tempted the eyes. Outside El Mercado in Monterrey mariachis serenaded as we drank Bohemias con limones and a tear or two crept unnoticed down cheeks. Along autostrade and highways, streets and alleys, indoors and beneath Caribbean stars, during countless moments in space where time sometimes almost came to a standstill, we ate and saw, we drank and tasted, we defecated and slept...and dreamed.

But with equal, perhaps even superior determination, she also surrounded me with unbearable, impenetrable metal bars. The lifeless cage into which I would be forever sentenced, surrendered to see, but not touch, be observed, while kept conveniently apart, distant. With one gracious hand she offers me tea and cucumber sandwiches on fine china in a lush, springtime-scented English garden. And with equal esprit de corps, physical closeness, pressing of the flesh, intimacies are rendered verboten by command and her intrinsic manic-depressive psyche. She stands, or should I say sits, between me and every person on this earth, isolating me to be forever apart from others. Could such a temptress-cum-jailer be the personification of evil, the devil, the antichrist? No, I'm afraid it's just a lousy, can't-live-without-you chair with wheels.

◆ ◆ ◆

When I married Daniela, I undoubtedly thought that I would no longer be alone in my metal mobile prison. I probably imagined that there would be a sense of freedom that once on a bed with my loved one, I would be closer to another human being; I would perhaps be one with her. But I am, and all people are, ultimately alone—whether isolated by the metal parts of a chair or locked within the thoughts of one's mind that cannot possibly be shared completely.

At times, I can feel so down, it's as though I'm still alone. When I'm in this funk, I feel as though I want from my wife a complete declaration of how she feels about me or how she cares for me. I can't seem to take her actions and be satisfied. I value her loyalty, commitment, kindness, attention, and her total focus on me. Why do I want some kind of extreme verbal expression of love? Down deep I know that expression, too, would be insufficient.

I am no different from many with severe disabilities who ask, "How could you love me just for myself when I'm so imperfect, cannot offer you what others can and I often can't even love myself?" There is no acceptable answer. Even though we cannot love ourselves, we can tolerate ourselves, because we can't leave ourselves. Others can leave us. So we get used to our imperfections, but we can't imagine that a spouse can.

I feel most alone when I think of our downward financial path since the sale of the company and the huge losses sustained from my go-it-alone investment in KJ Software. As I consider what else to do to ease our financial burden, like selling our expensive house, I feel my dear wife is not my partner but an obstacle to a joint sacrifice we must both make for the future. Yet, I would do anything to avoid becoming her enemy in these plans for the future. So we stumble into a kind of cycle, in which we are forever stepping back from each other. I tend to put off disturbing discussions and find other ways to prepare for the future.

Something that changed my routine of *storms*, jails and tempests was when my wheelchair took me to a Writing Class. It began one day when the sun had just snuck under the covers and chilled air pierced my bones, reminding me that the desert was where I had lived for these twenty past years. Follow-up phone calls, overland and electronic mail, setting new appointments, writing letters, re-registering for government contract work, going to the john, getting IDs and vehicle stickers, eating dinner too fast, rolling through a ten-hour day squeezed from twenty. The shattering orange-pink and purple sunset still stops my time, forgets my chill, and sequesters a sliver of sanity.

Grunting through the parking lot, then sidewalks meandering through lawns, people talking, walking, waiting alone, I wonder. Old and new buildings surround me until I encounter the open foyer. My chaotic gaze suddenly transfixes, as if a high-voltage switch has been tripped in my brain. She slowly descends the open foyer stairs. Perfect porcelain-white legs, enticingly revealed by a tailored miniskirt rivaling Calista Flockhart's Ally McBeal, trapped and coaxed my eyes over firm, prideful breasts, a swan neck, and the face of an enchantress—determined mouth, clever jade eyes and freckles, all ensconced in careless, flaming-red hair.

The only thing I remember next is sitting down at one of the dozen or so wobbly tables in this otherwise pabulum room, except for several walls splashed with photos of youngish, past-trendy women and men. Others enter, singly and in pairs or groups. The tables fill, mine—God likes me—with charming women.

Counterclockwise the room moves to greet each unraveling mystery. Coy gazelle Laura, a conflicted bank employee/movie star/corporate yuppie, would rather write screenplays than approve credit cards.

Cool-hand Luke Brian prefers devouring anything written down rather than the food he cooks and is already a published writer. Brian keeps multiple writing notebooks, including one with the magazines near his toilet, but I suspect that's only the tip of his iceberg's bizarreness.

Angela's granny glasses and school-marmish good looks can't disguise the smoldering charcoal beneath her skin. She's a technical writer, an enthusiastic reader who wants to be disciplined to commit to daily creative writing. Disciplined, eh?

Chris, an intense young man, passionate about many things, especially the arts, is the quintessential personification of Jay Leno's "scary stage hand."

Artie is a stonemason by trade and plays in a local Phoenix band by night. Artie wants to take a serious stab at writing.

Rick is notably quiet, reserved, and business-like. He's here because he wants to write.

We drift over to young guy Corey who exudes naiveté, but isn't. He thinks writing might help him get back in touch with his creative side.

Rick II is a student of philosophy who wants to write about it.

Andrew is a trained, working techie who is itching to write song lyrics.

Youthful Randy is a technical writer and engineer who wants to do something more creative than take orders from bean counters.

Effervescent girl/woman Jill is our very own Christina Applegate incarnate. She's here because she "thought it would be fun."

Serious Steven voraciously reads, plays drum and guitar, and chose this class as an elective on his way to better things. He's earning his certification as a physician's assistant. "Steven, where did you leave your pen?"

Jim is a hard-working druggist who's taught biology and wants to tune into his creative self. Drugs don't work anymore.

Can't-put-a-book-down Tami, devoted wife and mother of two daughters, is deluged by the many stories whirling around in her head. Now, if she could just get rid of the old man and those two brats.

Steamy Anabel, lover of reading and, I suspect, most things pertaining to the senses, writes intensely, especially the love of her life, poetry. Her pseudonym: Trashy Novel; her bank account: millions.

Yours truly, a.k.a. horny little Kenny, has taken a few dips, literally and figuratively, in art, business, entrepreneurship, consulting, government, and teaching, now writing to save his soul. If he makes as many mistakes writing as he has in his other endeavors, he'll need to stay alive until he's 105 to complete his first book.

Belinda is a no-grass-grows-under-this-hot-mama's-feet person chasing the many crazy stories in her cerebrum, but hasn't finished.

Teresa, another hot-mommy, has the look of a savvy, but not-yet-21 year old woman, but she already has a teenage daughter. Teresa is curious about her creative writing capabilities. No one present doubts the creative part.

Generous Kimberly shares with us that she's a voracious reader, all fired up to write. The aura spilling off Kimberly is filled with life and passion.

Robin, our no-nonsense business analyst is, so far, an undisciplined writer.

Professor Jed, jazz musician, teacher, giver of self, but often too much, is our book-and-life educated, superbly insightful instructor. Among many other things, Jed religiously keeps a daily journal, writing in it every morning, even if it's only gibberish. What's vital is that he and, if we're serious, *we* write every day.

The assignment is to write a miniature narrative and a few poetry exercises. Simple. Keep it simple, stupid. Drink six to eight glasses of water each day. Exercise and meditate daily. Write anything—just write.

What do *I* write about? "Anything, your daily life, a hole in a bucket, anything!" said the instructor.

One reason I wanted to learn to write was because I wanted to write about my Jacuzzi family and set the record straight, as I told my dear friend Pat. Pat had become a claims adjuster and had a very good understanding of medical conditions and needs. She had come to visit us in Arizona and for a time lived in the Valley of the Sun. She enjoyed visiting us and carried on about Daniela's cooking.

Pat told me frankly that she thought writing about the Jacuzzi business and family might bring only criticisms. She thought another facet might make my book more acceptable. I finally came to see it that way and focused on sharing the life of someone with a major disability in more of my writings. I wanted to clarify the problems that we create when we call people "handicapped," "disabled," etc.

Nobody says, "I'm cancerous;" they say "I have cancer." Well, we should not say, "I'm disabled." We should say, "I have a disability" like they say "I have high blood pressure."

As it turned out later, Pat began to suffer from pain, loss of flexibility and was diagnosed with a muscle disorder called polymyalgia rheumatica. She had to take that dreadful drug Prednisone and we shared miseries about the side effects from that drug. But ever so kindly, she said, "I may have pain and little flexibility, but I can't know what it's like not to be able to bathe myself."

For my class, I decided to write about a typical day in my life. The Good Day (La Belle Di) begins like this. The birthing light of day delicately kisses awakening shades of gray surrounding my breathing eyes; I slowly inhale peaches, clouds, harvest grain and swaying timbers. I lie awake for 20 minutes or so until Morning Edition fills the room with 6 a.m. sounds and begins to stir her. She snuggles close, resting her head on my right arm and whispers, "Just a few more minutes."

Because it takes me so much longer to do so many things, I'm driven to devour mornings, but I lie there content to listen to the latest Israel-Palestinian genocides, drifting in and out of a semi-sleep myself. Sometimes while she dozes, I lie there in the quiet morning and I consider the mystery to me that is my wife. But my reality, and ours, soon prompts me to gently nudge her from her mattinata nirvana.

Again, she sighs, "One more minute," which is really five or ten. The second or third nudge and "Sweetie, we've got a lot of things to do," usually does it. She awakens, flitting a kiss on my cheek followed by a froggy "buon giorno." Out of bed, the toilet for her, urinal for me. Sitting on the side of the bed, she slowly raises my legs above my head for my morning backstretch. Then, with my knees bent, she holds my feet and ankles firmly against the mattress while I huff and puff 20 partial sit-ups. Depending on the season, she slides over my rear a bathing suit or sweat pants, moves my feet and knees over the side of the bed, grabs my wrists and helps me to a sitting position on the bed's edge.

With a bear-hug embrace, as I breathe in the familiar scent between her soft breasts, she transfers me to the wheelchair. We're off to the kitchen. I then breakfast, if I have an early appointment, or read while she feeds the cats and waters the potted plants.

Then back to the bathroom. Another bear-hug embrace transfers me to the shower bench. While I'm brushing my teeth, she's putting aside the clothes I'll wear. I am like many people with disabilities in that my whole life is written as legibly on my clothing as a homeless vagrant. Anyone who looks at my odd clothing can see my autobiography as clearly as if it were written there on parchment. Ah, but that's another story.

Coming into the shower, she picks up the telephone showerhead and hoses my body from head to toe. Then, bar of soap in hand, she lathers my chest, neck, shoulders, and under arms; and next comes calves, thighs and all 'round and on my male parts, making sure they're lathered thick. At this point, I'm always torn between what feels better: her sudsing ministrations to my scalp or cock and balls. That ten second sleepless dream gets doused as soon as she starts hosing down all of the suds and foam. With an impish twinkle, she makes sure I don't start enjoying things too much. I have to pay something for making her get up at this ungodly hour.

I'm transferred to the wheelchair where she dries the rest of me with special care given to the private places where the sun doesn't shine. I raise my butt to help her slide on my bikini shorts and then its socks, shirt, pants, and shoes. I stand at her desk while she finishes adjusting my trousers and wheeling my power wheelchair up to my behind so that I can sit and get out of her hair for a while.

Daniela almost has to lift me. She's 57 now and several years ago had a tough bout with sciatica for four months, requiring injections into a herniated disc. My condition is hard on her and ages her faster than usual.

My schedule varies from day to day; I could be out or at home with clients, consulting, coaching, volunteering, or doing what I do on the computer, the telephone, or whatever. She, on the other hand, gardens, makes beds, washes and irons, opens mail, cleans vegetables, cooks, pays bills, volunteers with a homeless dining room and, periodically, gets her hair done and a pedicure. She does sometimes let the telephone take messages so that she can take an afternoon nap.

Around seven in the evening, we sit down for a god-awful-good dinner she's fixed. It can be as simple as spaghetti, mozzarella cheese, and a tossed salad, but the spaghetti sauce is homemade, the mozzarella bought fresh, and the salad from vegetables grown in her garden. Often, dinner's an elaborate work of art. Always it's a loving feast. While I am winding down my day, reading, watching the tube, or vegetating, with or without music, she's cleaning up the dishes and the pots and pans and doesn't start her R&R for another hour.

Something after 10 p.m., we head towards sleepy room. The bed gets turned down, Jay Leno turned on and both of us undressed by you know who. Then, I usually transfer to the pot to poop. Poop successful, she carefully cleans my bottom, helps me transfer back to the wheelchair. I rinse with Listerine, pop two Tylenols and plop, face down, my torso on the bed while she grabs my legs and lifts them up behind me. As if I weren't much bigger than the kitty cat who sleeps at the foot of our bed, she helps me flip around on my back and move up onto the pillow just right. She crawls in beside me. Minutes later, Leno and lights are silenced.

Oftentimes sleep suffocates us. Sometimes, her lips meet mine, our tongues dance. She moves each breast to my mouth so I can devour one and caress and squeeze the other with my crippled hands. Her secret lips are given me to kiss and inhale. She moves her full Italian thighs onto and all the way down my beam. Crystal beads of sweat dawn between her breasts, as she rhythmically rocks and consumes, illogical now, eyes disappear into our heads, breathing halts, whimpers. The night's silence is broken. We kiss, as we began, like children with a crush. Sleep comes. Kitty cat's purr caresses the night.

> In the beginning
> a big bang created earth's soil
> an orchid scents, sways, sings.

Gazing out at the unhurried but effortless pirouetting of the copper wind sculpture in our backyard patio, my most recent physical checkup began playing. *Do the wheels of injustice circle with the same faithful assurance as our wind-kissed sculpture?*

◆   ◆   ◆

"Hi, Ken, how're you doing?"

"I'm still breathing, Bill."

"Well, that's good. Why don't you follow me down the hall to the usual room? Ah, here we are. Let's see your chart. Anything new or different since you were last in? Has the arthritis been stable?"

"Same ol' pains from the arthritis. They're always there."

"Are you still taking only Tylenol for pain?"

"Ya, just Tylenol. No anti-inflammatories for me. Not after that duodenal ulcer business in '82."

"If the pain gets really rough, you might think about trying Celecoxib, this new super aspirin. It seems to be working with many patients and doesn't have aspirin's gastrointestinal side effects."

"You know me, Bill. I'll hold off as long as I can."

"Your capacity to live with pain always amazes me, Ken. I wish some of my other patients had some of your thick hide. I'll send Daniela in to help you get undressed and then the nurse will do your EKG. I'll be back after that."

"The EKG looks as good as a twenty-year-old's. Here, let me help you sit up. There. Are you balanced, comfortable, sitting on the edge of the table?"

"Yeah, I'm okay, Bill."

"Okay, good. When I shut off the lights, look in the direction of that photo so I can examine your eyes. Now look to the right over there. Fine. Any trouble with your eyes or hearing?"

"The hearing's fine, but the last time I had my eyes checked I had to notch up my reading glasses."

"Gettin' old like me, eh, Ken?"

"Have I told you to go to hell lately?"

"No, but we're all getting there. There's only so far away from your face you can hold a newspaper."

"Shit, tell me about it. Especially with my bent arms."

"Your ears are normal, no heavy wax. Let's take a look at the blood pressure. 120 over 70. God, you've got good blood pressure. Must be Daniela's Italian food."

"At least something works right."

"Okay, let's lay you back down again so I can examine your prostate."

"Your chance to get even, eh?"

"Let's say it's one of the fringes of the job. Well, now, your prostate is normal size. What did the urologist say last year?"

"He said everything checked out okay, no tumors or infections. And he said its size was normal, too, especially for a guy my age. He gave me Urised to help reduce the frequency, but it dried me up and made it harder to empty my bladder completely. I asked him if there was any herb or natural substance I could try, instead and he said that saw palmetto had helped many of his patients. But he said I'd have to take it 45 to 60 days before noticing a difference. I tried it and after a couple of months it was helping, without the drying out of the Urised. But I still have to go more frequently than 20 years ago."

"Welcome to the other club. Anything else goin' on?"

"Nothin' much else, except I'm still pretty stressed. The money situation hasn't gotten any better, but we're surviving. A couple of years back, when my insurance made me a part of an HMO, I thought I'd try getting them to okay you as my primary care doctor. What a joke! They said you weren't eligible and, besides, 'all of their primary care physicians were certified,' implying you weren't."

"That's a crock. I'm one of the members of the board that certifies physicians in Arizona."

"I know that, Bill. It's just more HMO bullshit. Anyway, I thought I'd give a stab at using the primary care physician they'd assigned me for my annual check-ups. I rather liked Dr. Hoshiwara. His office was about a mile from my house and, in a pinch, I could go with my motorized wheelchair. As you know, Hoshiwara did my checkup once. Then the HMO canceled his contract and assigned me a new doctor way the hell over in north Scottsdale.

"I called them, saying it was ludicrous and bad medicine moving me from physician to physician. Especially considering my long history of severe medical problems. Having to continuously re-educate a new doctor endangered my health, especially in emergencies. Some asshole, high-school dropout at the other end of the phone, said I could choose another doctor from their 'approved' list, but neither you nor Hoshiwara were on it.

"I then asked the son-of-a-bitch if Prudential could at least put your name on my medical insurance card, instead of the primary care physician *they* assigned me. I told him that if I was in an accident and couldn't speak, I'd want the paramedics or whomever to contact the doctor that knew intimately my illness and history. 'Sorry,' he said, 'Prudential just couldn't do that.' So I bought a Medic Alert medallion to hang around my neck and had your name and phone number engraved on it. Hopefully, the paramedics will see that before the insurance card."

"You don't know the half of it, Ken. The HMOs are destroying medicine. They don't care about good medical practice, just making money. You heard the lady coughing in the room next door, I'm sure. She's in her thirties and six months pregnant. She has a high fever and strep throat. Instead of letting us do her throat culture today in our lab, her HMO wants her to go to their laboratory, which can't see her until tomorrow. Every additional day that she's left untreated puts her and her baby that much more at risk. It's even stupid because they'll probably end up paying more than if they'd let me test her here in the first place. And that's only a fraction of the HMO crap I put up with daily. Those high-school dropouts you dealt with on the phone are the same people making the day-to-day medical decisions, not the doctors."

"You know, Bill, in Italy and the rest of Western Europe, where they have that *awful* socialized medicine, you're still allowed to choose your own doctor. Do you have to wait sometimes two or three months for elective surgery? Yeah, big deal! But how much do we wait and wait with our HMOs?"

"Don't even get me started on that subject, Ken. I can tell you hair-raising incidents where people have died because they were refused emergency care at some hospitals. And it was mostly the HMOs that dictated the policies of those offending hospitals. It's still no excuse, but it's what healthcare's become. I'm glad I'm retiring in a few years.

"Anyway, for an old guy you look great. When I get the results of your blood work back in a few days, I'll call you. But I expect that'll look good, too. Tell Daniela to keep giving you that good Italian food, just eat a bit less. You don't want to get too heavy. You remember the actor-director Orson Welles. His doctor told him to stop having intimate dinners for four, unless there were three other people.

"And don't worry about your medical insurance or money. You'll always be able to come here."

"Thanks, Bill, for everything. You're a good guy for an old fart."

"So are you."

To tell you the truth, I know that a doctor's job is to heal, not to maintain. If doctors can't solve a problem, they're frustrated. There's no room for some of the crazy things people want to do to feel alive. I jumped out of an airplane in 2001 to do a freefall celebrating my 60th birthday. Doctors don't know how to deal with maintaining health in weird disabilities like mine when I want to go out and do something crazy like a freefall.

Then there's the maintaining of a marriage. When I came up on 25 years of marriage, it shocked me that my union had survived so long, given the disappointments that people have in each other, themselves, life, and how alone we all feel at times. Despite everything, as Jean Paul Sartre said from his existentialist view of life, we are all basically alone. Who can ever climb inside our skin and see life as we see it? Nobody!

> Frigid night, me, and
> lonely science fiction brute
> yearning for spring girl.
>
> Mountains not climbed,
> not even toes and feet splashing,
> dancing on icy creeks.

Ancient Udine
at distant temple pew
kneeling devotion.

Chestnut eyes sparkling
magical symphonies while
cute mouth whispers all.

Prayers coming true,
but still with conflict's battle
before both say yes.

Nature's seasons shift
from snuggled in Frosty's bed,
summer barbecues.

Fighting families,
descending company fortunes,
lawsuits, money flows.

Acetic winds greet
us with dusty, ruby skies
peppery comfort.

An apprentice's
international schooling;
a father passes.

Fine wines endure life
becoming God's sweetest peach
as did lovely dulcet.

Fruit orchard harvested
honey, greenbacks run easy as
a software gamble.

Father and sister
return where P.J. winter sleeps
crystal rain, old leaves.

A fig tree succumbs
witnessing unhappiness
insecurity growls.

A mother falls ill
to the stars a brother flies
flowers groom backyard.

Kitties born, surgeons
cut flesh necklaces, another
mom joins heaven's wait.

So, I cannot fail
loving this sunshine, sapphire,
still bride, Daniela.

◆ ◆ ◆

My dear mother died in 1995. In her last years, she not only got a kick out of playing Scrabble with us and other friends and family, but she was a whiz at it. A typical afternoon might involve lunch, and sipping on a glass of wine while playing the word game. With her drink and tummy full, she frequently became a little sleepy and would doze off. We'd wake her for her turn and, without flinching, she'd quickly put down a word worth 60 points or so, and doze off again. It would make me and everyone else playing with her sit there dumbfounded! As age and medical conditions caught up with her, she required more and more frequent blood transfusions. Finally one day in 1994, she said she didn't want any more transfusions. A close friend, who also was frequently her caregiver, urged her to at least have one last transfusion to take her through the Christmas season, and she consented. She died peacefully, surrounded by much of her family, at age 86 on February 21, 1995.

Age was catching up with me, too. Now this doesn't happen every day but it happened. At least it got me out of my jailer, the wheelchair, and gave me something to write about.

> So, let me see if I've got this straight. You were born in Oakland, California, in 1941, on or about 5:45 a.m., April 22nd, the Year of the Snake. You got all crippled up by a nasty dose of systemic juvenile rheumatoid arthritis—"Still's Disease," to docs in the know—when you were two. The good ol' docs told your folks you'd be dead by the time you were three. You sure fooled the bastards!
>
> In less than two weeks you'll be 60! (This was in 2001). Six decades and counting! There you are, a gnat's ass over four feet tall, crippled as a drunken Methuselah, curled up and natty as any snake. And still horny—and alive. The quintessential exemplar of the fact that God, indeed, has a weird sense of humor.
>
> As I understand it, you won't be content with your usual celebratory pleasures: ice-cold Absolut vodka martinis, a sumptuous Italian feast, and getting your itty-bitty brains fucked inside out. No, not good enough.
>
> You're going to take that chunky, crippled ass of yours and hurl it out of some stupid, damn airplane at 13,000 feet. From there you're goin' to plunge—*freefall*, they call it—8,000 to 10,000 feet, in less than a minute. About as long as it'll take you to say one Our Father and three Hail Marys. Supposedly, a parachute will then open and gently bring your sorry ass down to terra firma. Maybe still in one piece. Maybe. If you're lucky.
>
> But, why not? You're 60. And you'll get a big fuckin' picture and certificate to prove you did it? So you can hang it on your wall? And you think this will prove something?

Matt, my tandem parachutist, tightens up one last time my pretzeled torso against his chest and asks if my clear plastic goggles are secured just right over my eyes.

I nod yes for my shallow voice cannot compete with the rushing wind of a half-opened fuselage.

Flying at an altitude of 13,000 feet.

As Matt crouches at the edge of the plane's gaping door he shouts one last instruction into my ear:

"As we freefall, don't let the wind overcome you—just breathe normally through your mouth and nose."

With thumb up,
    Me attached,
        Matt jumps

From
The
Plane!

Whistling winds sculpt my nutty-putty cheeks into one deeply-etched, ear-to-ear happy face, as the pastel green, yellow, brown patchwork quilt of earth.

For 50 seconds, what's below rushes towards me in slow motion so I can touch it with the tip of my finger.

"When the 'chute opens in about 10 seconds, you'll feel a slight jerk," Matt says loudly into my ear.

Whoooosh,

Snaps the parachute and Matt and I are reeled back into time and space

A very long fraction of a second and the universe snaps.

Another shutter open/close.

We are floating like silent lilies on a summer pond.

Then, we bank to the left.

"Look over there!" says Matt, in barely a whisper, "That's Phoenix!" As we circle and then bank to the right, Matt, pointing straight ahead, says, "Just beyond the Valley at the foot of that mountain lies Tucson."

Earth's pastels have now succumbed to the intense light and heat of land's surface, transforming into the radiant, hot desert colors of sandy orange, cactus yellow, and cotton green.

"Do you see the two rectangular shaped patches of green on either side of the airfield below?" asks Matt, nonchalantly.

And, as he points to the left, Matt continues, "Over there, on that green patch with the gray circle in the middle is where we're going to land." The earth is moving in faster now, but rather like a spectacularly grand, floating roller coaster.

As the loose gravel of our target zooms backward to meet outstretched feet, the only sounds slicing open the silence are the chirps from the birds flying in with us and the "Bravos" and "Right ons" and "Awesomes" of awaiting ground crew.

Nothing on the face of the earth, above or below it changes.

Babies are born, old people pass away, lovers hold hands and kiss.

Hearts are broken. Fortunes are wasted. Jobs are lost.

Health turns into disease, illness.

People steal. People hate. People kill. People destroy. People lie. People die.

A golden harvest moon lights early autumn nights.

There, see the morning dew sparkle like ice against the rosebud's tip.

The sweat from summer's noonday sun garnishes

The embrace of lovers lost to each other.

A host of birds fly from the clouds,
Filling mountain rivers with dancing fish,
A gray-headed veined pebble laughs at me.
Does God exist? What about Heaven?
Should I care now about death,
Afterlife, becoming
Ashes?

I am only an infinitely small part of a magnificently grand universe—
Vivaldi's, *Four Seasons*.

26

"Call No Man Happy Until He is Dead!"

Mirage: An optical illusion caused by light on objects seen through differing densities of air.

Am I happy? Some days and some moments, I am extremely happy. But there are so many things that make me unhappy.

I think of Daniela more often than of anyone else in the world. I'd have liked to have her for a sweetheart, wife, mother or sister—anything that a woman can be to a man. The idea of her is part of my mind. She influences my likes and dislikes, my tastes, everything. She is part of me. I've spent all my married years trying to love her, please her, understand her, be part of her and communicate with her. But I still have much to learn.

I did not realize, for example, how it changes the nature of a relationship when you have to be the ultimate caregiver for your lover. My wife tells me that her lack of interest in sex during these last years has not been lack of love. She said, "I'm so exhausted when I go to bed. And I'm getting older, you know."

Of course, my wife must lift my weight and bend in ways that prematurely age her and her back. It breaks my heart that I hurt those who love me most and that I love most, those who care for me in more ways than one.

Speaking of caregivers, I could write a whole chapter or a whole book on them and how important they are to those with disabilities. But, I'm unhappy to think we have made our government into a caregiver, albeit an impersonal and unsympathetic caregiver. For example, Medicare and some private insurers may provide a powered wheelchair so people who can't walk, like moi, can be mobile. But they don't pay for a bench or shower chair for taking a shower. I'm trying to design a mobile shower chair since I can no longer stand in a shower. I'm trying to make it into a manual push chair that I could also travel with, so I can use it in showers and elsewhere in and out of our house. Oh, and I am trying to do it for around a thousand bucks, retail. No easy task.

In fact, while I'm on the subject of caregivers, let me add that from my early 20s onward, I required the part-time or full-time help of a personal care assistant (PCA) to complete many of my activities of daily living, including bathing and dressing. To this day, there are times when I just wish with all my might that I didn't have to depend on the assistance of others for my self care. Ah, to be able to shit, shower, shave, and dress unassisted and then walk out into the day all by my lonesome. What an ecstatic moment that would be if it were indeed humanely doable. But it isn't.

On the other hand, I must also say that having a body and a life which requires the day-to-day assistance of a personal caregiver is a treasure that's impossible to put a value on. I have learned so very much from each and every one of the persons who assisted me. They have been people of different races, sexes, ages, cultures, religions, and economic backgrounds. Each and every one has had an impact on me, but some more so than others. Lasting friendships have evolved from these relationships, some others I long ago lost contact with and a few have since passed away. Certainly, when a caregiver cleans up the bowel movements, dresses the pressure sores and bathes your most intimate parts, it's almost impossible not to develop a mutual friendship and respect for each other.

The caregiver or personal care assistant can and usually does consist of multiple roles, including that of mother, brother, nurse, confessor, confessee and, in some cases, even lover. The job is physically and emotionally taxing and is rarely, if ever paid the value it's worth. It's also a very intimate relationship, with caregiver and person cared for developing an interdependency that's similar to the relationship between spouses or parent and child. When the primary caregiver is your spouse, as has been the case with me for the past 30 years, the relationship side of care-giving becomes even more difficult.

There's absolutely no way I can adequately thank the many wonderful people who have been there for me when I needed them. You have all given me so much, including new and wonderful ways to see, hear, taste, feel and experience the world in which we live. I hope in some small way I have touched, assisted you, too. The first names that follow represent some of the incredible people who assisted me over past 40 years. My 63-year-old brain doesn't permit me to recall the names of all of you.

"Anita," Lolita, Bill, Bruce the Beard, Wayne, Helen, Egidio, Marcia, Pasquale, Joseph, Susan, Steven, Bruno, Glauco, Guillermo, Pat, Ruth, Dave,

Sharon, "the Bird Lady," Warren, Ray, Abel. And Daniela—my arms and legs and heart.

But I'll return to some of the things that I'm not happy with. There is the "venerable" AARP, which doesn't really want to associate itself with seniors who have disabilities. In fact, "disability" is one of those no-no concepts when talking about the "active-dynamic-virile" senior lifestyle. Their "preferred" image is your typically physically active 75-year-old senior who looks 50 and has the body of a 25 year-old. Hey, I and 10 million other old farts want to be that, Babe! Yet as people age, they have trouble bending, walking, hearing, seeing, and even thinking. And they also lose strength and equilibrium in a variety of ways. The AARP could have been a spokesperson and advocate for *all* seniors but they chose not to do so, which makes me unhappy.

If you think I am feeding you some curdled cheese, just ask someone involved in the AAPD—the American Association of Persons with Disabilities—about how much cooperation they get from, or meaningful political action they are able to coordinate with, the AARP, and they'll likely say little or nothing.

The American Automobile Association (AAA) also seemed like an organization that could be helpful to seniors with disabilities who have the time in retirement to travel about the country. Seniors are looking for hotels, cruise ships, and destination venues that can accommodate their needs. AAA provides members with ratings according to amenities and prices and other things. Thus, one disability group that I worked with wanted to train AAA personnel to correctly evaluate hotels, etc. so that they would know how to rate them for accessibility. The decision makers at AAA weren't interested.

Now, years later, when a senior goes to AAA, he can receive help with planning a cruise on the right ship, or staying at the right hotel and even get advice on available price ranges, amenities, distance from tourist sites, breakfast availability, keeping pets, and even disabled access. The trouble is that the information on disabled access is mostly minimal, uninformed and frequently just plain wrong.

Speaking of AAA, they are involved with transportation. Specifically, AAA has been marketing itself for decades as the nation's leading organization which provides towing and aid when you are on the road and your motor vehicle breaks down or is involved in an accident. However, 99.99% of AAA's towing trucks are not equipped to handle and aid AAA members with disabilities who travel and also use wheelchairs and scooters, but become stuck somewhere in the middle of no man's land, like on Highway I-8, 75 miles east of Yuma, Arizona, or broken down 15 miles from home at 12 midnight. I'm not happy that AAA has limited their helpfulness when it would be so easy to be in the forefront of a movement to truly help all motor vehicle travelers.

Disabled people must learn to ask lots of questions. There are things available if you know to ask for them. But there are still many things that are not available and you must learn to fight for them. The ol' squeaky wheel gets the grease.

For example, as people develop vision problems, wouldn't it be helpful if restaurant menus were in a bold type font size 14 to 18, instead of the usual 10 or 12, and in light print? The publishing industry wants 10 or 12 for books, but some books (usually popular fiction) are now being printed in 14 or 16 large print. Product warnings—even those for potentially dangerous drugs—are legal as long as they are printed, so they usually get the smallest size print of all, about 4 or maybe 6. Phone books are 6 and newspapers are 8 so seniors turn more and more to television and/or radio for their news and information and directory assistance for their phone numbers.

You can get free directory assistance from your phone company if you have a legitimate disability, but you must ask for it and usually must provide proof of your disability. However, neither cable nor satellite dish companies offer a discounted rate for seniors and/or people with disabilities, regardless of their dependency on the broadcast media as their source for news and information.

It's very shortsighted on corporate America's side, too. A satellite company which markets to limited income persons and families at a nicely reduced rate would most likely gain a very sizable market niche in the process. This fight deserves being fought because such a pricing change would provide a double win for both customers and corporations involved. Those in corporate leadership could enlarge their customer base while enhancing customer satisfaction and loyalty.

In some ways, Europe now allows for disabilities better than the U.S., but when they began their journey, they still had the tendency to make decisions for you, as if you were not quite up to it. They didn't want much input. From what I have observed, they do not involve the community of people with disabilities nearly as much as they should in the decision-making process. For example, some of their airports, especially those in northern Europe, were among the first in the world to have adequately sized, unisex bathrooms that also provided good disabled access.

Their initial attempts to provide a few accessible rooms in some of their hotels produced results that were uneven and mostly provided less than satisfactory access. Here again, the mentality was that people with disabilities never traveled without a companion or nurse. Because of the recent (in comparison with the

United States) but rapidly growing involvement of the disability community in Europe in their access issues, much better accessibility is now provided. And they are gaining on the U.S. in some areas such as respite care for family caregivers and the dying. If there is a lesson here for the disabled, seniors, all of us—it is involvement.

If we are to be a democracy, we must represent the people, all people. We need good debate on all kinds of issues. The election process causes politicians to promise so many things that it becomes impossible for them to deliver on everything, so our electorate becomes disillusioned, deteriorates, and votes progressively less and less. However, the big problem with not voting in a democracy is that we are not holding our elected officials accountable—and democracy is all about accountability.

Even voting can be a problem, as Arizona Senator John McCain pointed out in 1999. He joined with Senator John Kerry to introduce the bill, "Improving Accessibility to Voting for Disabled and Elderly Americans." He noted that millions of disabled and elderly voters are faced with too many obstacles and said, "This is simply wrong. The vote is the heart and soul of our democracy."

Their bill established minimum guidelines for accessibility at polling places, allowed blind or visually impaired people to vote privately with technological assistance, and instilled enforcement to address the lack of accommodation by more than 20,000 polling places which are currently not accessible.

What would make me happier? Well, for one thing, that everyone—even those extreme far, far right and far, far left wacko-types—voted during each election. McCain pointed out when introducing his bill that voter turnout in the 1998 election was the lowest since 1942, only 36% of eligible voters participated.

Let me briefly consider health care, which I know intimately as a consumer. I believe that universal health care, especially single-payer universal health care, is a concept which has been demonized far too long by those in the health-care industry who are more interested in short-term profits than the long-term health of a nation.

The problems I have seen in health care make me feel that our nation needs to have an honest, prejudice-free dialogue about health care, including single-payer universal health care. If health care were provided to all Americans, independent of age, disability, or employment status:

> 1. The unemployed or laid off worker would be free to seek employment without having to worry about losing or reacquiring health-care coverage—it would always be there.

2. Labor mobility would be greatly enhanced for both the employer and employee.

3. Employers, as well as employees, would have a fixed, predictable cost for health-care coverage, similar to what now exists for unemployment insurance and Social Security.

4. Both the cost of administration and the total cost for health care as a percentage of gross domestic product (GDP) would be significantly reduced with a single-payer type of universal health-care system. (In the past two decades, health care costs as a percentage of GDP have increased 36%).

5. The debilitating worry and stress of not having health-care coverage would no longer be a burden for American families, as well as the corporations and businesses that hire them and/or lay them off when times get tough.

6. Universal health care would improve considerably our nation's health in vital areas like pre-natal care and infant mortality; the battle against infectious and preventable diseases; preventing or reducing the impact of the diseases and maladies of aging through early intervention; improving significantly our readiness to handle large, community-wide disasters brought on by new disease strains such as bird flu, catastrophes of nature or acts of terrorism.

Many in the health-care professions already know what quality universal health care could provide in the way of benefits to our country. It has been conservatively estimated that the implementation of a universal health-care system would result in approximately $300 billion in savings from what we have now. Furthermore, universal healthcare means that the United States would no longer have 40 plus million of its citizens who have no health care coverage at all and millions of other Americans who have inadequate coverage.

Senator McCain took up another issue in 1998. He learned that almost two-thirds of the 3.4 million children who were Medicaid-eligible and were uninsured were Hispanic and close to three-fourths of those children live in the South and the West. He said in a press release on April 27, 1998,

> I am deeply concerned about the children in our country who are currently lacking health-insurance coverage. More than 3 million children qualify for Medicaid health care coverage but are not enrolled, thus going without impor-

tant primary and preventive health care which is crucial for their healthy growth and development.

I support his efforts and agree with his goals but I would go one step further. There is no doubt that we can come up with a vastly improved health care delivery system if we demand it from our elected officials. It is up to us to tell our representatives and senators that we expect them to work diligently and in a bipartisan manner, in making quality health care for our families a reality. The health of every citizen cannot be separated from "life, liberty and the pursuit of happiness."

Thankfully, other politicians are recognizing these problems and these issues will not divide people along party lines. I was heartened by Senator Edward Kennedy's comments on January 16, 2003, about universal health care:

> There is no issue more important to the well-being of American families than access to high quality, affordable health care. While our ultimate goal remains universal health security for every American citizen, we can and will take smaller steps along the way to bring us closer to that goal.
>
> Yet, 41 million Americans now have no health insurance at all. Over the course of a year, 30 million more will lack coverage for an extended period. It is unacceptable that any American is uninsured. It is shameful that 41 million Americans are uninsured. And it is intolerable that the number of uninsured is now rising again and, if we do nothing, could reach more than 52 million by the end of the decade...
>
> One other part of the problem is the mushrooming cost of prescription drugs. One powerful engine to control costs is competition from generic drugs. Generic drugs account for 42% of all prescriptions, but account for only 8% of drug spending. When a generic competitor to a brand name drug is available, it typically cuts the cost to the consumer by half or more. But in recent years, some drug companies have manipulated the law to keep generic competitors off the market long after their patents have expired.
>
> It is time to close the loopholes that allow drug companies to exploit patients by blocking generic competition. It is time to regulate direct-to-consumer advertising more effectively, to assure that the freedom recently granted companies to advertise their products serves a useful public health purpose.

Not too long ago, Senator Orrin Hatch proposed legislation to deregulate all supplements sold in health-food stores and supermarkets. The public was crying out for the freedom to choose alternative medicines, including food supplements, vitamins, and herbs to treat their ills and diseases. So, for supporting that freedom of choice I supported the effort of Senator Orrin Hatch. This legislation eventually was passed by Congress and signed into law. However, where I disagree with the final bill that was signed into law was in the area of product integrity control. As is already done throughout most of Europe, Japan, and other industrialized countries, the FDA in the United States should certify herbal and other alternative medicine products as to their purity, potency and should require warnings where necessary, but it doesn't. Senator Hatch's legislation neglects this area of consumer protection completely. Rather than giving the consumer more choices the uncertainty as to product and content actually takes them away.

Military and/or national service is another area of national importance which, I believe, is not as equitable as it should be. I can hear you saying, "But Ken Jacuzzi never served in the military." That's exactly my point. It would certainly be in keeping with the spirit of national unity to encourage the disabled to participate in diverse areas of national service need.

Presently, we have an all-volunteer military, but the consequence of such a system is that those of us who have the least number of educational and economic options—the poorest among us—generally are those who join the military.

That fact by itself is not necessarily good or bad. However, military service to one's country is something that should not be borne by just one segment of the population. It is particularly unfair during times of conflict and war. Furthermore, the all-volunteer military makes the decision to go to war much easier, since war's prospects won't directly involve "me," just "them." Again, I think our present-day system tends to polarize the people of our country rather than unify them.

I think a viable, more equitable alternative would be a system requiring national military service of every physically and mentally fit young man and woman for a period of one to two years as well as many disabled individuals. Please note that I have combined the words "national" and "military" into one service, giving the individual the option to choose a non-combatant role when serving the United States.

I believe that if we are all required to serve our country for a period of time, we will witness many resulting benefits. An increased sense of shared responsibilities, purpose and national unity has been mentioned. We will also increase markedly our nation's capability of responding to major areas of need whether ongoing or brought on suddenly by disasters such as hurricanes, earthquakes, or fires.

I guess if someone were to suddenly anoint me "The Big Kahuna" or "Chief Mucky-Muck" of the U.S. government, I'd strongly stress to legislators the vital importance of passing laws that are essential, not frivolous, and that are created through a process of attentive listening to all sides and with due respect given to all concerned. An example of this is crazy drug laws that claim *any* drug use will lead to addiction and danger to self and others. That doesn't mean that we should not disagree, even quite heatedly, when appropriate. The key is maintaining respect of one another in the process, sticking to the issues at hand and refusing to descend to name calling and cheap shots which, after all, end up only diminishing both sides and not accomplishing a damn thing. But, I'm not Chief Mucky-Muck, so I'll just let it go for what it's worth and get on with the ending of this book.

Finally, I hope that I was able to convey in this book some of the very large fears, uncertainties, conflicts, even pandering—as well as a few of the upside possibilities that those with disabilities have to confront as they grow up and mature. I think the other remaining item on the top of my to-do list includes doing more of whatever I can to help adults and children with disabilities, and their parents, families, friends and caregivers better understand that what is going on, what's happening to them, is part of their lives. And while it may stink like unholy hell at times, it is and will be okay.

In fact, if I could give young people with disabilities a little advice, I would say "Remember to take no stinkin' badges in your quest to live your own life and be yourself." Don't try to be so brave that you don't get the help you need. Hopefully, your parents will reflect on what I just said, also.

Well, that's it. This is the caboose of this train. I can't add more right now because I've got stuff to do. Perhaps the reflections of a couple of other folks might help in wrapping up this book and shedding a bit more insight into the life of yours truly. One is a gospel according to Luke (no, it's not the story of the prodigal—wasteful—son, although that parable could also apply to me, too). The other is a poem written by my Dad, Candido, during the last years of his life.

If, after having read the very last word of this book, you are still a bit hazy, well, join the club. Given the situation, I don't know about you, but I think I know what I'm going to do. I am going to take my honey out for a romantic dinner and maybe....

◆ ◆ ◆

The following is the gospel according to Luke: 12:13–34.

> Someone in the crowd said to him, Teacher, tell my brother to share the inheritance with me.
> He replied to him, Friend, who appointed me as your judge and arbitrator?

Then he said to the crowd, Take care to guard against all greed, for though one may be rich, one's life does not consist of possessions.

Then he told them a parable. There was a rich man whose land produced a bountiful harvest.

He asked himself, What shall I do, for I do not have space to store my harvest?

And he said, This is what I shall do: I shall tear down my barns and build larger ones. There I shall store all my grain and other goods and I shall say to myself, Now as for you, you have so many good things stored up for many years, rest, eat, drink, be merry!

But God said to him, You fool, this night your life will be demanded of you; and the things you have prepared, to whom will they belong?

Thus will it be for the one who stores up treasure for himself but is not rich in what matters to God.

He said to (his) disciples; Therefore I tell you, do not worry about your life and what you will eat, or about your body and what you will wear. For life is more than food and the body more than clothing. Notice the ravens: they do not sow or reap; they have neither storehouse nor barn, yet God feeds them.

How much more important are you than birds? Can any of you by worrying add a moment to your lifespan? If even the smallest things are beyond your control, why are you anxious about the rest?

Notice how the flowers grow. They do not toil or spin. But I tell you, not even Solomon in all his splendor was dressed like one of them.

If God so clothes the grass in the field that grows today and is thrown into the oven tomorrow, will he not much more provide for you, O you of little faith?

As for you, do not seek what you are to eat and what you are to drink, and do not worry any more.

All the nations of the world seek for these things, and your Father knows that you need them.

Instead, seek his kingdom, and these other things will be given you besides.

Do not be afraid any longer, little flock, for your Father is pleased to give you the kingdom.

Sell your belongings and give alms. Provide money bags for yourselves and do not wear out an inexhaustible treasure in heaven that no thief can reach nor moth destroy.

For where your treasure is, there also will your heart be.

In closing, this is the poem my father wrote. It's about coming to America, the fortune he made, the fears and disappointments he experienced and the homeland he left behind.

La Terra Mia—My Homeland

Italian

Quel bel mattino di sole,
sulla mia vita splendeva.

Cuando dal genitor udii,
andar lontano io dovevo.

Terra dei primi natali lasciai,
senza volonta mia.

Io penso ancor di quel di,
che il treno mi porto via.

Ero giovane con molto
spirito e impaziente.

Quasi senza sculoa, sapevo
poco o niente.

Emigrai al di la del mar
in un' altra terra.

Dove trovai fortuna,
pane e Guerra.

Passaron moliti anni
di tanta nostalgia.

Per il mio paese nativo
dov'e l'origin mia.

Il tramontar del sol di nostra vita
e in vedetta.

Nella mia terra tornai
con la mia cara vecchietta.

Aspettando, contemplando
il nostro passato,

Per un riposo eterno
chissa se sara meritato.

Candido Jacuzzi

English

That beautiful sunny morning,
on my life was shining.

When from my father I heard,
I had to go far away.

I left the land where I was born
without any desire.

I still remember that day
when the train took me away.

I was young with much
spirit and impatience.

With little schooling, I knew
little or nothing.

I emigrated to the other side of the sea
in another land.

Where I found fortune,
bread and war.

Many years went by
with much homesickness.

For my native country
of my origin.

The sunset of our life
is on the outlook.

In my homeland I returned
with my dear old little woman.

Waiting, contemplating
our past.

For an eternal rest
who knows if it will be deserved.

Note the difference in just one of the stanzas from the above poem between Italian and Friulano (Furlan), which is not considered an Italian dialect, but a distinct language:

Italian: "Dove trovai fortuna, pane e Guerra."
Furlan: "Dula jo chata fortune, pan e vuere."
English: "Where I found fortune, bread and war."

Appendix A

RESOURCES

FINANCES:

Supplemental Security Income (SSI)

Supplemental Security Income (SSI) is a program administered by the Social Security Office. They pay monthly benefits to people with *limited income* and *limited resources*, who are "disabled, blind, or age 65 or older." Blind children or children with disabilities, as well as adults, can get SSI benefits.

As its name implies, Supplemental Security Income supplements a person's income up to a certain level. The level varies from one state to another and can go up every year based on cost-of-living increases.

Note: Once your income and/or personal assets reach a certain level (usually 2.5 times the poverty level or less) your ability as an adult to receive SSI income and benefits, including healthcare coverage, will, in most cases, soon disappear.

This is particularly problematical for adults who become disabled later in life after having worked for many years on a contractual basis. This kind of employment can often result in an insufficient number of "work" quarters, or trimesters, being paid into the Social Security system. Therefore, such employees or workers would not qualify for Social Security Disability Income (SSDI) until they have reached retirement age, usually 65 years of age or more. In the interval prior to retirement, which could be years or even decades, these disabled adult individuals will probably find themselves unqualified to receive either a Social Security income source and/or healthcare coverage.

Of course, if you are elected to the United States Congress and serve even just one term, you and your family are assured a lifetime pension income (adjusted by upward changes in the cost of living) and platinum-quality healthcare coverage.

The definition of "blind" in adults in Social Security disability programs means a central visual acuity of 20/200 or less in your better eye, even while you are wearing a correcting contact lens or glasses in that eye; or a limitation in the field of vision of your better eye so that you have a contraction of peripheral visual fields to 10 degrees from the point of fixation OR the widest diameter of your visual field subtends an angle no greater than 20 degrees.

An individual under age 18 is "disabled" if he/she has a medically determinable physical or mental impairment that results in marked and severe functional limitations and can be expected to result in death, or has lasted (and can be expected to last) for a continuous period of not less than 12 months. Again, the parent's income and assets are considered by the Social Security Administration in deciding if a child under 18 qualifies for SSI.

An adult over 18 is "disabled" if he/she has a medically determinable physical or mental impairment which results in the inability to engage in any substantial gainful activity and can be expected to result in death, or has lasted (or can be expected to last) for a continuous period of not less than 12 months.

When SSI states that it will pay benefits to those with limited income and/or resources, here is what they mean. "Limited income" includes money earned from work, received from other sources and free food, shelter or clothing. "Limited resources" includes cash/bank accounts, land, vehicles, personal property and life insurance. The SSI "limits" for resources that Social Security counts are these: Individual—$2,000, or Couple (two SSI eligible persons living together)—$3,000.

The Social Security disability insurance program for an average family is equivalent to a private disability insurance policy worth over $233,000. However, people need recent work to qualify for disability benefits. After age 30, a worker must have 20 credits (5 years) of work in the ten years before the disability started. In 2003, you earn one credit for every $890 in earnings, up to a maximum of four credits for the year. In 2004, that amount increased to $900.

Some people think that since their disability must be expected to last at least a year to qualify, they must wait a year to apply. Not true. You should apply for benefits as soon as you can. If you are approved, payments will begin after a five-month waiting period that starts with the month Social Security decides your disability began. You will receive benefits as long as your condition keeps you from working. Your case will be reviewed periodically to see if there is any improvement in your condition. If you still have a disability when you reach full retirement age, your disability benefit will be automatically converted to a retirement benefit of the same amount.

The list of impairments that Social Security considers to be disabling is contained in SSA Pub. No. 64-039, *Disability Evaluation Under Social Security.* This booklet is intended primarily for physicians and health professionals.

Unlike Social Security benefits, SSI benefits are not based on your prior work or a family member's prior work. In most states, SSI beneficiaries can get Medicaid (medical assistance) to pay for hospital stays, doctor bills, prescription drugs and other health costs. SSI beneficiaries may also be eligible for food stamps in every state except California. In some states, application for SSI benefits also serves as an application for food assistance.

Social Security (SS)

Social Security benefits are retirement benefits, calculated on your average earnings during a lifetime of work under the Social Security system. For most retirees, the 35 highest years of earning will be averaged. Social Security provides retirement benefits that last as long as you live and increase each year with increases in the cost of living. The Social Security Administration has estimated that these benefits are similar to a $354,000 insurance policy. You can receive an estimate of your potential monthly benefits by using their web site: http://www.ssa.gov/planners/faqs.htm.

Social Security Dependents benefits are payable to children under the age of 18 on the record of a parent who is collecting retirement or disability benefits from Social Security, or survivors benefits payable to children under the age of 18 on the record of a parent who has died. A child can continue to receive dependents or survivors benefits until age 19 if he/she is a full-time student in elementary or high school.

Social Security benefits for adults "disabled since childhood" require that an individual is the child of someone who gets Social Security retirement or disability benefits, or of someone who has died and that child must have a disability that began prior to age 22. It is considered a child's benefit because it is paid on the basis of a parent's Social Security earnings record.

Medicaid

Medicaid for employed people with disabilities (MEPD) allows persons with disabilities to work and continue to have access to medical assistance. To qualify, you must be "disabled." You are "disabled" if you receive Supplemental Security Income (SSI), Social Security Disability (SSD) benefits, or if you are eligible for

Medicare. You must be under age 65 and you must have earned income from employment or self-employment.

The monthly net family income must be less than 250% of the federal poverty level for your family size. (This level for a family size of one person is currently $1,846 per month). You will be required to pay a monthly premium when your monthly gross income is above 150% of the federal poverty level (currently $1,108). In addition, countable resources must be $12,000 or less for an individual and $13,000 or less for a couple.

If you make enough to pay a premium, you will be billed. The premium will be approximately $20 monthly if the gross income of the eligible person is $1123 to $1302. It continues to go up according to how much money you make. For example, if your gross income is $2021, you will pay a monthly Medicaid premium of about $110. If you make $2919 or above, your Medicaid premium may be about $201. In addition, these amounts can vary by state.

In the long run, Medicaid wants to help people with disabilities build their confidence that they can work, so they are not penalized as strongly as those without disabilities.

My Perspective on Social Security

The benefits for people with disabilities under Social Security are not insignificant and have in many cases not only preserved life, but helped create a better quality of life. However, there still remain many people with disabilities in the United States who have fallen through sizable cracks regulating Social Security and, consequently, receive neither income nor healthcare coverage benefits.

Furthermore, despite recent changes in Social Security regulations, such as the Ticket to Work program, which allows some individuals with disabilities to retain Medicare coverage if they go back to work, that option is unavailable to all disabled.

Additionally, other kinds of assistance provided under Medicaid (in Arizona it's called AHCCCS), such as Personal Care Assistants (PCAs), will no longer be provided to a person with a disability who goes back to work full time and begins earning a relatively small amount above minimum wage. It is the quintessential Catch-22 of disincentives for people with severe disabilities—the very people who cannot survive without the day-to-day help of a PCA—to seek employment full time.

Let's see, if Ms. Bunch gets a job full-time earning, let us say, $29,000, which is our state's average salary for teaching, she's going to need her PCA because she requires personal assistance with many of the activities of daily living. Now, however, Ms. Bunch is going to have to fully pay the PCA out of her own salary, which is over half of what her gross earnings would be.

Gee, Mabel, what would you do? Actually the problem is very serious and should not be taken lightly. Assuming Ms. Bunch represents most people with severe disabilities; she probably couldn't cover her expenses and would have to turn down the full-time teaching job. The Ticket to Work program is supposed to include provisions which take into account, at least somewhat, those costs that directly relate to a person's ability to sustain employment, However, with the exception of Medicare coverage, which can continue for a number of years after becoming employed, other benefits are quite limited, especially with respect to PCAs, and soon evaporate as a person's gross salary begins to reflect something more than entry-level responsibility.

I know of incidents where men and women with severe disabilities became so depressed over not being able to work because of benefits being lost that they committed suicide. The Ticket to Work program has addressed this but the problem is far from resolved. Such limited regulations are an excellent example of how government "bites off its nose to spite its face." Even under the hypothetical scenario that a severely disabled person becomes employed and will retain all prior benefits regardless of income, government coffers still benefit from the additional local, state, and federal taxes paid by the employed disabled person.

This problem goes back several generations to the creation of Social Security benefits for people with disabilities. The concept then was very simple: if you are severely disabled, you are too disabled to work and, therefore, you should be able to receive benefits under Social Security. The trouble is that while the Social Security system evolved, technology enabled many with severe disabilities to complete a university education and become qualified to fill important jobs. Jobs in architecture, science, engineering, marketing, teaching, finance...the list goes on. This is something that wasn't widely possible two or three decades ago.

I'll probably sound like a damned broken record but a quality universal healthcare system that truly covers everyone in this country would resolve the lion's share of these problems. Not only would universal healthcare be the most cost-effective solution, but it would also provide the most benefits to society, families, businesses and government. While universal health care does not automatically set to rest the problem regarding PCAs and similar issues for people with severe disabilities, it does create a framework that makes it much easier and less costly to create a sensible solution.

PRODUCTS/RESOURCES:

ABLEDATA, 8630 Fenton Street, Suite 930, Silver Spring, MD 20910; Tel: 1-800-227-0216. This is the name of a website where you can explore information on assistive technology and disability issues in general. It is a federally funded website of the U.S. Department of Education, operated by the National Institute on Disability and Rehabilitation Research (NIDRR). The website is: http://www.abledata.com/Site_2/Default.htm.

The database contains over 18,000 currently available products from over 2,000 different companies. Each product record contains a detailed description of the product as well as price, manufacturer and distributor information. You will find information on non-commercial prototypes, customized and one-of-a-kind products and do-it-yourself designs. You can also find listings for about 9,000 products that are no longer available for sale.

You can search the database by keyword, product type, company or brand name. There are also consumer reviews about products written by consumers like you. Resource Centers and disability news, conference listings, publications, classified ads and links are available on this website as well.

Society of Automotive Engineers (SAE); 400 Commonwealth Dr.; Warrendale, PA 15096-0001; Tel: 412-776-4841. Website: http://www.sae.org.

The SAE has established an Adaptive Devices Standards Committee relating to adaptive equipment standards and practices. Their goal is the advancement of the mobility community sharing technical information and development of all forms of self-propelled vehicles. They do innovative research on vehicle modification for drivers with physical disabilities.

MEDICINES:

American Society of Consultant Pharmacists (ASCP), 1321 Duke Street, Alexandria, VA 22314; Toll free Tel: 800-355-2727, 703-739-1300; Fax: 800-220-1321, 703-1321. Website: http://www.ascp.com E-mail: info@ascp.com

The ASCP is the international professional association that provides leadership, education, advocacy, and resources to advance the practice of senior care pharmacy. You can check to see where Senior Care pharmacists are located in your state.

Note: Aging truly ain't for sissies. But aging with a disability can really be a walk on burning coals that is intensified by each medication taken, including non-prescription and prescription drugs, herbs, nicotine, caffeine, street drugs, and even chocolate and grapefruit. This can be of great help in determining the interactions of the different substances you take. These sites are no substitute for an informed relationship between you and your primary healthcare provider and pharmacist, but serve as an educational and information resource to enable you to be responsible for your own health.

Medical Device Adverse Events Reporting at the Food and Drug Administration (FDA). Reporting Systems Monitoring Branch (HFZ-533), Med-Watch Office, 5600 Fishers Lane, HFD-410, Rockville, MD 20857; Fax: 301-827-7241. Website: http://www.fda.gov/medwatch/

This site provides warnings and recalls about medicines and equipment. You may report and ask questions of staff personnel about medicines or medical devices.

Note: Unlike many countries in Europe, the United States of America still does not have a law which requires direct patient notification of defective or recalled medical products. Additionally, there is no law which requires that a patient's primary care physician be notified of such recalls or defective products. To illustrate, my friend, should you be roaming around with a heart pacemaker installed in your chest, please be advised that the very device that is supposed to keep your heart going could have been declared potentially defective and you were never told about it.

This site may be able to provide information about medical devices you are thinking of using. If you and your physician contemplate a surgical procedure in which a medical device will be installed in your body, please make certain that you provide written instructions to your surgeon that you want your primary care physician and yourself immediately informed of any problems that may surface with respect to the device installed. You not only have the right to request this information, but it is your duty as an informed patient and the person responsible for your own health.

United States Pharmacopeia, Diane Cousins, Vice President Practitioner and Produce Experience Division, 12601 Twinbrook Pkwy, Rockville, MD 20852; Voice: 301-816-8215; Fax: 301-816-8532. Website: www.usp.org/index.html E-mail: ddc@usp.org

This site is for pharmacists, nurses, physicians and consumers worldwide. All medication errors are preventable as are many adverse drug reactions. One of the most important ways to prevent adverse drug events is to share information about them along with prevention recommendations. This site allows medical personnel to report medication problems.

ACCESSIBILITY DESIGN:

The Access Board, 1331 F Street, NW, Suite 1000, Washington, DC 20004-1111; Tel: (202) 272-0080 (voice); (202) 272-0082 (TTY); (202) 272-0081 (fax). This is a federal agency committed to accessible design. Website: http://www.access-board.gov/

This agency and website offer accessibility guidelines and standards under the Americans with Disabilities Act (ADA) and the Architectural Barriers Act (ABA). The Board and advisory committees deal with courthouse accessibility, space requirements for wheeled mobility aids, courses on designing accessible telecommunications products in compliance with standards, accessibility guidelines for recreation facilities, play surface treatments, evacuation and emergency planning that accommodates persons with disabilities, standards on classroom acoustics, a variety of on-line courses for accessibility training, enforcement, publications and links.

JOBS:

Let me remind you of some people with disabilities and the jobs they held or hold. Some people have had mobility limitations like me. Some of them became musicians like Rachel Barton, an American violinist, who was hurt in a commuter train accident in 1995 in which she lost her left foot and part of her right foot and played her violin from a wheelchair thereafter. Yitzhak Perlman, an Israeli violinist, uses leg braces because of polio at age four. My dear friend Diane Cummings, a former violinist with the Phoenix Symphony and watercolorist extraordinaire, is wheelchair mobile due to multiple sclerosis.

Other people with disabilities may have vision problems like my very dear friend Dr. Tom S., who earned two doctorate degrees, political science and law and had two careers. He first was a professor of political science at a Midwestern college and second as an attorney with expertise in Social Security and Disability

Law. Some became musicians like Ray Charles, singer, pianist and songwriter; singer Jose Feliciano; and Stevie Wonder, singer and songwriter.

People with severe hearing impairments included Beethoven who, despite being deaf, composed beautiful, passionate music. Thomas Edison, the Father of Electricity, continued to invent devices long after he became deaf. The Spanish painter, Francisco Goya, was a painter and print maker but not many know he was deaf. Marlee Matlin, an American actress, won the Academy Award for a performance in a role requiring her deafness. Helen Keller was a noted American author and lecturer who was not only deaf but also blind.

Others became involved in the arts such as Christy Brown, an Irish novelist and poet, who was almost completely paralyzed by cerebral palsy. He wrote an autobiography which was made into the movie, *My Left Foot*. And I am sure that unless you live in a cave, you have already seen and laughed over one or more of the irreverent, politically incorrect cartoons of another person I am proud to call friend, John Callahan, who became a quadriplegic from an auto accident. The Library of Congress lists him under several categories: cartoonist, quadriplegic, recovered alcoholic.

Frida Kahlo, a Mexican painter, was severely injured in a bus accident. She successfully and unsympathetically used her suffering, operations and hospitalizations in her paintings. Dorothea Lange became an American photojournalist documenting poverty in depression American; she contracted polio as a youth. Auguste Renoir became a painter and sculptor with a paint brush tied to his hands after he was paralyzed by rheumatoid arthritis. Toulouse-Lautrec, a French painter, was stunted by a childhood accident which resulted in undeveloped legs. Even though he was 100 times the artist I could ever hope to be, I think Toulouse and I had some things in common: we were/are both very short and really liked/like pretty girls.

Still others were in assorted careers such as Stephen Hawking, whom I mentioned earlier. He is the Nobel prize-winning British physicist and author who wrote *History of Time* and as a baby developed amyotrophic lateral sclerosis or Lou Gehrig's disease. John Wesley Powell, American geologist and ethnologist, explored the Grand Canyon by boat; he had previously lost an arm in a military battle. Jim Abbott, born with only one hand, became a New York Yankee pitcher and pitched a no-hitter on September 4, 1993.

Painter Georgia O'Keeffe turned to sculpture when her eyesight failed. American humorist and cartoonist James Thurber lost an eye as a child when his brother shot him with an arrow. Then he gradually lost sight in his other eye due to complications from the first injury and became known for his many writings including *The Secret Life of Walter Mitty.*

Other actors with vision problems included actor Sammy Davis, Jr., who lost an eye in a car accident; Sandy Duncan, who lost an eye following removal of a brain tumor; and Peter Falk, who lost an eye at age three from a tumor.

Some actors have become quadriplegics. Can you imagine, Christopher Reeve, a.k.a. Superman, gets flattened not by Kryptonite but by an otherwise gentle horse? Go figure. Anyway, Christopher—the man—evolved in his thinking over the course of time. His post-disability recovery transitioned into him becoming a passionate advocate for research to find a cure for spinal cord injury. This was a laudable goal, but only a relatively small component in the life of a person with a permanent, severe disability as, I think, Mr. Superman soon came to realize. Chris went back into acting in and making movies. The passion for the cure did not go away, but the real need to live a complete, fulfilled life with his disability kept him going every day until he died October 10, 2004. Heck, the only guy Hollywood would dare propose to play Superman today is none other than Jesus Christ himself (remember the actor who played Jesus in the movie *Passion of the Christ?)*

This list is only a tiny sampling of the careers people with disabilities have successfully pursued. But I must add the names of a few more departed souls before I leave this section. They have all made significant contributions to their professions and the disability and independent living movement—some may be well known while others less so—and I have been blessed by their friendship. They are: Russ Beeson, Karen Hubacher, Clint Smith, Ed Roberts, Roger Irving, Abe Jaffe, Rebecca "Charlie" Shepard, Hon. John Sticht, and Justin Dart.

Job Accommodation Network (JAN), P.O. Box 6080, Morgantown, WV 26506; Tel/TTY: 800-526-7234; 304-293-7186; Fax: 304-293-5407. Website: http://jan.wvu.edu/

The Office of Disability Employment Policy of the U.S. Department of Labor funds this organization. It is a free consulting service to increase employability of people with disabilities by helping employers prepare worksite accommodations and comply with ADA. Additionally, they educate callers about self-employment options, but they do not have a job-line service.

They describe tax incentives and funding to help employers install equipment and worksites to accommodate employees and they inform callers about the benefits and methods of working independently at home.

They suggest funding sources for the education of people with disabilities such as the Heath Resource Center of the American Council on Education, state-supported Vocational Rehabilitation offices, the U.S. Veterans Administration, the Social Security Administration's PASS (Plan to Achieve Self-Support) program and other public and private funding sources.

U.S. Department of Justice, Americans with Disabilities Act, ADA
Toll-free ADA Information Line, Tel: 800-514-0301; TDD: 800-514-0383; Website: http://www.usdoj.gov/crt/ada/adahom1.htm.

This site contains information for business about ADA, including publications, design standards, ADA regulations, employment, transportation, telephones, education, health care, labor, housing, parks and recreation, enforcement, technical assistance, building codes, etc. For example, a publication for Self-Serve Gas Stations instructs such businesses to provide access, at no extra charge, to those with disabilities by posting signs that encourage them to honk or signal employees for fueling assistance.

In addition, there are consumer guides such as *A Guide for People With Disabilities Seeking Employment.* That publication includes rights, "reasonable accommodation" by employers for employees with disabilities and what to do if ADA rights have been violated.

U.S. Equal Employment Opportunity Commission (EEOC); 1801 L Street NW, Suite 100, Washington, DC 20507-1002; Tel: 800-669-4000; 202-275-7377; TTY: 800-669-6820; 202-275-7518; Fax: 202-275-6834. Website: http://www.eeoc.gov

This site informs employees about their rights as an applicant or employee to suffer no discrimination on the basis of race, color, sex, religion, national origin, age, or disability. It instructs people about how to file a charge, how to use mediation to resolve problems, how to deal with local, state and federal agencies, and training for businesses about how to avoid claims charging discriminatory practices.

STATE PROGRAMS:

Many states have programs and invaluable resources for those with disabilities. In my state, Arizona, as in most throughout the nation, we have a very effective independent living center, ABIL. The **Arizona Bridge to Independent Living**

(ABIL) Phil Pangrazio, Executive Director, 1229 E. Washington Street, Phoenix, AZ 85034-1101, Tel: (602) 256-2245, Fax: (602) 254-6407, Email: azbridge@abil.org.

This organization provides a newsletter, "survival manual," job opportunities, events calendar, information and referrals, and programs. One service is the Ticket to Work Program. SSI/SSDI beneficiaries are able to receive up to 60 months of employment assistance at no charge. One can get training, a job, change jobs, advance in your career, all without risking losing your benefits, especially in the initial phases of your employment. (For further elaboration, see my additional comments under Social Security above).

The majority of the ABIL staff are people with disabilities and they negotiate accommodations you may need, as well as being your mentor and advocate. An employment coordinator who focuses on ability, not disability, will explain details. Contact ABIL at (602) 667-0277, Ext. 10.

Statewide Independent Living Council, Governor's (SILC), 2400 N. Central Ave., Suite 105, Phoenix, AZ 85004; Tel: 602-262-2900; Fax: 602-271-4100. Donna Powers, Chairperson; Tony DiRienzi, Executive Director.

This Arizona organization, made up almost entirely of persons with a broad spectrum of disabilities, facilitates systemic change that promotes independence, inclusion, non-discrimination, and dignity for all people with disabilities throughout the state. It also acts as an oversight and cooperative forward-planning body for the Independent Living Centers, including ABIL, in the state, is responsible to the governor and serves as a valuable resource for people with disabilities in Arizona. Each state of the union has its own SILC.

Independent Living Research Utilization Program (ILRU), 2323 S. Shepherd, Suite 1000, Houston, TX 77019; Tel: 713-520-0232; Fax: 713-520-5136; 713-520-5785. Website: http://www.ilru.org

This state program offers services mainly to Texans but has information available online to anyone. Services and programs include training, databases, grant writing resources, a film library, and personal assistance services.

TRAVEL/TRANSPORTATION:

There are many web sites about travel and transportation. When planning a trip, get all the information possible about the destination, transportation, and accommodations to avoid problems. Here are some books and web sites that may be of use to gain this information.

Rick Steves' Easy Access Europe is a 498-page book that covers only five destinations (Amsterdam, Bruges, London, Paris and the Rhine) but it's packed with useful advice for travelers with wheelchairs and slow walkers. A web site about the book is:
http://europeforvisitors.com/europe/articles/rick-steves-easy-access-europe.htm

The European Union has produced a series of 18 detailed country guides in PDF format to make Europe accessible that are well worth reading and printing. To view them, you'll need the free Adobe Acrobat Reader. The web site is:
http://europe.eu.int/comm/enterprise/services/tourism/policy-areas/guides.htm

Access-Able Travel Source is a web site where you can pick a country for information on airport accessibility, "equal access" travel agencies, 24-hour medical care and other services to travelers with disabilities. The web site is:
http://www.access-able.com

Accessible Journeys is a travel agency in Pennsylvania that offers group tours and independent programs for slow walkers and travelers with wheelchairs. The web site is: http://www.disabilitytravel.com

World Wide Cruises, Inc., is an agency that provides information about ships and cruises for people with disabilities. The web site is: http://www.wwcruises.com/html/cruises-disabilities.html

Global Access may be the web's most comprehensive source of travel information for people with disabilities. It has some articles about travel to Europe and web links, as well as reviews of campgrounds for van or motor home travelers in Spain, France and the Netherlands. The web site is: http://www.geocities.com/Paris/1502/

Disability Travel and Recreation Resources is an extensive on-line directory with links by category to travel planning, destinations, transportation, air travel, kids' sites, related books and more. The web site is: http://www.makoa.org/travel.htm

The Society for Accessible Travel and Hospitality tells what to do at security checkpoints, has a travel insurance checklist and a number of how-to's for traveling with arthritis, speech or vision impairment, traveling in a wheelchair and other tips for those with disabilities. The web site is: http://www.sath.org/

DisabilityWorld.com is an extensive United Kingdom-based directory to holidays, travel and leisure with thousands of links to accommodations, tours and excursions, and lots more information of interest to those with disabilities. The web site is: http://www.disabilityworld.com/

Gimp on the Go is an engaging on-line magazine edited by an American with a disability that provides travel reviews, visitor recommendations, photo gallery, bulletin board, related links and a U.S. travel database searchable by a variety of useful disability access criteria. The web site is: http://www.gimponthego.com/

Flying with Disability is a guide to air travel for those with disabilities with tips for preplanning, getting around the airport, plane accessibility, flying with a guide dog or wheelchair, plus travel links. The web site is: http://www.flying-with-disability.org/

Allgohere.com is a United Kingdom-centric directory of access-friendly hotels in England, Scotland, Wales and Northern Ireland, and boasts the world's only accessible airline directory with information on individual airlines' policies and services for those with disabilities. The web site is: http://www.allgohere.com

Note: If you have special requirements when traveling that are due to your disability, there is no substitute for knowing precisely what those requirements are and communicating your needs specifically with those providing you with travel services. These providers could be, for example, your airline or hotel. I hope the following true story serves as an illustration.

A divorced parent living in Phoenix, Arizona, needed to make arrangements for her 10-year-old child to fly back to New York to spend time with the child's father. The child had a severe allergy to peanuts and could go into anaphylactic shock even breathing the air in a closed environment, such as an airplane cabin, where peanuts were being consumed by others. So the parent making the travel arrangement contacted the airline in advance of this trip to explain her daughter's accommodation needs. America West Airline assured the mother and made certain that the snack food handed out on that particular flight did not include peanuts or related foods which could cause anaphylactic shock in the child traveling. The flight went off on schedule and without a hitch. Again, there is no substitute for knowing your own needs, how to best accommodate them and being seriously proactive about getting your needs met.

ORGANIZATIONS:

ADAPT, 201 S. Cherokee, Denver, CO 80223; Tel: 303/733-9324; or ADAPT of Texas, 1339 Lamar Square Dr., Austin, TX, 78704; Tel: 512/442-0252; Email: adapt@adapt.org

This is a premiere organization advocating the rights of people with disabilities and the elderly to live in the least restrictive environment possible. One of ADAPT's principal goals is for people with disabilities and the impaired elderly to be able to choose to continue living in their own homes, with appropriate personal care assistant services provided them in their homes instead of being institutionalized in nursing facilities.

For decades, people with disabilities, both young and old, have wanted alternatives to nursing homes and other institutions when they need long term services. Our long term care system has a heavy institutional bias. Every state that receives Medicaid MUST provide nursing home services, but community-based services are options. Seventy-five percent of Medicaid long term care dollars pay for institutional services, while the remaining 25% must cover all remaining community-based programs.

Whether a child is born with a disability, an adult has a traumatic injury or a person becomes disabled through the aging process, they overwhelmingly want their attendant services provided in their own homes, not nursing homes or other large institutions. ADAPT has drafted a bill which will fundamentally change our long-term care system and institutional bias that now exists. The critical fact about this legislation, AND allowing people who require assistance to stay in their own homes, is that it will end up costing the taxpayer CONSIDERABLY LESS money than placing the same people in nursing homes. For the nursing home industry, this legislation just isn't cool at all.

MiCASSA, the Medicaid Community Attendant Services and Supports Act, is that alternative! Instead of making a new entitlement, MiCASSA makes the existing entitlement more flexible. MiCASSA establishes a national program of community-based attendant services and supports for people with disabilities, regardless of age or disability. The two million Americans currently residing in nursing homes and other institutions would finally have a choice to return home to live if they wish to.

Just a thought. Perhaps you might want to ask your congressional representative or senators why the MiCASSA legislation is still not law, especially since the law is not only the right thing to do, but it also strengthens families while reducing in the long-haul Medicaid expenses for the American taxpayer.

The World Institute on Disability, 510 16th Street, Suite 100, Oakland CA 94612; Tel: 510-763-4100; TTY: 510-208-9496. Website: http://www.wid.org

This organization is an excellent resource for people with disabilities, on a wide range of issues including education, work, living independently, advocacy and political action. It is a non-profit research, training and public policy center promoting the civil rights and full societal inclusion of people with disabilities. Their website also includes programs, publications, events, training, news, resources and jobs. There are many publications about hiring and managing personal care assistants (PCAs) in the United States, Europe, Canada, and Scandinavia.

Sexual Health.Com. Website: http://www.sexualhealth.com/

This site is an excellent Internet information source for sexuality for both men and women with disabilities. Founder Mitch Tepper is unafraid to tackle any subject of intimacy. The website deals with disability, sexual activities and dysfunctions, sexual orientation, sexually transmitted diseases, illnesses, love and intimacy, and sexual education through articles, interviews, books and videos.

Paralyzed Veterans of America (PVA), 801 Eighteenth Street NW, Washington, DC 20006-3517; National Headquarters: 800-424-8200; Health Care Hotline: 800-232-1782. Website: http://www.pva.org/

This organization offers news about sports and recreation for paraplegics, information about living with spinal cord injuries, research, education, architecture, veterans benefits, job opportunities, wheelchair games, boating and fishing, shooting sports, publications, and a store.

Disabilities Rights Education and Defense Fund (DREDF). Main Office: 2212 Sixth Street, Berkeley, CA 94710; Tel/TTY: 510-644-2555; Fax: 510-841-8645. Government Affairs: 1730 M Street NW, Suite 801, Washington, DC 20036; Tel: 202-986-0375; Fax 202-833-2116. Website: http://www.dredf.org/

This organization was founded by people with disabilities and parents of children with disabilities to protect and advance the civil rights of the disabled through legislation, litigation, advocacy, technical assistance, training of attorneys and advocates. The website has news, legal cases, articles, newsletters and publications. They have been on the forefront in the creation and implementation of the Americans with Disabilities Act (ADA) and are one of the premier organizations of its kind in the world.

Disabilities Resources on the Web, Pioneer Library System, Patricia Stoker, Assistant Director, 4595 Rt. 21 North, Canandaigua, NY 14424; Tel: 585-394-8260. Website: http://www.pls-net.org/disability.html

This site offers statistics on disability, accessibility design, computers, legal advocacy, software and library services for those with disabilities. They also have sites for children to connect with other young people with disabilities or chronic illnesses as well as to peers and mentors without physical disabilities.

National Council on Independent Living; 1916 Wilson Blvd., Suite 209; Arlington, VA 22201; Tel: 703-525-3406; TTY: 703-525-41153; Fax: 703-525-3409; Tel/TTY/Toll free: 877-525-3400. Website: http://www.virtualcil.net/cils/

This website opens with a map of the U.S. Click on a state to be shown web sites and e-mail addresses for centers of independent living in your state. For example, in Arizona six centers are listed in six different cities, with access information.

American Association of People With Disabilities (AAPD), 1629 K Street NW, Suite 503, Washington, DC 20006; Voice/TTY: 202-457-0046; Fax: 202-457-0473; Toll free: 800-840-8844. Website: http://www.aapd-dc.org/

This organization was created to ensure economic and political empowerment of all people with disabilities; to further their productivity, independence and integration into all aspects of society; to foster leadership among people with disabilities; to support implementation and enforcement of ADA laws; to provide information to the disability community and to educate the public regarding issues affecting people with disabilities.

There is a quarterly newsletter, federal credit union, life and medical insurance plans, car rental discounts, mail-order prescription drug benefit, loan service, savings and checking accounts, credit cards, and travel services. This web site has the most extensive listing of available jobs, mostly federal, of any website for the disability community.

Note: Although the AARP still yields an inordinate amount of power and somehow manages to continue to do at least some things right with respect to the elder community, despite their repeated lapses (or relapses?) into a big-business mentality, the AAPD is much more agile and does a much better one-on-one job of serving the disability community. This is all the more commendable because the AAPD has a fraction of the resources of the AARP.

A good metaphor might be in observing the performance of the WNBA versus the NBA. The Megabucks Superstars of the NBA can perform, on occasion, with great talent and even sportsmanlike enthusiasm. But, alas, it is relatively easy to observe that such performance effort is sporadic and inconsistent game to game. The ladies of the WNBA do have their occasional off days, too, but their effort seems to be consistently more enthusiastic than that of their NBA compadres.

Moral: Check out the AAPD the next time you need help or information, especially with respect to issues relating to aging and disability. And, while you are at it, check out the WNBA, too. They play like the men should and overall they're better to look at.

EDUCATION:

IDEA, Center for Inclusive Design and Environmental Access, 378 Hayes Hall, School of Architecture and Planning, 3435 Main Street, University at Buffalo, Buffalo, NY 14214-3087; Tel: 716-829-3485; TTY: 716-829-3758; Fax: 716-829-3861. Website: http://www.ap.buffalo.edu/idea/indexwelcome.html.

This university architectural department is dedicated to improving the design of environments and products by making them more usable, safer and appealing to people with a wide range of abilities throughout their life spans. The web site describes their programs, special interests, publications, software, bright ideas, and links. Those who intend to enter the field of architecture stressing accessibility will find this college department most valuable.

Center for Universal Design, College of Design, North Carolina State University, 50 Pullen Road, Brooks Hall, Room 104, Campus Box 8613, Raleigh, NC 27695-8613; toll free: 800-647-6777; Tel: 919-515-3082; fax 919-515-7330. Website: http//www.design.ncsu.edu

This college department offers education, design, research, outreach, standards for accessible design, technical assistance, evaluation of public and commercial facilities, affordable and universal homes for independence, publications, and more. Installation guides can be purchased for curbless showers, how to add a ramp that looks good and works too, creating inclusive child care facilities, accessible stock house plans, transportation facilities, bathrooms, grab bars, kitchens, bedrooms, windows, entrances, and housing for the lifespan of all people. Those who intend to enter fields of work in accessibility will want this college program.

Raising Special Kids, 4750 N. Black Canyon Highway, Suite 101, Phoenix, AZ 85017-3621, Tel: 602-242-4366, 800-237-3007, Fax: 602-242-3406. Website: http//www.raisingspecialkids.org

This organization offers advocacy and help for parents of children with developmental disabilities. They offer a free lending library, newsletter, and training for parents and teachers of children with disabilities, as well as legislative news, event calendar, employment, and resources. Such organizations are available in many states.

Learning Disabilities Online, 2775 South Quincy Street, Arlington, VA 22206. Website: http://www.ldonline.org/

This organization describes learning disabilities, suggests readings, presents research results, and gives teachers and parents tips to help students with disabilities. They also give children opportunities to submit letters and artwork.

National Dissemination Center for Children with Disabilities (NICHCY), P.O. Box 1492, Washington, DC 20013; Tell: 800-695-0285; Fax: 202-884-8441. Website: http://www.nichcy.org/idea.htm

IDEA (Individuals with Disabilities Education Act) helps states and school districts provide special education and services to more than six million eligible children with disabilities. The organization offers training materials to inform people about the law, assure compliance, offers research results and publications and includes resources for every state. For example, under Arizona resources, the names and contact information for U.S. senators, representatives, governor, state department of education, programs for children with disabilities, state vocational rehabilitation agency and more are listed.

This website is funded by the U. S. Office of Special Education Programs. The website also includes interactive sections for children under the title

Zigawhat! Subtitles with cartoon characters are these: *Learn More About You, Connect With Other Kids, Tips Just For You, Tell Your Story* and *Fun and Games.*

Best Information on the Net, O'Keefe Library, St. Ambrose University, 518 W. Locust Street, Davenport, IA 52803; Tel: 563-333-6000. Website: http://library.sau.edu/bestinfo/disability/disindex.htm

This site offers resources such as adaptive technologies (computers and software for people with disabilities,) disability law, local and state resources (only for Illinois and Iowa,) about 15 organizations and institutes, and other useful sites such as sign language.

APPENDIX B

JACUZZI FAMILY TREE

Note: I want to give very special thanks to my cousin, Victor Jacuzzi, son of Aldo, grandson of Giuseppe (one of the original seven Jacuzzi brothers) for the work he has performed over more than two decades in maintaining and updating the entire list of Jacuzzi family members, their personal contact information and data. Quite obviously, this Jacuzzi Family Tree could not have been created if it were not for Victor's exceptional work which now reaches beyond five generations. Thanks Vic!

Note: Care was taken in the preparation of this Family Tree, but some omissions or errors in dates and names may have occurred. Please forgive. KJ

Generation No. 1

Giovanni Jacuzzi was born 10/5/1855 and died 3/19/1929. He married Teresa Arman on 1/30/1886. She was born 10/10/1865 and died 8/8/1943. They had:

    i. Rachele Jacuzzi born 11/11/1886, died 8/24/1937

    ii. Valeriano (Valerio) Jacuzzi born 12/16/1887, died 3/10/1973

    iii. Francesco (Frank) born 3/12/1889, died 9/24/1973

    iv. Giuseppe (Joseph) born 2/5/1891, died 1/5/1965

    v. Gelindo Jacuzzi born 1/31/1894, died 2/4/1950

    vi. Giocondo Jacuzzi born 7/5/1895, died 7/14/1921

    vii. Felicita Jacuzzi born 5/15/1897, died 11/17/1978

    viii. Angelina Jacuzzi born 11/23/1899, died 2/17/1990

    ix. Ancilla Jacuzzi born 11/8/1901, died 12/8/1949

x. Candido Jacuzzi born 2/24/1903, died 10/7/1986

xi. Cirilla Jacuzzi born 3/13/1905, died 5/15/2000

xii. Stella Jacuzzi born 4/3/1907, died 12/2/2003

xiii. Gilia Jacuzzi born 9/15/1908

Generation No. 2

1. Rachele Jacuzzi's family

Rachele (father=Giovanni Jacuzzi, mother=Teresa) married Olympia Calugi on 6/15/1916. She was born 6/22/1881 and died 5/22/1952. They adopted:

i. Giordano (Gordon) Charles Jacuzzi born 12/31/1927, died 3/22/1971

2. Valeriano Jacuzzi's family

Valeriano (father=Giovanni Jacuzzi, mother=Teresa) married Giuseppina (Pina) Piucco on 7/12/1919. She was born 12/16/1898 and died 2/2/1984. They had:

i. Virgilio (Virgil) Joseph Jacuzzi born 12/26/1919, died 4/26/2003

ii. Dante Paul Jacuzzi born 7/1/1921, died 5/17/1997

iii. Jaconda Jacuzzi born 3/5/1923

iv. Teresa Maria Jacuzzi born 10/29/1924

v. Mary Alice Jacuzzi born 11/25/1926

vi. Flora Margaret Jacuzzi born 9/20/1929, died 2/6/1990

vii. Remo Cesare Jacuzzi born 1/6/1936

viii. Rachel Joanne Jacuzzi born 5/19/1939

3. Francesco Jacuzzi's family

Francesco (father=Giovanni Jacuzzi, mother=Teresa) married Rena Villata on 6/21/1919. She was born 6/21/1901 and died 8/27/1995. They had:

i. Giocondo Frank Jacuzzi born 9/12/1921

ii. Ugo Jacuzzi born 11/27/1922

4. Giuseppe Jacuzzi's family

Giuseppe (father=Giovanni Jacuzzi, mother=Teresa) married Rena Beggio on 6/12/1920. She was born 4/15/1904, died 12/2/1990. They had:

i. Aldo Joseph Jacuzzi born 4/26/1921, died 2/21/1989

5. Gelindo Jacuzzi's family

Gelindo (father=Giovanni Jacuzzi, mother=Teresa) married Rosie Meinero on 12/14/1918. She was born 12/12/1903, died 8/4/1999. They had:

i. Lola Jacuzzi born 12/18/1919

ii. Olga Jacuzzi born 1/6/1922

iii. Tullio Jacuzzi born 5/28/1924

iv. Rodolfo Jacuzzi born 3/6/1926

v. Daniele Jacuzzi born 9/20/1928

6. Giocondo Jacuzzi's family

Giocondo (father=Giovanni Jacuzzi, mother=Teresa) married Mary Guarneri on 4/19/1919. She was born 1/12/1902, died 5/3/1990. They had:

i. Anna Jacuzzi born 2/20/1920, died 11/11/1984

7. Felicita's family

Felicita (father=Giovanni Jacuzzi, mother=Teresa) married Luigi Lanza on 1/30/1921. He was born 1/27/1890, died 5/1/1980. They had:

i. John Vincent Lanza born 10/8/1925, died 8/15/1995

8. Angelina's family

Angelina (father=Giovanni Jacuzzi, mother=Teresa) married Peter Tunesi on 1/30/1921. He was born 6/1/1897, died 1/5/1971. They had:

i. Doris Tunesi born 3/31/1924

ii. Edith Tunesi born 7/12/1928

9. Ancilla's family

Ancilla (father=Giovanni Jacuzzi, mother=Teresa) married Peter Bianchi on 12/23/1922. He was born 3/27/1895, died 6/25/1988. They had:

i. Leo Bianchi born 11/3/1923

ii. John Mario Bianchi born 3/31/1933

10. Candido's family

Candido (father=Giovanni Jacuzzi, mother=Teresa) married Inez Ranieri on 12/26/1925. She was born 11/21/1908, died 2/21/1995. They had:

i. Alba Gloria Jacuzzi born 10/13/1926

ii. John Bruno Jacuzzi born 8/28/1929

iii. Irene Benita Jacuzzi born 10/7/1935, died 12/11/1986

iv. Kenneth Anthony Jacuzzi born 4/22/1941, married Daniela G. Manzini on 3/10/1974. She was born 1/4/1948.

11. Cirilla's family

Cirilla (father=Giovanni Jacuzzi, mother=Teresa) married Joseph Benassini on 11/25/1922. He was born 10/10/1898, died 11/2/1963. They had:

i. Harold Joseph Benassini born 4/26/1924

ii. Lydia Margaret Benassini born 10/21/1925

iii. Norma Rose Benassini born 10/13/1938, died 9/27/1992

12. Stella's family

Stella (father=Giovanni Jacuzzi, mother=Teresa) married Rino Vitorio Marin on 8/22/1925. He was born 4/27/1900, died 11/14/1995. They had:

i. Silviano Marin born 3/8/1926, died 12/28/1991

ii. George Marin born 9/15/1934

13. Gilia's family

Gilia (father=Giovanni Jacuzzi, mother=Teresa) married Jack Peruzzo on 11/7/1925. He was born 5/11/1900, died 4/17/1979. They had:

i. Nilda Peruzzo born 2/13/1927

ii. Esther Delia Peruzzo born 7/6/1937

iii. Peter Anthony Peruzzo born 6/15/1945

Generation No. 3

1. Rachele's grandchildren, Giordano's family

Giordano Jacuzzi (father=Rachele Jacuzzi, mother=Olympia) married Eda Massoni (Mrs. Guido Biagi) on 4/25/1948. She was born 4/20/1927. They had:

i. Dennis Charles Jacuzzi born 2/14/1950

ii. Fred Gordon Jacuzzi born 12/28/1953, died 8/5/1968

2. Valeriano's grandchildren, Virgilio's family

Virgilio Jacuzzi (father=Valeriano Jacuzzi, mother=Giuseppina) married Beulah Jones on 5/31/1941. She was born 3/22/1918, died 9/29/2002. They had:

i. Beverly Ann Jacuzzi born 8/10/1937

ii. Lita June Jacuzzi born 6/19/1942

iii. Virginia May Jacuzzi born 5/19/1944

iv. Diana Jean Jacuzzi born 2/14/1946

v. Virgil Thomas Joseph Jacuzzi born 8/5/1950

vi. Susan Joan Jacuzzi born 2/3/1952

vii. Paul Vincent Jacuzzi born 4/13/1956

2. Valeriano's grandchildren, Dante Paul's family

Dante Paul Jacuzzi (father=Valeriano Jacuzzi, mother=Giuseppina) married Rosalyn Devoynne Underhill on 12/8/1945. She was born 5/17/1926. They had:

i. Dante Paul Jacuzzi Jr. born 11/12/1948

ii. Cheryl Christine Jacuzzi born 3/12/1952

iii. Charles Stephen Jacuzzi born 11/15/1954, died 5/21/2004

iv. Deborah Ann Jacuzzi born 6/10/1957

v. Mary Regina Jacuzzi born 11/19/1961

2. Valeriano's grandchildren, Jaconda's family

Jaconda Jacuzzi (father=Valeriano Jacuzzi, mother=Giuseppina) married Robert Wayne Hawkins on 9/27/1942. He was born 11/3/1919, died 11/10/1998. They had:

i. Robert Michael Hawkins born 12/29/1943

ii. Mary Margaret Hawkins born 5/1/1945

iii. Sharon Anne Hawkins born 3/2/1947

iv. Patrick Anthony Hawkins born 8/6/1951

v. Elizabeth Teresa Hawkins born 12/20/1957

2. Valeriano's grandchildren, Teresa Maria's family

Teresa Maria Jacuzzi (father=Valeriano Jacuzzi, mother=Giuseppina) married Donald Francis DeShields on 4/22/1946. He was born 12/25/1919. They had:

i. Josephine Anna DeShields born 1/18/1948

ii. Donald Anthony DeShields born 5/11/1949

iii. William Martin DeShields born 2/6/1951

iv. Anna Teresa DeShields born 12/3/1952

v. Timothy James DeShields born 7/2/1955, died 6/29/1972

vi. Teresa Carol DeShields born 3/4/1958

2. Valeriano's grandchildren, Mary Alice's family

Mary Alice Jacuzzi (father=Valeriano Jacuzzi, mother=Giuseppina) married James Sherwood Cline on 6/12/1949. He was born 2/18/1927, 11/10/1991. They had:

i. Valerie Anne Cline born 3/12/1950

ii. Marilyn Cline born 10/25/1951

iii. James Charles Cline born 4/30/1954

iv. Charles Brian Cline born 6/23/1955

v. Frederic Thomas Cline born 1/19/1957

vi. Michael Jon Cline born 5/19/1958

vii. Mary Janis Cline born 1/14/1960

viii. Matthew Alan Cline born 3/27/1961

ix. Gary Edward Cline born 8/17/1962

2. Valeriano's grandchildren, Flora Margaret's family

Flora Margaret Jacuzzi (father=Valeriano Jacuzzi, mother=Giuseppina) married Joseph Harold Nicoletti on 1/11/1953. He was born 3/22/1927. They had:

i. Jo Ann Nicoletti born 3/6/1954

ii. Joseph Michael Nicoletti born 7/19/1955, died 4/8/1990

iii. Janice Margaret Nicoletti born 5/9/1957

iv. Katherine Jane Nicoletti born 3/29/1959

v. Robert John Nicoletti born 5/10/1963

2. Valeriano's grandchildren, Remo Cesare's family

Remo Cesare Jacuzzi (father=Valeriano Jacuzzi, mother=Giuseppina) married Paula Putnam on 1/20/1957. She was born 5/31/1934. They had:

i. Remo Valerian Jacuzzi born 12/15/1957

ii. Jennifer June Jacuzzi born 6/29/1959

iii. Loretta Dawn Jacuzzi born 2/21/1961

iv. Gretchen Lynn Jacuzzi born 8/25/1962

v. Matthew Paul Jacuzzi born 3/15/1965

vi. Paulo Andrew Jacuzzi born 5/24/1969

2. Valeriano's grandchildren, Rachel Joann's family

Rachel Joann Jacuzzi (father=Valeriano Jacuzzi, mother=Giuseppina) married John Neil Bruce on 9/4/1970. He was born 4/7/1926. They had:

i. Neil Valerian Thomas Bruce born 12/30/1975

ii. Shawn Christopher Ian Bruce born 9/15/1978

3. Francesco's grandchildren, Giocondo Frank's family

Giocondo Frank Jacuzzi (father=Francesco Jacuzzi, mother=Rena) married Lillian Irene Mintzman on 10/13/1942. She was born 11/2/1922. They had:

i. Janice Paula Jacuzzi born 10/19/1943

ii. Marc Steven Jacuzzi born 1/25/1947

iii. Carol Ann Jacuzzi born 3/31/1951

3. Francesco's grandchildren, Ugo's family

Ugo Jacuzzi (father=Francesco Jacuzzi, mother=Rena) married Justine Rogers on 7/20/1947. She was born 2/7/1924. They had:

i. Nancy Jacuzzi born 4/3/1951

ii. Susan Lynn Jacuzzi born 4/28/1953

iii. Chris Saunders Jacuzzi born 9/7/1956

4. Giuseppe's grandchildren, Aldo Joseph's family

Aldo Joseph Jacuzzi (father=Giuseppe Jacuzzi, mother=Rena) married Granuccia Amadei on 4/26/1942. She was born 7/7/1922, died 11/11/2000. They had:

i. Roy Aldo Jacuzzi born 6/3/1943

ii. Victor Steven Jacuzzi born 10/29/1944

iii. Rita Carol Jacuzzi born 10/2/1953

5. Gelindo's grandchildren, Lola's family

Lola Jacuzzi (father=Gelindo Jacuzzi, mother=Rosie) married Lawrence (Bud) Fenolio on 9/14/1940. He was born 10/17/1916. They had:

i. Ronald Lawrence Fenolio born 2/25/1943

ii. Edward Lawrence Fenolio born 8/24/1947

5. Gelindo's grandchildren, Olga's family

Olga Jacuzzi (father=Gelindo Jacuzzi, mother=Rosie) married Richard Gilmour Gall on 7/24/1948. He was born 11/7/1916, died 9/10/1993. They had:

i. Richard Gilmour Gall Jr. born 1/6/1951

ii. Raymond Karl Gall born 7/1/1952

iii. Robert Charles Gall born 2/2/1954

iv. Marjorie Lynn Gall born 9/24/1956

5. Gelindo's grandchildren, Tullio's family

Tullio Jacuzzi (father=Gelindo Jacuzzi, mother=Rosie) married Clydia Lee Casey on 9/8/1946. She was born 8/31/1926. They had:

i. Linda Lee Jacuzzi born 8/11/1948

ii. Richard Steven Jacuzzi born 11/6/1949

iii. Kathleen Ann Jacuzzi born 2/1/1951

iv. James Tullio Jacuzzi born 7/13/1952

v. Jane Carol Jacuzzi born 9/1/1954

vi. Nancy Marie Jacuzzi born 10/11/1957

vii. Andrew Martin Jacuzzi born 5/17/1960

viii. Julie Lynn Jacuzzi born 8/26/1961

ix. Robert Casey Jacuzzi born 6/13/1964

5. Gelindo's grandchildren, Rodolfo's family

Rodolfo Jacuzzi (father=Gelindo Jacuzzi, mother=Rosie) married Mary Helen Bacon on 7/29/1949. She was born 7/4/1926. They had:

i. Marianne Jacuzzi born 11/25/1951

ii. Laura Lea Jacuzzi born 3/10/1954

iii. Douglas Reid Jacuzzi born 5/15/1957

iv. Leanna Marie Jacuzzi born 8/13/1963

v. Marc Lewis Jacuzzi born 2/22/1965

5. Gelindo's grandchildren, Daniele's family

Daniele Jacuzzi (father=Gelindo Jacuzzi, mother=Rosie) married Jean Louise Pfeiffer on 6/25/1950. She was born 12/13/1929. They had:

i. David Gelindo Jacuzzi born 12/3/1951

ii. Rosanne Jacuzzi born 6/27/1953

iii. Daniel Craig Jacuzzi born 8/4/1956

iv. Gail Lynn Jacuzzi born 5/17/1959, died 8/25/1996

6. Giocondo's grandchildren, Anna's family

Anna Jacuzzi (father=Giocondo Jacuzzi, mother=Mary) married Vincent Liotta on 7/28/1940. He was born 1/4/1916. They had:

i. Richard Eugene Liotta born 12/29/1943

ii. Bruce John Liotta born 12/24/1946

iii. David Howard Liotta born 1/31/1950

7. Felicita's grandchildren, John Vincent's family

John Vincent Lanza (father=Luigi Lanza, mother=Felicita) married Rosemary. They had:

i. John Wayne Lanza born 7/26/1948

ii. Thomas William Lanza born 9/24/1949

iii. Kathleen Jane Lanza born 8/18/1953

iv. Maureen Oliva Lanza born 10/17/1956

v. Ronald Louis Lanza born 9/30/1959, died 6/17/1999

vi. Terry Vincent Lanza born 6/16/1961

8. Angelina's grandchildren, Doris's family

Doris Tunesi (father=Peter Tunesi, mother=Angelina) married Joseph Adamo on 7/1/1943. He was born 1/4/1922. They had:

i. Philip John Adamo born 9/24/1948

ii. Robert Peter Adamo born 8/26/1949

iii. Christopher Joseph Adamo born 2/2/1951

iv. Thomas David Adamo born 2/15/1955

8. Angelina's grandchildren, Edith's family

Edith Tunesi (father=Peter Tunesi, mother=Angelina) married Mr. De Amicis. They had:

i. Marguerite Ann De Amicis born 10/11/1954

ii. Roger Peter De Amicis born 6/12/1956

iii. Carl Vincent De Amicis born 6/12/1956

iv. Paul James De Amicis born 11/11/1961

9. Ancilla's grandchildren, Leo's family

Leo Bianchi (father=Peter Bianchi, mother=Ancilla) married Helen Mary Pianto on 5/19/1946. She was born 9/22/1924, died 8/7/1993. They had:

i. Marcia Madeline Bianchi born 5/7/1947

ii. Barbara Anne Bianchi born 9/19/1949

iii. Linda Marie Bianchi born 6/13/1952

iv. Peter Stephen Bianchi born 7/9/1957

v. Laura Jean Bianchi born 12/19/1963

9. Ancilla's grandchildren, John Mario's family

John Mario Bianchi (father=Peter Bianchi, mother=Ancilla) married Elaine Marie Rodriguez on 6/10/1956. She was born 1/15/1935. They had:

i. John Mario Bianchi Jr. born 3/16/1957

ii. Becky Marie Bianchi born 2/26/1958

iii. Cindy Lou Bianchi born 7/8/1961

iii. Christina Lorraine Bianchi born 12/9/1967

iv. Noel Patrice Bianchi born 12/7/1978

10. Candido's grandchildren, Alba's family

Alba Gloria Jacuzzi (father=Candido Jacuzzi, mother=Inez) married Peter Louis Kosta on 9/23/1945. He was born 1/3/1925. They had:

   i. Stephen Peter Kosta born 11/28/1947

   ii. Candida Alba Kosta born 11/2/1949

   iii. Cynthia Ann Kosta born 9/8/1956

   iv. Jeffrey Louis Kosta born 8/20/1958

10. Candido's grandchildren, John Bruno's family

John Bruno Jacuzzi (father=Candido Jacuzzi, mother=Inez) married Margaret Andresen on 9/3/1955. She was born 8/5/1935. They had:

   i. Elizabeth Ann Jacuzzi born 7/8/1956

   ii. Patricia Jan Jacuzzi born 3/1/1958

   iii. John Bruno Jacuzzi Jr. born 3/28/1959

   iv. James Candido Jacuzzi born 2/3/1965

10. Candido's grandchildren, Irene's family

Irene Benita Jacuzzi (father=Candido Jacuzzi, mother=Inez) married Don Roescheise first and second Neil Davidson on 3/23/1974. He was born 1/22/1932. Irene had by her first marriage:

   i. Rosanna Inez Roescheise born 7/25/1956

   ii. Deborah Ann Roescheise born 11/28/1958

   iii. Cristina Ruth Roescheise born 8/19/1961

   iv. Raymond Don Roescheise born 10/18/1964

11. Cirilla's grandchildren, Harold Joseph's family

Harold Joseph Benassini (father=Joseph Benassini, mother=Cirilla) married Marcella Verdeene Rand on 6/2/1951. She was born 4/4/1930. They had:

   i. Joseph Arthur Benassini born 2/29/1952

   ii. Anne Theresa Benassini born 10/1/1953

iii. Lisa Mary Benassini born 8/11/1955, died 10/20/2003

11. Cirilla's grandchildren, Lydia Margaret's family

Lydia Margaret Benassini (father=Joseph Benassini, mother=Cirilla) married Frank Charles Negherbon on 7/2/1949. He was born 7/28/1920. They had:

i. Gary Joseph Negherbon born 5/28/1950

ii. Cheryl Marie Negherbon born 12/28/1951

11. Cirilla's grandchildren, Norma Rose's family

Norma Rose Benassini (father=Joseph Benassini, mother=Cirilla) married Caesar Nuti on 6/11/1960. He was born 10/27/33. They had:

i. Peter Joseph Nuti born 12/15/1961

ii. Gregory Caesar Nuti born 4/19/1963

iii. Suzanne Theresa Nuti born 10/14/1965

iv. Larry Stephen Nuti born 10/31/1969

v. Paul Michael Nuti born 1/22/1971

12. Stella's grandchildren, Silviano's family

Silviano Marin (father=Rino Marin, mother=Stella) married Jean Haslam on 8/9/1947. She was born 9/23/1928. They had:

i. Gregory Marin born 5/16/1949

ii. Douglas Marin born 1/2/1951

iii. Curtis Marin born 7/12/1952

iv. Janine Estelle Marin born 1/17/1954

12. Stella's grandchildren, George's family

George Marin (father=Rino Marin, mother=Stella) married Patricia Leiser on 2/2/1958. She was born 11/5/1935. They had:

i. Steven Craig Marin born 12/27/1960

ii. Karen Valerie Marin born 11/22/1962

13. Gilia's grandchildren, Nilda's family

Nilda Peruzzo (father=Jack Peruzzo, mother=Gilia) married John Daniel Rego on 11/12/1949. He was born 10/20/1927. They had:

    i. Jacqueline Marie Rego born 10/31/1950

    ii. John Daniel Rego Jr. born 9/22/1952

    iii. Michael David Rego born 8/11/1955

    iv. Charles Anthony Rego born 4/23/1958

    v. Frank Alan Rego born 3/12/1961

    vi. George Avery Rego born 2/12/1963

13. Gilia's grandchildren, Esther's family

Esther Peruzzo (father=Jack Peruzzo, mother=Gilia) married George Alfred Regula on 8/2/1958. He was born 6/24/1936. They had:

    i. David Michael Regula born 3/30/1960

    ii. Charles (Kale) Anthony Regula born 3/4/1964

    iii. Christina Marie Regula born 5/23/1968

13. Gilia's grandchildren, Peter's family

Peter Anthony Peruzzo (father=Jack Peruzzo, mother=Gilia) married Florence Sue Lowell on 7/11/1970. She was born 4/20/1947, died 10/2/2002. They had:

    i. James Patrick Peruzzo born 5/3/1972

    ii. Anthony David Peruzzo born 5/3/1975

Generation No. 4

1. Rachele's great grandchildren, Giordano's grandchildren, Dennis' family

Dennis Charles Jacuzzi (father=Giordano Jacuzzi, mother=Eda) married Judith Parker on 10/29/1977. She was born 11/22/1952. They had:

    i. Anthony Gordon Jacuzzi born 5/17/1979

ii. Natalie Rachele Jacuzzi born 1/21/1981

2. Valeriano's great grandchildren, Virgilio's grandchildren, Beverly's family

Beverly Ann Jacuzzi (father=Virgilio Jacuzzi, mother=Beulah) married Wiley Virgil Allgood first and then Bernard Claude Edgell on 11/3/2000. He was born 10/27/1935. She had by her first marriage:

i. Wiley Virgil Allgood Jr. born 2/20/1964

ii. Heidi Suzanne Allgood born 5/10/1965

iii. Holly Anne Allgood born 12/24/1967

2. Valeriano's great grandchildren, Virgilio's grandchildren, Lita's family

Lita June Jacuzzi (father=Virgilio Jacuzzi, mother=Beulah) married Joachim (Joe) Klaus Gitt on 2/9/1962. He was born 12/1/1936. They had:

i. Andrew Joseph Gitt born 2/23/1963

ii. Angela Susan Gitt born 7/14/1964

iii. Carol Ann Gitt born 6/11/1968

2. Valeriano's great grandchildren, Virgilio's grandchildren, Virginia's family

Virginia May Jacuzzi (father=Virgilio Jacuzzi, mother=Beulah) married John David Burgess on 7/10/1963. He was born 11/9/1941. They had:

i. Cynthia Clare Burgess born 1/31/1966

ii. Christine Ann Burgess born 4/29/1967

iii. Jennifer Lynne Burgess born 12/18/1969

iv. John David Burgess Jr. born 4/20/1975

2. Valeriano's great grandchildren, Virgilio's grandchildren, Diana's family

Diana Jean Jacuzzi (father=Virgilio Jacuzzi, mother=Beulah) married Robert Cameron McRae on 8/20/1966. He was born 10/14/1942. They had:

i. Robert Cameron Virgil McRae born 12/21/1974

2. Valeriano's great grandchildren, Virgilio's grandchildren, Virgil's family

Virgil Thomas Joseph Jacuzzi (father=Virgilio Jacuzzi, mother=Beulah) married and had:

i. Jacqueline Virginia Jacuzzi born 9/18/1980

ii. Matthew Stanley Jacuzzi born 11/8/1989

2. Valeriano's great grandchildren, Virgilio's grandchildren, Susan's family

Susan Joan Jacuzzi (father=Virgilio Jacuzzi, mother=Beulah) married Poul-Erik Hansen. He was born 11/20/1939. They had:

i. Fleming Poul Hansen born 2/20/1986

ii. Pia Danielle Hansen born 3/22/1991

2. Valeriano's great grandchildren, Virgilio's grandchildren, Paul's family

Paul Vincent Jacuzzi (father=Virgilio Jacuzzi, mother=Beulah) married Rosie Tomasic on 8/4/1979. She was born 1/25/1956. They had:

i. Robin Sarah Jacuzzi born 6/30/1989

2. Valeriano's great grandchildren, Dante's grandchildren, Dante Paul Jr.'s' family

Dante Paul Jacuzzi Jr. (father=Dante Paul Jacuzzi, mother=Rosalyn) married Susan Jordan on 7/5/1980. She was born 6/4/1959. They had:

i. Dante Paul Jacuzzi III born 7/12/1982

ii. Jordan Michele Jacuzzi born 9/27/1984

iii. Andrew Thomas Jacuzzi born 10/3/1990

2. Valeriano's great grandchildren, Dante's grandchildren, Cheryl's family

Cheryl Christine Jacuzzi (father=Dante Paul Jacuzzi, mother=Rosalyn) married Burt Gee Squires on 11/25/1981. He was born 5/29/1949. They had:

i. Kathryn Christine Squires born 12/19/1984

ii. Michael Burton Squires born 7/24/1987

iii. Erin Elizabeth Squires born 11/9/1989

2. Valeriano's great grandchildren, Dante's grandchildren, Deborah's family

Deborah Ann Jacuzzi (father=Dante Paul Jacuzzi, mother=Rosalyn) married Garran Dee Barker on 4/17/1981. He was born 2/5/1956. They had:

i. Alexander Dee Barker born 7/8/1989

ii. Lauren Marie Barker born 4/14/1998

2. Valeriano's great grandchildren, Dante's grandchildren, Mary's family

Mary Regina Jacuzzi (father=Dante Paul Jacuzzi, mother=Rosalyn) married Robert Cecil Allison, Jr. on 9/24/1988. He was born 11/22/1947. They had:

i. William Porter Allison born 10/13/1978

ii. Blake Carney Allison born 12/20/1982

iii. Lindsey Elizabeth Allison born 5/31/1991

iv. Kristen Nicole Allison born 11/3/1993

2. Valeriano's great grandchildren, Jaconda's grandchildren, Robert's family

Robert Michael Hawkins (father=Robert Hawkins, mother=Jaconda) married Virginia Louise Groseth on 4/1/1967. She was born 5/26/1945. They had:

i. Carolyn Jean Hawkins born 1/10/1968

ii. Mark Andrew Hawkins born 5/23/1969

iii. Sara Song Hawkins born 11/23/1975

2. Valeriano's great grandchildren, Jaconda's grandchildren, Mary's family

Mary Margaret Hawkins (father=Robert Hawkins, mother=Jaconda) married Robert Gene Moncur on 1/28/1967. He was born 6/12/1942. They had:

i. Timothy Robert Moncur born 8/7/1967

ii. Susanne Christine Moncur born 10/30/1968

iii. Michael John Moncur born 4/8/1970.

iv. Daniel Stephen Moncur born 12/15/1981

v. Maria Lynne Moncur born 2/24/1984

2. Valeriano's great grandchildren, Jaconda's grandchildren, Patrick's family

Patrick Anthony Hawkins (father=Robert Hawkins, mother=Jaconda) married Dorothy Michele Shoffner on 8/6/1977. She was born 5/17/1952. They had:

i. Rachel Elizabeth Hawkins born 1/23/1982

ii. Jennifer Megan Hawkins born 10/18/1983

2. Valeriano's great grandchildren, Jaconda's grandchildren, Elizabeth's family

Elizabeth Teresa Hawkins (father=Robert Hawkins, mother=Jaconda) married Michael Alan Kozlowski on 9/1/1984. He was born 5/30/1957. They had:

i. Anthony Hawkins Kozlowski born 10/13/1989

ii. Nicolas Hawkins Kozlowski born 1/2/1993

iii. Zachary Hawkins Kozlowski born 12/30/1995, died 1/22/1996

2. Valeriano's great grandchildren, Teresa's grandchildren, Josephine's family

Josephine Anna DeShields (father=Donald DeShields, mother=Teresa) married first Mr. Clare and then Chester Avery on 8/14/1984. He was born 9/22/1946. She had by Mr. Clare:

    i. Joshi Linn Clare born 12/31/1970

    ii. Sequoia Moon Clare born 4/5/1973

    iii. Stephanie Rose Clare born 10/3/1976

2. Valeriano's great grandchildren, Teresa's grandchildren, Donald's family

Donald Anthony DeShields (father=Donald DeShields, mother=Teresa). He had:

    i. Shane Anthony DeShields born 10/5/1971

    ii. Amy Jean DeShields born 10/8/1974

2. Valeriano's great grandchildren, Teresa's grandchildren, William's family

William Martin DeShields (father=Donald DeShields, mother=Teresa). He had:

    i. Justin Morgan DeShields born 10/13/1986

    ii. Alexandra DeShields born 10/31/1988

    iii. Madison Lucinda DeShields born 4/15/1994

2. Valeriano's great grandchildren, Teresa's grandchildren, Anna's family

Anna Teresa DeShields (father=Donald DeShields, mother=Teresa) married Diego Velasquez on 10/3/1981. He was born 10/18/1953. They had:

    i. William Francesco Velasquez born 4/3/1982

    ii. Timothy Alejandro Velasquez born 9/11/1985

    iii. Julianna Marie Velasquez born 7/7/1989, died 7/7/1989

    iv. Catherine Anne Marie Velasquez born 2/3/1996

2. Valeriano's great grandchildren, Teresa's grandchildren, Teresa's family

Teresa Carol DeShields (father=Donald DeShields, mother=Teresa) married John Whitton on 6/8/1984. He was born 11/27/1946. They had:

i. James Johnathan Whitton born 4/14/1988

ii. Carlynn Margaret Whitton born 4/19/1994

2. Valeriano's great grandchildren, Mary Alice's grandchildren, Valerie's family

Valerie Anne Cline (father=James Cline, mother=Mary) married Kim Porter on 4/23/1977. He was born 8/28/1950. They had:

i. Kelly Owen Porter born 2/4/1978

ii. Ian Michael Porter born 7/19/1982

iii. Caitlan Quinn Porter born 1/21/1994

2. Valeriano's great grandchildren, Mary Alice's grandchildren, Marilyn's family

Marilyn Cline (father=James Cline, mother=Mary) married Thomas Keenan on 8/11/1973. He was born 8/18/1948. They had:

i. Sara Nicole Keenan born 6/21/1977

ii. Alison Rose Keenan born 9/19/1979

iii. Thomas Martin Keenan born 6/28/1984

iv. Mary Catherine Keenan born 7/1/1986

2. Valeriano's great grandchildren, Mary Alice's grandchildren, James' family

James Charles Cline (father=James Cline, mother=Mary) married Joanna Lee Haase 9/30/1989. She was born 11/16/1960. They had:

i. Elizabeth Ann Cline born 6/22/1983

ii. Helen Alyssa Cline born 10/3/1997

iii. James Jonathan Cline born 1/11/2002

2. Valeriano's great grandchildren, Mary Alice's grandchildren, Charles' family

Charles Brian Cline (father=James Cline, mother=Mary) married Regina Ruthe on 3/30/1985. She was born 3/17/1955. They had:

i. Corie Anne Cline born 4/24/1986

ii. Charles James Cline born 2/1/1988

iii. Blake Edward Cline born 5/7/1990

2. Valeriano's great grandchildren, Mary Alice's grandchildren, Frederic's family

Frederic Thomas Cline (father=James Cline, mother=Mary) married Nancy Joan Bunting on 11/1/1986. She was born 6/15/1957. They had:

i. Frederic Ramsey Cline born 4/21/1987

ii. Nancy Emma Cline born 2/19/1989

iii. Hillary Claire Cline born 8/16/1990

iv. Megan James Cline born 1/4/1992

v. Elsie Marie Cline born 8/10/1993

vi. Mayme Christine Cline born 7/21/1995

vii. Henry Edward Cline born 9/9/1997

2. Valeriano's great grandchildren, Mary Alice's grandchildren, Michael's family

Michael Jon Cline (father=James Cline, mother=Mary) married Karen Jean Smith on 8/4/1990. She was born 5/25/1959. They had:

i. Olivia Marie Cline born 7/28/1992

ii. Maxwell Jon Cline born 8/8/1994

iii. Kevin Michael Cline born 6/7/1997

2. Valeriano's great grandchildren, Mary Alice's grandchildren, Mary's family

Mary Janis Cline (father=James Cline, mother=Mary) married Michael John Pfaff on 8/28/1993. He was born 2/21/1952. They had:

    i. Mary Josephine Pfaff born 6/17/1994

    ii. Michael Sherwood Pfaff born 3/16/1996

    iii. James Gordon Pfaff born 6/8/1997

2. Valeriano's great grandchildren, Mary Alice's grandchildren, Matthew's family

Matthew Alan Cline (father=James Cline, mother=Mary) married Erin Patricia Horan on 10/29/1994. She was born 8/11/1967. They had:

    i. Madeline Isabelle Cline born 9/21/1996

    ii. Margaret Alice Cline born 5/15/1998

    iii. Anna Marie Cline born 7/7/2001

2. Valeriano's great grandchildren, Mary Alice's grandchildren, Gary's family

Gary Edward Cline (father=James Cline, mother=Mary) married Maureen Cook on 8/11/1985. She was born 7/5/1962. They had:

    i. Amy Rooney Cline born 5/30/1982

    ii. Gary Thomas Cline born 6/21/1991

    iii. Thomas James Cline born 9/29/1994

    iv. Katrina Marguerite Cline born 8/6/1996

2. Valeriano's great grandchildren, Flora's grandchildren, Jo Ann's family

Jo Ann Nicoletti (father=Joseph Nicoletti, mother=Flora) married Marven Blaha on 6/17/1978. He was born 8/15/1952. They had:

    i. Rebecca Margaret Blaha born 4/4/1979

    ii. Leah Christina Blaha born 12/25/1980

iii. Andrew Joseph Blaha born 12/29/1982

iv. Matthew Thomas Blaha born 5/14/1985

2. Valeriano's great grandchildren, Flora's grandchildren, Joseph's family

Joseph Michael Nicoletti (father=Joseph Nicoletti, mother=Flora) married Ann Null on 7/3/1982. She was born 7/30/1959. They had:

i. Michael Joseph Nicoletti born 4/1/1983

ii. Joshua Christopher Nicoletti born 3/10/1985

iii. Jeremy David Nicoletti born 8/27/1986

2. Valeriano's great grandchildren, Flora's grandchildren, Janice's family

Janice Margaret Nicoletti (father=Joseph Nicoletti, mother=Flora) married Richard Jefferson 5/26/1984. He was born 3/15/1956. They had:

i. Kathleen Margaret Jefferson born 3/23/1985

ii. Emily Ann Jefferson born 1/11/1987

iii. Erin Susanna Jefferson born 6/10/1989

iv. Caroline Jefferson born 9/15/1991

v. Eleanora Jefferson born 8/5/1993

vi. Jennifer Christiana Jefferson born 2/2/1996

2. Valeriano's great grandchildren, Flora's grandchildren, Katherine's family

Katherine Jane Nicoletti (father=Joseph Nicoletti, mother=Flora) married David Joseph Tims on 8/9/1986. He was born 12/3/1960. They had:

i. Samson John Tims born 9/30/1988

ii. Maxwell Joseph Tims born 3/6/1990

iii. Emmet Jacob Tims born 1/15/1993

iv. Sadie Jane Tims born 3/12/1997

2. Valeriano's great-grandchildren, Flora's grandchildren, Robert John's family

Robert John Nicoletti (father=Joseph Nicoletti, mother=Flora) married Jody Ann Smith. They had:

i. Joseph Michael Nicoletti born 8/30/2003

2. Valeriano's great grandchildren, Remo's grandchildren, Remo's family

Remo Valerian Jacuzzi (father=Remo Cesare Jacuzzi, mother=Paula) married Lynn Marie Piere on 12/18/1982. She was born 12/10/1957. They had:

i. Nina Marie Jacuzzi born 6/2/1984

ii. Remo Alexander Jacuzzi born 10/12/1988

iii. Emily Ruth Jacuzzi born 12/6/1990

2. Valeriano's great grandchildren, Remo's grandchildren, Jennifer's family

Jennifer June Jacuzzi (father=Remo Cesare Jacuzzi, mother=Paula) married Daniel Mahan Peregrin on 8/1/1981. He was born 12/4/1957. They had:

i. Jacqueline Jacuzzi Peregrin born 8/27/1984

ii. Daniel O'Donovan Peregrin born 6/1/1988

iii. Madison Mahan Peregrin born 5/7/1990

iv. Anastasia Mikolaj Peregrin born 10/11/1993

2. Valeriano's great grandchildren, Remo's grandchildren, Loretta's family

Loretta Dawn Jacuzzi (father=Remo Cesare Jacuzzi, mother=Paula) married James Scott Stewart on 10/11/1986. He was born 9/27/1965. They had:

i. Seth Christian Stewart born 11/10/1988

ii. Katherine McKenzie Stewart born 12/31/1990

iii. Scott Ethan Stewart born 10/26/1994

2. Valeriano's great grandchildren, Remo's grandchildren, Gretchen's family

Gretchen Lynn Jacuzzi (father=Remo Cesare Jacuzzi, mother=Paula) married Dr. Tyson James Roe on 6/11/1988. He was born 7/6/1962. They had:

i. Addison Austin Roe born 4/25/1990

ii. Asher James Roe born 1/18/1992

iii. Hannah Laura Roe born 8/4/1994

2. Valeriano's great grandchildren, Remo's grandchildren, Paulo Andrews family

Paulo Andrew Jacuzzi (father=Remo Jacuzzi, mother=Paula) married Jennifer Bosley Amos on 7/10/2004. She was born on 9/6/1966. They had:

i. Mallory Erin Tarp born 5/11/1990

3. Francesco's great grandchildren, Giocondo's grandchildren, Janice's family

Janice Paula Jacuzzi (father=Giocondo Jacuzzi, mother=Lillian) married Mr. Pollio first then Martin Hussey. Janice and Mr. Pollio had:

i. Christine Marlene Pollio born 8/27/1965

ii. Michael Albert Pollio born 12/23/1966

iii. James Matthew Pollio born 3/7/1970

3. Francesco's great grandchildren, Giocondo's grandchildren, Marc's family

Marc Steven Jacuzzi (father=Giocondo Frank Jacuzzi, mother=Lillian) married Karen Kelly on 12/2/1978. She was born 2/7/1954. They had:

i. Rebecca Marie Jacuzzi born 11/3/1981

ii. Nicholas Bernard Jacuzzi born 6/29/1984

iii. Natalie Marie Jacuzzi born 7/31/1986

3. Francesco's great grandchildren, Giocondo's grandchildren, Carol's family

Carol Ann Jacuzzi (father=Giocondo Frank Jacuzzi, mother=Lillian) married Ray Lisai on 7/10/1983. He was born 4/13/1951. They had:

i. Paul Jacuzzi Lisai born 12/31/1983

ii. Jason Leonard Lisai born 8/19/1969

3. Francesco's great grandchildren, Ugo's grandchildren, Nancy's family

Nancy Jacuzzi (father=Ugo Jacuzzi, mother=Justine) married Mr. Nipkow. They had:

i. Nicole Nipkow born 1/28/1978

3. Francesco's great grandchildren, Ugo's grandchildren, Susan's family

Susan Lynn Jacuzzi (father=Ugo Jacuzzi, mother=Justine) married Michael P. Cochrane on 8/30/1975. He was born 7/27/1951. They had:

i. Patrick Saunders Cochrane born 6/18/1980

ii. Trevor Michael Cochrane born 9/25/1983

4. Giuseppe's great grandchildren, Aldo's grandchildren, Roy's family

Roy Aldo Jacuzzi (father=Aldo Joseph Jacuzzi, mother=Granuccia) married Dee-Ann Peterson Gunn. She was born 11/9/1958. They had:

i. Jonathan Joseph Jacuzzi

ii. Robert Jason Jacuzzi born 2/4/1970

iii. Lincoln Gunn Jacuzzi born 8/9/1987

iv. Giordano Petter Jacuzzi born 4/4/1994

4. Giuseppe's great grandchildren, Aldo's grandchildren, Victor's family

Victor Steven Jacuzzi (father=Aldo Joseph Jacuzzi, mother=Granuccia) married Sandra Kay Taylor on 4/2/2005. She was born 5/5/1953. They had:

    i. Shannon Lhea Jacuzzi born 6/1/1966

    ii. Stacey Suzanne Jacuzzi born 9/9/1967, died 7/9/2004

    iii. Victor Steven Jacuzzi Jr. born 10/2/1968

4. Giuseppe's great grandchildren, Aldo's grandchildren, Rita's family

Rita Carol Jacuzzi (father=Aldo Joseph Jacuzzi, mother=Granuccia) married Jeffrey Lynn Huber on 6/23/2001. He was born 10/16/1953. She already had:

    i. William Paxton Brinkley born 3/31/1975

    ii. Dayna Carol Brinkley born 5/2/1979

    iii. James Thomas McCann born 2/22/1983

5. Gelindo's great grandchildren, Lola's grandchildren, Ronald's family

Lawrence Fenolio (father=Lawrence Fenolio, mother=Lola) married Jeanne Marie Mudd on 5/9/1981. She was born 10/4/1949. They had:

    i. Christopher Lawrence Fenolio born 10/4/1981

    ii. Ronald Eugene Fenolio born 4/25/1983

    iii. Peter Gelindo Fenolio born 4/9/1986

5. Gelindo's great grandchildren, Olga's grandchildren, Richard's family

Richard Gilmour Gall Jr. (father=Richard Gilmour Gall, mother=Olga) married Maria Brunette. She was born 2/18/1960. They had:

    i. Mikaela Gall born 10/27/1989

    ii. Nikolas Ian Gelindo Gall born 12/17/1991

5. Gelindo's great grandchildren, Olga's grandchildren, Raymond Karl's family

Raymond Karl Gall (father=Richard Gilmour Gall, mother=Olga) married Van Thu Mai. She was born on 5/27/1963. They had:

i. Avalon Mai Gall born 5/19/2003

5. Gelindo's great grandchildren, Olga's grandchildren, Robert's family

Robert Charles Gall (father=Richard Gilmour Gall, mother=Olga) married Tina R. Katchen on 5/17/1986. She was born 10/27/1957. They had:

i. Alexander Ryan Gall born 7/29/1989

ii. Evan Michael Gall born 5/6/1994

iii. Sarah Ashley Gall born ll/21/1995

5. Gelindo's great grandchildren, Olga's grandchildren, Marjorie's family

Marjorie Lynn Gall (father=Richard Gilmour Gall, mother=Olga) married Richard Marshall Himes on 3/22/1986. He was born 1/23/1956. They had:

i. Christina Anne Himes born 6/8/1988

ii. Catherine Elizabeth Himes born 7/17/1990

iii. Caroline Rose Himes born 1/14/1993

iv. Camilla Louise Himes born 11/4/1996

5. Gelindo's great grandchildren, Tullio's grandchildren, Linda's family

Linda Lee Jacuzzi (father=Tullio Jacuzzi, mother=Clydia) married Lynn Emery on 11/26/1980. He was born 3/12/1953. They had:

i. James Anthony Emery born 10/12/1968

ii. Adrian Bozeman born 2/15/1974

5. Gelindo's great grandchildren, Tullio's grandchildren, Richard's family

Richard Steven Jacuzzi (father=Tullio Jacuzzi, mother=Clydia) married Patti Caver on 4/2/1982. She was born 5/23/1947. They had:

i. Richard Steven Jacuzzi Jr. born 6/13/1969

ii. Casey Caver Jacuzzi born 2/2/1984

5. Gelindo's great grandchildren, Tullio's grandchildren, Kathleen's family

Kathleen Ann Jacuzzi (father=Tullio Jacuzzi, mother=Clydia) married Larry Fluharty on 8/11/1984. He was born 4/5/1948. They had:

i. John Jones born 9/6/1970

ii. Benjamin Blakney Fluharty born 9/14/1986

iii. Daniel Casey Fluharty born 1/27/1989

5. Gelindo's great grandchildren, Tullio's grandchildren, James' family

James Tullio Jacuzzi (father=Tullio Jacuzzi, mother=Clydia) married Marilyn Jean Hill on 7/27/1974. She was born 7/24/1954. They had:

i. Gregory Alan Jacuzzi born 1/20/1978

ii. Phillip Randall Jacuzzi born 9/29/1981

iii. Kimberly Rebecca Jacuzzi born 1/13/1983

5. Gelindo's great grandchildren, Tullio's grandchildren, Jane's family

Jane Carol Jacuzzi (father=Tullio Jacuzzi, mother=Clydia) married John Chadwick Gavin on 5/16/1986. He was born 2/1/1955. They had:

i. Leanna Christine Gavin born 8/1/1994

5. Gelindo's great grandchildren, Tullio's grandchildren, Nancy's family

Nancy Marie Jacuzzi (father=Tullio Jacuzzi, mother=Clydia) married Patrick Nolan Davenport on 6/21/1997. He was born 1/15/1954. They had:

i. Heather Marie Atkins

5. Gelindo's great grandchildren, Tullio's grandchildren, Andrew's family

Andrew Martin Jacuzzi (father=Tullio Jacuzzi, mother=Clydia) had:

i. Hannah Alexandra Jacuzzi born 10/22/1994

5. Gelindo's great grandchildren, Tullio's grandchildren, Julie's family

Julie Lynn Jacuzzi (father=Tullio Jacuzzi, mother=Clydia) married Gary Lee Housholder on 12/1/1984. He was born 1/6/1958. They had:

i. Curtis Lee Housholder born 9/19/1986

ii. Laura Jane Housholder born 11/2/1988

iii. Olivia Jean Housholder born 3/19/1994

5. Gelindo's great grandchildren, Tullio's grandchildren, Robert Casey's family

Robert Casey Jacuzzi (father=Tullio Jacuzzi, mother=Clydia) married Michelle Leigh Raney on 10/26/1997. She was born 9/9/1971. They had:

i. Luke Christopher Jacuzzi born 3/4/2004

5. Gelindo's great grandchildren, Rodolfo's grandchildren, Marianne's family

Marianne Jacuzzi (father=Rodolfo Jacuzzi, mother=Mary) married Robert Arthur Mohr Jr. on 3/20/1982. He was born 12/28/1951. They had:

i. Patrick Thomas Mohr born 3/26/1982

ii. Brendan Robert Mohr born 6/16/1985

iii. Kieran Stephan Mohr born 1/8/1992

5. Gelindo's great grandchildren, Rodolfo's grandchildren, Laura's family

Laura Lea Jacuzzi (father=Rodolfo Jacuzzi, mother=Mary) had:

   i. Matthew Rodolfo Jacuzzi born 4/22/1981

   ii. Lea Marie Jacuzzi born 5/14/1990

5. Gelindo's great grandchildren, Rodolfo's grandchildren, Douglas' family

Douglas Reid Jacuzzi (father=Rodolfo Jacuzzi, mother=Mary) married Georgia Dee Hodges on 8/8/1992. She was born 12/15/1964. They had:

   i. Lola Dee Jacuzzi born 3/5/2001

   ii. Cielo Elizibeth Jacuzzi born 4/7/2003

5. Gelindo's great grandchildren, Rodolfo's grandchildren, Leanna's family

Leanna Marie Jacuzzi (father=Rodolfo Jacuzzi, mother=Mary) married Bradley Jonathan Thomas on 10/17/1998. He was born 12/3/1954. They had:

   i. Spencer Reid Thomas born 1/8/2000

   ii. Dylan Franklin Thomas born 2/28/2002

5. Gelindo's great grandchildren, Rodolfo's grandchildren, Marc's family

Marc Lewis Jacuzzi (father=Rodolfo Jacuzzi, mother=Mary) married Kaye Anne Anable on 6/24/1995. She was born 7/9/1968. They had:

   i. Cullen Reid Jacuzzi born 8/3/1998

   ii. Aidan Lewis Jacuzzi born 6/23/2000

   iii. Ava Alexandra Jacuzzi born 11/4/2004

5. Gelindo's great grandchildren, Daniele's grandchildren, David's family

David Gelindo Jacuzzi (father=Daniele Jacuzzi, mother=Jean) married Glorianne June Wong on 9/19/1981. She was born 6/13/1956. They had:

i. Matthew Ryan Wong Jacuzzi born 8/3/1992

ii. Lisa Nicole Wong Jacuzzi born 7/30/1995

5. Gelindo's great grandchildren, Daniele's grandchildren, Daniel's family

Daniel Craig Jacuzzi (father=Daniele Jacuzzi, mother=Jean) married Nan Ellen Karperos on 1/28/1989. She was born 11/8/1954. They had:

i. Thomas Marshall Jacuzzi born 7/14/1991

ii. Alec Michael Jacuzzi born 2/11/1993

6. Giocondo's great grandchildren, Anna's grandchildren, Richard's family

Richard Eugene Liotta (father=Vincent Liotta, mother=Anna) married Leonor Natalia Fortis on 6/6/1991. She was born 11/22/1959. They had:

i. Marc Anthony Liotta born 10/17/1970

ii. Dante Liotta born 7/23/1998

iii. Analisa Liotta born 7/15/2001

iv. Dario Liotta born 7/15/2001

6. Giocondo's great grandchildren, Anna's grandchildren, Bruce's family

Bruce John Liotta (father=Vincent Liotta, mother=Anna) had:

i. Gavin Bruce Liotta born 10/10/1983

6. Giocondo's great grandchildren, Anna's grandchildren, David's family

David Howard Liotta (father=Vincent Liotta, mother=Anna) married Rosanne (Rose) Farnesi on 6/21/1975. She was born 9/3/1949. They had:

i. Anthony David Liotta born 4/27/1983

ii. Michael Vincent Liotta born 9/30/1987

7. Felicita's great grandchildren, John Vincent's grandchildren, Kathleen Jane's family

Kathleen Jane Lanza (father=John Vincent Lanza, mother=Rosemary) married Jim Whirlow on 7/8/1973. He was born 2/11/1951. They had:

i. Kami Whirlow born 3/7/1974

ii. Chris Whirlow born 8/11/1975

iii. Anthony Whirlow born 12/22/1976

8. Angelina's great grandchildren, Doris' grandchildren, Christopher's family

Christopher Adamo (father=Joseph Adamo, mother=Doris) He had:

i. Domenic Christopher Adamo born 12/26/1983

ii. Sergio Try Adamo born 7/26/1985

iii. Emilio Peter Adamo born 4/30/1988

iv. Basevi Matteo Adamo born 7/18/1991

8. Angelina's great grandchildren, Doris' grandchildren, Thomas' family

Thomas David Adamo (father=Joseph Adamo, mother=Doris) Lorna Jones. They Had:

i. Derek Thomas Adamo born 1/1/1986

ii. Alexander Joseph Adamo born 9/24/1987

iii. Genavieve Christine Adamo born 8/6/1991

8. Angelina's great grandchildren, Edith's grandchildren, Marguerite's family

Marquerite Ann De Amicis (father=De Amicis, mother=Edith) married Christopher Bennet. He was born 4/26/1962. They had:

    i. Michele Marie Bennet born 5/11/1977

8. Angelina's great grandchildren, Edith's grandchildren, Roger's family

Roger Peter De Amicis (father=De Amicis, mother=Edith) married Liz Rose Taormina on 5/12/1984. She was born 6/8/1963. They had:

    i. Natalie Renee De Amicis born 2/13/1987

    ii. Lisa Marie De Amicis born 12/22/1989

    iii. Ryan Alexander De Amicis born 7/4/1992

8. Angelina's great grandchildren, Edith's grandchildren, Carl's family

Carl Vincent De Amicis (father=De Amicis, mother=Edith) married Ilene Cohen on 12/9/1990. She was born 4/7/1956. They had:

    i. Teresa Edith De Amicis born 2/26/1983

    ii. Richard T. De Amicis born 4/12/1985

    iii. Matthew Becker born 4/10/1985

    iv. Joshua De Amicis born 3/3/1994

9. Ancilla's great grandchildren, Leo's grandchildren, Marcia's family

Marcia Madeline Bianchi (father=Leo Bianchi, mother=Helen). She had:

    i. Gina Maria Barteletti born 8/22/1985

9. Ancilla's great grandchildren, Leo's grandchildren, Barbara's family

Barbara Anne Bianchi (father=Leo Bianchi, mother=Helen) married David Kirby on 5/26/1973. He was born 1/18/1950. They had:

    i. Jason Bianchi Kirby born 5/20/1980

ii. Valerie Bianchi Kirby born 3/30/1982

9. Ancilla's great grandchildren, Leo's grandchildren, Laura's family

Laura Jean Bianchi (father=Leo Bianchi, mother=Helen) married Jose Payne on 7/19/1986. He was born 3/13/1963. They had:

i. Joseph William Bianchi Payne born 7/11/1990

ii. Kathryn Helen Bianchi Payne born 12/14/1995

9. Ancilla's great grandchildren, John's grandchildren, John Jr's family

John Mario Bianchi Jr. (father=John Bianchi, mother=Elaine) had:

i. Michael John Bianchi born 7/18/1981

ii. Lara Michelle Bianchi born 1/5/1984

9. Ancilla's great grandchildren, John's grandchildren, Becky's family

Becky Marie Bianchi (father=John Bianchi, mother=Elaine) married Steven Petersen on 10/22/1977. He was born 8/12/1954. They had:

i. Matthew Steven Petersen born 11/26/1979

ii. Daniel James Petersen born 6/14/1983

iii. Timothy Joseph Petersen born 5/31/1986

10. Candido's great grandchildren, Alba's grandchildren, Stephen's family

Stephen Peter Kosta (father=Peter Kosta, mother=Alba) married Jeanne Meange on 9/2/1979. She was born 4/17/1948. They had:

i. Matthew S. Kosta born 3/21/1981

ii. Andrew P. Kosta born 2/1/1983

iii. Jennifer M. Kosta born 11/12/1986

10. Candido's great grandchildren, Alba's grandchildren, Candida's family

Candida Alba Kosta (father=Peter Kosta, mother=Alba) married David Shawver on 6/14/1975. He was born 6/8/1951. They had:

i. Katherine Lee Shawver born 6/10/1977

10. Candido's great grandchildren, Alba's grandchildren, Cynthia's family

Cynthia Ann Kosta (father=Peter Kosta, mother=Alba) married Robert Polizzi. They had:

i. Jessica Alba Polizzi born 6/12/1985

ii. Chelsea Michelle Polizzi born 5/22/1990

10. Candido's great grandchildren, John's grandchildren, Elizabeth's family

Elizabeth Ann Jacuzzi (father=John Jacuzzi, mother=Margaret) married Abel Guerra on 10/22/1977. He was born 5/25/1954. They had:

i. Elizabeth Guerra born 11/19/1979

ii. Evelyn Guerra born 6/30/1982

iii. Abel Guerra born 4/2/1984

10. Candido's great grandchildren, John's grandchildren, Patricia's family

Patricia Jan Jacuzzi (father=John Jacuzzi, mother=Margaret) married Angel Pasta and they had:

i. Carola Pasta born 1/3/1980

10. Candido's great grandchildren, John's grandchildren, John Bruno's family

John Bruno Jacuzzi, Jr. (father=John Bruno Jacuzzi, mother=Margaret) married Lorena Woo on 5/18/1985. She was born 10/2/1961. They had:

i. Giovanna Jacuzzi born 4/21/1989

10. Candido's great grandchildren, John's grandchildren, James Candido's family

James Candido Jacuzzi (father=John Bruno Jacuzzi, mother=Margaret) married Maribel Salazar on 4/24/1999. She was born 1/1/1970. They had:

i. James Jacuzzi born 11/18/1992

ii. Gian Jacuzzi born 5/12/2001

10. Candido's great grandchildren, Irene's grandchildren, Rosanna's family

Rosanna Inez Roescheise (father=Don Roescheise, mother=Irene) married David John Hanley on 1/16/1988. He was born 6/15/1954. They had:

i. David Christopher Hanley born 5/20/1989

ii. Elizabeth Irene Hanley born 1/16/1991

10. Candido's great grandchildren, Irene's grandchildren, Deborah's family

Deborah Ann Roescheise (father=Don Roescheise, mother=Irene) married Marc Brian Glazer on 3/8/1979. He was born 7/18/1956. They had:

i. Evan Lee Glazer born 1/4/1981

ii. Alesha Marie Glazer born 4/18/1984

iii. Ryan C. J. Glazer born 11/24/1986

iv. Travis Isaac Glazer born 6/25/1990

v. Shane C. J. Glazer born 2/4/1993

vi. Michele Debra Glazer born 8/28/1996

10. Candido's great grandchildren, Irene's grandchildren, Cristina's family

Cristina Ruth Roescheise (father=Don Roescheise, mother=Irene) married Frank Kuiper on 9/27/1986. He was born 4/20/1950. They had:

i. Brett Kuiper born 8/21/1973

ii. Justin Kuiper born 12/2/1977

iii. Kyle James Kuiper born 4/12/1988

iv. Derek Donald Kuiper born 1/5/1991

v. Mitchell Kenneth Kuiper born 2/2/1995

10. Candido's great grandchildren, Irene's grandchildren, Raymond's family

Raymond Roescheise (father=Don Roescheise, mother=Irene) and Lizabeth Westman had:

i. Adam Roescheise—Westman born 5/2/1988

ii. Tobias Roescheise—Westman born 5/2/1988

11. Cirilla's great grandchildren, Harold's grandchildren, Anne's family

Anne Theresa Benassini (father=Harold Benassini, mother=Marcella) married Rogelio Aranda on 4/18/1980. He was born 11/7/1943. They had:

i. Victor Daniel Aranda born 6/11/1983

ii. Silvia Jane Aranda born 5/11/1986

iii. Monica Elise Aranda born 5/11/1986

11. Cirilla's great grandchildren, Lydia's grandchildren, Gary's family

Gary Joseph Negherbon (father=Frank Negherbon, mother=Lydia) married Gertrude (Trudy) Ann Chapman on 8/19/1972. She was born 3/2/1951. They had:

i. Aaron James Negherbon born 11/13/1973

ii. Amanda Ann Negherbon born 4/25/1977

11. Cirilla's great grandchildren, Norma's grandchildren, Peter's family

Peter Joseph Nuti (father=Caesar Nuti, mother=Norma) married Stacy Gillock on 2/6/1988. She was born 11/16/1964. They had:

i. Arianna Michel Nuti born 10/10/1989

ii. Angelina Norma Nuti born 7/20/1994

iii. Dominic Joseph Nuti born 2/21/1997, died 5/3/2001

iv. Anabella Emma Nuti born 8/30/2002

11. Cirilla's great grandchildren, Norma's grandchildren, Gregory's family

Gregory Caesar Nuti (father=Caesar Nuti, mother=Norma) married Claire Jullien on 9/8/1990. She was born 9/21/1963. They had:

i. Grayson Gregory Nuti born 5/21/1992

ii. Cory Caesar Nuti born 4/17/1995

iii. Jenna Nicole Nuti born 7/16/1997

11. Cirilla's great grandchildren, Norma's grandchildren, Suzanne's family

Suzanne Theresa Nuti (father=Caesar Nuti, mother=Norma) married Paul Peterson on 6/13/1987. He was born 9/9/1963. They had:

i. Gregory Phillip Peterson born 6/21/1996

ii. Anneliese Rose Peterson born 5/20/1999

iii. Celeste Marie Peterson born 4/8/2002

11. Cirilla's great grandchildren, Norma's grandchildren, Paul's family

Paul Michael Nuti (father=Caesar Nuti, mother=Norma) married Elizabeth Goebel on 5/3/1997. She was born 2/24/1971. They had:

i. Julia Clare Nuti born 6/18/2002

ii. Emma Rose Nuti born 10/20/2004

12. Stella's great grandchildren, Silviano's grandchildren, Douglas' family

Douglas Marin (father=Silviano Marin, mother=Jean) married Carol Ann Dodd on 5/20/1972. She was born 5/15/1951. They had:

i. Scott Marin born 9/7/1984

ii. Will Marin born 1/13/1988

12. Stella's great grandchildren, Silviano's grandchildren, Curtis' family

Curtis Marin (father=Silviano Marin, mother=Jean) married Dianne Burror on 3/25/1977. She was born 4/25/1945. They had:

   i. Sharon Marin born 10/18/1977

   ii. Darren Marin born 7/11/1979

   iii. Daniel Marin born 1/3/1982

12. Stella's great grandchildren, Silviano's grandchildren, Janine's family

Janine Estelle Marin (father=Silviano Marin, mother=Jean) married Allan Fredrick Rose on 2/25/1978. He was born 1/26/1944. They had:

   i. Trevor Rose born 10/30/1983

   ii. Tristan Rose born 2/3/1987

12. Stella's great grandchildren, George's grandchildren, Steven's family

Steven Craig Marin (father=George Marin, mother=Patricia) married Roxanne Woods on 5/26/1991. She was born 2/1/1965. They had:

   i. Elizabeth Anne Marin born 12/9/1994

   ii. Patrick George Marin born 7/12/1996

   iii. Rebecca Lynne Marin born 6/11/1998

13. Gilia's great grandchildren, Nilda's grandchildren, John's family

John Daniel Rego, Jr. (father=John Rego, mother=Nilda) married Deborah Kahane on 5/5/1978. She was born 3/29/1953. They had:

   i. Joshua Adam Rego born 10/5/1986

   ii. Benjamin Daniel Rego born 8/20/1989

13. Gilia's great grandchildren, Nilda's grandchildren, Michael's family

Michael David Rego (father=John Rego, mother=Nilda) married Susan Van Nevel on 12/15/1979. She was born 11/19/1954. They had:

i. Joshua Sean William Rego born 5/25/1990

ii. Christopher Daniel Rego born 7/25/1992

13. Gilia's great grandchildren, Nilda's grandchildren, Charles' family

Charles Anthony Rego (father=John Rego, mother=Nilda) married Jennifer Johnston on 6/28/1980. She was born 9/3/1960. They had:

i. Jeffrey Ryan Rego born 3/29/1986

ii. Rebecca Katherine Rego born 9/8/1989

iii. Elizabeth Pauline Rego born 3/15/1998

13. Gilia's great grandchildren, Nilda's grandchildren, Frank's family

Frank Alan Rego (father=John Rego, mother=Nilda) married Bridget Gold on 9/10/1988. She was born 8/2/1962. They had:

i. Matthew Thomas Rego born 2/14/1990

ii. Zachary Daniel Rego born 10/15/1992

iii. Anna Mairead Rego born 8/28/1994

13. Gilia's great grandchildren, Esther's grandchildren, Christina's family

Christina Marie Regula (father=George Regula, mother=Esther) married Keith Hancock on 9/27/1991. He was born 5/4/1966. They had:

i. George Alexander Hancock born 12/9/1994

ii. Catherine Marie Hancock born 1/20/1999

Generation No. 5

2. Valeriano's great great grandchildren, Virgilio's great grandchildren, Beverly's grandchildren, Wiley's family

Wiley Virgil Allgood, Jr. (stepfather=Bernard Edgell, mother=Beverly) married Heidi Anne Boelts on 6/4/1988. She was born 6/16/1966. They had:

    i. Elizabeth Ann Allgood born 12/8/1992

    ii. Abigail Elyse Allgood born 11/29/1996

    iii. Wiley David Allgood born 10/5/2000

2. Valeriano's great great grandchildren, Virgilio's great grandchildren, Beverly's grandchildren, Heidi's family

Heidi Suzanne Allgood (stepfather=Bernard Edgell, Mother=Beverly) married Christopher Todd Stoneking on 12/16/1989. He was born 8/16/1964. They had:

    i. Emma Kathleen Stoneking born 1/8/1995

    ii. Sarah Nicole Stoneking born 5/11/1999

2. Valeriano's great great grandchildren, Virgilio's great grandchildren, Beverly's grandchildren, Holly's family

Holly Anne Allgood (stepfather=Bernard Edgell, Mother=Beverly) married Daniel Lynn Marlowe. They had:

    i. Hannah Christine Marlowe born 8/9/1996

    ii. Madison Lynn Marlowe born 3/30/1999

2. Valeriano's great great grandchildren, Virgilio's great grandchildren, Lita's grandchildren, Andrew's family

Andrew Joseph Gitt (father=Joachim Gitt, mother=Lita) married Ewa Jonsson on 6/24/1988. She was born 2/8/1957. They had:

    i. Caroline Lita Gitt born 8/30/1989

    ii. Natalie Ericka Gitt born 1/23/1991

    iii. Sabastian Lars Gitt born 2/12/1996

2. Valeriano's great great grandchildren, Virgilio's great grandchildren, Lita's grandchildren, Angela's family

Angela Susan Gitt (father=Joachim Gitt, mother=Lita) married Timothy Dennis Hemmen on 5/9/1992. He was born 11/14/1957. They had:

i. Sarah Caitlyn Hemmen born 7/14/1994

ii. Madeline Claire Hemmen born 5/23/1996

2. Valeriano's great-great-grandchildren, Virgilio's great-grandchildren, Lita's grandchildren, Carol Ann's family

Carol Ann Gitt (father=Joachim Klaus Gitt, mother=Lita) married Kenneth William Mahaffey on 10/12/2002. He was born 4/27/1963. They had:

i. Devin William Mahaffey born 6/2/2004

2. Valeriano's great great grandchildren, Virgilio's great grandchildren, Virginia's grandchildren, Christine's family

Christine Ann Burgess (father=John Burgess, mother=Virginia) married Mark Joseph Jany on 7/20/1991. He was born 5/8/1966. They had:

i. Laura Virginia Jany born 9/16/1995

ii. Catherine Anne Jany born 9/3/1997

2. Valeriano's great great grandchildren, Jaconda's great grandchildren, Robert's grandchildren, Sara's family

Sara Song Hawkins (father=Robert Hawkins, mother=Jaconda) had:

i. Isabel Rose Pelarski born 2/25/2000

2. Valeriano's great great grandchildren, Jaconda's great grandchildren, Mary's grandchildren, Timothy's family

Timothy Robert Moncur (father=Robert Moncur, mother=Mary) married Jennifer Lynn Villwock on 12/28/1991. She was born 10/19/1967. They had:

i. Sean Timothy Moncur born 2/6/2000

ii. Byrnn Rene Moncur 2/18/2002

2. Valeriano's great-great-grandchildren, Jaconda's great-grandchildren, Mary's grandchildren, Susanne's family

Susanne Christine Moncur (father=Robert Gene Moncur, mother=Mary) married Jukka Villa Kukkanen on 11/30/2002. He was born on 12/31/1972. They had:

    i. Sonja Eveliina Kukkanen born 4/22/2004

2. Valeriano's great great grandchildren, Teresa's great grandchildren, Donald's grandchildren, Amy's family

Amy Jean DeShields (father=Donald DeShields, mother=Patti) married Ben Zimmerman on 6/12/1999. They had:

    i. Emily Jean Zimmerman born 4/4/2000

    ii. Greta Teresa Zimmerman born 6/29/2003

2. Valeriano's great great grandchildren, Teresa's great grandchildren, Donald's grandchildren, Melanie's family

Melanie Rose DeShields (father=Donald DeShields, mother=Patti) married Raphael Costa on 10/21/1996. He was born on 3/2/1973. They had:

    i. Zoe Rose Costa born 1/5/1998

3. Francesco's great great grandchildren, Giocondo's great grandchildren, Janice's grandchildren, Christine's family

Christine Marlene Pollio (father=Joe Pollio, mother=Janice) married Robert Conolly Quinn on 9/27/1997. He was born 7/1/1962. They had:

    i. Robert Conolly Quinn, Jr. born 1/23/1989

    ii. Margert Deans Conolly Quinn born 6/6/1991

    iii. Lillian Grace Quinn born 4/9/1999

    iv. Nora Ruth Quinn born 6/26/2000

3. Francesco's great great grandchildren, Giocondo's great grandchildren, Janice's grandchildren, Michael's family

Michael Albert Pollio (father=Joe Pollio, mother=Janice) married Tara Anne Sobocinski on 9/18/1993. They had:

i. Kevin Francis Pollio born 3/8/1996

ii. Owen Michael Pollio born 12/13/1998

3. Francesco's great great grandchildren, Giocondo's great grandchildren, Janice's grandchildren, James' family

James Matthew Pollio (father=Joe Pollio, mother=Janice) married Tina Swett on 11/25/2000. She was born 8/24/1970. They had:

i. Matthew Xavier Pollio born 6/27/04

4. Giuseppe's great great grandchildren, Aldo's great grandchildren, Roy's grandchildren, Jonathan's family

Jonathan Joseph Jacuzzi (father=Roy Jacuzzi, mother=Vickie) married Lisa Marie Nuti on 4/25/1992. She was born 7/18/1967. They had:

i. Alexis Lynn Jacuzzi born 6/8/1996

ii. Rachel Elizabeth Jacuzzi born 6/9/1998

iii. Nicole Marie Jacuzzi born 12/20/1999

4. Giuseppe's great great grandchildren, Aldo's great grandchildren, Victor's grandchildren, Shannon's family

Shannon Lhea Jacuzzi (father=Victor Jacuzzi, mother=Nancy) married Russell James Berryhill. They had:

i. Stuart Russell Berryhill born 9/5/1991

ii. David Jacuzzi Berryhill born 5/1/1995

iii. Catherine Carter Berryhill born 9/23/1999

4. Giuseppe's great great grandchildren, Aldo's great grandchildren, Victor's grandchildren, Stacey's family

Stacey Suzanne Jacuzzi (father=Victor Jacuzzi, mother=Nancy) had:

   i. John Austin Antes born 8/18/1994

   ii. Justin Thomas Antes born 9/17/1996

4. Giuseppe's great great grandchildren, Aldo's great grandchildren, Rita's grandchildren, James's family

James Thomas McCann (father=McCann, mother=Rita) married Jessica Erin McCann on 6/28/2003. She was born 1/15/1982. They had:

   i. James David McCann born 9/3/2003

5. Gelindo's great great grandchildren, Tullio's great grandchildren, Linda's grandchildren, James' family

James Anthony Emery (father=Lynn Emery, mother=Linda) married Nicole Marie Copeland on 7/24/1993. She was born 8/29/1970. They had:

   i. Samantha Rose Emery born 11/4/1997

   ii. Michael Anthony Emery born 9/21/1999

   iii. David Alexander Emery born 5/16/2001

5. Gelindo's great great grandchildren, Tullio's great grandchildren, Linda's grandchildren, Adrian's family

Adrian Bozeman (father=Lynn Emery, mother=Linda) married Jaime Laine Hockaday on 10/17/1998. He was born 3/28/1977. They had:

   i. Gabriel Robert Bozeman born 4/15/1999

5. Gelindo's great great grandchildren, Tullio's great grandchildren, Richard's grandchildren, Richard Jr. family

Richard Steven Jacuzzi Jr. (father=Richard Jacuzzi, mother=Patti) married Kristine Alisha Booker on 6/8/1996. She was born 5/11/1973. They had:

   i. Isabella Catherine Jacuzzi born 4/18/2001

   ii. Grant Christopher Jacuzzi born 2/5/2003

5. Gelindo's great great grandchildren, Tullio's great grandchildren, Nancy's grandchildren, Heather's family

Heather Marie Atkins (father=Patrick Davenport, mother=Nancy) married Jason Ryan McKim on 6/23/2001. He was born 9/12/1982. They had:

    i. Callie Marie McKim born 11/28/2001

10. Candido's great great grandchildren, Alba's great grandchildren, Candida's grandchildren. Katherine's family

Katherine Lee Shawver (father=David Shawver, mother=Candida) married Matthew Milton June 2001. They had:

    i. Emma Alexis Milton born 4/6/2003

Sources

Aaseng, Nathan. 1989. *The Problem Solvers.* Lerner Publications: Minneapolis.

Biography of Candido Jacuzzi. *U.S. Patent and Trademark Office,* Arlington, Virginia.

Burd, Amy. 2000. Father to son. *Independent Newspapers,* Paradise Valley, AZ, October.

Cato, Loren. 1958. The Jacuzzi brothers: Rachele. *The Injector,* Jacuzzi Bros. Inc., (10:5) December.

Obituary of Candido Jacuzzi. 1986. *London Times,* 10 Oct.

Obituary of Candido Jacuzzi. 1986. *New York Times,* 10 Oct.

Obituary of Candido Jacuzzi. 1986. *Washington Post,* 10 Oct.

Obituary of Candido Jacuzzi. 1986. *Newsweek,* 20 Oct.

Obituary of Candido Jacuzzi. 1986. *People Weekly,* 27 Oct. (92–94)

Obituary of Candido Jacuzzi. 1988. *Contemporary Newsmakers.*

Palmer, Ted. 1952. A story of the Jacuzzi brothers, *Westward Magazine,* Kaiser Steel Corporation, May.

Rego, Nilda. 2003. Memories shared at Jacuzzi family reunion. *Contra Costa Times,* 5 Oct.

Scafetta, Jr., Joseph. History: wellspring of invention, Part I and II. *Franoi,* Chicago.

Ulmer, Christoph. 1999. *The Castles of Friuli: History and Civilization.* Udine: Konemann.

Note: Additional information about Rachele Jacuzzi was obtained from one of his nieces who was his last secretary, Lola Jacuzzi Fenolio, during a series of telephone interviews and correspondence conducted between 1992 and 1998.

Index

A

A Dash Through the Clouds 25
A Fire Next Time 167
A Hard Day's Night 182
A Romance in the Air 25
AAA 414
AARP 414, 442
Acapulco 209, 210, 211, 212, 290
Accessibility 107, 184, 373, 395, 414, 416, 432, 437, 438, 441, 442, 443
Al B. 344
Alice in Wonderland 396
Alioto, Joseph 141, 340
All That Jazz 206
Allen, Woody 206, 375
Anita 112, 113, 114, 115, 116, 117, 118, 119, 413
Ansani, Louis 99
Arbuckle, Fatty 25
Arman, Felicita 7
Armstrong, John 75, 247, 248
Astaire, Fred 198

B

Bailey, Jack 78, 136, 285
Baldwin, James 167
Balling the Jack 156
Barrett, Barbara iv
Beachey, Lincoln 25, 35
Beatles 172, 174, 185
Beckett, John xv
Beijing 307, 308, 356, 357, 358, 360
Benassini, Harold 101, 247, 267, 482

Benchley, Robert 109
Bill Haley and the Comets 139
Bob M. 175, 181, 183
Bogart, Humphrey 322
Bommersbach, Jana i
Bond, James 175, 181, 193, 198, 203, 396
Brando, Marlon 122
Brian 399, 451, 465, 481
Bruce C. 204
Bruno 259, 318, 319, 413, 448, 456
Bryan, Alfred 15
Burton, Richard 341
Byrd, James 384

C

Cabin monoplane iv, 29, 33, 35, 36, 38, 282
Calugi, Olympia 24, 446
Cantini, Professore 223
Caporetto 26
Capote, Truman 318
Carter, Jimmy 197, 364
Caruso, Frank 384
Casarsa 5, 6, 7, 8, 10, 13, 15, 17, 18, 19, 21, 30, 31, 38, 55, 241, 266, 305
Cecille 188, 189, 196
Chicago World's Fair 54
Cline Cellars 146
Cline, Fred 146
Clinton, Bill 85, 383
Coffee, Harold (Bud) 36
Concorde 347, 348, 350, 351
Cook, Judge Lyle E. 204
Cooper, Gary 197

Coquilini 242, 243, 301
Cortisone 111, 154
Cover, Wesley 383
Crisp, Donald 25
Cuevas, Cecilia xvi
Curtis, Tony 237, 238
Curtiss, Glenn 15

D

David xxix, 5, 35, 213, 277, 358, 359, 361, 363, 364, 454, 455, 458, 459, 467, 476, 477, 478, 480, 481, 485, 486, 489, 490, 491
Dean, James 262
DeConcini, Sen. Dennis i
Dempsey, Jack 24
DeSica, Vittorio 47
Detention camp 68, 131
DeWitt, John 81
Diane D. 184, 188, 190
DiMaggio, Joe 82
Don Quixote 204
Dylan, Bob 185

E

Easter Seals 190, 208, 252
Eastwood, Clint 205, 383
Egidio xvi, 220, 231, 232, 233, 234, 235, 297, 319, 413
Eisenhower, Dwight 106
Elliott, Milton 26
Ellis Island 14, 20, 21, 30, 31, 42, 82, 84
Elmer S. 105
Evans, George 12

F

Fisher, Fred 15
Flockhart, Calista 398
Florence Crittenden Home 162, 165
Flynn, Kay 125, 127, 140, 163
Fosse, Bob 206

Francis, Dr. J. Donald 123
Francisco xvi, 14, 23, 24, 30, 34, 35, 41, 43, 44, 46, 47, 64, 69, 73, 74, 75, 81, 82, 103, 121, 123, 128, 141, 159, 160, 162, 170, 173, 181, 182, 183, 189, 199, 200, 201, 203, 205, 209, 215, 221, 229, 233, 235, 237, 238, 239, 256, 296, 299, 325, 353, 354, 360, 433
French, Kenneth Junior 383
Friuli 6, 9, 12, 16, 19, 30, 39, 258, 263, 318, 322, 348, 493
Fulbright, J. William 192
Furlan 423

G

Gagarin, Yuri 163
Gardner, Ava 227
Garibaldi, Giuseppe 9
Gepetto 170, 171
Goodyear, Sarah 84
Gray, Nathan 140, 143, 247
Guaraldi, Vince xvii, 207

H

Hall, Bert 25
Hapsburg Empire 28
Harper, Randy xv
Hartmann, Bill 247
Hayworth, Rita 78
Helen 258, 292, 413, 433, 453, 455, 464, 478, 479
Henderson, Russell Arthur 379
Hennessy, David 35
Hepburn, Kathryn 7
High Noon 112
Hockenberry, John 372
Holloway, Diane xvi, xxi
Hoolihan, HotLips 126
Horan, Ray 247, 248, 259, 262, 352
Hoten, Mr. 106
Houdini, Harry 25

Hubbard Tank 66, 74
Hutton, Timothy 207

I

Ideal Marriage 111

J

Jackie 253, 254
Jacuzzi Family Tree 445
Jacuzzi Zinfandel 146
Jacuzzi, Aldo 259, 452, 470
Jacuzzi, Ancilla 445
Jacuzzi, Angela 5
Jacuzzi, Angelina 445
Jacuzzi, Candido xix, xxiv, 4, 41, 44, 61, 63, 137, 422, 446, 456, 493
Jacuzzi, Cirilla 39, 446
Jacuzzi, Francesco 446, 452
Jacuzzi, Gelindo 50, 445, 447, 452, 453, 454, 476
Jacuzzi, Gilia 446
Jacuzzi, Giocondo 37, 248, 282, 445, 447, 454, 469
Jacuzzi, Giovanni 5, 445, 446, 447, 448, 449
Jacuzzi, Giuseppe 447, 452
Jacuzzi, Gordon 449, 458
Jacuzzi, John 37, 480
Jacuzzi, Ken i, iii, iv, xix, xxi, xxxi, 137, 190, 273, 349, 372, 394, 419
Jacuzzi, Margaret 446, 451
Jacuzzi, Rachele 23, 54, 273, 445, 446, 449, 459, 494
Jacuzzi, Remo 101
Jacuzzi, Rose 204
Jacuzzi, Roy 489
Jacuzzi, Stella 446
Jacuzzi, Teresa 7, 98
Jacuzzi, Valeriano 146, 446, 449, 450, 451, 452
Jacuzzi, Virgil 247, 287
Jansen, Ralph xvi

Jet Charger pump 75
Joanne W. 177, 252
Jose 235, 236, 433, 479
Juanito 235, 236, 237
Julie xv, xvi, 150, 151, 152, 153, 154, 155, 156, 159, 162, 163, 165, 166, 169, 173, 188, 200, 202, 453, 474
Juvenile Rheumatoid Arthritis iii, xxiii, 64, 144, 159, 279, 366, 387, 409

K

Kauke, John 34
Kennedy, Jacqueline 189
Kennedy, John 161, 182, 189
Kennedy, Robert 25
Kennedy, Ted 238, 270, 364, 382
Kenny Packs 73
Kidd, James 383
King, Martin Luther 175, 185, 218
Kitch, Anne 381
KJ Software 355, 359, 361, 362, 363, 364, 365, 398
Koeth, Julie xv
Kosta, Alba 456, 480
Kosta, Peter xi, 43, 71, 249, 286, 456, 479, 480

L

LaBrie, Phil 381
Lavagetto, Cookie 77
Lemmon, Jack 246
Leno, Jay 399, 402
Lick Observatory 24
Lindbergh, Charles 49
Lisbon 215, 216, 218
Locklear, Ormer 26
Lolita 191, 192, 193, 194, 195, 413

M

MacArthur, Douglas 108
Mafia 35, 344

Malaga 231, 232, 236, 237
Mann, Thomas 7, 84
Mansfield, Jayne 78
Mantle, Mickey 77
Manuel 250, 251
Marcia 12, 226, 227, 228, 229, 230, 231, 234, 237, 238, 240, 295, 369, 413, 455, 478
Marin, George 204, 448, 457, 484
Marin, Rino 83, 247, 457
Marin, Silviano 126, 144, 448, 457, 483, 484
Marshall, George 84
Martin, Mary 84
MASH 126
Matt 379, 380, 381, 382, 383, 384, 409, 410
Mazzini, Giuseppe 9
McCahill, Tom 146
McCarthy, Joe 131, 161
McKinney, Aaron James 379
McLeish, A. Duncan 37, 282
McNally, Terrence 379
Mechanics Illustrated 146
Medicaid 417, 427, 428, 439, 440
Miller, George 186
Miller, Henry 169
Mondavi Winery 151
Monroe, Marilyn 78, 110

N

National Recovery Act 28
Negherbon, Lydia xvi
Nightingale, Florence 131
Nixon, Richard 161
Normand, Mabel 25

O

One Flew Over the Cuckoo's Nest 126
Ordinary People 207

Organizations xxix, 362, 439, 441, 443, 444
Out of the Air 25

P

P.J. 347, 348, 349, 350, 408
Panama Canal 23
Parrous, Ethel 383
Parrous, Pete 383
Pasley, Chastity Vera 379
Pasquale 220, 294, 413
Pat P. 110, 183
Pearl Harbor xxiii, 63, 80, 81, 83
Penny 91, 92, 93, 94, 104, 114, 127
Peters, Mrs. 127
Phelps, Fred 381
Physically Handicapped Memorial Foundation 181, 189
Pickford, Mary 25
Pinocchio 170
Pinza, Ezio 84
Praeger, Otto 33
Price, Kristen Leann 379
Products xx, xxviii, 49, 76, 98, 249, 250, 255, 257, 261, 333, 335, 353, 418, 419, 430, 431, 432, 442
Pufang, Deng 359

Q

Queen for a Day xix, 78, 136, 285

R

Rae Ann 123, 124
Ranieri, Inez 41, 448
Rapallo 41, 306
Raquelote, J. V. 53
Ratchet, BigNurse 126
Reagan, Ronald 271, 363, 364
Richard xvi, 120, 121, 123, 124, 161, 209, 341, 453, 454, 467, 471, 472, 473, 476, 478, 490
Robinson, Pat xi

Rodgers, Calbraith 35
Rolling Stones 185
Rome 14, 222, 223, 226, 228, 231, 238, 258, 293, 294, 295, 377
Roosevelt, Quentin 35
Roosevelt, Theodore 35
Rosenberg, Ethel 131
Russ B. 176

S

Sartre, Jean Paul 406
Scelsa, Joseph 85
Schwartz, Ray 77, 78, 247, 248
Scott, Lee 24
Secret of the Submarine 25
Sennett, Mack 25
Shepard, Dennis 381
Shepard, Judy 382
Shepard, Matthew 378, 380, 382
Shields, Ren 12
Sikorsky, Igor 33
Silva, Dick 247
Sister Mary Ellen 75, 134, 135, 136
Smith, Dean 34
Smithsonian Museum 76
South Pacific 84
SS 235, 427
SSI 425, 426, 427, 436
State programs 435
Steven 399, 413, 452, 453, 457, 469, 471, 473, 479, 484, 490
Stevenson, Adlai 106, 107
Stubbs, Kenneth Ray iv
Suntina 42, 43, 44

T

Tagliamento 8, 26, 241, 246
Taylor, Elizabeth 341
Tenney, Jack 82
The Bicycle Thief 47
The Flying Torpedo 25
The Fortune Cookie 246
The Girl of Yesterday 25
The Grim Game 25, 26
The Sky Pirate 25
The Skywayman 26
The Sweetheart of Sigma Chi 170
The Thief 112
The Thirteenth Apostle 169
The Three Faces of Eve 126
Thomas, Terry 237
Thoreau, Henry David 213
Tijuana 141, 244
Titanic 21
Tom S. xxx, 79, 157, 161, 169, 244, 342, 432
Tom Sawyer 204, 206
Toothpick 25
Torremolinos 235, 238, 298, 299
Transportation 11, 36, 68, 414, 435, 436, 437, 443
Travel xv, xxix, 14, 42, 62, 72, 85, 89, 185, 204, 205, 209, 216, 244, 245, 325, 348, 376, 393, 413, 414, 436, 437, 438, 441
Tresca, Carlo 84
Trieste 6, 8, 221, 319
Tropic of Cancer 169
Twain, Mark 371

U

Udine 6, 11, 21, 220, 258, 320, 323, 407, 493
Una Storia Segreta 85
Uncle Miltie 135

V

Veltro, R. J. 54
Venice 6, 7, 220, 318, 323, 348, 350, 351
Verdi, Giuseppe 9
Von Stroheim, Erich 25

W

Wake, Aaron v
Waldie, Jerome 186
Watts, Alan xxvi, 169
Wayne 251, 256, 257, 258, 291, 292, 413, 450, 454
Welles, Orson 406
Whirlpool bath iv, xix, xxiv, xxix, 4, 51, 73, 74, 76, 77, 78, 94, 95, 97, 98, 136, 137, 175, 245, 246, 248, 249, 255, 256, 257, 262, 284, 286, 344, 352, 353, 365
Whitmarsh, Phil xvi
Willard, William 35
Wizard of Oz 123, 186
Woodward, Joanne 126
Wright, Frank Lloyd 375
Wright, Orville 12, 15
Wright, Wilbur 39

X

Xiaoping, Deng 359

Z

Zedong, Mao 359
Zelig 206
Zoppola, Count 12

978-0-595-37097-9
0-595-37097-7

Printed in the United States
43869LVS00005B/13-36